INDIA AND THE RESPONSIBILITY TO PROTECT

Rethinking Asia and International Relations

Series Editor: **Emilian Kavalski**,
Australian Catholic University (Sydney)

This series provides thoughtful consideration both of the growing prominence of Asian actors on the global stage and the changes in the study and practice of world affairs that they provoke. It offers a comprehensive parallel assessment of the full spectrum of Asian states, organisations, and regions and their impact on the dynamics of global politics.

The series encourages conversation on:

- what rules, norms, and strategic cultures are likely to dominate international life in the 'Asian Century';
- how will global problems be reframed and addressed by a 'rising Asia';
- which institutions, actors, and states are likely to provide leadership during such 'shifts to the East';
- whether there is something distinctly 'Asian' about the emerging patterns of global politics.

Such comprehensive engagement not only offers a critical assessment of the actual and prospective roles of Asian actors, but rethinks the concepts, practices, and frameworks of analysis of world politics.

Other titles in this series

Managing Global Risks in the Urban Age
Singapore and the Making of a Global City
Yee-Kuang Heng

The China–Japan Border Dispute
Islands of Contention in Multidisciplinary Perspective
Edited by Tim F. Liao, Kimie Hara and Krista Wiegand

Risk State
Japan's Foreign Policy in an Age of Uncertainty
Edited by Sebastian Maslow, Ra Mason and Paul O'Shea

China's New Governing Party Paradigm
Political Renewal and the Pursuit of National Rejuvenation
Timothy R. Heath

India and the Responsibility to Protect

ALAN BLOOMFIELD
The University of New South Wales, Australia

Routledge
Taylor & Francis Group
LONDON AND NEW YORK

First published 2016 by Ashgate Publishing

2 Park Square, Milton Park, Abingdon, Oxfordshire OX14 4RN
711 Third Avenue, New York, NY 10017

Routledge is an imprint of the Taylor & Francis Group, an informa business

First issued in paperback 2017

British Library Cataloguing in Publication Data
A catalogue record for this book is available from the British Library

The Library of Congress has cataloged the printed edition as follows:
Bloomfield, Alan.
India and the responsibility to protect / by Alan Bloomfield.
pages cm. – (Rethinking Asia and international relations)
Includes bibliographical references and index.
ISBN 9781409468721 (hardback)
1. India–Foreign relations–1984-. 2. India–Foreign relations–Philosophy. 3. Humanitarian intervention–Côte d'Ivoire. 4. Humanitarian intervention–Syria. 4. Humanitarian intervention–Libya. 5. Responsibility to protect (International law)

DS449.B55 2016
341.5/84–dc23

2015026590

ISBN 978-1-4094-6872-1 (hbk)
ISBN 978-1-138-57655-1 (pbk)

Contents

To my parents, John and Noelene, whose love and support have made this most rewarding of careers possible

Preface

The genesis of this book lay in what turned out to be, with hindsight, a revelatory conversation I had in late 2011 with a distinguished older colleague, Dr Theodore Gabriel. I was teaching a Middle East politics course at the overseas campus of Canada's Queen's University – located in the idyllic Herstmonceux Castle, near Eastbourne in the UK – and I had been following the 2011 Libyan crisis closely with my students. It was early November 2011, less than two weeks since Colonel Gaddafi's death, and I now realise I had in some ways become caught up in the wave of youthful exuberance my students displayed when this brutal dictatorship collapsed. I declared to Theodore over lunch that this event marked an important turning point in the fortunes of the responsibility to protect (R2P) norm – a positive one – and that it was also an important step along the road towards what I thought would be a more democratic future for the Middle East.

But Theodore was less sure. An acknowledged expert in religious studies, he had devoted decades to studying Islam and the Middle East. He is also an Indian, and while he has lived and worked in the UK for many years, he remained closely connected to his family back in India. He alerted me to the fact that Indians were not nearly so positive about events in the Middle East, especially in Libya, and I might want to look into this. I asked him why this was so – 'wasn't India a true democracy?' I recall saying – on the assumption that being so ('surely' was another word I think I used) meant Indians perceived a dictator's fall little differently to the way I viewed it. He responded by agreeing that India was democratic, for all its flaws, but this did not necessarily mean Indians viewed the fall of an Arab regime to a coalition of Western powers positively, or that democracy would necessarily be advanced in the wake of such events. He urged me to begin reading some of the Indian press reactions to Gaddafi's downfall to get a better feel for the 'unique subcontinental worldview, shaped as it is by the long shadow of colonialism', as I recall him putting it. I questioned him a little further, but we both had to depart for afternoon classes soon. Still, the conversation had started me thinking.

I had never taken much more than a general interest in India until that point, other than knowing that it was a rising power (and one whose people shared, with many of my fellow Australians, a deep love of cricket). But I did take Theodore's advice a few days later when the English weather turned bad. I spent my Saturday in the office instead of shopping in Brighton as planned, and because I didn't really feel like doing any 'real' work I read the Indian press reports about Libya which had appeared in the days and weeks after Gaddafi's death. And while it would be a gross exaggeration to say that what I saw in those articles precipitated a sort of 'road to Damascus moment', it is fair to say that this book would not have been written had I not spoken to Theodore (and, perhaps, if the skies had not turned ominous that weekend).

In those articles I saw a fundamentally different worldview on display. I am thoroughly Western. I grew up in Australia, I have travelled widely in Europe and North America in my youth, I have lived in Canada, and I was now in 'the Old Country', as Australians often put it. And while I had over the years become thoroughly familiar with the history of Western empire and the decolonisation era which followed it I had only read about it in books penned by Westerners. For the first time, however, I was reading about events which I was thoroughly familiar with – I had followed the Libyan war closely, after all, in the Western press and in the pages of international relations journals (which are still dominated by Western authors) – but these events were being interpreted very differently by Indians. These viewpoints were more sceptical of than celebratory towards the impact R2P was having on the world, and in particular, there were many dark prognostications of 'trouble to come' in Libya.

I was working on other research interests at the time, mainly Australian foreign policy and models for understanding how a state's strategic culture affects its foreign policy. But over the next six months or so I watched as Libya's transition to democracy began to falter. I also continued to watch how Indians were responding to the ever-growing litany of bad news, and I talked on several more occasions to Theodore about the matter; he urged me to throw the net wider and begin reading works by Indian historians who have dissected India's colonial experience. I did so – and also dived into the rapidly burgeoning literature on emerging India's foreign policy – and so I took the first steps towards gaining a greater insight into the Indian worldview and, more generally, towards looking at R2P somewhat differently. In particular, I began to appreciate better – or at least not dismiss entirely – the sorts of developing-world critiques of R2P which sometimes portray it as the thin end of a wedge which might ultimately lead to a sort of 'colonialism 2.0'. I was not convinced that R2P was really just a smokescreen for the cynical reimposition of Western dominance – and I remain unconvinced – yet I began to realise these sorts of viewpoints at least need to be taken seriously and investigated further.

Another milestone on the journey towards this book came in July 2012. At the Oceanic Conference for International Studies in Sydney I saw Ian Hall, a noted Australian expert on Indian foreign policy, deliver an excellent paper which argued that when Indians debated NATO's Libyan intervention they tended to 'tilt at windmills'; in other words, they did not necessarily debate the merits of or problems with intervening in a particular humanitarian crisis like the one in Libya directly, but instead they tended to oppose R2P on the basis that it was just another form of colonialism, or they supported it by arguing that doing so would raise India's stocks in Western capitals (etc.). Ian graciously provided me a copy of his conference paper, I read it that night, and I became almost instantly convinced that this topic – India's position on R2P generally, especially given it was at the time sitting on the Security Council – was one which deserved sustained attention. Days later I met Emilian Kavalski, the editor of the series this book is a part of.

He had contacted me weeks before and we had agreed to meet to discuss the possibility of me writing a book about my strategic culture research. But I instead pitched to him over coffee at Badde Manours – a café in Sydney where the staff famously treat customers brusquely – my idea for a book on India and R2P. He agreed it was something he and the people at Ashgate might be interested in. They were, and this book is the result.

There are many persons who deserve acknowledgment for assisting with the preparation of this book. I should first acknowledge the assistance rendered – and especially the patience shown – by Brenda Sharp at Ashgate. I missed several deadlines, some by wide margins, as I struggled to learn those lessons that all junior academics must internalise (mainly how to 'say no' to invitations to join other research agendas – to 'just write a chapter in my edited book' – in short, I kept on getting diverted by side-projects). The same thanks must also be extended to Emilian. I also owe thanks to a number of my colleagues at the University of New South Wales who read parts of this manuscript or who offered advice about conducting field work in India, including Monika Barthwal-Datta, Tanya Jakimow, Christian Downie, Jeni Whalan and Shirley Scott. I also owe thanks to Nicolas Blarel, who helpfully commented on an ISA paper which eventually became Chapter 5, and to Kudrat Virk who did something similar. And, of course, I owe many thanks to Theodore for setting me on this path in the first place, and to Ian, whose paper crystallised my thoughts and who also offered me some very helpful advice, in person, in mid-2013 before I travelled to India.

Finally, I owe special thanks to a number of Indians. First, to Gopal, the manager of the Rainbow Residency, the hotel where I stayed for three months in late 2013; without his assistance my time in busy New Delhi would have surely been far less productive. Second, thanks must also go to the score of Indian scholars who graciously consented to let me interview them; without the benefit of their special expertise in Indian foreign policy this book would have been significantly less rigorous and insightful (with special thanks to the scholars at the Institute for Defence Studies and Analyses, who graciously gave me access to their fantastic library and who were unfailingly generous with their time). Third, I must thank the doctors and nurses at Max Super Speciality Hospital in New Delhi: I was told by 'old India hands' before I left that there was a 50/50 chance of ending up in hospital given how long I would be in India for, and I ended up on the wrong side of that coin toss (I caught pneumonia). But I was back on my feet within four days after their excellent care. Finally, I want to thank India's *aam aadmi* – the 'common man', or more precisely the common *people*, because many women helped me too – who drove me to and from my interviews in Delhi, who explained maddeningly complex train timetables to me, who guided me through a tiger reserve (safely), and who cooked me all of those wonderful meals. India is dazzling and exciting one moment, then frustrating and exasperating the next. It confronts many pressing problems, yet unquestionably has great potential. It is, above all, vibrant and alive and bustling (sometimes too much so … at least for this boy from sleepy Perth, Western Australia). I look forward to many returns to chart its course as it emerges as one of the world's most influential international actors.

Introduction
India and the Responsibility to Protect

India began its seventh stint as a non-permanent member of the UN Security Council in 2011 expecting to focus in that year and the next on advancing the cause of Council reform. At the early meetings in January India began speaking to the various issues before the Council, starting with a strong expression of solidarity with the Palestinian cause,[1] then it sought to leverage its record as the most ardent and consistent supporter of peacekeeping to push for reform of several relevant UN agencies and processes.[2] A few days later it noted it was in both India's and the international community's interests to better coordinate anti-piracy operations in the Gulf of Aden.[3] It was a good, steady start to India's campaign to burnish its image as a credible and responsible rising great power and a prime candidate for elevation to that most august and influential of international clubs, permanent membership of the Security Council.[4]

Then India was blind-sided by a series of acute humanitarian crises which came to dominate the Council's agenda during 2011 and 2012. One such crisis broke out in early 2011 in West Africa, in Côte d'Ivoire, but it was the turmoil engulfing the Middle East, popularly known as the Arab Spring, which really derailed India's grand plans. Tunisia's government fell on 14 January 2011; the first big demonstrations began in Cairo's Tahrir Square on 25 January; on 15 February the Libyan uprising began; and protests erupted in Syria on 15 March. These last two uprisings morphed into brutal wars featuring serious human rights abuses and atrocities, which in turn sparked fierce international debates about whether Security Council-authorised military interventions inspired by the emerging Responsibility to Protect (R2P) norm should take place. An intervention which was broadly consistent with the tenets of R2P took place in Libya in 2011, while by the time India left the Security Council at the end of 2012 nothing comparable had taken place in Syria despite the ostensibly similar circumstances (indeed, the scale of atrocities was significantly *worse* in Syria). This seeming inconsistency or alleged 'selective application' of R2P has provoked fierce debates about the nature and viability of the R2P norm which continue to rage through academic and diplomatic circles. And India was by virtue of its presence on the Council at this crucial time at the centre of the storm, meaning it was forced by circumstances to grapple as it

1 S/PV.6470, 19 January 2011.

2 S/PV.6472, 21 January 2011.

3 S/PV.6473, 25 January 2011.

4 Rohan Mukherjee and David Malone, 'India and the UN Security Council: An Ambiguous Tale', *Economic and Political Weekly* 48:29 (2013), 110.

had never done before with the thorny debates about whether the R2P norm should structure and inform international responses to grave humanitarian crises.

India as an International Actor: Increasing Influence, Shifting Stance?

This book examines India's attitudes and policies towards R2P, and especially its most controversial component, Pillar III (by which the international community purportedly has the responsibility to intervene, including by the threat or application of military force, to prevent atrocities in a sovereign state). Two key 'meta debates' in contemporary international relations provide the background context for the project. The first is the 'BRICs[5] narrative' about the emergence of rising powers and their impact on the international system, while the second is the debate about the nature of modern sovereignty which presently includes controversies surrounding the meaning and status of R2P. The intersection of these debates produces questions about whether the emerging powers, including India, will support or oppose the sorts of changes to global governance structures that R2P advocates.

India has traditionally favoured relatively conservative, non-interventionist interpretations of the sovereignty norm for most of its history as an independent state. But ever since the economic reforms precipitated by the turbulent crises it suffered in the early 1990s India arguably remains in a sort of transitional period – most notably economically and demographically – but also diplomatically in the sense that there has been a discernible shift towards New Delhi becoming more prepared to engage with the prevailing Western-dominated international system. This book examines one discrete aspect of India's engagement with the contemporary Western-shaped international system – namely, its engagement with the R2P norm – but to do so it is necessary to understand what sort of international actor India is more broadly in the early twenty-first century, which in turn requires understanding how India has changed over the past half-century or so.

Indian foreign policy-making was dominated by its first prime minister, Jawaharlal Nehru, in the first few decades after it attainted independence in 1947. Nehru's worldview was forged by a complex mix of admiration for Western democratic values and scientific progress, resistance to Western Imperialism, and a firm belief in the inherent greatness of Indian civilisation. He has been described as an 'internationalist' whose reading of history led him to conclude that Western imperialism was the root cause of the international conflicts which convulsed the world in the first half of the twentieth century, but also that these conflicts could be tempered and maybe even solved by the promotion of Asian values, like respect

5 'BRICs' refers to the 'original four' – Brazil, Russia, China and India – identified in 2001 by economist Jim O'Neill, and not to the institutional structure known by the acronym 'BRIC***S***' (i.e. including South Africa); 'Building Better Global Economic BRICs', *Global Economics Paper* 66, Goldman Sachs, 30 November 2001.

for harmony and commitment to peaceful coexistence.[6] He thus saw India's attainment of independence as a great moment in history; India, he thought, could lead other nations out of colonial subjugation by example and towards 'the great design of promoting peace and progress all over the world' or his vision of 'One World' (i.e. a federation of free states presided over by the United Nations).[7] Specifically, his foreign policy rested on five key principles: anti-imperialism; non-alignment; India could and should play a mediatory role; global disarmament (especially nuclear); as well as peaceful co-existence and mutual non-interference (i.e. the *Panchscheel* Doctrine).[8]

Unfortunately, and despite his great efforts to advance this agenda globally, Nehru's grand design largely failed; Cold War tensions fuelled a nuclear arms race and caused both superpowers to meddle incessantly in the affairs of newly-independent states, which in turn caused Nehru's most cherished project, the creation of the Non-Aligned Movement, to fracture and slide into general irrelevance.[9] As a result in the turbulent 1960s 'Indian leaders graduated from a liberation movement with idealistic notions about how the world ought to run [because] they had to learn to deal with the harsh realities of international politics'.[10] An especially harsh lesson was delivered by India's shock defeat by China in the 1962 border war. Nehru had invested considerable hope in a Sino-Indian partnership to shape the new international order, and the war was a cruel blow which greatly diminished his standing at home and abroad. India's defeat and Nehru's humiliation is widely seen as opening the door to a more pragmatic or realist shift in Indian foreign policy, yet we should not overstate this; for example while many scholars acknowledge Indian foreign policy became somewhat more muscular and non-alignment was partially abandoned in favour of a tilt towards the Soviet Bloc in the two decades after 1962,[11] Nehru's daughter, Indira Ghandi, did not abandon her father's foreign policy preferences altogether during her tenure as prime minister.[12]

---

6 Nehru, *India's Foreign Policy: Selected Speeches, September 1946–April 1961* (New Delhi: Ministry of Information, 1961), 23.

7 Ibid., 248–256.

8 S. Kalyanaraman, 'Nehru's Advocacy of Internationalism and Indian Foreign Policy', in Kanti Bajpai, Saira Basit and V. Krishnappa (eds), *India's Grand Strategy: History, Theory, Cases* (Routledge: New Delhi, 2014), 167–173.

9 Ibid., 174.

10 C. Raja Mohan, 'Rising India: Partner in Shaping the Global Commons?', *Washington Quarterly* 33:3 (2010), 136.

11 Rahul Sagar, 'State of Mind: What Sort of Power will India Become?', *International Affairs* 85:4 (2009), 813; David Malone, *Can the Elephant Dance?: Contemporary Indian Foreign Policy* (Oxford: Oxford University Press, 2011), 130–134.

12 Mohan, 'Rising India', 137; David Malone and Rohan Mukherjee, 'Polity, Security and Foreign Policy in Contemporary India', in T.V. Paul (ed.), *South Asia's Weak States: Understanding the Regional Insecurity Predicament* (Stanford: Stanford University Press, 2010), 148.

But India would continue to change as a foreign policy actor: 1991 in particular was a watershed year marked by the confluence of two momentous events. The first was the abrupt collapse of the Soviet Union and the ending of the Cold War with the West victorious, which shocked and disoriented Indian policy-makers of all stripes.[13] Then, more-or-less contemporaneously with this event (and indirectly caused by it[14]) India suffered an acute balance of payments crisis which precipitated a general economic crisis. But India's policy-makers responded with a bold package of reforms and in the following two decades India left behind the much-maligned so-called 'Hindu growth rate' (i.e. a tortuously slow one).[15] While much attention has been paid to this economic growth story, interest in exploring changes to India's foreign policy has also grown strongly.

Raja Mohan's 2003 thesis of how and why India changed as an international actor has been particularly influential. He argued that India had traditionally favoured idealism because it had been relatively weak, but that as it grew stronger in the 1990s it 'crossed the Rubicon' and became a 'normal' state which pursued its national interests rationally, leaving behind the high-minded idealism, the knee-jerk Third Worldism and the socialist develop model which had condemned it to decades of relative economic decline.[16] In other words, while India's international alignment had not changed radically – it had not wholeheartedly dived into the Western camp – it was no longer defining its Self against the Western Other as antagonistically as it had for much of the Cold War. As Mohan put it,

> India was the only liberal democracy in the world that stood apart from and often against the West throughout the Cold War … . Its attempts to reconcile with the West had run against the entrenched [domestic] sources of antagonism … [like] the anti-imperialist tradition, the nativist ideologies [etc.] … This story [i.e. the one told in his book] of Indian foreign policy in the 1990s is about the struggle to overcome the sources of opposition to the West.[17]

---

13 Baldev Raj Nayar and T.V. Paul, *India in the World Order: Searching for Major-Power Status* (Cambridge: Cambridge University Press, 2003), Chapter 6; Deepa M. Ollapally, 'The Evolution of India's Relations with Russia: Tried, Tested, and Searching for Balance', in Sumit Ganguly (ed.), *India's Foreign Policy: Retrospect and Prospect* (New Delhi: Oxford University Press, 2010), 229; Bajpai et al., *India's Grand Strategy*, 8.

14 In the sense that Soviet weakness contributed to the outbreak of the 1991 Gulf war, which sent oil prices souring, draining India's foreign currency reserves: N.S., Sisodia, 'Economic Modernisation and the Growing Influence of Neoliberalism', in Bajpai et al., *India's Grand Strategy*, 178.

15 Arvind Pangariya, *India: The Emerging Giant* (New York: Oxford University Press, 2008).

16 *Crossing the Rubicon: The Shaping of India's New Foreign Policy* (New York: Palgrave Macmillan, 2003), xi–xxii. See also Ganguly, *India's Foreign Policy*.

17 Mohan, ibid., xv.

Since then the debates about what sort of international actor India is (or should be) have run hot. They are far too voluminous for this introductory chapter to consider in full, but broadly speaking fellow realists like Harsh Pant and others[18] have agreed that India has at least begun the process of becoming a normal great power, and they typically argue that it must continue to align itself closer to the West, especially given the serious challenge to India posed by the rise of China.[19] But others disagree and instead emphasise the virtues of India continuing to play the 'role of conscience-keeper of the world';[20] in particular, instead of the older non-alignment strategy being entirely discredited and abandoned it arguably has such deep roots in India's identity that it has instead morphed into a determination to retain 'strategic autonomy'. This has in turn found expression in a broad preference for India to continue to maintain some distance from the West and instead work with other emerging states – including, for some, with China – to forge a multipolar world order.[21]

Thus the broader outcome of these debates about what sort of international actor India is or should be remains uncertain, but one thing does seem clearer: India has become a less-peripheral, more-influential international actor than it was. While China's rise has undoubtedly attracted more attention, ever-more interest is paid to India's rise too,[22] especially since the publication of Stephen Cohen's *India: Emerging Power* alerted the American audience in 2001 to the India's impressive turnaround in the 1990s.[23] India's rapprochement with the West has been particularly aimed at one actor – the United States – given that American post-Cold War pre-eminence means that India has much to gain directly from

18 For example: Harsh V. Pant (ed.), *Indian Foreign Policy in a Unipolar World* (New Delhi: Routledge, 2009).

19 Harsh V. Pant, *The China Syndrome: Grappling with an Uneasy Relationship* (New Delhi: HarperCollins, 2010); Bharat Karnad, 'An Elephant with a Small Footprint: The Realist Roots of India's Strategic Thought and Policies', in Bajpai et al., *India's Grand Strategy*, 219–228.

20 Rajiv Sikri, *Challenge and Strategy: Rethinking India's Foreign Policy* (New Delhi: Sage, 2009), 298. For an overview of the debate see: Deepa Ollapally and Rajesh Rajapagolan, 'The Pragmatic Challenge to Indian Foreign Policy', *Washington Quarterly* 34:2 (2011), 145–162.

21 S.M. Krishna, 'Address by EAM [External Affairs Minister] at the Editors Guild Meeting', New Delhi, 10 September 2009; Pratap Bhanu Mehta, 'Still Under Nehru's Shadow? The Absence of Foreign Policy Frameworks in India', *India Review* 8:3 (2009), 209–233; Sunil Kilnani, Rajiv Kumar, Pratap B. Mehta, Prakash Menon, Nandan Nilekani, Srinath Raghavan, Shyam Saran and Siddharth Varadarajan, *Nonalignment 2.0: A Foreign and Strategic Policy for India in the Twenty First Century*, Centre for Policy Research, Working Paper, January 2012. Available at: <http://www.cprindia.org/sites/default/files/NonAlignment%202.0_1.pdf>.

22 Ian Hall, 'The Other Exception? India as a rising Power', *Australian Journal of International Affairs* 64:5 (2010), 601–611.

23 Washington: Brookings, 2004.

closer relations (especially economically, in the form of technology transfers and investment, but also diplomatically given Washington's unrivalled influence). At the same time the United States has increasingly seen India as a potential partner – if probably not an ally: Americans are typically well aware of the latent strength of India's attachment to the principle of strategic autonomy – which might be enlisted in Washington's broader effort maintain its preeminent global position and to hedge against China's rise.[24]

That India is objectively speaking a 'weightier' international player is no longer seriously disputed; its average growth rate over the past two decades has been second only to China's,[25] and it has almost become a cliché to observe that if the present trends continue India will boast the world's third largest economy by 2030.[26] Indeed, its superior demographic profile (and other supposed advantages, like more English speakers, a more flexible democratic system, and a more robust rule of law) might mean India's long-term growth potential is superior to China's, although there are plenty of reasons to be wary of expecting these trends to simply continue in a linear fashion.[27] Nevertheless, all of this interest in India's growing capabilities has given rise to speculation about how India currently *uses* its power; in other words, questions are asked about how *influential* India has become. In particular, questions continue to be raised regarding whether India does now – and also whether it will in future – use its growing power *responsibly*. Again, this debate is far too large to engage with properly here save to say that Amrita Narlikar has concluded that India is *not* a responsible power – at least not yet – because it is

> a veto-player rather than an agenda setter … . [T]here are only a few instances in which India has successfully managed to influence outcomes in its own favour … . I argue that if its rising power and behaviour is anything to go by, we must take issue with both India's willingness and also its ability to take on the responsibilities that accompany rising power.[28]

---

24 Mohan, 'Rising India'; C. Christine Fair, 'India and the US: Embracing a New Paradigm, in Pant, *Indian Foreign Policy*; Malone, *Can the Elephant*, Chapter 7.

25 Sisodia, in Bajpai et al., *India's Grand Strategy*; Gurcharan Das, 'The India Model' *Foreign Affairs* 85:4 (2006), 2–16.

26 Satya Pattanayak, 'India as an Emerging Power', *India Quarterly* 63:1 (2007), 79–110.

27 Charles Wolf, Jr., Siddhartha Dalal, Julie DaVanzo, Eric V. Larson, Alisher Akhmedjonov, Harun Dogo, Meilinda Huang and Silvia Montoya, *China and India, 2025: A Comparative Assessment* (Santa Monica: RAND Corporation, 2011), 103–110; Holy A. Bell, 'Status of the "BRICs": An Analysis of Growth Factors', *International Research Journal of Finance and Economics* 69:2 (2011), 19–25; Pranab Bardam, *Awakening Giants, Feet of Clay: Assessing the Economic Rise of China and India* (Princeton: Princeton University Press, 2012).

28 'Is India a Responsible Great Power?', *Third World Quarterly* 32:9 (2011), 1608.

Raja Mohan, for one, substantially agrees: he has certainly called for India to shoulder more international burdens,[29] and we will see as the study progresses that the perceived failure of New Delhi to do so is one of his favourite gripes with the Indian foreign policy-making community generally, including in the R2P context.

But we will also see in the pages which follow that this bald conclusion – that India is not a responsible power – is contestable, not least because the question of what 'responsible' means is a more complex one than it first appears to be. Much hinges on how one defines responsibility and Indians do not always judge this matter with reference to the same criteria as Western actors, especially those Western actors who actively promote the *responsibility* to protect norm as a standard of appropriate behaviour for all states to adhere to when humanitarian crises break out. Others have noted that India still labours under significant constraints, especially the enormous burden of internal development, which 'distract' it from international affairs or make it a 'reluctant' international actor in many respects.[30] But for our purposes, and at this stage of the book, it seems reasonable to simply note that India is an actor whose steady growth means it is 'well placed to help shape the international order to an unprecedented degree' if it so chooses,[31] and that it has become somewhat more receptive to, or at least less likely to automatically react with hostility towards, Western efforts to reform key international norms than it was previously.

India has therefore become an increasingly important player in the ongoing debates about R2P. This is not to say India is the *most* important player: the United States, a long-established liberal democracy and still clearly the single most powerful state – and therefore the 'most likely intervener' in humanitarian crises – is obviously more important, and its two most enthusiastically interventionist allies, France and Britain, also arguably matter more than India does; China and Russia, both powerful states with questionable human rights records, ties to many repressive regimes, and the holders of Security Council vetos – so the 'most likely blockers' of efforts to intervene in humanitarian crises – also unquestionably matter more than India. And perhaps a few key non-state actors like the UN Secretary-General, NATO's Secretary General, maybe the African Union and, more recently, the League of Arab States might influence debates about R2P more than India.

Nevertheless India is already an important international actor, and one whose stake in and influence over debates about the management of global affairs, including debates about R2P, seems likely to increase. And while the Libyan and Syrian crises – and especially the fact they occurred while India was present on the Security Council – have recently begun to spark some interest in India's position

29 'Rising India'.

30 Pratap Bhanu Mehta, 'Reluctant India', *Journal of Democracy* 22:4 (2011), 101–113.

31 Kanti Bajpai, Saira Basit and V. Krishnappa, 'Introduction', in Bajpai et al., *India's Grand Strategy*, 9; Ramesh Thakur, 'R2P after Libya and Syria: Engaging Emerging Powers', *Washington Quarterly* 36:2 (2013), 61–76.

on R2P,[32] India's role in the debates about R2P have still been generally neglected in the international relations literature. These matters deserve more sustained consideration, so this book takes up the challenge.

Finally, while India's attitudes and policies towards humanitarian intervention back as far as the early 1970s are not ignored, this book focuses on the years 2011 and 2012, when India sat on the Security Council. There are good reasons for doing so. The Indian government has never produced much policy about the practice of humanitarian intervention or the R2P norm. But during 2011 and 2012 India voted when a number of draft resolutions concerning the three crises in Côte d'Ivoire, Libya and Syria came before the Security Council, meaning it was essentially forced to repeatedly reveal its position on R2P in more detail than ever before. Indians paid more attention to debates about R2P and the meaning of sovereignty more generally during this period, meaning an unprecedented amount of source material is available from the years 2011 and 2012. This material is also supplemented in later chapters with data from interviews conducted with foreign policy experts in New Delhi in late 2013.

The general picture presented by this evidence is relatively clear: despite occasional calls for India to live up to its oft-expressed and much-emphasised liberal-democratic ideals and traditions and support R2P wholeheartedly, anti-Western elements and an influential cadre of realists typically urge the opposite, or at least they urge India to support only parts of the R2P norm, namely, Pillar I and to some extent Pillar II, and to remain opposed to Pillar III in the main. Indeed, this study argues that India's opposition to Pillar III hardened as a result of its tenure on the Security Council, which generally speaking does not bode well for R2P advocates' wider effort to entrench this norm. Instead, by the end of 2014 –

---

32 Articles which deal squarely with India and R2P were rare before 2011: a 2003 review article discussed the 2001 International Commission on Intervention and State Sovereignty report (presenting R2P), and cites several 1990s-era articles about India's reaction to the 1999 Kosovo war; M.S. Rajan, 'Sovereignty of States and Intervention', *International Studies* 40:3 (2003), 277–281. A small but significant – considering the virtual silence before then – burst of commentary appeared after 2011, including: C. Raja Mohan, 'India, Libya and the Principle of Non-Intervention', *ISAS Insights*, 122, 13 April 2011; Satish Nambiar, 'The Emerging Principle of the Responsibility to Protect: An Asian Perspective', *Strategic Analysis* 35:6 (2011), 955–965; Dipankar Banerjee, 'India and R2P: Reconciling the Tension Between Intervention and State Sovereignty', in *The Responsibility to Protect – From Evasive to Reluctant Action? The Role of Global Middle Powers* (Johannesburg: United Litho, 2012); Kudrat Virk, 'India and the Responsibility to Protect: A Tale of Ambiguity', *Global Responsibility to Protect* 5:1 (2013), 56–83; Ian Hall, 'Tilting at Windmills? The Indian Debate over the Responsibility to Protect after UNSC Resolution 1973', *Global Responsibility to Protect* 5:1 (2013), 84–108; Kadira Pethiyagoda, 'India's Approach to Humanitarian Intervention and the Responsibility to Protect', *Oxford Institute for Ethics, Law and Armed Conflict Working Paper*, November 2013; Madhan Mohan Jaganathan and Gerrit Kurtz, 'Singing the Tune of Sovereignty? India and the Responsibility to Protect', *Conflict, Security and Development* 14:4 (2014), 461–487.

when this book's analysis finishes – India's international identity continued to be constituted primarily by relatively strong conceptions of the sovereignty norm, meaning it supported only those elements of R2P which were compatible with state sovereignty and not those which, in New Delhi's view, undermined it.

What Follows

Chapter 1 examines the R2P norm in detail, starting with its predecessor, humanitarian intervention. Despite the fact this latter practice or norm emerged and seemed to steadily gain acceptance in the 1990s, this chapter shows that disquiet and resistance steadily built as the decade advanced and came to a head over the 1999 Kosovo war, prompting the efforts in the early 2000s to establish a more precise doctrine to regulate when the international community could intervene to protect human rights (i.e. what would become R2P). The evolution of R2P after the seminal International Commission on Intervention and State Sovereignty (ICISS) report in 2001 – through the World Summit in 2005, the 2009 UN Secretary General's report, etc. – is then examined later in the chapter. Key questions about the nature and status of the R2P norm in 2010 – like what are its key features?; what is its status in international law?; to what degree have global governance structures been reformed to reflect or facilitate its application in humanitarian crises? – are answered by the end of Chapter 1, allowing for some consideration in the concluding pages of the book regarding the effect the three humanitarian crises in 2011 and 2012 had upon the efforts to entrench R2P as a recognised feature of global governance.

Chapter 2 explains the philosophical and theoretical framework which informs the later empirical analyses. R2P is conceptualised as a 'complex norm' with several component parts and more generally as a sort of 'global-level discourse' which, along with competitor norms/discourses (chief amongst them the sovereignty norm) interacts with domestic Indian 'identity discourses' to shape India's responses to particular humanitarian crises. The primary analytical focus is on these latter domestic-level discursive structures – the identity discourses – because they actually constitute India's foreign policy decision-makers, meaning they shape India's responses to humanitarian crises more directly than the global-level norms do. The working hypothesis which drove research was that various identity discourses competed to define 'who and what India is and does' (more accurately, who or what India *should* be and do; adherents to each argue their interpretations is the 'correct' or 'authentic' one). This book therefore treats India's identity as fundamentally *contested*; in other words, it is assumed that competition between the identity discourses affects the way in which India's interests are formulated and so how India responds to humanitarian crises (subject to the particular circumstances of each crisis).

More specifically, three key interrelated hypotheses drove the study's data-collection efforts. First, given India is a proud democracy, and because democracies are usually assumed to be supporters or protectors of human rights, might a *liberal-democratic identity discourse* shape India's policy-responses to humanitarian crises and predispose policy-makers in New Delhi to favour interventionist responses consistent with the R2P norm? But India is also a former colony, a leading member of the Non Aligned Movement, and it has traditionally opposed Western 'meddling' in the developing world, so perhaps an *anti-imperial identity discourse* shapes India's policy responses in ways which mean New Delhi is inclined to oppose R2P-inspired interventions? Finally, India, as a rising power, pursues an ever-growing list of crucial national interests. Maybe, then, a *great power identity discourse* shapes India's policy responses in ways which mean New Delhi's support for or opposition to R2P-inspired interventions is shaped by hard-headed calculations about what best enhances India's security, prosperity or its diplomatic influence? Importantly, other potentially relevant identity discourses were also examined, although the data ultimately demonstrated that the three primary discourses – including somewhat different 'strains' or variants within them – exerted the greatest shaping influence on India's policy-responses to the three humanitarian crises which broke during 2011 and 2012.

But the question of linkage or causation – whether a particular discourse caused a particular policy response – is a tricky one; in particular, the nature of the evidence available makes process-tracing difficult. Nevertheless, the Indian media and academic debates are lively, relatively voluminous and, importantly, they are *available* to scholars, as one would expect in a healthy democracy. These sources yield plenty of evidence about how contributors to the public debates – who are called 'policy-shapers' in later chapters – interpreted the various humanitarian crises which broke out while India sat on the Security Council, and they subsequently offered advice about how India should respond. In other words, the various identity discourses are treated in this study as 'shaping' India's policy towards particular humanitarian crises; we cannot be certain that one or more discourses strictly *caused* a particular policy-response but we can be relatively confident that they *shaped* the response, if only in subtle but still very important ways. By the end of Chapter 2, therefore, the conceptual framework which drove the study will have been made clear.

The empirical analysis begins in Chapter 3 with consideration of India's responses to R2P and its predecessor, the practice or norm of humanitarian intervention, before India took up its Security Council seat in 2011. The chapter begins with discussion of India's intervention in what was then East Pakistan (now Bangladesh) in 1971; then India's trying Sri Lankan adventure in the late 1980s is explored; following that India's reactions to the various humanitarian interventions of the 1990s are considered; and exploration of India's interventions in the debates about R2P between 2001 and 2010 end Chapter 3. The analysis is structured throughout with reference to the identity discourses identified in Chapter 2, and a sort of 'baseline' is established: in other words, knowing India's position on R2P in 2010 enables conclusions to be drawn in later chapters about how India's experiences during its Security Council tenure affected New Delhi's position on R2P.

The empirical analysis continues in Chapters 4, 5 and 6 where India's responses to the three humanitarian crises are assessed in detail. India's response to the crisis in Côte d'Ivoire is examined first, in Chapter 4, although that discussion ultimately demonstrates that this crisis was relatively unimportant from New Delhi's perspective. Accordingly, Chapter 4 is relatively short simply because there was very little Indian debate about this crisis, and few formal policy responses. But the volume of Indian debates about the crises in Libya (Chapter 5) and Syria (Chapter 6) was orders of magnitude greater, making theses chapters much longer. And while Chapter 6 is primarily focused on the Syrian crisis during 2011 and 2012 it also considers what occurred thereafter, especially the chemical attack in August 2013 and the intervention in Iraq which began in July 2014. Together these three empirical chapters constitute the heart of the book.

The implications to be drawn from the empirical analysis chapters are presented in a final concluding chapter. The primary purpose of the study as a whole is to determine India's position on R2P, and especially its Pillar III component, by examining New Delhi's responses to humanitarian crises. Accordingly, this final chapter is dominated by assessment of India's position on R2P put in the broader context of the challenge posed by the R2P norm to traditional interpretations of the meaning of sovereignty. Finally, some thoughts about what India's position on R2P may mean for the *global* fortunes of the R2P doctrine more generally are presented briefly, along with some more speculative insights about the prospects of India's international identity changing in future.

Chapter 1

Humanitarian Intervention and the Responsibility to Protect Before 2011

This chapter broadly explores the wider or global status and fortunes of the humanitarian intervention practice or norm and its successor, the responsibility to protect (R2P) norm before 2011; India's position on these matters up to and including 2010 is the subject of sustained treatment in Chapter 3, while Chapters 4, 5 and 6 examine India's engagement with R2P thereafter.

How much R2P differs from humanitarian intervention continues to be a matter of fierce debate, especially after the regime change which followed NATO's intervention in Libya in 2011. R2P is *supposed* to be different from humanitarian intervention, at least as the latter was practiced in the 1990s. Indeed, R2P was specifically designed by the International Commission on Intervention and State Sovereignty (ICISS) in 2001 as a more effective and less controversial replacement for the practice or norm of humanitarian intervention; the conventional narrative is that R2P emerged out of efforts to 'regulate' humanitarian intervention – to establish criteria to determine when interventions could or should occur – especially in response to criticism of NATO's war in Kosovo in 1999. It is therefore important to note that there are key differences between the practice or norm of humanitarian intervention and the R2P norm; in particular, R2P is 'wider' in the sense that it encompasses state- and capacity-building initiatives (Pillar I and Pillar II) to ensure vulnerable populations can be protected without the need for military intervention (Pillar III). These finer points of difference are discussed in greater detail later in the chapter.

Nevertheless, a definition of humanitarian intervention is offered immediately below on the assumption that R2P – particularly its Pillar III – resembles the older practice or norm enough to warrant treating them as essentially part of the same normative tradition. Doing so also enables the latter two-thirds of this chapter to be organised in a chronological narrative which examines the practice or norm of humanitarian intervention first before R2P is considered; in other words, the R2P norm is treated as 'evolving' out of the older tradition. But before this narrative can commence, the first third of the chapter is organised thematically because it briefly sketches some of the philosophical arguments for and against humanitarian intervention.

Philosophical Arguments For and Against Humanitarian Intervention

At the outset the author must clarify why humanitarian intervention was referred to above as a 'practice or norm'. This formulation was preferred because humanitarian intervention was always a somewhat fuzzy or indistinct concept, at least compared to the R2P norm. It was certainly practiced by some states (especially in the 1990s, as the discussion below shows), and those states typically gave various justifications for doing so which can be treated as evidence that their behaviour was informed or shaped by 'a norm' (i.e. 'a standard of appropriate behaviour for actors with a given identity'[1]). But it is also true that humanitarian intervention was not ever codified, or at least it was never 'stated as precisely' as the R2P norm has been in various documents between 2001 and 2009.

Nevertheless, it is necessary to define 'humanitarian intervention' as precisely as possible to avoid confusion. A typical humanitarian intervention (i.e. including an intervention of the sort contemplated by, or possible under, Pillar III of R2P) occurs when three essential elements are met. First, there must be military action, or the threat of it, by one or more international actors – usually states because they are the primary strategic actors today – which influences events inside the borders of another actor. Second, the actor intervened in (also typically a state which would otherwise enjoy sovereign immunity) must not consent to the intervention, or its consent must have been extracted by coercion or pressure. Of course, sometimes a state's government requests foreign military intervention, which confuses matters somewhat, but usually people mean the non-consensual variety when they talk of humanitarian intervention. Finally, the intention of the intervening actors must have substantially been to prevent or alleviate large-scale atrocities.[2]

This last aspect of humanitarian intervention – the intent of the intervener – is especially controversial because of the 'problem of other minds'; put simply, we can never know with perfect confidence whether what another actor tells about their motives or intentions is true. We also know that humanitarian intervention principles have been *abused*, to 'smokescreen' or justify the pursuit of other more traditional national interests: Adolf Hitler's annexation of Sudentenland in 1938 is perhaps the classic example. A related critique is that the humanitarian intervention norm can be *applied selectively*, and in particular the choice of when and where to intervene is typically tainted by inequalities of power.[3] In other words, powerful

1 Martha Finnemore and Kathryn Sikkink, 'International Norm Dynamics and Political Change', *International Organization* 52:4 (1998), 891.

2 D.J.B. Timms and Brendan Simms, 'Towards a History of Humanitarian Intervention', in D.J.B. Timms and Brendan Simms (eds), *Humanitarian Intervention: A History* (Cambridge: Cambridge University Press, 2011), 4; Adam Roberts, 'The So-Called "Right" of Humanitarian Intervention', in *Yearbook of International Humanitarian Law* 2000, Vol. 3 (The Hague: T.M.C. Asser, 2002), 3.

3 Mohammed Ayoob, 'Humanitarian Intervention and State Sovereignty', *International Journal of Human Rights* 6:1 (2002), 86.

states cannot be held to the same standards because intervening in them is simply not realistic.

As we will see later in the book these two critiques of humanitarian intervention, and now of R2P, are typically the strongest and loudest. Nicholas Wheeler characterises the abuse and selectivity critiques as 'realist',[4] although not all those who level these accusations self-describe as realists; Noam Chomsky, for example, assumes *Western* states are typically abusers of humanitarian intervention and R2P, grounding his argument more in Marxist and/or postcolonial premises than strictly realist ones.[5] But another critique is more distinctively realist in the sense of being grounded, as Hans Morgenthau puts it, in the 'moral principle of national survival', meaning that in a world of sovereign states the highest moral duties are owed to one's own community.[6] Thus Samuel Huntington argued against humanitarian intervention in Somalia in 1993 because, as he put it, American soldiers sign up to defend *America*, and it is both unwise and immoral to risk their lives unless vital national interests are at stake (which they weren't in Somalia, at least according to Huntington).[7]

Wheeler usefully illustrates the dilemma posed and the controversy stirred by humanitarian intervention in a world of sovereign states with reference to the venerable debate about the relationship between order and justice.[8] Drawing on Hedley Bull's pluralist/solidarist distinction,[9] Wheeler has argued that the pluralist moral position – which generally opposes humanitarian intervention – privileges the maintenance of international order over justice; in other words, because conceptions of what constitutes justice differ between states and societies they should generally tolerate each other's differences on this question.

Bhikhu Parekh notes the debt this position owes to J.S. Mill's 'harm principle' and his notion that societies only 'mature' by learning to manage their own affairs, so non-intervention should be the norm and intervention should occur only very rarely.[10] This broad, pluralist 'live and let live' attitude has both a moral foundation

---

4 *Saving Strangers: Humanitarian Intervention and International Society* (Oxford: Oxford University Press, 2000), 30–32.

5 'The Skeleton in the Closet: The Responsibility to Protect in History', in Philip Cunliffe (ed.), *Critical Perspectives on the Responsibility to Protect: Interrogating Theory and Practice* (Oxon: Routledge, 2011).

6 *Politics Among Nations: The Struggle for Power and Peace*, 5th ed., (New York: Alfred A. Knopf, 1948), 10; Jennifer M. Welsh, 'Taking Consequences Seriously: Objections to Humanitarian Intervention', in Jennifer M. Welsh (ed.), *Humanitarian Intervention and International Relations* (Oxford: Oxford University Press, 2004), 58–60; Adrian Gallagher, 'A Clash of Responsibilities: Engaging with Realist Critiques of the R2P', *Global Responsibility to Protect* 4:3 (2012), 337–339.

7 'New Contingencies, Old Roles', *Joint Forces Quarterly* 2 (Autumn 1992), 38–43.

8 *Saving Strangers*, 11–13.

9 'The Grotian Conception of International Society', in Herbert Butterfield and Martin Wight (eds), *Diplomatic Investigations* (London: Allen & Unwin, 1966), 51–74.

10 Bhikhu Parekh, 'Rethinking Humanitarian Intervention', *International Political Science Review* 18:1 (1997), 52.

– if conceptions of justice differ, who is to say which should apply universally? – and two pragmatic bases, namely, if interventionism became too common general instability would harm all, and if societies are not generally left alone to sort out their own problems those problems are just stored up for the future. International order is therefore best preserved, so this line of reasoning goes, when states' rights are privileged over individuals' rights. Hedley Bull, for example, while refusing to definitively privilege order over justice in all circumstances still felt maintaining order was and logically must be the prime goal of international society – especially in light of the sorry history of international conflict during the turbulent twentieth century – which ultimately led him (in the 1980s) to dismiss the notion that a humanitarian intervention norm was or should be an accepted feature of international society.[11]

This pluralist logic underpins the traditional, relatively strict conception of state sovereignty – especially the self-determination and non-intervention aspects of the sovereignty norm – which has for several centuries formed the basic organising principle of the international system.[12] Consider Vincent and Suganami's 'egg-box' analogy: the international system, so the pluralist position maintains, should act like an egg-carton, cushioning and protecting the eggs/states and allowing them to find their own solutions to their internal-stability problems rather than interfering with and breaking them.[13] In other words, while proponents of pluralism might concede sometimes strong sovereignty norms may lead to atrocities, they nevertheless maintain that most states, most of the time, adequately protect most of their citizens from harm.

By contrast the solidarist position favours 'relaxed' definitions of state sovereignty more amenable to the humanitarian intervention norm. The moral dimension of the solidarist position is based on the belief that contemporary political and cultural divisions are to some extent arbitrary and historically contingent; solidarists therefore believe some principles of justice – in this case basic human rights – *are* universally valid, which means we all owe at least some basic moral obligations to each other, even to 'strangers' or non-members of our own group. R.J. Vincent defined these basic rights as those which protect persons from arbitrary violence and ensure a minimum subsistence,[14] and he concluded it may be moral to intervene to protect strangers' rights to both in the most extreme of circumstances. The pragmatic basis of the solidarist position rests on the insight that justice and order are not necessarily forever in tension, and instead carefully designed institutions can ensure they become mutually supportive. Unjust orders tend to cause resentment, misery and desperation, and eventually revolution; over-privileging order, so the argument goes, actually *undermines* order in the long run.

11 *Intervention in World Politics* (Oxford: Oxford University Press, 1984), 193.

12 Hedley Bull and Adam Watson (eds), *The Expansion of International Society* (Oxford: Clarendon Press, 1984).

13 R.J. Vincent, *Human Rights and International Relations* (Cambridge: Cambridge University Press, 1986), 123.

14 Ibid., 14.

Solidarists typically have to finesse their way around the various critiques of humanitarian intervention which confront them. For example, to counter the scepticism inherent in the abuse critique Michael Walzer counters that 'there are only mixed cases where the humanitarian motive is one amongst many',[15] and James Pattison notes both the 'realist position that states will always act purely on the basis of self-interest and the view that states can possess purely humanitarian motives are too crude'. Indeed, he thinks it may be *desirable* that potential interveners are partly self-interested by non-humanitarian motives to ensure an intervention actually goes ahead, and effectively, saving more lives than a 'pure' but half-hearted, easily-abandoned intervention (or a decision to not intervene at all).[16] Thomas Weiss agrees, arguing 'while the ethical humanitarian rationale need not be exclusive or even foremost, it should be explicit and prominent'.[17] Wheeler even rejects the absolute necessity of humanitarian motives or intentions, and instead focuses on outcomes: 'even if an intervention is motivated by non-humanitarian reasons', he contends, 'it can still count as humanitarian provided the motives, and the means employed, do not undermine a positive humanitarian outcome'.[18]

Solidarists also must typically finesse their way around the selectivity critique, which is a powerful one because selective application runs counter to the practice of equality before the law, a crucial component of any rule-of-law system which is itself inherent in the notion that human rights exist at all. Obviously if decisions to launch humanitarian interventions occurred too selectively – based on an arbitrary coin-toss, or informed only by racism, etc. – this would be a major problem. Solidarists counter the selectivity critique by invoking the intuitively attractive yet still conceptually slippery notion that just because we cannot *always* intervene to protect human rights, it does not necessarily follow that we should *never* do so.[19] Pattison provides several other justifications for allowing some degree of selectivity in the application of humanitarian intervention principles, like situations in which potential interveners may have insufficient resources if faced with several humanitarian crises at once.[20] Still, selectivity remains a problem for solidarists because it exposes them to accusations of hypocrisy and, more generally, means the victims of certain crises are left to suffer while other victims in different crises are protected.

---

15 *Just and Unjust Wars: A Moral Argument with Historical Illustrations* (New York: Basic Books, 1977), 101.

16 James Pattison, *Humanitarian Intervention and the Responsibility to Protect: Who Should Intervene?* (Oxford: Oxford University Press, 2010), 159–160.

17 *Humanitarian Intervention*, 2nd ed. (Cambridge: Polity Press, 2012), 8.

18 *Saving Strangers*, 38–39.

19 International Commission on Intervention and State Sovereignty (ICISS), *The Responsibility to Protect: Supplementary Volume* (Ottawa: International Development Research Centre, 2001), 150.

20 Pattison, *Humanitarian Intervention*, 170–171.

Ultimately the pluralist position, which essentially represents a status quo and prudentially cautious position, is a difficult one to overcome. Accordingly, the solidarist position is typically not presented in the potentially radical form it could take, namely, abolishment of sovereignty and imposition of a universal rule-of-law under a world state (although a few scholars have come perilously close to advocating such[21]). Instead, solidarists typically take G.K. Chesterton's warnings about the dangers of 'virtue run amok' seriously[22]; Chesterton famously argued that during the Thirty Years War which wracked seventeenth century Europe, intervention by states in their neighbours' affairs to protect co-religionists' human (and spiritual) rights became an entrenched, destabilising dynamic which caused more suffering than would have occurred if non-interference had been the norm. Not coincidentally, of course, the sovereignty norm arose in the wake of these terrible wars.[23]

Solidarists therefore typically accept, simply put, the need to work within the limits set by a deeply entrenched sovereign state system.[24] For example, pro-intervention solidarists typically warn against *unilateral* humanitarian interventions, and instead prefer multilateral decision-making processes to provide a degree of constraint and greater legitimacy[25] even if this means likely delays or even failure to act in some crises. They debate the trade-offs between seeking a strong-interventionist – but therefore controversial – norm, or a watered-down but more widely-acceptable norm, and whether criteria should guide action or if a case-by-case approach is better, etc. These matters will be taken up again later in the chapter when we examine the debates about the meaning and scope of the R2P norm after 2001.

Keeping all of these complex and difficult issues in mind, advocates of the R2P norm have therefore typically limited themselves to calling for a *reconceptualisation* of the sovereignty norm, or the creation of a 'recognised exception' to it. At the core of their arguments is the notion that sovereignty implies *responsibilities* to protect 'the values of individual life and communal liberty'[26] and not just a hard or inflexible right of absolute non-interference. Chris Brown, for example, disputes that sovereignty implies an absolute right of non-interference by asserting 'if

---

21 Heather Roff, *Global Justice, Kant, and the Responsibility to Protect: A Provisional Duty* (Oxon: Routledge, 2013). Note that B. Sharon Byrd and Joachim Hruschka have called for the creation of a world government, but their paper was not exclusively concerned with humanitarian intervention: 'From the State of Nature to the Juridical State of States', *Law and Philosophy* 27:6 (2008), 599–641.

22 Oliver P. Richmond, 'The Problem of Peace: Understanding the Liberal Peace', in Ashok Swain, Ramses Amer and Joakim Öjendal (eds), *Globalization and Challenges to Building Peace* (London: Anthem Press, 2008).

23 Daniel Philpott, *Revolutions in Sovereignty* (Princeton: Princeton University Press, 2001), Part Two.

24 Weiss, *Humanitarian Intervention*, 32–33.

25 Michael J. Smith, 'Humanitarian Intervention: An Overview of the Ethical Issues', *Ethics and International Affairs* 12:1 (1998), 67.

26 Walzer, *Just and Unjust Wars*, 108.

diversity entails that states have the right to mistreat their populations, then it is difficult to see why such diversity is to be valued'.[27]

The philosophical debates for and against humanitarian intervention cannot be accorded full justice in this book, which is focused on examining *India's* policy towards R2P. But they cannot be ignored entirely because the Indian debates about R2P are 'nested' in a wider web of global-level discourses and abstract philosophical debates about human rights, the meaning of sovereignty, global stability, etc. Discussion therefore returns to them at times, but most of the rest of this chapter examines how humanitarian intervention remained nascent for decades before flowering in the post-Cold War world of the 1990s, which in turn provoked considerable controversy and subsequently led to the emergence of the R2P norm after 2001.

Finally, because most treatments of humanitarian intervention until quite recently asked 'is it acceptable under international law?',[28] the discussion addresses this question in the next two sections which examine the pre-2001 period. But since then debate has shifted somewhat to consideration of global *norms* – it is often asked whether R2P is an 'entrenched *norm*' – so the terminology shifts later in the chapter after the relationship between laws and norms is conceptualised more fully.

Humanitarian Interventions Before 1990

Common sense in debates about humanitarian intervention holds it was a distinctive practice of the post-Cold War world. This is substantially true in that it was usually viewed as 'inconsistent with the conventional pattern of international relations' before 1990.[29] Still, Michael Ignatieff's blunt claim that humanitarian intervention began in 1991[30] is somewhat misleading. The Spanish jurist Vitoria, Calvinists in Basel, and the Dutch jurist Grotius all endorsed roughly similar doctrines in the sixteenth century.[31] Edmund Burke also mixed humanitarian and national security concerns when arguing for British intervention in Revolutionary France.[32] And the

27 *International Relations Theory: New Normative Approaches* (Hemel Hempstead: Harvester Wheatsheaf, 1992), 15.

28 Walzer, *Just and Unjust Wars*; Vincent, *Human Rights*, etc.

29 R.J. Vincent, *Nonintervention and International Order* (Princeton: Princeton University Press, 1974), 13.

30 *Empire Lite: Nation-Building in Bosnia, Kosovo and Afghanistan* (London: Vintage, 2003), 57.

31 D.J.B. Trim, '"If a Prince Use Tyrannie Towards his People": Interventions on Behalf of Foreign Populations in Early Modern Europe', in D.J.B. Timms and Brendan Simms (eds), *Humanitarian Intervention: A History* (Cambridge: Cambridge University Press, 2011).

32 Jennifer M. Welsh, 'Edmund Burke and Intervention: Empire and Neighbourhood', in Stefano Recchia and Jennifer M. Welsh (eds), *Just and Unjust Military Intervention: European Thinkers from Vitoria to Mill* (Cambridge: Cambridge University Press, 2013).

historical examples of humanitarian intervention most commonly cited occurred when nineteenth century European powers intervened to protect Christians in the Ottoman Empire (i.e. Greeks in 1827, Syrian Maronites in 1860, Slavs in the late 1870s, etc.).[33]

By the end of the nineteenth century some international jurists felt humanitarian intervention was acceptable, although they were in a minority.[34] Their position was, however, shot through with implicit racist prejudices: no interventions were suggested, let alone took place, to protect Tasmanian Aborigines from settler-genocide or native Congolese from King Leopold's depredations; as 'uncivilised' peoples they were not considered suitable candidates.[35] It was only in the twentieth century that the long-standing civilised/barbaric distinction began to break down and fully-human status was assigned to non-white persons and groups. When asserting a right of humanitarian intervention to stop 'arbitrary and persistent abuse' in 1921, for example, Ellery Stowell did not rule out the possibility that one European colonial power might intervene in another European state's colony to protect colonial subjects from atrocities.[36] But it was Nazi atrocities during World War II that fatally undermined the old racist assumptions. The United Nations was formed in 1946 and a number of non-European societies were admitted into the society of states and afforded equal sovereign status, with many more to follow, and the Universal Declaration of Human Rights (signed in 1948) explicitly recognised the inherent equality of all humanity.

Yet in the following decades the prospects of humanitarian intervention becoming a recognised component of international law actually *receded*. Logically speaking Nazi atrocities could have been interpreted not just as a motivation to remove racial prejudices and to accept non-Europeans – and their states – as equals, but also as a reason to institutionalise humanitarian intervention to prevent future Holocausts. But, as Hersch Lauterpacht put it in 1946, 'conceived in the spirit of realism, the [UN] Charter in many respects preferred order to law'[37] and it was decided the international 'use of force' was only legal in two very specific circumstances, namely, in self-defence (without Security Council authorisation: Article 51) or to 'maintain or restore international peace and stability' (requiring the Council's authorisation: Article 42). Article 55(c) does call on the UN to 'promote … universal respect for, and observance of, human rights', but it is not linked explicitly to Article 42.

33 Wheeler, *Saving Strangers*, 45; Weiss *Humanitarian Intervention*, 35; Gary Bass, *Freedom's Battle: Origins of Humanitarian Interventionism* (New York: Alfred A. Knopf, 2008).

34 Weiss, *Humanitarian Intervention*, 37.

35 Thomas M. Franck and Nigel S. Rodley, 'After Bangladesh: The Law of Humanitarian Intervention by Military Force', *American Journal of International Law* 67:2 (1973), 281.

36 *Intervention in International Law* (Washington: John Byrne & Co, 1921), 53

37 'The Grotian Tradition in International Law', *British Year Book of International Law* 23:1 (1946), fn. 2.

So, while a predominantly internal humanitarian crisis featuring atrocities may acquire an international dimension – like when refugees flood across a border and threaten the peace in another state – and thus trigger a Council-authorised intervention, a literal reading of Article 42 suggests mass atrocities occurring within a state would not typically constitute a threat to '*international* peace and security'. This interpretation dominated for most of the Cold War despite occasionally vigorous debate.[38] Various reasons are advanced for this. First, notwithstanding the awful atrocities perpetrated by the Nazis and others, most of the death and destruction during World War II was caused by straightforward interstate conflict, suggesting the newly-minted UN should focus on eliminating the 'greater of two evils'.[39] Second, newly-independent ex-colonies lacked 'positive sovereignty' – actual control over their territories – and remained very weak compared to their erstwhile colonial masters, so they collectively emphasised 'negative sovereignty', or the right of non-interference.[40] Finally, because most states aligned with one or the other nuclear-armed superpower after 1945 prudence dictated both sides avoid regular, overt intervention in each other's client-states lest a wider and potentially species-threatening conflagration erupt.[41]

Nevertheless, several Cold War-era interventions can be interpreted as humanitarian. For example, Wheeler paid particular attention to India's 1971 intervention in what became Bangladesh, Vietnam's overthrow of Cambodia's Pol Pot regime in 1979, and Tanzania's intervention in Uganda, also in 1979, in his influential 2001 book *Saving Strangers*. He found them to all be valid examples of humanitarian intervention – despite the fact that none of them were motivated *primarily* by humanitarian principles – because positive humanitarian *outcomes* were achieved. But these outcomes provided no real boost to the legal status of the humanitarian intervention norm; indeed, quite the opposite occurred because there was widespread resistance by other states (as Wheeler puts it, 'precedent setting was the dominant objection'[42]). Specifically, prevailing international opinion held that India had acted unilaterally and, in effect, encouraged separatism in East Pakistan while stretching the meaning of self-defence,[43] despite citing humanitarianism as a motivation for its intervention. Vietnam's case for self-defence was more clear-

38 Richard Lillich, *Humanitarian Intervention and the United Nations* (Charlottesville: University Press of Virginia, 1973).

39 Adam Roberts, 'The United Nations and Humanitarian Intervention', in Jennifer M. Welsh (ed.), *Humanitarian Intervention and International Relations* (Oxford: Oxford University Press, 2004), 72.

40 Robert Jackson, *Quasi-States: Sovereignty, International Relations and the Third World* (Cambridge: Cambridge University Press, 1990).

41 Weiss, *Humanitarian Intervention*, 38.

42 *Saving Strangers*, 135.

43 Ibid., 72: regarding self-defence, Pakistan *did* initiate hostilities with air-strikes, but India had been arming the rebels and was mobilising its own forces, threatening invasion; Summit Ganguly, 'The Indo-Pak Conflict', in Atul Kohli and Prema Singh (eds), *Routledge Handbook of Indian Politics* (Oxon: Routledge, 2013).

cut,[44] but Hanoi never offered humanitarian justifications and the resulting near-universal condemnation of its intervention owed much to geopolitical politicking.[45] Only Tanzania avoided sustained criticism – it had been blatantly attacked by Idi Amin's Uganda, and the subsequent intervention in Uganda was essentially a continuation of the Tanzanian counter-attack from within its own borders – but this incident was still not widely considered a proper instance of humanitarian intervention.[46]

Customary international law is recognised with reference to two broad criteria: first, state practice – and roughly speaking 'the more the better' – which follows certain patterns that suggest they were 'following a rule', and second, *opinio juris* must be found, or evidence that states *believed* their actions were legally justifiable (without too many objections by other states).[47] Before releasing the 2001 report which presented the earliest form of the R2P norm the ICISS examined the three cases mentioned above and seven additional, potential cases of humanitarian intervention during the Cold War.[48] But given that only ten such (potential) humanitarian interventions took place – and all were considered dubious or contestable examples at best[49] – while millions of civilians died in dozens of conflicts between 1945 and 1990, many at the hands of their own governments, the evidence that states practiced humanitarian intervention during the Cold War is thin at best. And the evidence of *opinio juris* is even thinner. As noted above, some interveners, like Vietnam, never claimed humanitarianism as a motivation for their intervention in neighbouring states; and typically plenty of other states loudly condemned these interventions, thereby affirming the prevailing strict interpretation of sovereignty.[50] International Court of Justice decisions in the *Corfu Channel* (1949) and especially the *Nicaragua* (1986) cases reaffirmed the prevailing strict interpretation of the meaning of sovereignty and its corollary,

44 Over several years Pol Pot's forces repeatedly raided Vietnam, killing thousands of villagers. Vietnam invaded in October 1977 but then unilaterally withdrew. Cambodian provocations continued and after its attempts to foment rebellion in 1978 failed, Vietnam finally invaded 'properly' in late December 1979.

45 *Saving Strangers*, 108: America was still smarting from defeat in the Vietnam War and its allies supported it against its former enemy; ASEAN states feared a resurgent, unconstrained Vietnam; China and its allies backed the Khmer Rouge, etc. Only the Soviet Union and its clients backed Vietnam.

46 *Saving Strangers*, 136.

47 Shirley V. Scott, *International Law in World Politics*, 2nd ed. (Boulder: Lynne Rienner, 2010), 5–7.

48 International Commission on Intervention and State Sovereignty (ICISS), *The Responsibility to Protect: Research, Bibliography, Background* (Ottawa: International Development Research Centre), 150.

49 Simon Chesterman, *Just War or Just Peace: Humanitarian Intervention and International Law* (Oxford: Oxford University Press, 2001), 84.

50 Roberts, 'The United Nations', 78.

non-intervention.[51] And, crucially, none of the ten potentially humanitarian interventions which the ICISS examined was authorised by the Security Council. Therefore before the 1990s the notion of humanitarian intervention was just that, a notion promoted by a few academics and occasionally deployed by a state – alongside a slew of other reasons – to justify an intervention (which then typically provoked much condemnation).

Humanitarian Intervention in the 1990s

The situation changed noticeably in the 1990s. This is not to say humanitarian intervention became a fully accepted component of international law, because it didn't, it remained vigorously contested. Still, the end of the Cold War led to interventions which could be said to have been – at least in part – humanitarian in nature or intent becoming more common, meaning it is at least arguable that they were motivated by an emerging humanitarian intervention norm.

There were a number of reasons for this. Systemically, fears that overly-zealous interventionism would spark a nuclear war receded as the Cold War faded into history. The fact the *Soviet Union* collapsed in 1991 also mattered profoundly; at minimum, it is difficult to imagine a wave of humanitarian interventions would have followed an *American* collapse. The 1990s were also marked by multiple state-failures in many conflict-ridden societies as superpower (especially Soviet) support for their governments ended abruptly. The result was a burst of small-arms proliferation, and a sharp rise in low-intensity conflicts – what Mary Kaldor famously called the 'New Wars'[52] – in which civilians became explicit targets, causing waves of refugees in Africa, the Middle East, Central Asia and even in Europe. In Western states the so-called 'CNN effect' – constant, harrowing images of suffering on TV screens – also precipitated a boom in civil society organisations dedicated to easing the plight of strangers. Western states and their key institutions – especially NATO – also began searching for new forms of legitimacy and unity, finding it partly by committing their now under-utilised militaries to humanitarian missions.[53] The Security Council also became less polarised after the end of the Cold War and therefore somewhat less gridlocked[54] meaning that internal conflicts were more commonly found to be threats to international peace and security.

For the humanitarian intervention practice or norm to have become an entrenched component of international law in the 1990s would have required

51 Weiss, *Humanitarian Intervention*, 38.

52 *New and Old Wars: Organized Violence in a Global Era* (Stanford: Stanford University Press, 1999).

53 Jennifer M. Welsh, 'Introduction', in Welsh (ed.), *Humanitarian Intervention*, 2–3; Weiss, *Humanitarian Intervention*, 42; Smith, 'Humanitarian Intervention', 64–69.

54 Roberts, 'The United Nations', 81.

several things: first, more instances of behaviour consistent with it and supporting *opinio juris*, over a range of somewhat different circumstances and over time; second, some sort of codification (preferably in an international treaty or, ideally, by amending the UN Charter); and third, reform of global governance structures in a way which facilitated (by authorising and resourcing) particular humanitarian interventions. As the 1990s advanced there *were* more humanitarian interventions and more *opinio juris* (i.e. intervening states arguing they were justified or obliged to intervene to protect human rights). Importantly, however, the interventions continued to encounter resistance from other states, meaning the humanitarian intervention practice or norm was not really codified and global governance structures were not substantially reformed. The R2P norm itself was, of course, introduced in 2001 to remedy these shortcomings and entrench the practice of humanitarian intervention more deeply into international law.

The first real humanitarian intervention of 1990s came after the main battles of the Gulf War had ended with Iraq's defeat and Kuwait's liberation. UN Security Council Resolution 688 of 5 April 1991 condemned 'the repression of the Iraqi civilian population [i.e. mainly Shias and Kurds] … the consequences of which threaten international peace and security'. Masses of refugees fled – especially into Turkey – which arguably gave this crisis an international dimension; in other words, international peace and security was arguably being threatened, which could have justified action under Chapter VII of the UN Charter (i.e. Article 42). Still, the subsequent intervention was not strictly-speaking taken under Chapter VII; there were no *explicit* enforcement provisions included in Resolution 688 after China and Russia threatened to veto an earlier draft. But several weeks later Western states declared and then enforced 'safe zones' and 'No-Fly Zones' over Iraq. Wheeler says they were 'advancing a new claim: the use of force could be justified to enforce compliance with an existing Security Council resolution that demanded respect for human rights' even if this pre-existing resolution did not *specifically* authorise them to do so.[55]

The intervention in Somalia in 1993 also responded to an internal human rights tragedy – but this time with no massive refugee component – which was nevertheless also characterised as a threat to international peace and security by the Council. The resolution also contained a Chapter VII authorisation to deploy 'all necessary means to establish … a secure environment for humanitarian relief operations'.[56] While few states objected forcefully to the intervention in Somalia, the resolution recognised its own 'unique' and 'exceptional' nature and, technically, it was neither a consensual nor a non-consensual intervention because there was no functioning government to request or oppose it.[57] Still, efforts to prevent a

55 'The Humanitarian Responsibilities of Sovereignty', in Welsh (ed.), *Humanitarian Intervention*, 33.

56 SC/Res/794, 3 December 1992.

57 Adam Roberts, 'Humanitarian War: Military Intervention and Human Rights', *International Affairs* 69:3 (1993), 429–449.

precedent being treated as such are never wholly effective: the action taken *was* humanitarian in intent; and some states delivered *opinio juris* consistent with humanitarianism (the *weight* of such a precedent is, however, another matter). Yet, the deaths of 18 US troops in what is now known as the 'Blackhawk Down' incident cooled American ardour for similar 'pure' humanitarian interventions thereafter (i.e. as noted earlier, Huntington argued that the US had few pressing 'traditional' interests in Somalia, and this interpretation came to be widely accepted).

Several other humanitarian crises broke out nearly simultaneously. In 1992 the Liberian civil war was declared a threat to international peace and security, although intervention was limited to an arms embargo. Then early in the Bosnian War the Security Council declared the 'continuation of this situation constitutes a threat to international peace and security', although intervention was again initially limited to an arms embargo[58] and it took some time for more interventionist measures to be imposed.[59] But the war intensified until NATO's *Operation Deliberate Force* (September 1995). These bombing missions against the ethnic Serbian militias who had been perpetrating many of the atrocities had some Security Council backing – a No-Fly Zone had been imposed in 1992, for example[60] – but previous NATO efforts to deploy force had typically been hampered by glacial approval processes and a (self-confessed[61]) tendency for UNPROFOR (i.e. the UN peacekeeping mission) and its contributing states to privilege soldiers' over civilians' safety. NATO had been authorised to 'coordinate' with the UN, and the Secretary-General had even requested some specific strikes on occasion,[62] but after the July 1995 Srebrenica massacre the Council was not consulted again, meaning *Operation Deliberate Force* in its full coercive glory, so to speak, took place without specific authorisation.

Precedents for the view that once the Council declared a threat to international peace and stability (and used the words 'all necessary means') states were entitled to determine on their own *how to implement* the resolution were beginning to stack up. But events in Rwanda, where 800,000 people died in 1994 despite a UN presence, showed that the question of *whether* states would always follow through after the Council had ruled was a live one. As the mass-killings intensified, on 21 April the Security Council actually *reduced* UNAMIR from 2,500 to 270.[63] A month later a threat to international peace and stability was declared by the Council,[64] but UNAMIR was increased agonisingly slowly and the veto-powers

58 SC/Res/713, 25 September 1991.

59 SC/Res/749, 7 April 1992; SC/Res/ 836, 4 June 1993.

60 SC/Res/ 781, 9 October 1992.

61 A/54/549, *Report of the Secretary-General Pursuant to General Assembly Resolution 53/35: The Fall of Srebrenica*, 15 November 1999, 480–483.

62 Nicholas Morris, 'Humanitarian Intervention in the Balkans', in Jennifer M. Welsh (ed.), *Humanitarian Intervention and International Relations* (Oxford: Oxford University Press, 2004), 109.

63 SC/Res/912.

64 SC/Res/ 918, 17 May 1994.

studiously avoided using the word 'genocide' while also declining to take concrete steps to intervene. On 22 June the Security Council (ironically) demanded an 'urgent' response which was, however, also called 'unique'. France's subsequent *Operation Turquoise* and a rebel offensive ultimately ended the genocide,[65] leading Simon Chesterman to declare in 2001 that

> [i]mplicit in many of the arguments for a right of humanitarian intervention is the suggestion that [state sovereignty] is preventing interventions that should take place. This is simply not true. Interventions do not take place because states do not want them to take place. Fear of international condemnation did not prevent any state intervening in Rwanda: televised images of a downed US Ranger being dragged through the streets of Somalia [during the Blackhawk Down incident] did.[66]

Still, he conceded there was in the 1990s a 'general shift away from reliance on transboundary implications of a situation [towards] greater preparedness to view an internal conflict as a threat to peace and security'.[67] The 1999 East Timor intervention is illustrative: the refugees who fled the violence perpetrated by government-backed militias did not cross any borders. This intervention has been called 'so particular that its lessons may be hard to generalize': Indonesia ultimately consented to the intervention which ended the atrocities, but only after it had faced a considerable degree of international pressure; and East Timor had been invaded in 1975, so 'Indonesia's claim to sovereignty ... was not [widely] recognised' anyway.[68] But any case can technically serve as a precedent (again, its weight is another matter), and this one saw the initial deployment of INTERFET with Security Council authorisation.[69]

Therefore by 1999 it was at least arguable that a humanitarian intervention norm had become part of customary international law. Not everyone examines the same precedents – Roberts[70] and Weiss[71] examine nine, although their lists vary marginally, while Chesterman[72] examines 11 – but these scholars nevertheless all broadly agreed that state practice showed humanitarian intervention had at least become more common. Regarding *opinio juris*, on the one hand the mere fact the Council regularly found humanitarian concerns constituted threats to international peace and security suggests customary law was being shaped to reflect new, relaxed

65 SC/Res/929.

66 *Just War or Just Peace*, 231.

67 Ibid., 151.

68 Ian Martin, 'International Intervention in East Timor', in Welsh (ed.), *Humanitarian Intervention*, 142.

69 S/RES/1264, 15 September 1999.

70 'The United Nations', 81.

71 *Humanitarian Intervention*, 46.

72 *Just War or Just Peace*, Chapter 4.

understandings of sovereignty. On the other hand, there was plenty of opposition to this new interpretation: the Somalia mission was labelled 'exceptional' at Zimbabwe's and India's behest;[73] Russia disputed NATO's authority to carry out *Operation Deliberate Force* in Bosnia;[74] suspicion of French motives in Rwanda meant *Operation Turquoise* was both delayed and hedged around with restrictions;[75] and China, Russia and the G77 carefully demanded Indonesia's sovereignty be respected in East Timor.[76]

This opposition to humanitarian intervention came to a head in Kosovo in 1999. Resolution 1160 of 31 March 1998 had established that the growing conflict in Kosovo posed a threat to international peace and stability, although both Russia and China had abstained, with China in particular expressing concerns about the accumulations of precedents in support of humanitarian intervention.[77] Russia later voted for Resolution 1199 on 23 September 1998 (China abstained again) which 'demanded' Yugoslavia withdraw troops from Kosovo, but Moscow also said it understood that the resolution did *not* authorise intervention.[78] Six months later NATO intervened without a further resolution, leading even strong advocates of humanitarian intervention like Adam Roberts to concede NATO's actions rested on only 'a crumb of legal comfort' (i.e. Russia's effort to explicitly condemn NATO's bombing campaign in the Council failed on 26 March 1999[79]).

This is the clearest instance of failure to clearly establish *opinio juris* for a humanitarian intervention in the 1990s; 17 states and a leading regional organisation (NATO) deployed force to protect the Kosovars' human rights, yet only the UK and the Netherlands cited humanitarianism as their *primary* grounds and most NATO members instead cited threats to stability more prominently.[80] Germany was particularly uncomfortable,[81] telling the Security Council on the eve of war that EU members had only a 'moral obligation' – not a legal obligation – to act.[82] Then condemnations came thick and fast. Russia was 'profoundly outraged', China called it a 'blatant violation of ... international law', and India argued that 'arbitrary and unilateral military action [threatened] a return to anarchy, where might is right'.[83]

Kosovo was therefore the crucial point at which simmering resentment of a decade's worth of humanitarian interventions finally boiled over. For states like

73 Wheeler, 'The Humanitarian Responsibilities', 35.

74 Wheeler, *Saving Strangers*, 255.

75 Chesterman, *Just War or Just Peace*, 147.

76 Martin, 'International Intervention', 161.

77 S/PV/3868, 31 March 1998.

78 S/PV/3930, 23 September 1998.

79 'NATO's "Humanitarian War" Over Kosovo', *Survival* 41:3 (1999), 105.

80 Chesterman, *Just War or Just Peace?*, 210.

81 Catherine Guicherd, 'International Law and the War in Kosovo', *Survival* 41:2 (1999), 26.

82 S/PV.3988, 24 March 1999.

83 Ibid.

China, Russia, India and developing-world organisations like the G77 and the Non-Aligned Movement[84] it seemed a line in the sand had to be drawn. Senior UN figures openly bickered in New York; divisions cut across the divide between the developed and the developing world[85]; and squabbles about the wording of memos and reports broke out in the UN Secretariat itself.[86] Radical voices like Noam Chomsky's proliferated: he argued America used the humanitarian intervention norm as a legitimising ideology to prop up its global hegemony.[87] Mohamed Ayoob also began deploying a battery of sophisticated arguments against humanitarian intervention – it 'conjures up images of colonial domination'; Western states had historically consolidated themselves with liberal applications of violence, making their current position on newer states using violence against restive populations hypocritical; rebels would 'forcibly challenge state authority' to precipitate intervention, etc. – in addition to the conventional ones (i.e. risks of international anarchy, states best provide justice, etc.). But Ayoob also conceded the 'considerable moral force' of the humanitarian argument and ultimately asserted:

> a new procedure should be devised to determine the need for humanitarian intervention … . [T]he UN Charter [should] be amended to include provisions which define 'humanitarian crises', that list the conditions under which humanitarian intervention may be permissible, and that specify the mechanism through which such intervention ought to be conducted.[88]

As the smoke cleared a consensus soon emerged that NATO had acted illegally in Kosovo. For opponents of humanitarian intervention the matter largely ended there. Advocates clung to more nuanced positions, like asserting the war had been 'illegal but legitimate'.[89] Catherine Guicherd perhaps summed up this position best:

> Military action was necessary on moral and political grounds. The legal question, however, is important … . NATO regards itself as an alliance of democratic nations, whose political system[s are] based on the rule of law … . Presumably

84 Final Document of the XIII Ministerial Conference, Cartagena, Colombia, 9 April 2000, 41.

85 John Ruggie (American) and Iqbal Riza (Pakistan) urged Secretary-General Annan to endorse NATO; but Kieran Prendergast (UK) and Shashi Tharoor (India) urged the opposite.

86 Alex J. Bellamy, *Responsibility to Protect: The Global Effort to End Mass Atrocities* (Cambridge: Polity Press, 2009), 29.

87 *The New Military Humanism: Lessons From Kosovo* (Monroe: Common Courage Press, 1999).

88 'Humanitarian Intervention and International Society', *Global Governance* 7:3 (2001), 228.

89 Independent International Commission on Kosovo, *The Kosovo Report: Conflict, International Response, Lessons Learned* (Oxford: Oxford University Press, 2000), 4.

> respect for the rule of law domestically should be joined by a similar respect for the [international] rule of law … . [I]nternational law [clearly] has serious gaps … . Advocates and adversaries of the NATO operations should focus on consolidating embryonic practices into a clear body of law to allow intervention on humanitarian grounds.[90]

The UN Secretary-General, Kofi Annan, was painfully aware of the bickering in his own offices and conscious of being stuck in the diplomatic crossfire – the Russians knew he had basically supported the intervention in Kosovo; the Americans wanted him to say so openly – but he would soon seize the opportunity to start the debate which eventually led to the R2P norm. But before the discussion can return to the narrative about the emergence of the R2P norm from the practice or norm of humanitarian intervention, we must address more directly the questions of the relationship between law and norms.

Norms and Laws

As noted above, before 2001 debates about humanitarian intervention tended to ask 'is it a part of international law?', but after then debates about R2P have more often asked 'is it a strong or entrenched norm?'. The change was not an abrupt one – articles in international law journals unsurprisingly often still favour legal analysis when they examine R2P – but International Relations (IR) scholars have tended to either treat R2P primarily as a norm,[91] or to explore the relationship between norms and laws and their respective status in or effect on the structures of global governance.[92]

The reasons for this shift are difficult to pin down and may in part reflect 'academic fashions', especially the steady rise of constructivism after 1990; norms feature prominently in this IR paradigm. Alternatively, approaching the shift *ironically* may help. Consider that before 2001 the humanitarian intervention practice or norm was objectively *less* 'law-like' than R2P is now: it had not been codified so its legal basis rested entirely in the more contestable realm of customary international law, few institutional reforms to facilitate humanitarian interventions had occurred, etc. But – and here is the irony – perhaps the very fact R2P continues to be fiercely contested even *after* it was codified at the 2005 World

---

90 Guicherd, 'International Law', 19–20.

91 Tim Dunne and Jess Gifkin, 'Libya and the State of Intervention', *Australian Journal of International Affairs* 65:5 (2011), 515–529; Jennifer M. Welsh, 'Norm Contestation and the Responsibility to Protect', *Global Responsibility to Protect* 5:4 (2013), 365–396.

92 Marie-Eve Loiselle, 'The Normative Status of the Responsibility to Protect after Libya', *Global Responsibility to Protect* 5:3 (2013), 317–341; Ramesh Thakur, *The Responsibility to Protect: Norms, Laws and the Use of Force* (Oxon: Routledge, 2011).

Summit (see below) and some reforms to global governance structures had taken place to ostensibly make it more 'law-like' may explain the shift from talking about law to talking about norms. In other words, the continued contestation over R2P's status suggests it is better to speak of it as an *emerging norm* that still has some way to go before it can be considered fully entrenched in international law.

To explain a little further, consider that a common understanding of the relationship between norms and laws sees norms as more informal, less coercive standards of what *ought* to be done or not done – hence the definition offered earlier of a norm as 'a standard of appropriate behaviour for actors of a given identity' – while laws are more formal statements of what *must* be done/not done, which implies the potential for them to be enforced by a legitimate authority.[93] The shift in the tone of the discourse about R2P from laws to norms may therefore reflect a growing realisation that international law itself is actually not very law-like, so treating R2P like a norm is preferable.

This book henceforth discusses R2P using the conceptual language of norms. The author must also confess to being among those who exhibit a degree of scepticism about the very notion of international law more generally; having worked as a solicitor in a domestic legal system where laws are voluminous, precise, applied consistently, enforceable, and their provenance is considered legitimate, he suspects many international laws fall well short of what is usually understood by the term 'law', especially in the security or strategic realm where military force can be used or threatened. But even if one assumes that it *is* meaningful to talk of international law generally, it is submitted that at present *R2P* is not very law-like: its substantive content is meagre; its meaning is vague; its application is selective; there are few consequences for non-compliance; and concerns about its legitimacy abound.

For these reasons R2P is henceforth treated as an emerging norm which remains contested and is, at best, 'becoming law-like' (or perhaps it only has the potential to do so). This means we must use different standards other than the 'compliance-testing' methods which are usually applied to evaluate the effectiveness of domestic laws when we consider the effect of norms like R2P on states' behaviour. Michael Barkun[94] commented long ago on the inappropriateness of subjecting international laws to compliance testing – assessing their effect by only examining to the extent to which actors comply with them – while Friedrich Kratochwil,[95] and Jutta Brunnée and Stephen Toope more recently,[96] have argued that to acknowledge international laws and/or norms cannot be enforced does

93 Thakur, ibid., 3.

94 *Law Without Sanctions: Order in Primitive Societies and the World Community* (New Haven: Yale University Press, 1968), 26.

95 *Rules, Norms and Decisions: On the Conditions of Practical and Legal Reasoning in International Relations and Domestic Affairs* (Cambridge: University of Cambridge, 1989).

96 *Legitimacy and Legality in International Law* (Cambridge: Cambridge University Press, 2010).

not mean they have *no effect* on the behaviour of states. Instead, norms (and laws, even the ones that can't be strictly enforced) have *constitutive* effects too; in other words, their qualities of 'oughtness' may motivate states to behave in accordance with them, or to restrict states from breaching them, because doing so will likely still entail paying a price even if not the overwhelmingly heavy one that enforcement mechanisms make malefactors who breach domestic laws pay. Chapter 2 engages with the question of how norms enable and constrain certain types of state behaviour in more detail.

The Responsibility to Protect: Getting to the 2005 World Summit

After this brief diversion into conceptual matters the rest of this chapter discusses the evolution of the R2P norm since 2001 as its advocates struggled to entrench it. To do so we must return to 1999, when Secretary-General Kofi Annan took steps to advance the cause of humanitarian intervention following the intense controversy generated by Kosovo.

In September 1999 Annan wrote in *The Economist* about how 'sovereignty, in its most basic sense, is being redefined' – thereby delivering a spirited statement of the 'sovereignty as responsibility' argument[97] – and a few days later he addressed the General Assembly to elaborate:

> one might ask … in the context of Rwanda: if … a coalition of states had been prepared to act … but did not receive prompt Security Council authorization, should [they] have stood aside and allowed the horror to unfold? [Regarding Kosovo]: is there not a danger of such interventions undermining the imperfect, yet resilient, security system … and of setting dangerous precedents … without clear criteria?

By calling for better *regulation* of humanitarian intervention Annan sought a way past the Scylla of indifference to suffering and the Charybdis of international instability (i.e. which might be caused by too much interventionism). He therefore sought to reconcile 'two equally compelling interests – universal legitimacy [i.e. sovereign equality] and effectiveness in defence of human rights'.[98]

The effect was immediate, with ad-hoc rebukes being delivered in several speeches in reply to Annan's address and disruptions at subsequent UN social events later that night. But Annan had emboldened Canada to set up the ICISS, the panel of international experts which produced the landmark 2001 report which first introduced R2P.[99] It was co-chaired by Gareth Evans from

97 'Two Concepts of Sovereignty', *The Economist*, 18 September 1999.

98 Speech, 'Annual Report of the Secretary-General to the General Assembly', New York, 20 September 1999.

99 Bellamy, *Responsibility to Protect*, 32.

the developed world (Australia) and Mohammed Sahnoun from the developing world (Algeria), with other members representing a wide array of regions. It was also supported by a dedicated research directorate, and 11 roundtables were held to seek opinions. Several complementary precursor and parallel processes (i.e. the 'Pugwash Workshops', the 'Rio Group', etc.) were also organised by civil society groups.

These discussions were voluminous,[100] but some key points stand out. First, criteria to guide decisions about if, when and how to intervene to protect human rights were discussed at length. Criteria could both *enable* particular interventions and also serve to *restrain* abuses, and if followed consistently criteria would blunt the selectivity critique. But they also generated controversy. Sceptics of humanitarian intervention felt if the Security Council failed to authorise, but the criteria 'seemed satisfied', some states may proceed with unauthorised, even unilateral interventions anyway. Western states – France in particular – were also worried that states would simply bicker about how to interpret the criteria, while rumblings from America suggested it, as the state with the greatest military capacity to intervene, was worried about its freedom of action being curtailed.

The matter of authorisation also generated much heat. The idea of a 'conflict verification' body staffed with experts to objectively advise the Council was floated early; later a body more representative of states – a standing committee of the General Assembly with rotating membership – was proposed; the notion of regional organisations taking a greater, even a leading role, was discussed; and America tended to favour the idea that authorisation should be 'preferable, not necessary'. But a consensus emerged for a somewhat *reformed* Security Council retaining its paramount authorising role: there was, for example, discussion of a 'code of conduct' to guide the deliberations of veto-members when responses to humanitarian crises were being considered.

A third controversial issue – perhaps the most important with hindsight – was the more abstract matter of changing the 'tone' or 'tenor' of the debate about reconciling sovereignty and human rights. The ICISS had been inspired by the success of the Brundtland Commission which, in the 1980s, had reconciled the seemingly contradictory goals of economic development and environmental protection with the notion of 'sustainable development' which continues to shape discussions about responses to climate change.[101] Developing-world contributions to the ICISS's deliberations revealed how much 'baggage' humanitarian intervention had accumulated; in particular, the notion of a 'right' of humanitarian intervention – a right seemingly only available to Western states, and implying a prerogative or discretionary choice – was especially galling to developing states. Disquiet over this matter had underpinned the abuse and

---

100 Bellamy provides an excellent short discussion: *Responsibility to Protect*, 38–51; the ICISS provided longer summaries in a supplementary volume: *The Responsibility to Protect: Research*, Part III.

101 Bellamy, *Responsibility to Protect*, 36.

selectivity critiques generally, and had also animated much of the opposition to the specific intervention in Kosovo.[102]

R2P advocates therefore realised early on that the 'frame of discourse' needed changing, and Gareth Evans argued for reframing the whole debate in terms of a *responsibility* to protect. The genesis of this notion lay in the context of protecting internally displaced persons (associated with Francis Deng and Roberta Cohen[103]), and Kofi Annan had already raised analogues to this sovereignty as responsibility argument. So the idea of multiple and linked responsibilities developed: of states to their people, of states to other states, and of the international community assuming responsibility, if necessary, etc. The military aspects of intervention were also toned down in favour of a more 'holistic' approach which included prevention and reconciliation strategies; these latter features of R2P are, of course, what most obviously distinguishes it from the old humanitarian intervention practice or norm.

The ICISS's report was released on 18 December 2001 and three components of the nascent R2P norm were emphasised. The first was the *responsibility to prevent* mass atrocities: said to be 'the single most important dimension',[104] the report acknowledged that it was 'first and foremost the responsibility of sovereign states' to assume responsibility for their citizen's human rights, but the ICISS also said that 'strong support from the international community is often needed' including development aid, good governance initiatives, conflict mediation and early warning mechanisms.[105]

Next was the *responsibility to react*, which most closely resembled the old humanitarian intervention practice or norm, although its contingent nature was stressed: intervention should only occur, the ICISS stressed, 'when preventative measures fail' and if 'a state is unable or unwilling to redress the situation'. Remedies 'may include political, economic or judicial measures and in extreme cases they may also include military action'. The primacy of sovereignty was also reaffirmed:

> the starting point should be the principle of non-intervention. This is the norm from which any departure has to be justified. All [states] have an interest in maintaining an order of sovereign, self-reliant, responsible yet independent states … . [This is usually] best served if all states … abstain from intervening … in the domestic affairs of other states … . [This] rule not only protects states and governments: it also protects peoples and cultures, enabling societies to maintain the religious, ethnic and civilizational differences that they cherish.

102 Louise Arbour, 'The Responsibility to Protect as a Duty of Care in International Law and Practice', *Review of International Studies* 34:3 (2008), 447.

103 *Masses in Flight: The Global Crisis of Internal Displacement* (Washington: Brookings, 1998).

104 ICISS, *The Responsibility to Protect*, xi.

105 Ibid., 19–22.

The extreme cases in which sovereignty could be violated therefore included:

> when conflict and repression are so violent that civilians are threatened with massacre, genocide or ethnic cleansing on a large scale … . [T]hese exceptional circumstances must … so genuinely 'shock the consciousness of mankind' or present such a clear and present danger to international security that they require coercive military intervention.[106]

The ICISS then delivered criteria – 'precautionary principles' – to guide the deliberations about whether an intervention should take place in particular cases. They were analogous to the just war tradition, and included: right authority; just cause; right intention; last resort; proportional means; and reasonable prospects.[107]

Discussion of right authority took all of Chapter 6 of the ICISS report. It declared 'the UN … is unquestionably the principal institution for building, consolidating and using the authority of the international community', and 'the Security Council [is] at the heart of the international law-enforcement system, [and] is the only organization with universally recognised authority to validate such operations'. The ICISS concluded 'the task is not to find alternatives … but to make the Security Council work much better'.[108] More controversially, the report also noted 'it has been said it is unconscionable that one veto can override the rest of humanity on matters of grave humanitarian concern', so it called on the veto-powers to agree to a 'code of conduct' whereby 'in matters where [their] vital national interests were not claimed to be involved, [they] would not use a veto to obstruct … what otherwise would be a majority decision'.[109] The report then discussed possible alternatives if the Council failed to act, including: action by the General Assembly (if a two-thirds majority could be secured); action by regional organisations (but only in extreme circumstances); and action by *ad-hoc* coalitions (as an absolute last resort).[110] Unsurprisingly, these latter recommendations have been especially controversial and, at the risk of foreshadowing what follows, none have been implemented.

Finally, the ICISS report canvassed a third element of R2P, the *responsibility to rebuild*, by which interveners must show a 'genuine commitment to helping build a durable peace' after an intervention. Specific duties followed, like providing security, rebuilding governance and justice structures, encouraging reconciliation, and promoting economic development. Authority, it was said, must also be handed back to locals quickly.[111] The inclusion of this third responsibility – and, equally, the responsibility to prevent – was clearly designed to reduce the impression

106 Ibid., 29–31.
107 Ibid., 32–38.
108 Ibid., 48–49.
109 Ibid., 51.
110 Ibid., 53–55.
111 Ibid., 39–45.

that military intervention was being over-emphasised (and, again, together they mark the clearest differences between the R2P norm and the old humanitarian intervention practice or norm).

Reactions to the ICISS report varied considerably. Many observers hailed R2P as a significant breakthrough – Kofi Annan was especially pleased[112] – but some felt it went too far, or didn't go far enough, or they felt it was too vague.[113] Reactions from states varied considerably too. The Canadians were very pleased,[114] but the veto-powers' reactions were mixed: the US was dismissive of the precautionary principles; China and Russia strongly rejected the discussion of interventions possibly proceeding in the absence of Council authorisation; and while Britain and France both formally endorsed the report they also queried whether just asking for 'good faith' and 'political will' would actually end up delivering such. The NAM – led by a prominent member, India – also expressed concerns (often, and vocally) that R2P seemed just a repackaging of the old humanitarian intervention (which New Delhi claimed was illegal).[115]

Then, as 2002 progressed, the US (and several allies) prepared to invade Iraq. The primary justifications tendered focused initially on Iraq's (alleged) possession of Weapons of Mass Destruction (WMD), and especially the risk that Iraq might proliferate WMD given its (again, alleged) links to terrorists.[116] Accordingly, humanitarian arguments were not raised in Council deliberations at all, and were only ever raised in informal settings.[117] But after the invasion, when the claims about WMD and terror-links proved difficult to substantiate, the invaders' began to rhetorically invoke humanitarianism as a justification. Then, when Michael Ignatieff (who had sat on the ICISS and helped draft its 2001 report) endorsed this position,[118] a tide of criticism followed,[119] including from Gareth Evans; he later said this linkage of R2P with the Iraq war 'almost choked it at birth'.[120]

112 Speech, 'The Responsibility to Protect', at the International Peace Academy, New York, 15 February 2002.

113 Bellamy, *Responsibility to Protect*, 59–64.

114 Paul Heinbecker, 'Canada Launches Report of the ICISS', press release, 18 December 2001.

115 Bellamy, *Responsibility to Protect*, 67–69.

116 Adam Roberts, 'Law and the Use of Force after Iraq', *Survival* 45:2 (2003), 39–40.

117 Alex J. Bellamy, 'Responsibility to Protect or Trojan Horse? The Crisis in Darfur and Humanitarian Intervention after Iraq', *Ethics & International Affairs* 19:2 (2005), 37 (fn. 41).

118 'Why Are We in Iraq? (And Liberia? And Afghanistan?)', *New York Times Magazine*, 7 September 2003. He later changed his mind and withdrew his endorsement: Bellamy, *Responsibility to Protect*, 68.

119 Nicholas J. Wheeler and Justin Morris, 'The Cure is Worse than the Disease', in W.P.S. Sidhu and Ramesh Thakur (eds), *The Iraq Crisis and World Order: Structural, Institutional and Normative Challenges* (New York: United Nations Press, 2006).

120 Speech, 'When Is It Right to Fight? Legality, Legitimacy, and the Use of Military Force', Cyril Foster Lecture, Oxford University, 10 May 2004.

Subsequently some erstwhile supporters of the R2P norm began to back away from their previous positions: for example, when Britain and Canada proposed a draft communique endorsing R2P at a conference of social democratic party leaders in July 2003, Germany, Argentina and Chile would only agree to a version which called for more discussion on the matter.[121] The best 'spin' on this unhappy Iraq War–R2P linkage was delivered by Badescu and Weiss, who noted at least we now know when R2P *shouldn't* apply.[122]

Nevertheless, Canada continued to promote R2P, seeking 'like-minded friends' – both states and NGOs – and by deploying the classic middle power traits of persuasion and technical proficiency to drive a 'norm building strategy'.[123] Key UN reports from the High-Level Panel (HLP) in 2004[124] and Kofi Annan in 2005[125] gave further impetus to the effort to not let R2P simply fade away into obscurity, although these reports collectively caused aspects of R2P to be diluted somewhat to allay the concerns which had arisen as a result of the Iraq War. For example, the notion that intervention might take place without Security Council authorisation was dropped altogether; the code of conduct for veto-powers was shelved (the HLP suggested they merely 'declare their position' before voting); and the precautionary principles were presented as only a source of *guidance* for the Council's deliberations (i.e. less 'binding' than had been previously indicated).

These promotional efforts ensured R2P featured prominently in the negotiations before the 2005 World Summit. While some developing states opposed R2P, and many developed states were strong supporters, the true situation was more complex than a simple North/South division over the issue: for example, American support was half-hearted at best while George W. Bush occupied the White House; on the other hand, in 2003 the Constitutive Act of the new African Union provided, in Article 4(h), 'the Right of the Union to intervene in a Member State … in respect of grave humanitarian circumstances' (although non-intervention was also codified in Article 4(g)). Accordingly, as negotiations about the Outcome Document continued before the World Summit a sort of 'grand bargain' was thrashed out whereby developing states would allow R2P 'in' if developed states agreed to relatively robust development goals

121 Kevin Word, 'Process Needed so Countries Know When to Intervene', *CBS (Canada)*, 13 July 2003.

122 I.e. 'misuse can advance norms … through contestation and conceptual clarification': Christina G. Badescu and Thomas G. Weiss, 'Misrepresenting R2P and Advancing Norms: An Alternative Spiral?', *International Studies Perspectives* 11 (2010), 355.

123 Bellamy, *Responsibility to Protect*, 71–74. For discussion of middle powers see: Andrew F. Cooper, Richard A. Higgott and Kim Richard Nossal, *Relocating Middle Powers: Australia and Canada in a Changing World Order* (Carlton: Melbourne University Press, 1993).

124 High Level Panel, *A More Secure World: Our Shared Responsibility* (New York: United Nations, 2004).

125 Kofi Annan, *In Larger Freedom* (New York: United Nations, 2005).

being included too. The first draft of the R2P-related paragraphs, for example, characterised intervention as a 'last resort' (i.e. because R2P provided that states had the primary responsibility to protect their citizens), it asked veto-powers to 'restrain' their use of vetos, and it used the words 'obligation' and 'shared responsibility' when discussing intervention. But at American insistence criteria were not included, not even as a device to guide the Council's deliberations.

Then John Bolton was appointed as America's UN Ambassador three weeks before the World Summit. He tried to renegotiate dozens of clauses in the Outcome Document and while his preferred changes to R2P were relatively minor,[126] this led several R2P-sceptics – China, Russia, India, the G77 and NAM, etc. – to renew their attacks. India's critique was particularly strident: its UN Ambassador, Nirupam Sen, had opposed R2P since the beginning and he now called it 'patronising' and 'offensive' while lambasting its legal and moral foundations. Ultimately, however, he overplayed his hand and was overruled by India's prime minister who wanted to avoid blame for scuttling the entire World Summit over this single issue. Bolton was also overruled for similar reasons.[127]

These last-minute objections nevertheless caused the final version of R2P which appeared in the World Summit Outcome Document (in paragraphs 138 and 139) to be weakened further. Instead of intervention becoming possible when a state was 'unable or unwilling' to protect human rights, intervention could now only occur after evidence of 'manifest failure' to protect. And instead of such failure triggering a 'shared responsibility' to intervene, the final document instead noted states were 'prepared to take collective action, in a timely and decisive manner, through the Security Council, in accordance with the Charter, including Chapter VII, on a case-by-case basis'. No criteria appeared (i.e. the 'case-by-case basis' reference) and no restrictions were placed on the veto-powers. Bellamy, however, warns us not to lose sight of the achievement this represented:

> The R2P which emerged ... amounted to an important formal recognition of the responsibility of sovereigns to their own citizens, a reaffirmation of the idea that the Security Council has the authority to intervene if it sees fit to do so [and] ... a commitment to develop institutional capacities and behaviours to prevent genocide and mass atrocities ... . True, this was much less than had been envisaged by the ICISS, but it marked an important milestone in the normative development of international society.[128]

Returning briefly to the realm of international law, it was noted earlier that 1990s-era humanitarian intervention might have become entrenched if one or more of three things had taken place; more practice may have created customary international

126 James Traub, *The Best Intentions: Kofi Annan and the UN in an Era of American Power* (London: Bloomsbury, 2006), 372–375.

127 Ibid., 386.

128 *Responsibility to Protect*, 91.

law; codification might have occurred; and global governance structures might have been reformed. The inclusion of R2P in the Outcome Document was a 'sort of codification': all 191 then-members of the UN agreed to the final wording of paragraphs 138 and 139, and no substantial reservations[129] were lodged against them. Commentary from the International Law Commission on the law of treaties notes

> an agreement as to the interpretation of a provision [i.e. in another treaty] reached after the conclusion of a treaty represents an authentic interpretation by the parties which must be read into the treaty for the purposes of its interpretation.[130]

It is not clear, however, whether paragraphs 138 and especially 139 of the Outcome Document fundamentally changed the interpretation of Article 41 of the UN Charter to mean internal human rights abuses constituted a threat to international peace and stability of the sort which places an *obligation* on the Council to authorise armed intervention to prevent such atrocities. Welsh and Banda[131] believe it does, but others are less sure.[132]

It would obviously have been preferable (for R2P's advocates at least) if the UN Charter had been amended – doing so would have constituted a much 'stronger', virtually unquestionable form of codification – and it is worth noting that a General Assembly vote of the sort which endorsed the Outcome Document is not strictly analogous to an international treaty; it is certainly less binding than a formal treaty because Assembly resolutions are advisory only, unlike Council resolutions. But the Outcome Document nevertheless expresses the consensus of states at an important international summit. It is probably therefore best seen as 'an interpretive aid which suggests the Security Council should seriously consider whether atrocities within a state constitute a threat to international peace and security in terms of Article 41' and, more generally, it is 'evidence of the collective intention of international society to operate in accordance with, if not be strictly bound by, the R2P norm'.

So, the first criteria for R2P becoming entrenched in international law, codification, had arguably been partially satisfied: but only partially. Whether the second and third criteria were satisfied – whether state practice reflected R2P and whether global governance structures were reformed to reflect and accommodate the R2P norm after the 2005 World Summit – is considered later. The next section accordingly explores the fortunes of R2P after 2005 and before India joined the Security Council in 2011.

---

129 Some states reiterated their support for 'traditional sovereignty' but none rejected them outright.

130 *Yearbook of the International Law Commission 1966, Vol. II* (New York: United Nations, 1967), 221.

131 Jennifer M. Welsh and Maria Banda, 'International Law and the Responsibility to Protect', *Global Responsibility to Protect* 2:3 (2010), 213 and 230.

132 Andres Henriksen and Marc Schack, 'The Crisis in Syria and Humanitarian Intervention', *Journal of the Use of Force and International Law* 1:1 (2014), 132–133.

The Responsibility to Protect: After the 2005 World Summit

Despite the fact the inclusion of R2P (albeit a very watered-down version) in the World Summit Outcome Document was a notable achievement – or perhaps because of it – resistance to the R2P norm reappeared immediately; Gareth Evans memorably characterised this resistance as 'buyer's remorse'.[133] Efforts to have the Security Council endorse paragraphs 138 and 139 to further entrench R2P ran into resistance from China, Russia, Algeria, Brazil and the Philippines, who argued states had only committed to discuss R2P further at the World Summit.[134] Only after the Security Council's membership rotated was Resolution 1674 passed on 28 April 2006, which 'reaffirmed' paragraphs 138 and 139. But China then argued again that

> there are still differing understandings and interpretations of this concept … . The Security Council should therefore refrain from invoking the concept of the responsibility to protect [and] should respect and support the General Assembly in continuing to discuss the concept in order to reach a broad consensus.[135]

As a result, over the next few years R2P was referred to in two resolutions[136] but it was left out of several others when, logically speaking, one would have expected references to it (i.e. in circumstances in which serious atrocities were being committed, most notably in Sudan's Darfur region). Resistance also manifested itself in other ways. Gareth Evans, for example, was heckled and harassed at several public speaking events in Sri Lanka in 2007 for his 'crackpot ideas' and 'neo-imperialist tactics'.[137] Then, after the Human Rights Council's (HRC) High-Level Mission penned a report in 2007 which found Sudan had 'manifestly failed' to protect its citizens in Darfur, the Arab and Asia Groups and the Organization of Islamic Conference, with Chinese and Russian support, blocked discussion of the report until all references to R2P were removed.[138]

Crucial battles also took place in two UN forums. First, the new Secretary-General, Ban Ki-Moon, was determined to reform global governance structures to facilitate the implementation of R2P,[139] and he started by appointing a Special

---

133 Speech, 'The Responsibility to Protect: An Idea Whose Time has Comes … and Gone?', David Davies Memorial Institute, Aberystwyth, 23 April 2008.

134 S/PV.5319, 9 December 2005.

135 S/PV.5703, 33 June 2007.

136 S/RES/1706, 31 August 2006; S/RES/1894, 11 November 2009.

137 Ramesh Thakur and Thomas G Weiss, 'R2P: From Idea to Norm – and Action?', *Global Responsibility to Protect* 1:1 (2009), 22–53.

138 Alex J. Bellamy, *Global Politics and the Responsibility to Protect: From Words to Deeds* (Oxon: Routledge, 2011), 30.

139 SG/SM/10842: speech, to Centre for Strategic Studies, Washington, 16 January 2007.

Advisor for the Responsibility to Protect and attempting to make the existing Special Advisor for the Prevention of Genocide a permanent, fully-resourced post. But his efforts were resisted strenuously over several years in the General Assembly's 5th Committee (i.e. which sets the UN budget), meaning both offices were at times funded by civil society donations until 2010 when Venezuela's final attempt to defund them was defeated 68 to 17. But the fact 51 states had abstained still troubled R2P advocates.[140]

Second, resistance also emerged in the General Assembly, especially during a key plenary session in July 2009. The President of the General Assembly, Miguel Brockmann of Nicaragua, initially resisted placing R2P on the agenda; then he ignored Secretariat requests regarding the timing of debates; eventually, he scheduled the debate for when the Secretary-General would be overseas, forcing Ban to revise his travel arrangements; then Brockmann tried to suppress information about R2P being distributed before the plenary session; and he issued a 'concept paper' (likely written by India's former Ambassador Nirupam Sen) which was highly critical of R2P. Then, at the plenary session itself Brockmann's opening address characterised R2P as 'redecorated colonialism', and he invited fierce R2P critics Noam Chomsky and Jean Bricmont to speak.

The outcome was basically a snub to Brockman, with only four of 94 countries (Venezuela, Sudan, Cuba and Nicaragua) calling for R2P to be rolled back, while 27 states called for its advancement. States which had hitherto expressed scepticism about, or which had practiced outright resistance to R2P like Brazil, India, South Africa and Indonesia also expressed qualified support.[141] Overall, the consensus at this plenary session supported taking steps to implement R2P, not renegotiate it, using Secretary-General Ban's 2009 report *Implementing the Responsibility to Protect* to guide the process. The notion that the R2P norm is composed of three fundamental component parts or 'pillars' first emerged in this report. Pillar I asserts states have the 'enduring responsibility' to protect their citizens; Pillar II declares that states have the responsibility to offer assistance to other states who are struggling to fulfil their Pillar I responsibilities; and Pillar III sets out the international community's responsibility to respond 'in a timely and decisive manner when a state manifestly fails to provide such protection', including with force if necessary.[142] This characterisation was not especially innovative – echoes can be found in the 2001 ICISS report – but the simplicity and clarity of the three-Pillar terminology has made it the predominant way of thinking about R2P.

---

140 Edward C. Luck, 'The R2P: The First Decade', *Global Responsibility to Protect* 3:4 (2011), 387–399.

141 Badescu and Weiss, 'Misrepresenting R2P', 357; Global Centre for the Responsibility to Protect, *Implementing the Responsibility to Protect: The 2009 General Assembly Debate: An Assessment*, August 2009. Available at: <http://www.globalr2p.org/publications/42>; Bellamy, *Global Politics*, 43–44.

142 A/63/677, 12 January 2009, 8–10.

This report also contained other important clarifications of R2P. First, it contextualised R2P more coherently into the web of existing international laws and global governance structures, like the Convention against Genocide and the Human Rights Council. Second, the 2009 report explicitly decoupled – or at it least *attempted* to decouple – the R2P norm from the old humanitarian intervention practice or norm and instead situated R2P overtly in the sovereignty as responsibility tradition; the 2009 report stated boldly that R2P 'is an ally of sovereignty, not an adversary'[143] (although not everyone was convinced). The 2009 report further argued the primary focus of efforts to advance R2P should be on Pillar II, helping states to protect their citizens, and that Pillar III interventions should be rare. Third, and to reinforce the previous point, the report reiterated that all three Pillars only apply to the most serious atrocities, namely, genocide, war crimes, ethnic cleansing and crimes against humanity, but many non-intrusive remedies (early warning systems, development aid, election monitors, etc.) could be deployed. In other words, while the *scope* of R2P was said to be narrow, the means of implementation should be *deep*. The following and final section considers to what degree Ban's efforts were successful before India joined the Security Council in 2011.

The Responsibility to Protect in 2010

Because the *Implementing the Responsibility to Protect* report was presented to the General Assembly during the July 2009 plenary session presided over by Brockmann and subsequently endorsed by a majority of the 94 participating states it is tempting to see it as the 'definitive statement' of R2P in 2010, on the eve of India's ascension to the Council. But doing so would be misleading because, as ever in international politics, the reality is more complex. For example, while the report provided many details about when and how implementation should occur, these were presented as examples of 'best practice' which states should deliberate further, and not as 'directives'.

Yet some broad conclusions about R2P's status in 2010 can be drawn. First, resistance had softened somewhat compared to the situation in the mid-2000s. In 2013 Patrick Quinton-Brown usefully divided states into 'rejectionists' – of which he found 14, none of which were especially powerful or influential (except Iran) – and 'cautious supporters'; he found 16 of these, including influential states like India, China, Russia, Indonesia, South Africa and Brazil (the remaining 160-odd states were, by implication, supporters; although Quinton-Brown admitted that many of these have not actually commented on R2P specifically since the 2005 World Summit).[144] Second, there was much more support for Pillar I and to a lesser

143 Ibid., 7.

144 'Mapping Dissent: The R2P and its State Critics', *Global Responsibility to Protect* 5:3 (2013), 260–282.

extent, Pillar II, than there was for Pillar III, which is unsurprising given Pillar III most closely resembles the old humanitarian intervention practice or norm. For example, none of the cautious supporters were very supportive of Pillar III (and some, like China, remained outright hostile). Still, as Edward C. Luck claimed in 2011, while plenty of controversy remained about implementing R2P at least the key conceptual aspects of the norm had been settled by 2010.[145]

Third, some reforms of global governance structures had taken place – modest, to be sure – and R2P had been endorsed at the World Summit, by the Security Council, and in an ever-increasing range of reports (especially from the UN Secretariat, but also the HRC and other UN agencies), providing evidence – again, modest, but there nonetheless – that the 'codification process' was continuing. Put simply, by 2010 the effort to entrench R2P as an international norm seemed to have some *momentum* behind it. But, fourth and finally, state practice did not yield clear evidence of regular compliance with the R2P norm, and while there was some accompanying *opinio juris* (i.e. evidence states believed they were obligated to comply) it was far from overwhelming and plenty of counter-examples, including outright criticism of R2P, were available to those who wanted to cast doubt on the claim that R2P was a part of international law.

Thus the question of R2P's status had not been fully settled in 2010. It had made advances, to be sure, but it had also met plenty of resistance and the effort to entrench it in international law had suffered serious setbacks. Most importantly, the second (reform of global governance structures to reflect R2P) and third (state practice in conformity with R2P) criteria which must be satisfied before it can be said that R2P has the status of law were, like the codification criteria, only partially or incompletely satisfied. This suggests R2P had not been unambiguously entrenched before 2011 as a principle of customary international law, nor had a new interpretation of Article 41 of the UN Charter which reflected the R2P norm been widely accepted.[146]

As we will see in later chapters, events after 2010 – especially the aftermath of NATO's 2011 Libyan intervention – were to substantially arrest the momentum R2P had built up prior to 2011. The very nature of R2P itself might be part of the problem. Jennifer Welsh calls R2P a 'complex norm', noting its three pillars leave it 'vulnerable to contestation'. For example, a state's failure to fulfil its Pillar I obligations is supposed to trigger Pillar III intervention. Or is it? Some states may argue Pillar II remedies must be tried first and thereby frustrate efforts to apply Pillar III in a timely manner by demanding sequential application of the three pillars. States may also question how and when the 'triggers' are actually *triggered*: they may object that Pillar I had 'not been breached enough' to warrant moving

145 'The Responsibility'.

146 Henriksen and Schack, 'The Crisis', 133; *Yearbook of the International Law Commission*, 222; J. Craig Barker, 'The Responsibility to Protect: Lessons from Libya and Syria', in Robert P. Barnidge (ed.), *The Liberal Way of War: Legal Perspectives* (Farnham: Ashgate, 2013), 13.

to Pillar II, and later quibble about whether enough assistance (and time for such to yield results) under Pillar II had been given to justify moving to Pillar III.[147] Finally, some states may broadly say 'we support R2P' at a summit or at one of the Assembly's plenary sessions to secure side benefits and/or to avoid the sort of opprobrium which is typically levelled by R2P's supporters against its critics. But during a crisis – when push comes to shove, so to speak – these states might then backslide by declaring that 'actually, we only meant Pillar I', and then decline to provide Pillar II assistance and/or oppose a proposed Pillar III intervention.

Perhaps the best that can be said, as noted above, is that in 2010 R2P was an emerging norm with some momentum behind it, but certain aspects of the norm – especially Pillar III – remained very controversial; R2P's scope, and the contexts in which it should be applicable, also remained hotly contested. But exploration of R2P's more recent travails after the 2011 Libyan crisis must wait; the next chapter, Chapter 2, provides a more comprehensive exploration of the conceptual framework which animates the later analytical chapters of this book (Chapters 3, 4, 5 and 6), meaning consideration of R2P's fortunes at the end of 2014 – after the crises in Côte d'Ivoire, Libya and Syria – will have to wait until the book's concluding remarks.

147 Welsh, 'Norm Contestation', 384.

Chapter 2
Discourses, Norms and Conceptual Models

This chapter presents the conceptual framework which informs the later chapters' empirical analyses of India's position on the responsibility to protect (R2P) norm. The discussion therefore proceeds as follows: the philosophical basis of the study is examined first; then the meaning of 'identity' is explored to explain why domestic-level identity discourses are made the primary explanatory devices in later chapters; after that the relationship between these identity discourses and global norms like R2P and state sovereignty is theorised, which leads to some consideration of the norm dynamics literature. These discussions occupy about one third of the chapter.

In the remainder of the chapter the specific Indian identity discourses which shape India's position on R2P and its responses to humanitarian crises are introduced and discussed. The core logics of each of these identity discourses, and how they can be distinguished from one another across three 'axes of difference', are explained in detail. Because they are conceptualised as discursive structures which 'nest' within a wider web of meanings, the relationship between the identity discourses and other related discursive structures at both the Indian-domestic and the global level – including global norms like R2P, but others too – is examined. Finally, the chapter ends with some discussion of the sources the study draws upon and the methodologies deployed to analyse those sources.

Philosophical Basis of the Argument

This study is grounded in the *constructivist* tradition of International Relations (IR). Constructivists argue that the social world is, as Wendt famously put it, 'as we make it' because agents and structures are mutually constituted.[1] Accordingly, the study is grounded in the scientific realist philosophical position[2] in that it

1 Alexander Wendt, 'Anarchy is What States Make of It: The Social Construction of Power Politics', *International Organization* 46:2 (1992), 391–425; Alexander Wendt, 'The Agent-Structure Problem in International Relations Theory', *International Organization* 41:3 (1987), 335–370. See also Emanuel Adler, 'Seizing the Middle Ground: Constructivism in World Politics', *European Journal of International Relations* 3:3 (1997), 319–363; Anthony Giddens, *The Constitution of Society* (Cambridge: Blackwell, 1984).

2 Ian Shapiro and Alexander Wendt, 'The Difference that Realism Makes: Social Science and the Politics of Consent', *Politics and Society* 20:2 (1997), 211; Roy Bhaskar, *A Realist Theory of Science* (New York: Humanities Press, 1975).

assumes policy-makers in New Delhi act on the basis of prevailing, predominant collective meanings or discursive structures which are not directly observable but which nevertheless are discernible by the application of reason.[3] These collective meanings or discursive structures exist inter-subjectively; they are not just the aggregation of individual beliefs or preferences, they are *shared* or public in character and they define social reality itself, setting the parameters for and goals of action.[4] And they *constitute* actors by giving the actors who accept them and work within and reproduce them particular properties. These properties create 'conceptions of possibilities' for action, meaning particular actions are only made possible in the context of those discursive structures; they *enable* or make some actions conceivable or 'proper', and also *constrain* and make other actions seem 'improper'.[5]

Adopting a constructivist approach has two important implications. First, the scholar should be prepared to find that different actors have different understandings of what might seem to be ostensibly the same context because those actors might be constituted by different discursive structures.[6] Thus 'reality' is not experienced the same way by every actor because, as Peter Winch puts it, 'our idea of what belongs in the realm of reality is given for us in the concepts which we use',[7] which can differ across societies; indeed, as this book shows, they can differ *within* a society – India – too. Second, humans should be treated as *reflexive* creatures, able to understand that their past actions were caused by their being constituted by particular discursive structures. Then, if the consequence of these past actions – the 'feedback' from the external world, so to speak – was unfavourable, the fact humans are sentient enables them to reflect on and decide to discard those discursive structures for others which they expect – or just hope – will produce more desirable consequences.[8]

---

3 Brian Fay, *Social Theory and Political Practice* (London: George Allen & Unwin, 1975), 85; Albert Yee, 'The Causal Effect of Ideas on Policies', *International Organization* 50:1 (1996), 97.

4 Clifford Geertz, *Negara: The Theatre State in Nineteenth-Century Bali* (Princeton: Princeton University Press, 1980), 135; Adler, 'Seizing', 327.

5 Mark Laffey and Jutta Weldes, 'Beyond Belief: Ideas and Symbolic Technologies in the Study of International Relations', *European Journal of International Relations* 3:2 (1997), 201.

6 Jutta Weldes, 'Constructing National Interests', *European Journal of International Relations* 2:3 (1996), 285.

7 *The Idea of a Social Science* (London: Routledge and Kegan Paul, 1958), 15.

8 Ian Hacking, *The Social Construction of What?* (Cambridge: Harvard University Press, 1999), 32–35; Jeffrey W. Legro, 'The Transformation of Policy Ideas', *American Journal of Political Science* 44:3 (2000), 419–432.

Identity Discourses

To capture the way discursive structures give meaning to external objects they have been called 'structures of signification'[9] or 'representations'[10] or 'shared mental models'[11] or 'interpretive filters'[12] by IR scholars. They are akin to what psychologists (and now some IR scholars[13]) call 'schemas': schemas/discursive structures are interpretive devices which affect perceptions about the circumstances actors find themselves in, inform attributions of causality, and shape behavioural responses.[14] Discursive structures are ubiquitous and all-pervasive because nothing in the world – neither material objects nor other external socially-constituted collective actors like foreign states – has meaning without them. This study, however, ignores countless types of discursive structures (like aesthetic discourses which tell us which clothes are fashionable) and instead focuses on *identity discourses*.

The concept of identity can be slippery,[15] but Abdelal et al. define it as a description of the essential properties of a collective actor like a state:

> Identity is a social category that varies along two dimensions – content and contestation ... Content describes the *meaning* of a collective identity ... [and] contestation refers to the degree of *agreement* within a group over the content of the shared category (emphasis in original).[16]

Regarding content, Abdelal et al. say collective[17] identities contain information about the actor which distinguishes it from other actors, and which informs the

---

9 Jennifer Milliken, 'The Study of Discourse in International Relations: A Critique of Research and Methods', *European Journal of International Relations* 5:2 (1999), 229.

10 Weldes, 'Constructing National Interests', 281–283.

11 Arthur Denzau and Douglass North, 'Shared Mental Models: Ideologies and Institutions', *Kyklos* 47:1 (1994), 3–31.

12 Janis G. Stein, 'Political Learning by Doing: Gorbachev as Uncommitted Thinker and Motivated Learner', *International Organization* 48:2 (1994), 155–184.

13 James Goldgeier and Philip E. Tetlock, 'Psychology and International Relations Theory', *Annual Review of Political Science* 4, (2001), 83.

14 John R. Anderson, *Cognitive Psychology and its Implications* (New York, Freeman, 1990); Bradd Shore, *Culture in Mind: Cognition, Culture and the Problem of Meaning* (New York: Harper, 1996).

15 James D. Fearon, 'What is Identity (as we now use the word?)', unpublished manuscript, Stanford University, 3 November 1999. Available at: <https://web.stanford.edu/group/fearon-research/cgi-bin/wordpress/wp-content/uploads/2013/10/What-is-Identity-as-we-now-use-the-word-.pdf> accessed 16 August 2014.

16 Rawi Abdelal, Yoshiko M. Herrera, Alistair Iain Johnston and Rose McDermott, 'Identity as a Variable', *Perspectives on Politics* 4:4 (2006), 696.

17 Identity is also used by social scientists to explain an individual's sense of self-worth and dignity: Fearon, 'What is Identity', 11.

basic attitudes it has towards others (i.e. friendship and respect, enmity and mistrust, indifference, etc.).[18] In other words, identities 'tell you and others who you are and they tell you who others are'.[19] Constructivists also accept that 'interests flow from identities'. So for Weldes, a state's interests 'are already entailed within [its identity] representations … . [O]nce a situation has been described the national interest has already been determined – it emerges out of the representations of identities and relationships'.[20]

This study therefore assumes domestic Indian actors – 'policy-shapers' as they are called herein – promote various identity discourses. Each identity discourse contains a somewhat distinct 'core logic' or somewhat different assumptions about India's identity and the identity of other actors India interacts with; these identity discourses are therefore different notions about what sort of international actor India 'is' (more precisely, what it *should* be; these are rival *interpretations* of reality). Each policy-shaper *competes* against the others by claiming its favoured identity discourse is 'the most authentic' and should supply all or most of the content or properties of India's identity as an international actor (and therefore shape India's interests). This conceptual model is consistent with the second part of Abdelal et al'.s definition of identity, namely, that the content of an identity is typically contested; as Weldes puts it, 'a multiplicity of discourses [or] … "codes of intelligibility" [form] … a field on which are fought battles over meaning'.[21] Hopf calls this 'societal constructivism' as opposed to Wendt's 'systemic constructivism' by which states' identities are formed during interaction with one another. Hopf does not deny the latter occurs, but instead he – and this study – also theorises about how domestic actors compete to define their state's identity.[22]

To clarify further, the identity discourses deployed in this study are not treated as analogous to India's 'general' or 'over-arching' international identity. Instead, these are *R2P-specific* identity discourses, and while they might be related to, borrow from, or affect the identities India has in other contexts, the content of India's identity is likely to be somewhat different in each foreign policy issue-area (climate change, trade relations, Sino-Indian bilateral relations, etc.) if only

18 Abdelal et al., 'Identity as a Variable', 696.

19 Ted Hopf, 'The Promise of Constructivism', *International Security* 23:1 (1998), 175; Weldes, 'Constructing National Interests', 282.

20 Weldes, ibid., 283.

21 Jutta Weldes, Mark Laffey, Hugh Gusterson and Raymond Duvall (eds), *Cultures of Insecurity: States, Communities, and the Production of Danger* (Minneapolis: University of Minnesota Press, 1999), 2; Elizabeth Kier, 'Culture and French Military Doctrine Before World War II', in Peter J. Katzenstein (ed.), *The Culture of National Security: Norms and Identity in World Politics* (New York: Columbia University Press, 1996), 38; Anja Dalgaard-Neilsen, 'The Test of Strategic Culture: Germany, Pacifism and Pre-emptive Strikes', *Security Dialogue* 36:3 (2005), 339–359.

22 *Reconstructing the Cold War: The Early Years, 1945–1958* (Oxford: Oxford University Press, 2012), 12.

because the substantive issues and the relevant external actors – the context or circumstances – are a little different in each.

This conceptual model covers what one might call the 'ordinary direction of causation'. It is falsifiable because we can 'see' identity discourses other than the one which informed or shaped the policy-response 'out there' in the public sphere – in newspaper articles or expert reports or speeches in parliament – being promoted by policy-shapers competing for influence over India's policy responses (and perhaps failing to exert much). Yet we can also conceive of circumstances in which an uninfluential identity discourse might rise in influence and actually shape policy.[23] In other words, the finding that one identity discourse exerted the most influence over a particular policy response, while others didn't, can be 'tested' by several means, including finding correlations between the core logics of various identity discourses and the justifications given by Indian officials for their policy responses, or by hypothesis testing and counterfactual analysis.[24] These matters are discussed in more detail at the very end of the chapter.

Much of the following analysis examines this ordinary direction of causation, but because Indian policy-makers are human and so capable of reflection it is entirely possible that the influence of the various identity discourses might change relative to one another over time. For example, an unexpected – especially a *negative* – outcome might *undermine* the validity of the dominant identity discourse which informed the policy response that led to that outcome, or perhaps shifts in global power occur, undermining the 'general validity' of the dominant identity discourse. Such circumstances may allow another identity discourse to rise in influence, so the analyses in later chapters are sensitive to this 'reflexive direction of causation' too.[25]

Of course, Indian society may change for reasons substantially unrelated to the debates about R2P or particular crises; 'deep' sociological changes of this sort may also affect the relative influence of the identity discourses vis-à-vis each other and India is, of course, experiencing profound demographic and cultural shifts in the contemporary era.[26] But the time period being closely analysed in this study is relatively short (mainly the years 2011 and 2012, with some consideration of 2013 and 2014). Accordingly, while these deeper, longer-term societal changes are given some consideration in Chapter 3 when India's historical responses to humanitarian intervention and R2P are explored

---

23 Ted Hopf, *Social Construction of International Politics: Identities and Foreign Policies, Moscow, 1955 & 1999* (Ithaca: Cornell University Press, 2002), 24.

24 For general discussion of falsifiability and testing, see: Martin Hollis, *The Philosophy of Social Science*, 2nd ed. (Cambridge: Cambridge University Press, 2002 [1994]), 71–77.

25 Legro, 'The Transformation', 426–429.

26 Ben Doherty, 'India: A Nation at the Crossroads', *The Age*, 1 February 2014; 'India's Demographic Challenge: Wasting Time', *The Economist*, 11 May 2013; I-10 ('Interviewee number 10'), New Delhi, 10 November 2013.

over several decades, their potentially confusing effect on the relative shaping influence of the identity discourses is largely put to one side in the main analytical chapters (i.e. 4, 5 and 6).

While this study focuses on domestic-level Indian identity discourses to explain India's policy responses to R2P, it must obviously also consider what global norms are and what they do (or what their policy-shaping promoters are *attempting* to do). Their relationship with the various domestic identity discourses therefore requires sustained consideration.

Global Norms and Domestic Identity Discourses

Finnemore and Sikkink have defined a norm as 'a standard of appropriate behaviour for actors with a given identity'.[27] Norms therefore constitute actors' identities in substantially the same manner as identity discourses do and thereby 'make possible' or enable some actions, and they also 'regulate' or constrain other actions. Yet there is a crucial conceptual difference between the way norms and identity discourses are understood in this study: norms are meant to be *widely applicable*, they are intended to apply to a range of actors with a particular identity; for example, norms like R2P or sovereignty are meant to apply to actors identified as 'states'. Norms are therefore one type or sub-category of discursive structures, while domestic identity discourses are another, but the latter are only 'relevant to' a single actor (in this study, India).

Thus the relationship between identity discourses and global norms can be conceptualised in the following way. Norm entrepreneurs – actors who promote new global norms[28] – try to *diffuse* a norm widely, to ensure it is internalised by all or most states. The dynamic competition within a particular state between policy-shapers promoting various domestic identity discourses is affected by the presence of a new global norm because policy-shapers may use it or become constituted by it (see below for more discussion of this distinction). In the process particular identity discourses may be altered or displaced, or at least the competition between them may be affected by, the pressure from or presence of the new norm, possibly altering states' identities, interests, and actions (Theo Farrell calls this process, if successful, 'norm transplantation'[29]). To clarify, this study treats identity discourses as the discursive structures which shape policy-making most

27 'International Norm Dynamics and Political Change', *International Organization* 52:4 (1998), 891. See also Ronald L. Jepperson, Alexander Wendt and Peter J. Katzenstein, 'Norms, Identity and Culture in National Security', in Peter J. Katzenstein (ed.), *The Culture of National Security: Norms and Identity in World Politics* (New York: Columbia University Press, 1996), 38.

28 Finnemore and Sikkink, ibid., 895.

29 'Transnational Norms and Military Development: Constructing Ireland's National Army', *European Journal of International Relations* 7:1 (2001), 65.

directly because policy-makers are constituted by them; these actors are primarily encultured or socialised by the domestic society in which they mature and operate and not the international society in which (foreign) norm entrepreneurs are located. Accordingly, norms are assumed to have a more indirect effect on policy (i.e. by affecting the competition between the identity discourses which shape policy-making more directly). This conceptualisation helps us understand what is happening at both the global- and domestic-level between the R2P norm and the sovereignty norm on the one hand, and the relevant domestic identity discourses on the other.

Regarding the global level first, states are states because the sovereignty norm largely defines what 'being a state means', and the traditionally dominant interpretation favours a relatively strict interpretation of sovereignty which stresses non-interference (see Chapter 1). Thus sovereignty is an essential element of states' identities, which in turn *prescribes* or enables certain types of interests and actions, in particular the right to more-or-less exclusive jurisdiction over affairs within their borders. This might mean – or at least it has occasionally meant in the past – that some states have felt it was possible to abuse, or more properly that those states' governments felt they have had an *interest* in abusing, their citizens' human rights. At the same time, the non-interference aspect of sovereignty *regulates* or rules out other states intervening to prevent such atrocities. The effort to diffuse R2P is thus intended to alter the meaning of sovereignty – to promote a 'sovereignty as responsibility' interpretation – meaning it is supposed to change the way all states are constituted and thus their identities and interests. Specifically, R2P is intended to regulate/rule out states grossly abusing their citizens (Pillar I), to prescribe/enable other states to offer assistance to those states which are struggling to fulfil their Pillar I obligations (Pillar II) and, in extreme circumstances, to prescribe/enable some states to intervene (Pillar III) when one state severely abuses its citizens' human rights.

Regarding the domestic-level, traditional interpretations of sovereignty have typically informed or supported domestic-level identity discourses which substantially conform with or are constituted by the sovereignty norm, causing that state's policy-makers to define the state's interests accordingly (i.e. empowering the state to reject and resist efforts by other states to interfere in its domestic affairs). So norm entrepreneurs trying to diffuse R2P globally have essentially been trying to *delegitimise* domestic-level identity discourses which are inconsistent with the R2P norm's core logic. Some domestic actors – policy-shapers in this study – thus agitate for identity discourses compatible with R2P (i.e. these might be thought of as 'R2P-friendly' identity discourses). If they succeed – if that state's policy-makers substantially accept these new R2P-friendly identity discourses – that state's identity would change and its interests would be redefined; specifically, it would not consider it to be in its interests to abuse its citizens (Pillar I) and, ideally, it would believe it was in its interests to help other states (i.e. Pillar II) or, in extreme cases, to intervene to prevent atrocities in other states (Pillar III).

Many scholars have explored this process by which norms diffuse into states. Cortell and Davis, for example, measure the effectiveness of norm diffusion efforts by seeking evidence that the norm's core logic appears more frequently in political discourse within the target state, and also by exploring whether institutions and/or policies change in ways consistent with the norm; the more the global norm changes domestic discourse, institutions and policy, they say, the higher the degree of 'salience' it has achieved with domestic discourses.[30] Jeffrey Checkel takes a slightly different approach, noting the degree of *initial* 'cultural match' between the norm and the domestic discursive environment affects the norm's *prospects* of diffusing – obviously low cultural match negatively affects such prospects – or, at minimum, the degree of cultural match effects *how* the global norm diffuses and the tactics norm entrepreneurs can or should adopt when they try to diffuse the norm into states.[31]

The motives of the domestic actors who support the diffusion of a particular global-level norm have been conceptualised in broadly two ways in the norm dynamics literature. For one, some scholars have found that domestic actors *use* a global norm 'to legitimate their self-interested preferences' by appealing to it in their internal squabbles with other actors; in other words, they *use* the norm to 'win' on a contentious issue, perhaps to change an institution or to entrench a favoured policy which benefits them.[32] Or, alternatively, other scholars argue that actors *accept* and sincerely believe in the 'rightness' of the norm, becoming constituted by it and promoting it for altruistic reasons.[33] Arguably in the R2P context the latter 'sincere belief' motivation might seem the most obvious explanation; offering aid to or military intervening in other states necessarily involves expending scarce national resources to protect 'strangers'. But we should never rule out the self-interested dimension either because successfully promoting R2P may increase a policy-shaper's professional influence, enhancing their status and career prospects. Equally, it is probably too cynical to conclude that when a domestic actor agitates for a global norm which might benefit them – when they seem to be using it – they do so entirely selfishly. Even if one suspects that they have 'conveniently convinced themselves' of the norm's validity one must still concede they 'believe in it' to some extent, that it has come to constitute them to some degree, even if a relatively limited or somewhat superficial sense. The norm literature splits over which description – using or sincerely believing – is best,

30 Andrew P. Cortell and James W. Davis, 'Understanding the Domestic Impact of International Norms: A Research Agenda', *International Studies Review* 2:1 (2000), 69–71.

31 Jeffrey Checkel, 'Norms, Institutions, and National Identity in Contemporary Europe', *International Studies Quarterly* 43:1 (1999), 87.

32 Andrew P. Cortell and James W. Davis, 'When Norms Clash: International Norms, Domestic Practices, and Japan's Internalisation of the GATT/WTO', *Review of International Studies* 31:1 (2005), 25.

33 Charlotte Epstein, *The Power of Words in International Relations: The Birth of an Anti-Whaling Discourse* (Cambridge, Mass.: MIT Press, 2008), 6.

although no scholar has argued that this is a sharp either/or distinction,[34] meaning which predominates in a particular context becomes an empirical question.

Regarding strategies norm entrepreneurs deploy to diffuse global norms, the norm dynamics literature pays particular attention to *grafting* and *framing*. Grafting means the new norm is 'associated with' – so, grafted onto – an existing, widely-accepted global norm. Richard Price has shown how advocates for a ban on landmines (whose campaign eventually produced the Ottawa Treaty) grafted their new anti-landmines norm onto the well-established 'military discrimination' norm.[35] If the existing global norm is already accepted locally then the prospects of the new norm diffusing into that state should be reasonably good. Framing is a similar process, but involves associating the new global norm with a pre-existing and influential *local* discursive structure; Audie Klotz, for example, showed how campaigners for the global anti-Apartheid norm successfully framed their campaign as similar to the domestic Civil Rights campaign in America, and how they persuaded a range of institutions (especially those representing the African-American community) to join. They thus generated significant support for the anti-Apartheid norm within America, which ultimately changed that state's interests significantly. This came to be reflected in Washington's policy towards South Africa, which in turn contributed to the demise of the Apartheid regime.[36]

Amitav Acharya has noted, however, that studies of both grafting and framing have typically been characterised by an inherent bias; Western norm entrepreneurs were assumed to be active 'givers' of norms and non-Westerners were passive 'takers' with limited agency. He offered a 'norm localisation' model to describe how local non-Western actors often *adapted* the global norms they were being pressured to adopt to better fit their local circumstances (in the South East Asian cases he examined the global norms were basically 'substantially watered-down').[37] Acharya subsequently explored other processes and potential outcomes of the norm diffusion process. One is what he calls 'norm subsidiarity', which involves local or regional actors *rejecting* new global norms by reaffirming or only slightly reformulating well-established domestic or regional norms – like the traditionally strict definitions of state sovereignty that underpin ASEAN – to protect their autonomy.[38] He has also offered a 'norm circularity' model by which

---

34 Matthew J. Hoffmann, 'Norms and Social Constructivism in International Relations', in Robert A. Denemark (ed.), *The International Studies Encyclopedia* (Blackwell Publishing, 2010). Available at: <http://www.isacompendium.com>.

35 I.e. militaries should discriminate between combatants, who are legitimate targets, and non-combatants, who are not; it obviously helped that landmines are inherently indiscriminate weapons: 'Reversing the Gun Sights: Transnational Civil Society Targets Land Mines', *International Organization* 52:3 (1998), 627–631.

36 *Norms in International Relations: The Struggle Against Apartheid* (Ithaca: Cornell University Press, 1999).

37 'How Ideas Spread', *International Organization* 58:2 (2004), 239–275.

38 'Norm Subsidiarity and Regional Orders: Sovereignty, Regionalism, and Rule-Making in the Third World', *International Studies Quarterly* 55:1 (2011), 95–123.

local actors reformulate new global-level norms to better fit pre-existing local discursive priors – as described by norm localisation – before they 'feed them back' to the global level.[39] In this last study Acharya examined R2P and found the controversial Libyan crisis caused various actors to reformulate R2P and feed it back to the global level (for example, Brazil's so-called 'responsibility while protecting' formulation), stimulating another round of debates about the norm's content and scope.

Thus identity discourses and global norms do not exist in strict isolation from one another, and neither are they static, unchanging entities. Instead, the identity discourses this study deploys as its primary explanatory devices are 'nested' in the complex, ever-shifting wider 'web of meanings' or discursive structures that Ludwig Wittgenstein, Clifford Geertz and Brian Fay tells us constitute all societies of meaning-oriented humans, including the international society which IR scholars examine (and, of course, the state of India too).[40] Thus domestic identity discourses are informed by or draw support from global norms which constitute – or in R2P's case are *trying* to constitute – international society. But the domestic actors promoting their favoured identity discourses also draw on 'extant cultural raw materials or linguistic resources'[41] – pre-existing domestic-level discursive structures – which constitute their discrete societies too.

This section has engaged in abstract discussion of the relationship between identity discourses and norms. The next section is more focused on India. The identity discourses themselves are introduced, the relationships between them and both global norms and other domestic discursive structures they nest within are explored, and the core logics of each identity discourse are distinguished across three broad 'axes of difference'.

India's R2P-Specific Identity Discourses

To recap, the argument so far is that Indian identity discourses constitute and so shape the preferences of persons in the wider foreign policy community – the policy-shapers – who comment on and offer advice about proper or appropriate responses to particular humanitarian crises, and try to influence policy-makers. This is not a particularly controversial position in the Indian context; Jaganathan and Kurtz claim, for example, that 'individual differences [vis-à-vis R2P] reflect larger debates within the Indian strategic community and the

39 'The R2P and Norm Diffusion: Towards a Framework of Norm Circulation'. *Global Responsibility to Protect* 5:1 (2013), 466–479.

40 Wittgenstein, *Philosophical Investigations* (Oxford: Blackwell, 1953), II.226; Geertz, *The Interpretation of Cultures: Selected Essays* (New York: Basic Books, 1973); Fay, *Social Theory*, 76–78.

41 Weldes, 'Constructing', 284–287.

administration',[42] and many studies have found that various 'schools' competed to shape Indian foreign policy-making; Kanti Bajpai found three (Nehruvian, neoliberal and hyperrealist),[43] Stephen Cohen found four (classical-Nehruvian, militant-Nehruvian, conservative realism and Hindu revivalism),[44] and Rahul Sagar also found four (moralist, Hindu-nationalist, strategic and liberal).[45] In the most recent comprehensive survey of Indian grand strategic thought Bajpai, Basit and Krishnappa found six schools; 'three minor schools … Marxism, Hindu nationalism or Hindutva, and Ghandianism', and 'three major schools … Nehruvianism, Neoliberalism and Hyperrealism'.[46] They found that despite dominating for most of India's post-independence history 'Nehruvianism has lost ground … leaving the three major schools more or less equal in their influence', while the three minor schools tended to only shape India's foreign policy occasionally or in relatively narrow policy-contexts or issue-areas.[47]

This study was originally inspired by these sorts of studies, although as noted above it is more narrowly focused; it is interested only in examining R2P-specific aspects of India's identity, not its overall foreign policy identity. Accordingly, three hypotheses were initially posed to guide the data-gathering process. First, maybe a *liberal-democratic* identity discourse predisposes India to support a proposed R2P-inspired intervention in a particular humanitarian crisis? Indians are typically proud of their democratic traditions and system, and liberal-democrats are, generally speaking, promoters and defenders of human rights. Second, maybe an *anti-imperial* identity discourse predisposes India to oppose a proposed intervention in a particular humanitarian crisis? Western actors are the most prominent promoters of R2P and it is they who typically carry out the interventions inspired by the R2P norm after all. And, finally, maybe a *great power* identity discourse predisposes India to carefully and dispassionately consider how best to secure its broader national interests before it decides to support or oppose a proposed intervention? In other words, while realists do not traditionally regard 'saving strangers' as a pressing national interest, they may nevertheless support (or oppose) a proposed intervention if India was able to secure side-benefits by doing so.

---

42 Madhan Mohan Jaganathan and Gerrit Kurtz, 'Singing the Tune of Sovereignty? India and the Responsibility to Protect', *Conflict, Security and Development* 14:4 (2014), 478.

43 *Future Strategic Balances and Alliances* (Carlisle: Strategic Studies Institute, 2002), 245–303.

44 *India: Emerging Power* (Washington: Brookings Institution, 2001), Chapter 2.

45 'State of Mind: What Kind of Power will India Become?', *International Affairs* 85:4 (2009), 801–816.

46 Kanti Bajpai, Saira Basit and V. Krishnappa, 'Introduction', in Kanti Bajpai, Saira Basit and V. Krishnappa (eds), *India's Grand Strategy: History, Theory, Cases* (Routledge: New Delhi, 2014), 16.

47 Ibid., 20.

The data-gathering process did indeed demonstrate that identity discourses broadly conforming with these three types were discernible in the Indian public debates about how to respond to the humanitarian crises in Côte d'Ivoire, Libya and Syria, although it also became clear as investigations proceeded that somewhat distinct 'strains' existed within each of them, especially within the great power identity discourse. Other potentially relevant identity discourses were also explored; while these were found to be much less influential they are mentioned below to demonstrate the study did not fixate on just a few pre-determined identity discourses and artificially 'squeeze' the data into conceptual boxes delimited by them.

Finally, and as noted earlier, each identity discourse contains different assumptions about what the proper content of India's R2P-specific identity should be; in other words, each contains different *core logics* or assumptions about what or who India is, who or what other actors are, the appropriate relationship between them and India, etc. Put another way, each identity discourse answers important questions like 'who is to blame?' for a crisis, 'whose side we are on?' and 'what should we do?' in fundamentally different ways.[48] We therefore need to be able to distinguish between the various identity discourses, which is done below with reference to three basic axes of difference, namely: its adherents' views about the correct *interpretation of history*; what international *role* they believe India should play; and which other international actors they think India can or can't *trust*.

Turning to the *liberal-democratic* identity discourse first, policy-shapers who adhere to this interpret history as meaning India – and by extension, all states – are better off liberal and democratic because democracies typically protect their citizens' human rights. Regarding India's proper international role, and given the liberal-democratic discourse privileges multilateralism,[49] India's role is to strongly support an international rule of law and to promote human rights through such. Finally, they are broadly predisposed to trust Western states and the UN Secretariat (or the Human Rights Council, etc.) when these actors claim a particular military intervention is necessary and is motivated by humanitarianism.

Generally speaking, this identity discourse shapes Indian debates in ways which suggest India should *support* the R2P norm and R2P-inspired interventions in particular humanitarian crises. Importantly, because adherents to this discourse are basically motivated by solidarist morality (i.e. all human lives are considered equally valuable), they typically claim human rights should be protected whenever and wherever they are threatened; they do not, as a result, tend to discriminate much between a proposed humanitarian intervention which would occur far away and one which would take place in India's immediate region.

48 These distinctions emerged as the consideration of the textual sources proceeded, meaning while not every axis of difference was apparent in every text, they were common, recurring themes.

49 Speech, 'Welcome remarks by External Affairs Minister during the visit of UN Secretary General', S.M. Krishna (Minister of External Affairs), New Delhi, 27 April 2012; Sagar, 'State of Mind', 814.

The liberal-democratic identity discourse nests within or draws support from other domestic Indian discursive structures. Some of these are ancient texts or traditions which remain influential: Nalini Kant Jha, for example, notes parallels between modern liberal concerns for human rights and tolerance and Indians' 'preference for the third way'; as he puts it, 'compromise is the hallmark of Indian tradition and culture'.[50] Others note the enduring influence of the great Mauryan Emperor Ashoka's 'Edicts' (third century BCE) which urged tolerance and promulgated basic universal rights,[51] and the emphasis Sanskrit classics like the *Gita* and *Mahabhrata* place on ethical international relations.[52] Ramachandra Guha, for his part, emphasises instead the deep institutional roots of the 'rights culture' bequeathed to India by Britain and notes Indians take great pride in being 'the world's largest democracy'.[53] Even the brief lapse into semi-autocracy – the 1975–1977 Emergency – is often spun into a success,[54] and Indians like comparing themselves favourably to the democratic failings of other former colonies (the contrast with Pakistan, in particular, elicits plenty of *schadenfreude*[55]). There is accordingly a reasonable degree of salience or cultural match between the R2P norm and a various pre-existing domestic Indian discursive structures; some have very deep, ancient roots and others, while technically bequeathed by the British, became integral to Indian nationalists' efforts to achieve independence and have been celebrated ever since.[56]

The fact democratic and liberal discourses have strong roots in India and are simultaneously powerful global-level norms illustrates what is meant by the notion that a particular identity discourse exists within a wider web of meanings: there is a fundamental interconnectedness of domestic and external norms/ discourses meaning adherents to a particular identity discourse – including those who attempt to shape how India responds to humanitarian crises – can use and/ or sincerely believe in global-level norms. Obviously R2P itself is the primary external norm which constitutes or influences domestic actors who promote the liberal-democratic identity discourse. But other global norms play similar roles. For example, Nehru championed the Universal Declaration of Human Rights and

---

50 'The Cultural and Philosophical Roots of Indian Foreign Policy', *International Studies* 26:1 (1989), 46.

51 David Malone, *Can the Elephant Dance?: Contemporary Indian Foreign Policy* (Oxford: Oxford University Press, 2011), 24–26.

52 Radha Kumar, 'India as a Foreign Policy Actor – Normative Redux', *CEPS Working Document* No. 285, February 2008, 2.

53 *India After Ghandi: The History of the World's Largest Democracy* (New York: Harper Perennial, 2008), Chapter 6.

54 For example, three historians have said 'the Indian people passed the test with a distinction if not full marks' at the 1977 election: Bipan Chandra, Aditya Mukherjee, Mridula Mukherjee (eds), *India After Independence* (New Delhi: Penguin, 1999), 260.

55 Maya Tudor, *The Promise of Power: The Origins of Democracy in India and Autocracy in Pakistan* (Cambridge: Cambridge University Press, 2013).

56 Bipan Chandra, Aditya Mukherjee and Mridula Mukherjee (eds), *India After Independence* (New Delhi: Penguin, 1999), Chapter 5.

campaigned stridently against Apartheid South Africa because it offended anti-racism norms.[57] And contemporary India promotes the Protection of Civilians norm (and is, accordingly, a major contributor to peacekeeping operations),[58] it supports humanitarian aid efforts,[59] and it has supported reforming the UN Human Rights Council.[60] Indeed, many related human rights treaties and good-governance norms at the global level – too many to list – provide external support to the liberal-democratic identity discourse.

One final observation should be made before we consider the next identity discourse. The 'full' or 'complete' liberal-democratic identity discourse conceptualised here is one which generally supports the use of military force – or at least relatively *interventionist* policies like sanctions and arms embargos, etc. – to protect human rights. But as later chapters show plenty of Indian policy-shapers adhere to a 'soft' or 'incomplete' version which means while they are supportive of democracy and human rights and would prefer, generally speaking, that such advance globally, they stop short of advocating the use of military force (or intrusive sanctions, etc.) to achieve such.

R2P encounters significant resistance from Indian policy-shapers who adhere to the second broad identity discourse, *anti-imperialism*. For them, history is interpreted broadly as a tale of injustice and (Western) interference and domination, while India's own history is interpreted through a victimisation narrative.[61] By implication, then, they believe India's international role is or should be to promote justice – *between* states in preference to within them – and to resist alleged (Western) neo-colonial impulses. For example, they often interpret the spread of capitalism through globalisation as essentially a neo-colonial enterprise, and they therefore remain suspicious of it. India, according to them, should trust other former-colonies, not Western states, and express solidarity with those states' representative bodies, like the Non-Aligned Movement (NAM), Arab League, African Union (AU) etc., while distrusting NATO, the IMF, and other 'Western tools' (often including the UN Secretariat).

The core logic of the anti-imperial discourse is therefore opposition to interventionism, pitting it profoundly against the R2P norm. Importantly, however, its adherents do tend to discriminate to some degree; they typically resist *Western* interventions and tend to be less resistant to interventionism by former-colonies or the regional organisations which represent them. We will see in later chapters, for

57 C. Raja Mohan, 'Rising India: Partner in Shaping the Global Commons?', *Washington Quarterly* 33:1 (2010), 135.

58 Statement, Manjeev Singh Puri (Deputy Ambassador to UN, India), Security Council Open Debate on Protection of Civilians, May 2011.

59 Urvashi Aneja, 'India, R2P and Humanitarian Assistance', *Global Responsibility to Protect* 6:2 (2014), 239.

60 Statement, Dushyant Singh (MP), to Third Committee of UNGA, 18 October 2011.

61 Manjari Chatterjee-Miller, *Wronged By Empire: Post-Imperial Ideology and Foreign Policy in India and China* (Stanford: Stanford University Press, 2013).

example, that India has been more comfortable with interventions in African states when such were authorised by the AU, even when Western troops were involved.

The anti-imperialism discourse also finds fertile ground in India's domestic discursive structures, reducing R2P's salience or cultural match. Some of these discursive structures are very ancient; for example the *Gita*, mentioned above as a potential resource Indians may invoke to justify ethical foreign policy (i.e. potentially including the active protection of human rights) also features the god Arjuna categorically rejecting his fellow-god Krishna's claim that war is a necessary and temporary evil.[62] And Kadira Pethiyagoda claims Ghandi's 'passive resistance' strategy (*satyagraha*[63]) was inspired by *Amhisa*, an ancient Buddhist and Hindu doctrine of absolute commitment to non-violence; Pethiyagoda claims 'dominant cultural values' like these explain in part why some Indians resist R2P, or at least its more intrusive elements like Pillar III.[64]

This identity discourse is given a more anti-*imperial* texture by various modern post- or anti-colonial discourses; for example, Nehru claimed 'the whole mental outlook of India [is] inherent in the condition of the mind during the freedom struggle'.[65] Specifically, adherents recall being colonised in the name of civilisation before (and so equate R2P with the 'white man's burden' discourse[66]) and that India, the 'jewel in the crown' of the British Empire, was systematically exploited (and so they subscribe to the 'drain theory'[67]). Overlaying all these discourses was the struggle, spearheaded by the Indian National Congress and arguably still very much a work-in-progress, to create a discourse of Indian nationalism which obviously rejects the interventionist colonial mind-set.[68]

A far-left strain of the anti-imperial identity discourse is even more antagonistic towards Western states. The Communist Party of India (Marxist) (CPI(M)) publishes *People's Democracy*, and its international news pages are typically shot through with insights from Lenin's *Imperialism*[69] and/or dependency theory.[70] The party also traditionally rejected Nehru's more-moderate anti-imperialism: for example,

62 Kumar, 'India', 2.

63 Literally 'truth insistence': Chandra et al., *India After Independence*, 173.

64 'India's Approach to Humanitarian Intervention and the Responsibility to Protect', *Oxford Institute for Ethics, Law and Armed Conflict – Working Paper*, November 2013, 10.

65 Lok Sabha debate, 9 December 1958, in *India's Foreign Policy, Selected Speeches, September 1946 – April 1961* (New Delhi: Ministry of Information, 1961), 80.

66 Mohammed Ayoob, 'Third World Perspectives on Humanitarian Intervention and International Administration', *Global Governance* 10:1 (2004), 101.

67 John Keay, *India: A History* (London: HarperPress, 2010 [2000]), Chapter 18.

68 Partha Chatterjee, *Nationalist Thought and the Colonial World: A Derivative Discourse* (Minneapolis: University of Minnesota Press, 1986); Chandra et al., *India's Struggle for Independence*.

69 Vladimir Lenin, *Imperialism, The Highest Stage of Capitalism* (Chippendale: Resistance Books, 1999 [1917]).

70 Andre Gunder Frank, *The Development of Underdevelopment* (Boston: New England Free Press, 1966).

Taufiq Nizami called Nehru a 'running dog of imperialism', and India's Cold War-era non-alignment grand strategic posture 'immoral' because it failed to align India with 'good' (communism) against 'evil' (capitalism).[71] The way the Indian far-left deploys Marxist discourses demonstrates again the interconnectedness of domestic identity discourses and global-level norms; despite the fact that Marxist norms and discourses have become somewhat discredited in the contemporary era they certainly haven't disappeared in India.

Many other related external, global-level norms also support the anti-imperial identity discourse, like those associated with the NAM (especially the *Panchsheel* principles[72]), anti-racism norms – which were manifested historically in opposition to Apartheid, but remain influential – and discourses which call for economic autarky and semi-socialist 'guided development' strategies. Indeed Nehru, and his minister V.K. Menon and adviser Prasanta Mahalanobis, played leading roles promoting these discourses globally during the Cold War.[73] More generally, non-aligned solidarity has meant rights of states – especially former-colonies' rights of self-determination – were privileged over individual rights.[74] Urvashi Aneja explains this as an innate preference amongst Indians for pluralist conceptions of justice and sovereignty over the solidarist discourse which underpins the R2P norm.[75] Obviously the global-level sovereignty norm also provides crucial support for and/or constitutes adherents to the anti-imperial identity discourse (subject to what was said above about India being somewhat less sensitive to interventions by regional organisations representing former-colonies); the ultimate goal of the entire anti-colonial effort in India and elsewhere was of course to ensure sovereignty was applied universally and not just to Western societies.

As the study progressed at least two strains of anti-imperialist logic became discernible; one emphasised implacable resistance to Western states (i.e. especially when such sought to intervene in another developing state) while a second emphasised solidarity with fellow developing-world states. These two are obviously related to one another but, as later chapters show, they actually advance somewhat different policy-claims in the context of particular humanitarian crises. In other words, the dynamics between them may affect the way India *discriminates*

71 *The Communist Party and India's Foreign Policy* (New Delhi: Associated Publishing House, 1971).

72 This doctrine was promoted in particular by Nehru in the 1954 Sino-Indian pact and the 1955 Bandung Conference. The principles states should adhere to in their dealings with other states are: mutual respect for each other's territorial integrity and sovereignty; mutual non-aggression; mutual non-interference in domestic affairs; equality and mutual benefit; peaceful co-existence; Jawaharlal Nehru, *India's Foreign Policy: Selected Speeches, September 1946–April 1961* (Delhi: Publications Division, Ministry of Information and Broadcasting, 1961), 101.

73 Stephen P. Cohen, *India: Emerging Power* (Washington: Brookings, 2004), 37–40; Guha, *India after Ghandi*, Chapters 8 and 10;

74 C. Raja Mohan, 'Balancing Interests and Values: India's Struggle with Democracy Promotion', *Washington Quarterly* 30:3 (2007), 91–93.

75 'India, R2P'.

between humanitarian crises; for example, the implacably anti-Western strain would suggest virtually all humanitarian interventions should be opposed if Western states are intervening but the aspect which emphasises solidarity with the developing-world may soften Indians' opposition if the AU, for example, invited Western troops to participate in an intervention in an African state.

Finally, a *great power* identity discourse also competes to shape India's response to R2P and humanitarian crises. Its adherents tend to self-describe as 'realists', and it too draws support from related Indian cultural resources, some of them ancient. For example, drawing parallels between realism and the third century BCE classic *Arthashastra* – authored by 'India's Machiavelli', Kautilya – is very common.[76] Michael Liebig explored this phenomenon – the 'active "re-use" of endogenous politico-cultural resources' as he puts it – and he claimed 'virtually everyone in India "knows" Kautilya' and applies their interpretations of the *Arthashastra* to understanding international politics.[77] More recently, Indian realist-historians have concluded India's relative backwardness and cultural heterogeneity made it an 'object of external intervention and aggrandizement' for centuries, meaning India's primary goal now must be to strengthen its power relative to other states to avoid a similar fate in future.[78] And the formative thinker of the modern doctrine of Hindutva (which roughly translates as 'Hindu-ness' or perhaps is better thought of as 'Hindu Nationalism') Vinayak Savarkar, blamed India's weakness on the enervating influence of pacifist Jainsim and Buddhism and called for 'all Hindus to get … reborn into a martial race'.[79] Hindutva's promoters typically want India to be 'assertive' and 'manly',[80] illustrating how the great power discourse nests amongst various complimentary domestic discursive structures; Kautilya's writings, the realist-historians' writings, and Hindutva all emphasise *power* as the crucial factor in international politics.

Obviously the sovereignty norm also offers crucial external support for the great power identity discourse. Ian Hall notes 'inspirations for India's new realism were both indigenous and Western in origin – a mixture of Kautilya and Kissinger',[81] demonstrating that global-level discourses or norms,[82] in this case varieties of

76 Rashed Uz Zaman, 'Kautilya: The Indian Strategic Thinker and Indian Strategic Culture', *Comparative Strategy* 25:3 (2006), 231–247; J.N. Dixit, *India's Foreign Policy, 1947–2003* (Delhi: Picus Books, 2003); Cohen, *India*, 41; Malone, *Can the Elephant Dance?*, 310.

77 'Kautilya's Relevance for India Today', *India Quarterly* 69:2 (2013), 99–116.

78 Discussed in Ashok Kapur, *India: From Regional to World Power* (Oxon: Routledge, 2006), 15–18.

79 *Hindutva* (New Delhi: The Central Hindu Yuvak Sabha, 1938), 201.

80 Priya Chacko, *Indian Foreign Policy: The Politics of Postcolonial Identity from 1947 to 2004* (Oxon: Routledge, 2012), Chapter 7.

81 'The Other Exception? India as a Rising Power', *Australian Journal of International Affairs* 64:5 (2010), 602.

82 IR theories, including realism, are just another form of discourse akin in some ways to norms (i.e. they are intended to be widely applicable and contain assumptions about causality, appropriate behaviour, etc.)

realist theory which themselves are partially constituted by the sovereignty norm, also constitute or are used by adherents to the great power discourse. As Chapter 1 showed, for example, realists like Hans Morgenthau and Samuel Huntington reject the notion that states owe any duties or responsibilities to foreigners and instead assert they are morally obliged to pursue and protect only their citizens' interests.

Conventional wisdom holds Nehru's principled or idealist foreign policy collapsed after India's defeat in the 1962 Sino-Indian War, opening the door to realism.[83] George Tanham concluded in the 1990s that India had no 'overall foreign policy template' to work from[84] and, notably, while some Indians still agree,[85] they are typically realists who (unsurprisingly!) offer realism as the remedy. While 13 of 16 interviewees this author spoke to during field work agreed realism had steadily become more influential since 1962 only eight agreed it 'clearly dominated' contemporary Indian foreign policy. Still, realist principles are readily apparent in major policy statements; for example, External Affairs Minister S.M. Krishna declared in 2009:

> India's main foreign policy challenge lies in creating and maintaining a regional and international environment which would enable us to sustain a high rate of economic growth ... to realise its vast, latent potential. The pursuit of enhanced investment trade, investment inflows, technology transfers, energy security and other economic imperatives has become an overarching imperative of our foreign policy.[86]

As noted earlier research for this study began with the working hypothesis that attention to liberal-democratic, anti-imperial and great power identity discourses might explain India's policy responses to R2P. As the research continued somewhat different 'strains' within each became apparent. This was so vis-à-vis the liberal-democratic identity discourse (i.e. 'soft' versus 'robust' liberal-democratic logics) and also the anti-imperial identity discourse (i.e. especially the hard-leftists who are implacably anti-Western and a softer variety which values developing-world solidarity but which also exhibits less automatic antagonism towards Western actors). But the presence of two distinct strains is most evident regarding the great power identity discourse.

---

83 Sagar, 'State of Mind', 813; Cohen, *India*, 41–43.

84 *Indian Strategic Thought: An Interpretive Essay* (Santa Monica: RAND Corporation, 1992).

85 E.g. C. Raja Mohan, *Crossing the Rubicon: The Shaping of India's Foreign Policy* (New Delhi: Viking, 2003); Harsh V. Pant (ed.), *Indian Foreign Policy in a Unipolar World* (New Delhi: Routledge, 2009); see discussion in Pratap Bhanu Mehta, 'Still Under Nehru's Shadow? The Absence of a Foreign Policy Framework in India', *India Review* 8:3 (2009), 209–233.

86 'EAM's Statement in Rajya Sabha on workings of MEA', Ministry of External Affairs, 31 July 2009.

The first is a 'hard-realist' strain tightly focused on pursuing India's national interests and enhancing its relative power and influence. Drawing primarily on neorealism[87] and offensive realism,[88] it is particularly sceptical of the potential for international institutions to create the conditions for advancing India's interests (classic examples can be found throughout Harsh Pant's edited volume *Contemporary Debates in Indian Foreign and Security Policy*[89]). Hard-realists also take Morgenthau's advice about treating prudence as a cardinal foreign policy virtue very seriously, meaning they typically advise India to respond to foreign events cautiously and, if possible, to avoid direct involvement in humanitarian crises if India's specific interests are not imperilled by such.[90] The 'enlightened-realist' strain, however, draws its inspiration more from defensive realism,[91] meaning its adherents are more prepared to accept the possibility of inter-state cooperation through international institutions.

To complicate matters further, as the study progressed a split within the enlightened-realist camp became discernible too, but it is less over the basic assumptions which inform their worldview than a difference over the interpretation of evidence. Some may accept it is in India's interests to support R2P lest vicious human rights abusers, left unchecked, undermine global stability to India's detriment. Some also argue that India should 'strategically' support particular R2P-inspired interventions to boost New Delhi's standing as 'serious global player'; in other words, they may advocate *using* R2P to extract side-benefits. Raja Mohan and others, for example, regularly advise India to become a *responsible* power, including by abandoning what they see as a knee-jerk anti-Western predisposition against interventionism.[92]

Yet enlightened-realist support for R2P is contingent upon it *actually* contributing to global stability: accordingly, some enlightened-realists are less willing to accept that R2P promotes stability and instead they suspect it does the opposite. Later chapters show policy-shapers applying what is basically enlightened-realist logic to come to different conclusions about this question of whether R2P enhances or undermines stability; the conduct and outcome of the

87 Kenneth K. Waltz, *The Theory of International Politics* (Reading: Addison-Wesley, 1979).

88 John Mearsheimer, *The Tragedy of Great Power Politics* (New York: Norton & Norton, 2001).

89 Harsh Pant (ed.), *Contemporary Debates in Indian Foreign and Security Policy* (New York: Palgrave Macmillan, 2008).

90 *Politics Among Nations: The Struggle for Power and Peace*, 5th ed. (New York: Alfred A. Knopf, 1978 [1948]), 10–11.

91 Charles Glaser, 'Realists as Optimists: Cooperation as Self-Help', *International Security* 19:3 (1994/5), 50–90.

92 *Crossing the Rubicon*; 'Rising India'; Rajesh Rajagopalan and Varun Singh, 'India and the Great Powers: Strategic Imperatives, Normative Necessities, *South Asian Survey* 15:5 (2008), 5–32; Amrita Narlikar, 'Is India a Responsible Great Power?', *Third World Quarterly* 32:9 (2011), 1607–1621.

crisis in Libya in particular affected the balance between these two interpretations (the R2P-pessimists generally gained the upper hand in this 'domestic dispute'). And none of the enlightened-realists are starry-eyed idealists: if an intervention directly imperilled India's interests they would oppose it.

Regarding the three axes of difference, both the hard-realists and the enlightened-realists accept history ebbs and flows as states' relative-power fluctuates, and both want to remedy India's relative weakness and enhance its global influence. But they differ more on India's proper international role: hard-realists urge the single-minded pursuit of India's interests, interpreted narrowly, while enlightened-realists may accept India's interests might be served by promoting *common* interests. These differences tend to be reflected, for example, in different attitudes towards international law; hard-realists dismiss it as relatively meaningless while enlightened-realists take it more seriously. They also differ regarding the degree to which India – indeed, any state – can or should trust others. Hard-realists resist trusting other international actors and typically advise India to dispassionately gauge if its interests align with others' interests in particular contexts, and to accept there are no enduring international friendships (nor enmities, for that matter). The enlightened-realists, however, are more willing to entertain trusting Western states and international institutions (if, that is, those Western actors behave in a responsible and stability-enhancing manner).

These discourses therefore have slightly different effects on the R2P norm's salience in India: the hard-realist strain reduces its salience and suggests the cultural match between R2P and pre-existing discursive structures is relatively low. Generally speaking, while its adherents may not urge India to actively *oppose* an R2P-inspired intervention – they readily admit India is relatively weak – they would likely advise not supporting it either unless India's specific interests were directly advanced by doing so. This hard-realist strain of the great power identity discourse therefore constitutes India's identity in ways which suggest India's interests are not served by intervening to protect the human rights of foreigners; its adherents don't consider positive humanitarian outcomes sufficient reason to risk India's precious resources, so they are most likely to urge New Delhi to stay on the sidelines. The enlightened-realist discourse, however, arguably increases R2P's salience, meaning policy-shapers who deploy this sort of logic are somewhat more disposed to support R2P; but, again, only if they accept R2P enhances stability and/or if supporting an R2P-inspired intervention enhances India's profile or influence, and so thereby serves India's interests. This strain of the great power identity discourse therefore competes to constitute India's identity in ways which mean its interests are formulated in 'longer' or perhaps 'broader' terms than their hard-realist stable-mates would prefer.

These strains of the great power discourse also differ when it comes to how they discriminate between humanitarian crises. The hard-realists, because they focus tightly on India's direct interests, may be prepared to support an intervention or even urge India to actively intervene in crises close to India, or in a vital region (i.e. like the Persian Gulf, where most of India's energy comes from). The corollary is that they are likely to be less concerned by crises further away or in less-sensitive regions. The enlightened-realists, however, because they are more concerned with enhancing general global stability and/or India's status as a responsible power might be somewhat more prepared to support interventions in far-flung regions.

So much for the three primary identity discourses (and the variants within them). But we should also ask whether other identity discourses present in India's public sphere might shape its policy-responses to humanitarian crises; this possibility was considered during the data-collection process to ensure the study remained falsifiable.

The most obvious 'fourth candidate' was Hindutva, although formulating a hypothesis to guide research was hard; perhaps, because it is a nationalist discourse which calls for India to be strong and respected, such an identity discourse predisposes India to care little about the sufferings of foreigners? Or maybe (and even more tentatively) it may predispose India to care less about the sufferings of *Muslim* foreigners?[93] Hindutva is certainly not characterised by respect for universal human rights as these are conventionally understood, and elements within the various Hindutva-promoting civil society institutions, like the Rashtriya Swayam Savek (RSS) and Shiv Sena, are openly hostile to Muslims (both Indian and foreign – especially Pakistani). The modern BJP party is built on Hindutva values, and it is affiliated with the RSS and Shiv Sena, amongst others: these latter groups represent 'hard Hindutva' while the BJP itself follows a sort of 'soft Hindutva' for diplomatic and electoral reasons.[94] Yet the BJP has arguably shown a propensity for relatively tougher, national security-sensitive foreign policy stances than Indian governments led by the Congress Party; this distinction should not be drawn too sharply, but at minimum it would seem reasonable to claim the BJP is more interested in pursuing 'traditional security interests' than in forging a foreign policy agenda predicated on the defence of universal human rights.[95]

It is not immediately clear, however, what implication this interpretation of history and the robust international role advocates of Hindutva want India to play may have for R2P. Perhaps it suggests a hard-headed realism? Maybe, but post-colonial angst is never far from the surface either even though the BJP is definitely not a left-party. Perhaps the social orientation inherent in a Hindutva identity discourse, the belief that only Hindus are 'authentically Indian'[96] – which still finds wide currency today – may suggest indifference towards the suffering of others, especially Muslim-others? Or perhaps it predisposes India against trusting

93 Some very hard-line Hindu nationalists may view atrocities against Muslims positively although, and to jump ahead, the data-gathering process yielded no evidence of such sentiments being aired publically.

94 Kapur, *India*, 206.

95 Chacko, *Indian Foreign Policy*, Chapter 7; Rahul Sagar, '"Jiski Lathi, Uski Bhains": The Hindu Nationalist View of International Politics', in Bajpai et al., *India's Grand Strategy*.

96 Savarkar, *Hindutva*, 147; Sagar, ibid., 250–252.

other Muslim states more generally, and not just Pakistan? Or maybe its adherents mistrust the West because they sees its Christian (or its secular?) values as a threat to the traditional Hindu values they cherish, and they still harbour resentments against the West for subjugating India for several centuries? Perhaps, but at times the proponents of Hindutva have acknowledged the crucial role the West played in ending India's humiliation under the Muslim yoke.[97]

Ultimately all of these questions became largely moot as the research proceeded because there was almost no evidence a Hindutva identity discourse shaped India's policy responses to humanitarian crises. To clarify, the research revealed that Hindutva significantly shapes India's *wider* foreign policy identity – especially vis-à-vis Indo-Pakistan relations, and Sino-Indian relations, and in the sphere of nuclear weapons policy (which is, of course, tied closely to both these bilateral relationships) – but not when it came to R2P. At most the Hindutva identity discourse may 'lend some support' to the great power identity discourse, especially the hard-realist strain, and perhaps also to the anti-imperialist discourse, in particular contexts.

The author also considered whether ethnic or regional identities may affect India's response to humanitarian crises. Most obviously, ethnic Tamils have long sympathised with their ethnic kin across the Palk Straits. The data indicated clearly that this sentiment shaped India's responses to certain humanitarian crises; the historical analysis in Chapter 3 reveals that India's (unhappy) experience intervening in Sri Lanka in the late 1980s delivered important lessons, and in 2009 the long-running Sri Lankan civil war came to a bloody end, with ethnic Tamils the most conspicuous victims of the carnage. Later chapters therefore sometimes consider the shaping effect of what might usefully be called an ethnic-Tamil identity discourse. But, importantly, this is a highly discriminatory identity discourse because while it shapes Indian policy in the very specific context of Indo-Sri Lankan relations, the spill-over effect into the broader R2P-context is relatively minor (apart from the lessons of the late 1980s).

Because India is a bewilderingly diverse mix of ethnicities, some of which have kin across borders in other states, other similar tightly-focused ethnic-based identity discourses occasionally play a minor role – to be clear, less than the ethnic-Tamil identity discourse, but a role nonetheless – in shaping policy in R2P-contexts. Ethnic Guajaratis in touch with their far-flung trading diaspora were upset by South African Apartheid and alarmed by Uganda's expulsion of Indians in the 1970s. Bengali-speakers have become agitated by the sufferings of fellow-Bengali speakers in what was East Pakistan (now Bangladesh); this was most obviously the case in 1971 (see Chapter 3). Apparently 200,000 Shia Muslims volunteered in 2014 to defeat Islamic State *jihadis*' murderous campaign against Shias in Iraq,[98]

97 M.S. Golwalkar, *Bunch of Thoughts* 3rd ed. (Bangalore: Sahitya Sindu Prakahana, 1996).

98 Stephanie March, '200,000 Indians Volunteer to Join Effort Against Islamic State Militants in Iraq, Mosque Says', *ABC News*, 6 October 2014.

and a few contributions to the public debate from the Urdu (so, 'Muslim') press are considered briefly in Chapter 5. But compared to the primary identity discourses the shaping effects of these ethnic-identity discourses was found to be negligible, and they are largely ignored other than their brief mention here.

Methodology

Before the analysis proper can begin in Chapter 3 discussion must return briefly to abstract matters. Choosing to ground a study in a particular philosophical tradition implies certain types of sources are favoured and certain methodologies are likely to be deployed to analyse such. This final section therefore examines both of these issues.

The discussion early in this chapter established that this study rejects strict-positivism. Yet it also rejects the opposite end of the 'philosophy of social science spectrum', so to speak: the 'strong-interpretivist' position.[99] Instead, this is what Ted Hopf calls a 'conventional constructivist'[100] study, meaning it accepts there is what Milja Kurki has called 'a "producing" connection between things [namely] discourses and human behaviour and thought'.[101] Thus discourses 'cause' states' policy responses in the sense that policy-makers are exposed to and become aware of and are affected by the discourses which are presented to them by policy-shapers (i.e. during their education, or when reading the newspapers, etc.), and these policy-makers interpret the 'raw data' and pressure from external objects 'through' the discursive structures, producing 'reasons for action' which they then act upon.[102] There are, however, some *practical* difficulties proving *linkage* between the identity discourses and the policy-responses peculiar to *this study*.[103]

99 Robert W. Cox, 'Realism, Positivism and Historicism' Robert W. Cox and Timothy J. Sinclair (eds), *Approaches to World Order* (Cambridge: Cambridge University Press, 1996), 87; David Campbell, *Writing Security: United States Foreign Policy and the Politics of Identity* (Minneapolis: University of Minnesota Press, 1992); R.J.B. Walker, *Inside/Outside: International Relations as Political Theory* (Cambridge: Cambridge University Press, 1993).

100 'The Promise', 181–185.

101 'Causes of a Divided Discipline: A Critical Examination of the Concept of Cause in International Relations Theory', *Global Politics Network* (2002), 18. Available at: <http://globalpolitics.de/essays>.

102 Milja Kurki, 'Causes of a Divided Discipline: Rethinking the Concept of Cause in International Relations Theory', *Review of International Studies* 32:2 (2006), 189–216; Alexander Wendt, 'On Constitution and Causation in International Relations', *Review of International Studies* 24:5 (1998), 101–117; Cynthia Enloe, *Bananas, Beaches and Bases: Making Feminist Sense of International Politics* (Berkley: University of California Press, 1990), 16.

103 John L. Campbell, 'Ideas, Politics and Public Policy', *Annual Review of Sociology* 28:1 (2002), 25; Ole Holsti, 'Public Opinion and Foreign Policy', *International Studies Quarterly* 36:4 (1992), 453.

Accordingly, the chapters which follow explore *correlations* between the logics inherent in the identity discourses and India's explanations for its policy responses; India produced many such explanations when voting on various draft resolutions presented to the Security Council regarding humanitarian crises in Côte d'Ivoire, Libya and Syria during 2011 and 2012. The analysis treats correlations between identity discourses and explanations for policy responses as 'suggestive' of the relative influence of the identity discourses on particular policy responses; we cannot, of course, be absolutely sure the reason India gave (i.e. which might *prima faecie* correlate with an identity discourse) was the only, or even the main, reason for its policy response. Therefore hypothesis testing – which involves counterfactual analysis – also complements the search for correlations; it might be possible to infer a policy response was consistent with the core logic of one or more of the identity discourse given what we know from general theories of how states behave and/or general understandings about India's understandings of its interests, even if India declines to mention that reason explicitly. This method is especially important if no official explanation for a particular policy response is tendered, but even when this is provided other motivations might have gone unmentioned (i.e. they might have been controversial).

Deployment of a process tracing method would be an ideal way to determine the precise connections between the logics inherent in the various identity discourses and the discrete policy outcomes.[104] For example, the transcript of a Cabinet debate may reveal certain ministers operating under assumptions consistent with the core logic of one identity discourse, while others seem to have preferred different assumptions consistent with a rival identity discourse, meaning it might be possible to find which of the alternative understandings actually drove the policy response which the Indian Prime Minister – or whoever made the final decision – ultimately chose to implement.

Unfortunately the nature of the evidence available to this study makes process tracing relatively difficult because, as noted in the introduction, India's government is notoriously 'quiet'; it produces very little formal policy, like white papers, and Indian ministers rarely hold press conferences, at least compared to the practice in developed states. While this is the case regarding all aspects of state policy it is especially true of foreign policy,[105] which is typically conducted in substantial secrecy; Raja Mohan has declared bluntly, for example, that 'when it [comes] to the making of foreign policy … the South Block [is] a closed shop'[106]; and Harsh Pant has explained how persistent chronic under-funding and under-institutionalisation

104 Ted Hopf, *Reconstructing the Cold War*, 24–28.

105 Deepa Ollapally, 'India: the Ambivalent Power in Asia', *International Studies* 48:3&4 (2011), 203.

106 'South Block' refers to the southern wing of the Cabinet Secretariat in New Delhi which houses the Prime Minister's Office, the Ministry of Defence and the Ministry of External Affairs: 'The Making of Indian Foreign Policy: The Role of Scholarship and Public Opinion', *ISAS Working Paper* 73, 13 July 2009, 11.

of foreign policy-making in India typically produces ad-hoc, chaotic decision-making.[107] India's parliament is also famously fixated on domestic affairs; it engaged in only two sustained discussions (i.e. over 30 minutes) of foreign policy in all of 2011. And scholars, especially foreigners like this author, are routinely denied access to serving-bureaucrats, meaning these persons can't be directly asked about their policy choices or the advice they tendered to their political masters (note that several of the interviewees – see directly below – were retired policy-makers; but none were directly involved in policy-making during 2011 and 2012). Finally, because the period under examination occurred so recently, archival materials like diplomatic cables or Cabinet records are obviously unavailable.

This study does not, therefore, argue that identity discourses *strictly determine* India's responses to humanitarian crises, so much as compete to constitute India as an actor, meaning they *shape* India's policy-responses, making certain policy options seem *possible* and proper, while *constraining* or ruling out others. Thus while the search for correlations and the testing of hypotheses enables us to draw reasonable inferences that particular identity discourses were more influential than others in certain contexts, and even that one tends to dominate over relatively long periods, we cannot be absolutely sure, or we should at least resist the temptation to conclude such with unwarranted certainty.

Regarding the sources from which data is extracted, discourse analysis is undertaken of newspaper (especially op-ed) and magazine articles, academic opinion, expert reports and government back-benchers' and/or opposition members' contributions to parliamentary debates; evidence from these sources is presented to demonstrate the existence of the identity discourses 'out there' in the public space, being presented by policy-shapers and therefore competing to influence policy-makers. The explanations for India's policy responses are gleaned from ministerial statements in parliament, senior policy-makers' speeches in other venues, Ministry of External Affairs press releases and, in particular, addresses by India's UN Ambassador when UN Security Council resolutions were voted on. Eighteen interviews were also conducted in New Delhi in 2013 with scholars at four universities[108] and four policy institutes.[109] Some of these are presented to aid interpretation of the textual sources and also to answer more general questions like 'How did the conduct and outcome of the Libyan crisis affect the way R2P is perceived in India?'.

The basic idea animating the analyses in the later chapters is therefore to understand how the authors of these sources – both policy-shapers and policy-makers, and the various interviewees too – understood R2P-relevant contexts (i.e. humanitarian crises in which, *prima faecie*, the application of R2P would

107 'A Rising India's Search for a Foreign Policy', *Orbis* 53:2 (2009), 250–264.

108 Jawaharlal Nehru University, University of Delhi, South Asian University and Jamia Millia Islamia.

109 Institute for Defence Studies and Analyses, Observer Research Foundation, Centre for Policy Research and Indian Council of World Affairs.

seem warranted), which can reveal why India responded as it did. But, equally, feedback may provide pressures or incentives for Indian policy-makers to revise their interpretations and understandings, so the same types of sources – op-ed articles, academic papers, policy-makers' speeches, interviews, etc. – also yield plenty of evidence of Indians reflecting on the outcomes of crises and drawing lessons from them.

Finally, the possibility of carrying out a content analysis to determine the statistical weighting of articles reflecting the relative frequency of each identity discourse was considered, but was ultimately discarded over sampling and coding concerns. It was decided instead that only the six largest-circulation English-language papers – *The Hindu*, *Times of India*, *Hindustan Times*, *Indian Express*, *New Indian Express* and *The Asian Age* – would be reviewed using the *Factiva* database, along with the most influential weekly political magazine, *Frontline*. Luckily for this monolingual English-speaking author, Indian academic articles and reports about foreign policy matters are *always* produced in English, parliamentary debates (especially about foreign policy) are almost entirely conducted in English (when speakers switch to Hindi momentarily translations are usually provided), and all of India's explanations for policy responses – whether in the Security Council, major speeches, or Ministry of External Affairs press releases – are also always presented in English. The study therefore only considered English-language sources, with one very minor exception: at one point an English-language newspaper report which surveyed stories from the Urdu press was considered.

So too clarify, this data was not used to provide quantitative assessments of the relative frequency of the appearance of the identity discourses in the public debates about the various humanitarian crises relative to one another. Indeed, statistics of this nature may provide a misleading impression of the relative influence of the identity discourses; further to sampling and coding problems, frequent mentions in the press do not *prove* an identity discourse is especially persuasive in policy-making circles (although elected policy-makers probably cannot ignore public opinion entirely; India is a democracy after all). Instead, this data is used to show that the various identity discourses were present in the public sphere when Indians debated foreign policy, meaning the author could, by searching for correlations and testing hypotheses, reasonably infer that the core logics of one or more identity discourses were more influential than others when policy responses were formulated.

Chapter 3
India and Humanitarian Intervention, and R2P, Before 2011

This chapter provides an historical overview of India's policy responses towards the humanitarian intervention practice or norm before 2001 and the R2P norm between 2001 and 2010; later chapters focus much more narrowly on the years 2011 and 2012 when India sat on the Security Council (Chapter 6 also considers events in 2013 and 2014 briefly). This chapter therefore provides some historical context and establishes a sort of 'baseline' – an understanding of India's position on the R2P norm – just before it took up its seat on the Council.

The chapter is divided into three sections. The first examines the Cold War era, with particular focus on India's direct involvement the crises in East Pakistan in 1971 and in Sri Lanka in the late 1980s. The second considers how India reacted to the humanitarian interventions of the 1990s, with special attention to the 1999 Kosovo crisis. The final section explores how India responded to the R2P norm after the International Commission on Intervention and State Sovereignty (ICISS) delivered its 2001 report. References to the various identity discourses (discussed in Chapter 2) are scattered throughout, and by the end a determination is made regarding which were the most influential were shaping factors.

India and Humanitarian Intervention during the Cold War

It is usually accepted that India was predisposed against humanitarian intervention during the Cold War. This is not surprising given, as explained in Chapter 1, most states and IR scholars rejected the notion that humanitarian intervention was acceptable in this period. It is more precise, however, to claim India was predisposed against *interventionism* per se, and especially against *Western* interventionism.[1] This too should not surprise anyone given India only threw off

1 Dipankar Banerjee, 'India and R2P: Reconciling the Tension Between Intervention and State Sovereignty' in *The Responsibility to Protect – From Evasive to Reluctant Action?* (Johannesburg: United Litho, 2012), 92–93; Ian Hall, 'Tilting at Windmills: The Indian Debate over the Responsibility to Protect after UNSC Resolution 1973', *Global Responsibility to Protect* 5:1 (2013), 87–89; Kudrat Virk, 'India and the Responsibility to Protect: A Tale of Ambiguity', *Global Responsibility to Protect* 5:1 (2013), 58–60; Madhan Mohan Jaganathan and Gerrit Kurtz, 'Singing the Tune of Sovereignty? India and the Responsibility to Protect', *Conflict, Security and Development* 14:4 (2014), 462.

the colonial yoke in 1947. India's first Prime Minister, Jawarharlal Nehru, loudly and repeatedly declared the non-intervention component of the sovereignty norm must be the most fundamental organising principle of the newly-forming post-1945 international system,[2] making it the central plank of his trademark *Panchsheel* doctrine.[3] The distinctly anti-Western character of India's grand-strategic stance was demonstrated by its furious reaction to Britain and France's intervention in Egypt during the 1956 Suez crisis after having virtually ignored the ostensibly very similar Soviet intervention in Hungary weeks earlier.

Newly independent India was also keenly aware of its relative weakness, especially compared to Western powers;[4] but it was also determined to remedy this weakness, in part by asserting sovereignty over all the territory it considered to be rightfully India's. Specifically, it wanted to settle the restive provinces in the north-west (Kashmir) and the north-east (Assam), assert its claims over the former princely states which were resisting incorporation (especially Hyderabad), and to seize Portugal's colonies on the Indian subcontinent (Goa was the largest). India was therefore not just predisposed against interventionism for historical or principled reasons but it had direct and pressing interests in preventing external meddling in what it considered to be its 'internal' affairs.[5] The 1961 occupation of Goa in particular seems *prima faecie*, interventionist – Portugal certainly thought so – but, notably, the Soviet Union vetoed attempts by Western powers to condemn India in the Security Council. America's President John F. Kennedy accused India of hypocrisy, telling the Indian Ambassador:

> You spend the last fifteen years preaching morality to us, and then you go ahead and act the way any normal country would behave ... People are saying the preacher has been caught coming out of the brothel.[6]

Obviously the anti-imperial identity discourse – especially the leftist strain which urged solidarity with the Soviet Bloc[7] – was shaping these policies. Clearly the great power identity discourse also shaped India's grand-strategic stance, and in particular its views on when Indian interventionism was legitimate – namely, when it was in *India's* grand-strategic interests – early in the Cold War. The liberal-

2 Nehru, in Victor H. Wallace (ed.), *Paths to Peace* (London: Cambridge University Press, 1956), Foreword.

3 I.e. 'five principle of peaceful co-existence', codified in the *Agreement (with Exchange of Notes) on Trade and Intercourse between Tibet Region of China and India*, signed in Beijing, 29 April 1954.

4 Pratap Bhanu Mehta, 'Do New Democracies Support Democracy?: Reluctant India', *Journal of Democracy* 22:4 (2011), 103.

5 Virk, 'India', 59; Mohan and Kurtz, 'Singing the Tune', 464.

6 Dennis Kux, *India and the United States: Estranged Democracies, 1941–1991* (Washington, Diane Publishing, 1993), 198.

7 Banerjee, 'India and R2P', 93; Virk, 'India', 59.

democratic identity discourse, by contrast, tended to only shape policy when its core logic aligned with another identity discourse; for example, Nehru campaigned loudly for black South Africans' human rights but had little to say when other Africans suffered under tyrants.

But in 1971 India found itself intervening in East Pakistan. It is difficult to overstate the importance of this event and the enduring impact of the lessons India drew from it – especially from the reactions of Western states – and it is no exaggeration to claim these lessons continue to profoundly shape many Indians' attitudes towards R2P today.

The seeds of this crisis lay in the overwhelming dominance enjoyed by Urdu-speaking West Pakistanis over Bengali-speaking East Pakistanis in the decades after the partition of British India in 1947. Given they were a demographic majority in unified Pakistan Bengali-speakers were determined to secure more autonomy, so when the Awami League won a majority in the National Assembly in the 1969 election ethnic-Bengalis expected to wield more influence. But the League was prevented from forming a government by the Urdu-speaking President Yahya Khan and rancorous negotiations throughout 1970 eventually broke down irrevocably; on 25 March 1971 Pakistani security forces struck precipitously and killed hundreds of prominent East Pakistani politicians, causing popular resistance to manifest immediately which led to Army reprisals and soon to mass atrocities. The exact death toll is uncertain; the figure of 300,000 is usually considered the lowest reliable estimate[8] while Bangladesh claims about 3,000,000 died.[9] Many scholars assume the eventual death toll was around 1,000,000.[10]

India's parliament described the situation as 'amounting to genocide',[11] and New Delhi allowed a government-in-exile to establish itself while secretly offering assistance to the East Pakistani resistance.[12] Crucially, over the course of 1971 at least 8,000,000 refugees streamed into India[13] and when India did eventually invade[14] in December 1971 the primary declared motive was self-defence against

8 Donald W. Beachler, *The Genocide Debate: Politicians, Academics, and Victims* (New York: Palgrave Macmillan, 2011), 16.

9 Banerjee, 'India and R2P', 93.

10 Nicholas J. Wheeler, *Saving Strangers: Humanitarian Intervention in International Society* (Oxford: Oxford University Press, 2000), 74.

11 Robert Jackson, *South Asian Crisis: India-Pakistan-Bangladesh* (London: Chatto & Windus, 1975), 36.

12 Ramachandra Guha, *India After Ghandi: The History of the World's Largest Democracy* (New York: Harper Perennial, 2007), 453.

13 Ibid., 452.

14 Technically, Pakistani air raids on India on 3 December 1971 opened hostilities. Many Indians claim they were the victims of aggression, but Srinath Raghavan explains how India steadily escalated pressure on Pakistan, provoking it into initiating hostilities; as he puts it 'the War of 1971 was started by India': *1971: A Global History of the Creation of Bangladesh* (Ranikert: Permanent Black, 2013), 205.

'refugee aggression'.[15] India had on 9 August 1971 signed a pact with the Soviet Union, meaning it felt it would be shielded from direct American or Chinese intervention on Pakistan's behalf.[16] U.S. President Richard Nixon did send the aircraft carrier *USS Enterprise* into the Bay of Bengal on 12 December about a week after Indian forces had crossed the border – provoking some immediate panic in New Delhi and decades of angst directed against America thereafter – but India crushed the Pakistani forces in East Pakistan decisively by 17 December, capturing 90,000 prisoners and enabling an independent Bangladeshi state to emerge.[17]

As noted above, India claimed its primary motivation for invading East Pakistan was to relieve the severe economic burden (and law-and-order concerns) caused by the refugee influx; India had, after all, struggled for much of the 1960s to feed itself and the states hosting the refugees, mainly West Bengal and Assam, were amongst the very poorest in India. Grand-strategic reasons, in particular carving off something over 60 per cent of its great rival's population and ending unified-Pakistan's encirclement of India, were obviously also important motivations.[18] Securing all these traditional security interests suggests the great power discourse substantially shaped the decision to invade (but, of course, India never invoked these grand-strategic motivations publically).

But the liberal-democratic identity discourse arguably also shaped India's response. India's UN Ambassador Samar Sen, when addressing the Security Council as Indian troops were crossing the border, asked what had happened to the 'conventions on genocide, human rights, self-determination and so on?', declared 'so long as we have any light of civilised behaviour left in us, we shall protect [civilians]', and claimed India had 'the purest of motives and the purest of intentions; to rescue the people of East Bengal'.[19] Of particular concern for India was that perhaps 80 per cent of the refugees were Hindus, and Pakistan had declared that they would never be allowed to return.[20]

Franck and Rodley claimed in 1973 'the Bangladesh case is an instance, by far the most important in our times, of the unilateral use of military force justified … on human rights grounds',[21] suggesting humanitarian intervention was part of international customary law. Nicholas Wheeler, writing in 2000, disagreed, noting

---

15 Wheeler, *Saving Strangers*, 61; Virk, 'India', 59; Raghavan, *1971*, 206.

16 Raghavan, *1971*, 209.

17 For detailed discussion of the diplomatic to-and-fro during the war, see ibid., Chapters 9 and 10.

18 Summit Ganguly, 'The Indo-Pak Conflict', in Atul Kohli and Prema Singh (eds), *Routledge Handbook of Indian Politics* (Oxon: Routledge, 2013), 333.

19 Security Council Official Records (SCOR), 1606th Meeting, 4 December 1971.

20 Raghavan, *1971*, 209.

21 Thomas M. Franck and Nigel S. Rodley, 'After Bangladesh: The Law of Humanitarian Intervention by Military Force', *American Journal of International Law* 67 (1973), 303.

there was simply too much resistance from other states.[22] But he nevertheless concluded that:

> [a]lthough India's intervention was not motivated by primarily humanitarian reasons, it counts as a humanitarian [intervention], because ... the security reasons that led it to intervene and the means employed did not undermine the humanitarian benefits of the intervention ... [because India] quickly withdrew its forces and did not try to make Bangladesh a satellite state.[23]

Wheeler therefore felt India had not cynically invoked humanitarianism; while noting 'India's humanitarian argument failed' to convince the majority of other states, he felt:

> what is important is that India felt able to raise this claim in the first place. Without the human rights norms in the 'justice part' of the UN Charter and the Genocide Convention, India would have lacked the normative language to name Pakistan's repression as a 'shock to the conscience of mankind'.[24]

Put in terms of this study's conceptual model, human rights norms in international treaties were used by – and/or partially constituted – Indian policy-makers, who felt ending mass atrocities was at least one reason to invade East Pakistan. In other words, a liberal-democratic identity discourse arguably contributed to shaping India's policy response.

The international response to India's actions in 1971 still affects contemporary Indian attitudes towards R2P profoundly. India was condemned by all the major players – except its Soviet ally – for breaching Pakistan's sovereignty. In America, Henry Kissinger called the human rights abuses 'internal problems of a friendly country': and all development aid to India was cancelled. India responded furiously, and when Nixon offered to resume aid payments in 1972 to mend fences he was angrily rebuffed.[25] The fact Western powers – the very states which continually condemned Soviet-bloc states as human rights abusers – opposed India in 1971 created a powerful impression of hypocrisy which 'continued to engage and infuriate Indians for decades',[26] meaning 'the lesson learned was ... long-lasting: a healthy scepticism of major power humanism'.[27] Anti-imperialist logic

22 Wheeler, *Saving Strangers*, 74.

23 Ibid., 75.

24 Ibid., 74.

25 David Malone, *Can the Elephant Dance?: Contemporary Indian Foreign Policy* (Oxford: Oxford University Press, 2011), 161.

26 S. Paul Kapur, 'India and the United States from World War II to the Present', in Summit Ganguly (ed.), *India's Foreign Policy: Retrospect and Prospect* (New Delhi: Oxford University Press, 2010).

27 Banerjee, 'India and R2P', 94.

was therefore boosted significantly by the 1971 crisis; in particular, America's image in India was tarnished for a generation,[28] and despite bilateral relations improving in recent years significant sections of the Indian elite still harbour deep resentments.[29] The shaping influence of the great power discourse was also boosted as Indians concluded that states pursued their traditional interests with little regard for human rights outcomes. Obviously the influence of the liberal-democratic identity discourse suffered in the aftermath of the crisis; Indians felt they had been hypocritically criticised for doing the right thing. Of the 11 interviewees asked about the 1971 war, all 11 agreed it delivered a powerful lesson which still resonated in contemporary India. For example, one claimed 'the lesson was that interests matter, not concern for human rights',[30] while another said 'the criticism was a major reason for realism cementing itself in Indian foreign policy circles',[31] while a third, a scholar who self-described as a Marxist, said '1971 proved – and we still see it today with R2P – that when Western states claim they value human rights they are just mouthing a legitimising discourse, not explaining their motivations'.[32]

Later events reveal the extent to which Indian attitudes were affected by the 1971 war. For example, India offered only the mildest critiques of the Soviet invasion of Afghanistan in 1979[33] while continuing to launch powerful rhetorical assaults against any Western intervention, like the US intervention in Grenada in 1983.[34] But, it seemed, India's success in 1971 may have precipitated a degree of overconfidence and India's intervention in Sri Lanka in the late 1980s provided another crucial lesson; put simply and colloquially, India 'got its fingers burnt' just as humanitarian intervention was about to become more common in the 1990s.

The roots of the conflict which tore apart Sri Lanka for three decades before 2009 lay in ethnic-Singhalese majority discrimination against ethnic-Tamils.[35] In response militant Tamils began assassinating Singhalese and moderate Tamil government officials, and they occasionally ambushed Sri Lankan army units in the late 1970s. The conflict escalated in the 1980s as the Liberation Tamil Tigers

28 Stephen P. Cohen, *India: Emerging Power* (Washington: Brookings Institution, 2001), 136.

29 C. Raja Mohan, *Crossing the Rubicon: The Shaping of India's New Foreign Policy* (New York: Palgrave Macmillan, 2003), 83–84; S. Paul Kapur, 'India and the United States from World War II to the Present', in Ganguly, *India's Foreign Policy*; David Malone, *Does the Elephant Dance*, Chapter 7.

30 I-1 (i.e. 'interviewee number 1'), New Delhi, 30 October 2013.

31 I-4, New Delhi, 5 November 2013.

32 I-2, New Delhi, 30 October 2013.

33 Virk, 'India', 59.

34 India sponsored the General Assembly resolution condemning the invasion as a 'flagrant violation of international law … and sovereignty', which passed 108 votes to 9; A/RES/38/7, 2 November 1983.

35 Neil Devotta, 'When Individuals, States and Systems Collide: India's Foreign Policy Towards Sri Lanka', in Ganguly, *India's Foreign Policy*.

of Eelam (LTTE) eliminated their rival Tamil political and insurgent organisations and openly campaigned for independence. Sri Lankan army operations became ever-larger, culminating in Operation Liberation in mid-1987 which put Jaffna, the main city in the north, under siege. India's intelligence service, the Research and Analysis Wing (RAW), had covertly assisted Tamil rebel groups (including the LTTE) since 1983, and when it seemed that Jaffna may fall India air-dropped food and medicine into the besieged city. Electoral pressures in India's southern-most state of Tamil Nadu – then home to 50,000,000 Tamils, and one of India's largest states – were a key motivating factor, suggesting the strong influence of the ethnic-Tamil identity discourse, although some scholars have claimed the so-called 'Indira Doctrine' also played a part; according to the doctrine India claimed the right to exclude external powers from and to manage the South Asian region,[36] suggesting the great power discourse shaped the decision to intervene in Sri Lanka too (i.e. New Delhi 'used' the humanitarian crisis to assert itself as the regional hegemon[37]).

The Indian intervention pressured Sri Lanka's government into peace talks, which resulted in the deployment of the Indian Peace Keeping Force (IPKF) to provide security in the north. Unfortunately, India was soon caught in the middle of an increasingly complex and violent conflict. On the one hand, the LTTE was not included in the negotiations and it soon began to attack IPKF units, precipitating an IPKF offensive that culminated in a gruelling battle for Jaffna that killed 800 Indian soldiers (and thousands of civilians) in October 1987; but the LTTE leadership melted away and resumed operations elsewhere.[38] On the other hand, a revolutionary Marxist organisation in the Singhalese south, the Janatha Vimukthi Peramuna, attacked both the IPKF and the Sri Lankan army, forcing Sri Lanka's government to recognise the rising tide of anti-Indian nationalist sentiment amongst Singhalese and begin agitating against India's IPKF.[39] One interviewee, an expert on Indo-Sri Lankan bilateral relations, advised that there are persistent rumours (but still little hard evidence) that elements of Sri Lanka's government directly assisted LTTE operations against the IPKF on occasion.[40]

By the end of 1989, and with an election looming, Colombo asked India to remove the IPKF.[41] With Indian parliamentary elections also approaching and the Dravida Munnetra Kazhagam (DMK) Party – an ethnic-Tamil party – now campaigning against the intervention, Prime Minister Rajiv Ghandi announced

36 Devin T. Hagerty, 'India's Regional Security Doctrine', *Asian Survey* 31:4 (1991), 351–363.

37 Devotta, 'When Individuals', 35, 43–45; Cohen, *India*, 149.

38 Hagerty, 'India's Regional', 358.

39 Bryan Pfaffenberger, 'Sri Lanka in 1987: Indian Intervention and Resurgence of the JVP', *Asian Survey* 28:2 (1988), 137–147.

40 I-8, New Delhi, 6 November 2013.

41 Sankaran Krishna, 'India and Sri Lanka: A Fatal Convergence', *Studies in Conflict & Terrorism* 15:4 (1992), 277.

the 80,000-strong IPKF force would be reduced if Congress won.[42] Put in terms of the study's conceptual model, by this point adherents to the ethnic-Tamil discourse believed the intervention negatively affected their kin across the Palk Straits; IPKF forces, untrained in anti-insurgency operations, tended to rely on heavy artillery and intrusive 'sweep' operations which alienated many Sri Lankan Tamils.[43] Adherents to the great power discourse were also opposing India's intervention, believing it was undermining, not advancing, India's grand-strategic regional interests. But Ghandi lost the 1989 election – notably, Congress suffered a heavy defeat in Tamil Nadu – and the new coalition government under V.P. Singh withdrew the IPKF in March 1990 after more than 1,000 Indian soldiers had died. Perhaps the single most devastating blow came on 21 May 1991 when Rajiv Ghandi, campaigning before the 1991 Indian federal election, was assassinated by a female LTTE suicide bomber. India had been thoroughly humiliated, and parallels were drawn with America's unhappy experience in Vietnam.[44]

This episode therefore also delivered a stark and still oft-discussed lesson, namely, that 'all the goodwill and force in the world was inadequate in a civil war'.[45] Of the 12 interviewees asked about the matter, 11 agreed it delivered a powerful cautionary lesson. For example, I-8, the Indo-Sri Lankan expert, listed four lessons: don't intervene without a solid domestic consensus (the episode badly weakened the Congress government); have a clear mandate in mind before intervening; be prepared to fight recalcitrant elements of the population you are there to protect (and if you aren't, don't intervene); and work closely with the local government (i.e. 'support, don't undermine the sovereignty of the state you intervene in'). I-8 also noted how, in personal conversations with colleagues in 2012 and 2013, parallels were commonly drawn between the Sri Lankan experience and the contemporary Syrian crisis (with the obvious implication that India should not support intervention in Syria).[46]

India took a while to digest these lessons, but by the late 1990s the so-called Gujral Doctrine was proclaimed to allay its neighbours' fears about Indian heavy-handedness; it established that 'India does not ask for reciprocity but gives all that it can in good faith and trust' and that no regional state (including India) should 'interfere in the internal affairs of another'.[47] Just as India's Sri Lankan adventure was ending in disaster, of course, the end of the Cold War was transforming the international system and causing a steady rise in humanitarian intervention (see Chapter 1). This was a turbulent period for India for other reasons too, as the following section explains.

---

42 Devotta, 'When Individuals', 45.

43 Hagerty, 'India's Regional', 357.

44 Cohen, *India*, 149.

45 Banerjee, 'India and R2P', 94.

46 I-8, New Delhi, 6 November 2013.

47 Miriam Prys, *Redefining Regional Power in International Relations: Indian and South African Perspectives* (Oxon: Routledge, 2012), 68.

India and Humanitarian Intervention during the 1990s

The early 1990s was a very trying time for India. Indian politics began to splinter, with the Congress Party losing much of its traditional dominance and, while the BJP rose to become a serious contender nationally, it couldn't secure a majority in the Lok Sabha (India's lower house) until Narendra Modi's thumping 2014 victory. Accordingly, for the 25 years after 1989 the rise of regionally-focused parties (i.e. the DMK), caste-based parties (like the Bahujan Samaj Party, or BSP, representing Dalits) and a range of smaller nationally-competitive parties meant coalition governments in New Delhi became the norm. This added significant complexity to federal policy-making; in particular, and as we saw vis-à-vis the DMK in Tamil Nadu, sometimes foreign policy-making was directly impacted by regional politics.[48]

Then a severe economic crisis broke in 1991. Its roots went back decades, arguably to Jawarharlal Nehru's policies of the 1950s which created a mixed capitalist/command economy which, it is commonly claimed, produced the infamous 'Hindu growth rate' (i.e. a sluggish one).[49] Rajiv Ghandi had initiated some limited reforms in the mid-1980s, but the turbulent politics of the late 1980s which culminated in three general elections in an 18 month period[50] meant much needed reforms were neglected. Spiralling fiscal deficits and anaemic growth of barely 1 per cent in 1991 resulted. The final blow came when an acute balance of payments crisis forced India to seek IMF assistance; in a particularly humiliating blow for gold-obsessed Indians New Delhi was forced to air-lift 67 tons of gold to Europe as collateral. The new Congress-led coalition government headed by P.V. Narasimha Rao after the June 1991 election initiated a sweeping reform programme led by the former-Finance Minister (and later Prime Minister) Manmohan Singh, freeing up investment and trade, reforming the financial system, modernising the tax system, selling many state-owned enterprises and introducing a floating exchange rate.[51] Soon India's economic performance began to improve markedly and several decades of impressive growth followed; but the early 1990s were a bleak period for India.

Just as the economic crisis was unfolding the Cold War abruptly ended with the Soviet Union's collapse. Nehru had followed a non-alignment policy,[52] but his

48 Suhas Palshikar, 'Regional and Caste Parties', in Kohli and Singh, *Routledge Handbook*; Cohen, *India*, 106–112.

49 Supriya Roy Chowdhury, 'Political Economy of India: A Selected Literature Review', in Samir Kumar Das and Achin Vanaik (eds), *ICSSR Research Surveys and Explorations: Political Science – Volume 1, The Indian State* (New Delhi: Oxford University Press, 2013), 86; Ramesh Thakur, 'India after Nonalignment', *Foreign Affairs* 71 (1992), 166–168.

50 2 December 1989, 10 November 1990, 21 June 1991.

51 Malone, *Does the Elephant*, 81–82.

52 'India's Foreign Policy', in *Selected Speeches, September 1946–April 1961* (Delhi: Ministry of Information and Broadcasting, 1983), 38.

daughter Indira Ghandi edged away from it and began to align India in various ways with the Soviets even before the signing of the 1971 treaty.[53] But India had always assiduously avoided falling too far into the Soviet orbit; as George Tanham put it:

> The Soviet–Indian alliance was not [actually] an alliance; in fact, over the next 20 years, each government interpreted the treaty to serve its own interests at any given time … . relations grew closer [but] India nevertheless maintained its independence.

Tanham nevertheless conceded that the 'sudden disintegration of the Soviet Union shocked Indians and in some ways left them feeling unprotected'.[54] The general consensus is that the event was traumatic and deeply discomforting for India's elites.[55] Several scholars have argued Indian policy-makers soon realised these circumstances created opportunities too (i.e. to improve relations with the West, especially with America)[56] although, at least initially, Indian foreign policy-making was quite confused, leading to accusations of 'ad-hocism' and 'drift'.[57]

This was reflected in India's reaction to Iraq's invasion of Kuwait in 1990, the subsequent US-led (and UN-authorised) campaign to dislodge it, and the efforts in 1991 to protect vulnerable Kurds and Shias from a battered but still belligerent Saddam Hussein. Prime Minister V.P. Singh at first vehemently opposed America's diplomatic manoeuvrings to build a coalition by deploying classic Cold War-era 'Third World solidarity' language; but when he realised the teetering Soviet Union would not back its Iraqi client he was thrown completely off his game and fell silent; when war broke out his replacement, Chandra Shekar, over-corrected and invited U.S. Air Force planes to refuel in Bombay, but after a storm of domestic criticism he rescinded the offer.[58] India joined the Security Council as a non-permanent member in January 1991, and a few months later it spoke against the draft resolution seeking to impose No-Fly Zones over Iraq, asserting the international community 'should be concerned enough to offer succour … [but] not prescribe what should be done,

---

53 C. Raja Mohan, 'Balancing Interests with Values: India's Struggle with Democracy Promotion', *Washington Quarterly* 30:3 (2007), 101.

54 'Indian Strategic Thought: An Interpretive Essay', in Kanti Bajpai and Amitabh Mattoo (eds), *Securing India: Strategic Thought and Practice* (New Delhi: Manohar Publishers, 1996), 64–65.

55 J. Mohan Malik, 'India Goes Nuclear: Rationale, Benefits, Costs and Implications', *Contemporary Southeast Asia* 20:2 (1998), 193; Baldev Raj Nayar and T.V. Paul, *India in the World Order: Searching for Major-Power Status* (Cambridge: Cambridge University Press, 2003), Chapter 6; Deepa M. Ollapally, 'The Evolution of India's Relations with Russia: Tried, Tested, and Searching for Balance', in Ganguly, *India's Foreign Policy*, 229.

56 Mohan, *Crossing the Rubicon*, xiii; Harsh V. Pant, 'A Rising India's Search for a Foreign Policy', *Orbis* 53:2 (2009), 253.

57 Malone, *Does the Elephant*, 72.

58 Thakur, 'India'.

for that would impinge on the internal affairs of states';[59] but India then abstained when it was voted on (it passed and became Resolution 688).

Kudrat Virk argues the fumbling indecision on display had its root causes in the economic crisis gripping India because it took a while for New Delhi to appreciate both the depth of the crisis and that America's goodwill was crucial to securing the much-needed IMF assistance.[60] This pragmatism – a concession on the matter at hand (i.e. abstaining when Resolution 688 came before the Council) to secure important side-benefits – is suggestive of the great power identity discourse shaping India's response. But not every Indian was convinced. Some, displaying clear anti-imperial sentiments and a flair for conspiracy theorising, concluded America had deliberately encouraged Iraq's invasion, seeking a pretext for a war to both cement its hegemony over the region's oil reserves and to deliver a fatal body blow to the weakening Soviets.[61]

India was still on the Security Council when the humanitarian crisis in Somalia deteriorated sharply in 1992, and it voted for Resolution 794 which authorised the 'use of all necessary means' to distribute humanitarian aid. India called the crisis a 'unique challenge' because Somalia was 'a country without a government', confirmed it only voted 'yes' because the situation demanded 'an immediate and exceptional response', but also stressed the mission must 'not set a precedent'.[62] India committed peacekeepers to the subsequent UN mission, UNSCOM II, but it refused to let them undertake the 'hard peacekeeping' which US forces engaged in (which ultimately led to the so-called 'Black Hawk Down' incident, precipitating America's withdrawal). The absence of a Somalian state to give or withhold consent was the crucial determining factor for India, and it also helped that a range of regional organisations supported the intervention too.[63] Arguably the logic inherent in the liberal-democratic identity discourse provided the impetus for India's policy response, while anti-imperial logic – especially the developing-world solidarity component of such – added support, or at least this aspect of it neutered the anti-Western logic otherwise inherent in the anti-imperial identity discourse which otherwise might have led India to oppose intervention.

As the 1990s progressed, India, preoccupied with internal reforms and worried by an ever-more restive Kashmir and the ultimate source of that problem, Pakistan, and no longer sitting on the Security Council, became a less active player in global affairs. India did support a Non-Aligned Movement (NAM) proposal to reinforce the small UN Mission in Rwanda as the terrible genocide there gained momentum, although it also demanded a Security Council mandate before it acted[64] (which

59 S/PV.2982, 5 April 1991.

60 'India', 67.

61 Samir Amin, 'US Hegemony: Need to Reshape European Politics', *Economic and Political Weekly* 34:21 (1999), 1247–1248.

62 S/PV.3145, 3 December 1992.

63 Wheeler, *Saving Strangers*, 184–185.

64 Jaganathan and Kurtz, 'Singing the Tune', 467.

Chapter 1 showed came far too late). India also seconded Lieutenant-General Satish Nambiar to command UNPROFOR in Bosnia in 1992, although he quit in frustration in 1993 at the UN's refusal to supply him with sufficient resources to protect the so-called 'safe areas' properly. Nambiar held a UN command and was not technically answerable to New Delhi, but the Indian government expressed discomfort with his calls for more robust 'peace enforcement' activities, which reportedly also influenced his decision to resign.[65] India did not take part in, or openly support, NATO's Operation Deliberate Force air-strikes which played a crucial role in ending the conflict (but, equally, India did not stridently oppose them; at least the author's efforts to find a formal statement either way proved fruitless).

India later joined the humanitarian intervention in Sierra Leone in 1998 and committed 3,000 troops. As atrocities mounted, the Security Council (without India's input) authorised UNAMSIL to use force to protect civilians. But then, in May 2000, rebels captured about 500 peacekeepers, including 12 Indians. India became involved in efforts to free them, and while it counselled against authorising a more intrusive intervention (citing the case of Somalia as warning), it also opposed withdrawal because 'to leave now would be to abandon the people of Sierra Leone to a terrible fate' and 'because the credibility of the United Nations is at stake'.[66] The Indian hostages were eventually released in June 2000, but after New Delhi suffered domestic criticism for wasting resources in a region where India had few interests, the troops were withdrawn later in 2000.

There is, accordingly, clear evidence for all three identity discourses shaping India's response to this crisis. Arguably the motivation to enter and stay in Sierra Leone for several years was provided by various logics inherent in the liberal-democratic identity discourse (i.e. both protecting human rights and supporting multilateral global governance), by the developing-world solidarity aspect of the anti-imperial identity discourse[67] (i.e. ECOWAS, the West African regional organisation, had requested India's participation), and the enlightened-realist identity discourse too; India was seeking a permanent Security Council seat and needed to demonstrate its credentials as a responsible power.[68] But hard-realists queried whether India had any interests in West Africa, and despite New Delhi claiming India's withdrawal would allow another nation to 'do its bit' in UNAMSIL, it coincided with UN Secretary-General Kofi Annan's push to have UN-blue-capped forces engage in more robust peace enforcement activities;[69] in other words, this was probably a step too far for India and raised the hackles of adherents to both the anti-imperialist and great power identity discourses who typically favour strong interpretations of the sovereignty norm.

---

65 I-10, New Delhi, 7 November and 9 December 2013.

66 S/PV.4139, 11 May 2000.

67 'India had no Strategic Interests in Sierra Leone', *The Hindu*, 18 August 2000.

68 Alan Bullion, 'India in Sierra Leone: A Case of Muscular Peacekeeping?', *International Peacekeeping* 8:4 (2001), 84.

69 Ibid., 79.

Then India's commitment to traditional interpretations of sovereignty was really tested – and strongly reinforced by – the 1999 Kosovo crisis. Chapter 1 showed how the Kosovo crisis generated significant resistance to humanitarian intervention generally, and India was one of the states which protested most loudly, profoundly affecting its attitude towards the R2P norm which emerged shortly thereafter.

Understanding the Kosovo crisis requires placing it in the wider context of post-Cold War Balkan unrest, especially the Bosnian war. Put simply, Western nations (especially the Europeans, and in particular the Germans) had been hesitant to deploy military force to stop the ever-worsening atrocities in Bosnia until the conscience-shocking 1995 Srebrenica massacre. Subsequent NATO air-strikes (i.e. *Operation Deliberate Force*) seemed to deliver the decisive blow which ended the conflict, or at least this was the lesson Western states learned[70] (a simultaneous Croatian offensive was also important). The atrocities in Kosovo therefore drew a faster and more decisive military response which ended with the Milosevic regime capitulating, Kosovo being occupied by NATO and, eventually, the establishment in 2008 of an independent state (which India still refused to recognise in 2014).

India was incensed by NATO's intervention in Kosovo for a number of reasons. For one, Kosovo was in 1999 unquestionably part of the rump-Yugoslavian state, while Bosnia had been widely recognised, including by India, as an independent sovereign state when *Operation Deliberate Force* took place in 1995; India argued that neither NATO nor the UN had any 'role in the settlement of the domestic political problems' inside Yugoslavia in 1999. For another, NATO's 1999 Kosovo operation had no Security Council authorisation, while there was some basis for arguing the 1995 air-strikes in Bosnia had UN sanction (see Chapter 1).

India was not sitting on the Council in 1999, although it (with Russia and Belarus) tabled a resolution to condemn NATO, and it condemned NATO's actions as 'completely illegal' (but the draft resolution was defeated 12–3).[71] India also made the rhetorically innovative but legally meaningless argument that because it, Russia and China had opposed the intervention in Kosovo, NATO was defying the wishes of 'half of humanity'.[72] New Delhi was also upset about the pre-war negotiations held at Rambouillet Conference in early 1999, especially the way Western powers had presented an ultimatum that Yugoslavia must accept a peacekeeping (as India put it, 'occupation') force or prepare for war; India had at the time counselled the West to recall what had occurred in Somalia earlier in the decade, noting that a 'peacekeeping operation forced upon a reluctant government or population stands little chance'.[73]

70 Wheeler, *Saving Strangers*, 242.
71 S/PV.3988, 24 March 1999.
72 S/PV.3989, 26 March 1999.
73 S/PV.3988, 24 March 1999.

Virk usefully explains how domestic politics also affected India's policy response to the Kosovo crisis. The BJP was at the time leading a shaky coalition, making their response 'overdetermined'; in other words, given that it was patently clear China and Russia would veto any attempt to secure Security Council authorisation some of the Indian response was posturing because it wasn't strictly necessary.[74] But India was at the time under Western sanctions after testing a nuclear device in 1998, and the government was therefore under pressure to not back down; for example, an editorial in a major Indian newspaper advised that New Delhi must 'be seen as being capable of defying the West'.[75] And Virk also notes that India was also motivated by other concerns. Specifically:

> In general terms, NATO's unilateral action was emblematic of the dangers inherent in an unbalance system … . [it] threatened a 'return to anarchy where might is right' … . In specific terms, concern centred in the first instance on Kashmir. Further, India was at the time under sanctions and itself fending off considerable pressure, not unlike [Yugoslavia] … . It is telling that while India condemned NATO forcefully, it did not offer any condemnation of the [Yugoslavian] government's actions against the Kosovars.[76]

General Nambiar – in retirement by then – wrote in the aftermath of the Kosovo intervention that there was 'near unanimity' amongst Indian policy-making circles that failure to robustly oppose NATO would have established a precedent with dire consequences for India's direct interests, especially in Kashmir, and global stability more generally.[77] Many Indian scholars concluded that NATO's claims of humanitarian motives were a smokescreen to justify the pursuit of traditional strategic interests, threatening to damage Indian interests, the UN, and the entire international order.[78] In other words, adherents to both strains of the great power identity discourse opposed the Kosovo intervention, and this sentiment also reflected deep-seated anti-imperial sentiments; for example, M.S. Rajan called NATO's actions 'plainly chauvinistic' and noted that what is 'now called "ethnic cleansing" … has happened all over the world in previous centuries … and mostly by white nations against coloured peoples'.[79] Accordingly, and as Virk alluded to,

---

74 Virk, 'India', 72.

75 'Foreign Policy Transition', *The Hindu*, 2 September 1999.

76 Virk, 'India', 72.

77 'India: An Uneasy Precedent', in Albrecht Schnabel and Ramesh Thakur (eds), *Kosovo and the Challenge of Humanitarian Intervention* (Tokyo: United Nations University Press, 2000), 263.

78 Rahul Rao, 'The UN and NATO in the New World Order: Legal Issues', *International Studies* 37:3 (2000), 157–181; Ninan Koshy, 'Sidelining the United Nations', *Economic & Political Weekly* 35:15, (8–14 April 2001), 1243–1244; B.K. Shrivastava and Manmohan Agarwal, 'Politics of Intervention and the Bosnian-Herzegovina Conflict', *International Studies* 40:1 (2003), 83.

79 'The New Interventionism', *International Studies* 37:1 (2000), 32.

the liberal-democratic identity discourse seemingly did not shape India's response to Kosovo in any significant way.

By the end of the 1990s, then, India was generally opposed to humanitarian intervention. Of course, some justifications given for India's support for or participation in various interventions – Somalia, Bosnia and Sierra Leone – suggest logic consistent with the liberal-democratic identity discourse played a shaping role at times. But there were typically other reasons too, consistent with the core logics of the other identity discourses. Developing-world solidarity logic would seem to have been a particularly strong motivation, shaping Indian participation in several crises, and occasionally logic consistent with enlightened-realism seems to have motivated India to support some interventions to boost India's responsible-power credentials. Nevertheless, India was always wary of crossing the line from supporting teetering states into more overt interference in those states' domestic affairs. Jaganath and Kurtz, when summing up India's policy responses both during the 1990s and thereafter (i.e. after the emergence of R2P) found Indian policy displayed 'remarkable consistency'. Specifically,

> The central tendency of India's stance is revealing: a clear privileging of the principle of sovereignty and territorial integrity and its corollary, non-interference in the internal affairs of states … . India's tilt has been towards the side of caution, which implies that, above all, it favours the principle of sovereignty.[80]

Put in terms of this study's conceptual model, during the 1990s the sovereignty norm was clearly used by and/or it constituted Indian policy-makers very strongly, muting the shaping effect of the democratic-liberal identity discourse on Indian policy. While the core logic of 'soft' liberal-democratic logic may have provided at least some initial motivation for India to support or participate in certain interventions, whenever it looked like an intervention would – or especially when it actually did – tip over into an intervention consistent with 'robust' liberal-democratic logic, India either abstained (Iraq), claimed the intervention was an exception (Somalia), tried to influence Indian officers in UN command positions against engaging in peace-enforcement activities (Bosnia), pulled its forces out (Sierra Leone), or vehemently opposed (Kosovo). In other words, whenever it looked like an intervention might undermine the sovereignty norm the shaping effects of what were called in Chapter 2 'sovereignty-friendly' identity discourses would intensify and overwhelm any humanitarian urges Indian policy-makers may have initially harboured.

It is worth briefly considering the arguments India levelled against humanitarian intervention just before the R2P norm was presented to the world in 2001, because the war in Kosovo precipitated a stream of formal statements of India's position. First, India repeatedly asserted humanitarian intervention was not recognised in international law; indeed, in India's opinion to 'press for such would be to violate

80 'Singing the Tune', 477.

… international humanitarian law' because the way humanitarian intervention was being practiced by the West in the 1990s was reminiscent of colonialism.[81] Instead, only consensual intervention was legal.[82] Second, responding to those who argued Security Council practice during the 1990s had established that an internal conflict could be judged a 'threat to international peace and security' consistent with Article 42 (see Chapter 1), India attacked the legitimacy of the Council in its present form and claimed resolutions of the more-representative General Assembly affected customary law to a greater degree.[83] Third, India queried whether the cure might be worse than the disease in two senses; primarily, an intervention might directly cause suffering; and additionally, it might indirectly do so by prolonging a conflict. India repeatedly raised what had occurred in Somalia earlier in the 1990s to drive home this point.[84] Fourth, India argued humanitarian intervention undermined states' abilities to protect their citizens' human rights when 'governments [were] already under violent internal stress' (i.e. from rebels or terrorists).[85] India was particularly wedded to this argument given how restive Kashmir was in the 1990s. Fifth, India claimed entrenching humanitarian intervention in international law would undermine global stability, encouraging cynical abuse by states pursing traditional strategic interests.[86] Sixth, India worried humanitarian interventions would bleed the UN dry as it spent its limited resources on expensive military ventures and alienated many states, causing them to withhold crucial funding.[87] Finally, India claimed humanitarian intervention undermined traditional peacekeeping and humanitarian aid efforts.[88]

As noted in Chapter 1, controversy stirred up by the Kosovo war led to efforts to reformulate humanitarian intervention – and these efforts, of course, produced the R2P norm – and India, as one might imagine from the discussion above, was not well disposed towards R2P initially. The course of India's engagement with R2P before the year 2011 is therefore the topic of the next and final section of this chapter.

India and the Responsibility to Protect: 2001 to 2010

Before the ICISS delivered its report it held various roundtables to gauge attitudes towards humanitarian intervention (see Chapter 1). One was held in Delhi in

81 S/PV.3980, 22 February 1999.

82 S/PV.4109 (Resumption), 9 March 2000; S/PV.4037 (Resumption 1), 25 August 1999.

83 Ibid.; Virk, 'India', 74.

84 S/PV.4109 (Resumption), 9 March 2000.

85 S/PV.3980, 22 February 1999.

86 A/54/PV.27, 6 October 1999.

87 S/PV.3875 (Resumption 1), 24 April 1998.

88 S/PV.4223 (Resumption 1), 15 November 2000.

July 2001 and the participants were perhaps less hostile than might have been expected given what was has just been said about India's 'general attitude' towards humanitarian intervention around the turn of the millennium. Special interest was shown in the possibility of Security Council reform and also in criteria to guide and restrain humanitarian interventions.[89] Notably, regarding criteria it was decided by the participants at the Roundtable that 'if at all possible, intervention should only occur … [after] invitation',[90] which suggests a marginal softening of the previously absolute requirement for consent had taken place. But transcripts of an informal roundtable discussion between Indian scholars are not the same as a formal statement from the Indian government; this came in 2002 when India told the General Assembly R2P 'has not found acceptance among the vast majority of [states]' and that 'discussion of this subject would, in our view, be infructuous'.[91] Jaganathan and Kurtz concluded that India 'perceived R2P as "humanitarian intervention by any other name", which is to say New Delhi was highly sceptical'. Western states accordingly came to regard 'India as "the worst of the recalcitrant"' when R2P was discussed in international forums over the next few years.[92]

As the 2005 World Summit approached India's UN Ambassador, Nirupam Sen, first successfully lobbied the NAM to flatly reject R2P because international law, as he put it, 'should protect weak and vulnerable states from the arbitrary exercise of power by the strong'.[93] He then told the Security Council India was opposed to:

> intrusive monitoring and finger pointing while dealing with specific human rights situations in individual countries … [because India had] made it clear that any discussion which is used as a cover for conferring legitimacy on the so-called "right of humanitarian intervention", or making it the ideology of some kind of "military humanism", is unacceptable.[94]

As negotiations over the Outcome Document proceeded Sen's opposition became more vociferous; he even criticised the phrase 'responsibility to protect' as 'patronising and offensive'.[95] Sen only bent marginally under sustained Western pressure by conceding that it might be permissible to occasionally intervene to

89 Ramesh Thakur, *The United Nations, Peace and Security: From Collective Security to the Responsibility to Protect* (Cambridge: Cambridge University Press, 2006), 269; Alex J. Bellamy, *Responsibility to Protect: The Global Effort to End Mass Atrocities* (Cambridge: Policy Press, 2009), 40.

90 ICISS, 'Regional Roundtable Consultation with Nongovernmental and Other Interested Organisations', New Delhi, 10 June 2001.

91 A/57/PV.58, 25 November 2002.

92 'Singing the Tune', 469.

93 A/59/2005, 20 April 2005.

94 'Statement by Mr Nirupam Sen, on the Role of the Security Council in Humanitarian Crises, at the Security Council', 12 July 2005. Available at: <https://www.pminewyork.org/adminpart/uploadpdf/45939ind1118.pdf>.

95 Bellamy, *Responsibility*, 88.

prevent atrocities (but doing so may only be 'morally advisable', and could not be made a legal requirement). Ultimately he stressed that only the very most extreme circumstances could warrant such, and that UN authorisation plus the active consent and participation of the relevant regional organisation were absolutely required. Finally, he argued that because India retained deep reservations about the Council's legitimacy more generally it would not support R2P without the permanent members accepting they could not exercise a veto if the General Assembly voted for intervention.[96] Without these conditions being met, Sen declared, India would oppose including R2P in the Outcome Document. As we saw in Chapter 1, however, India's Prime Minister Singh overruled Sen at the last minute, fearful that India would be blamed for scuttling the entire World Summit over this single issue.

Jaganathan and Kurtz have argued that India was predisposed against R2P because Indian policy-makers were strongly constituted by the sovereignty norm – as they put it, 'non-intervention is construed not just as a foreign policy objective rooted in rational considerations but a deeply ingrained moral value' – and they also point to two other factors. One is the 'presence of the so-called regional parties and other political parties in coalition governments' (this factor has already been canvassed above), but they also discussed 'the role of individual decision-makers' and, unsurprisingly, they focused on Nirupam Sen who they describe as a 'left leaning diplomat' and as an 'ambassador with anti-American leftist views'.[97]

Jaganathan and Kurtz explain Sen's influence in New Delhi with reference to three factors. First, his views resonated with other developing-world states which made his political masters wary of reining him in too publically for diplomatic reasons. Second, his views resonated with the Left Front parties which supported the Congress Party-led government between 2004 and 2008, meaning 'Sen could feel comfortable in voicing his socialist views because of coalition dynamics' in New Delhi. Third, the under-resourced and poorly-institutionalised Indian foreign policy-making apparatus (see Chapter 2) meant that 'tensions in India's foreign policy-planning are often not resolved officially'; in other words, individual officials sometimes 'go rogue', or at least they make policy without strict oversight from New Delhi.[98] Indeed, the Foreign Secretary Shyam Saran later complained Sen repeatedly and (in Saran's view) unnecessarily antagonised Western states with his constant agitation against R2P, damaging India's wider diplomatic interests, and that India had in fact supported R2P – with reservations, of course, but less stringent ones than Sen insisted on – all along.[99] Several interviewees gave similar accounts: for example, I-10 confirmed that 'Sen fell into the anti-imperial mindset you [i.e. the author of this book] describe, which sometimes upset others

96 Jaganathan and Kurtz, 'Singing the Tune', 469.
97 Ibid., 462.
98 Ibid., 478.
99 Ibid., 470.

in the MEA [Ministry of External Affairs]',[100] while I-11 advised that 'R2P is not terribly important [in the wider context of Indian foreign policy-making], giving UN ambassadors like Sen more leeway, and his leftist disposition might have meant he got a little bit carried away at times'.[101]

Nevertheless, and given R2P is considered a relatively low-priority issue in New Delhi (as several other interviewees confirmed[102]), Sen's career was not significantly impacted by his behaviour at the World Summit[103]; he remained in the job until 2009 and continued agitating against R2P at every opportunity. For example, when UN Secretary-General Ban Ki-Moon's efforts to institutionalise R2P encountered resistance in the Fifth Committee Sen was heavily involved,[104] and Sen also helped block the Human Rights Council's High-Level Mission's 2007 report on Sudan's Darfur region (see Chapter 1).

Still, Sen couldn't overturn India's formal support for R2P at the World Summit, and in early 2009 – just before his retirement– Indian policy-makers began to edge closer to deploying R2P-like rhetoric when responding to the violent end of the Sri Lankan conflict. Under pressure from the DMK in Tamil Nadu, officials in New Delhi repeatedly expressed concern about the 'humanitarian situation'[105] in 2008, and by April 2009 when the conflict was reaching its bloody climax New Delhi used language consistent with Pillar I of R2P by pointedly and publically reminding Sri Lanka's government that it 'had a responsibility to protect its own citizens'.[106]

This last statement is an important qualification to the general theme of much of the discussion above; direct invocation of R2P by New Delhi in the context of the Sri Lankan conflict suggests important figures in the MEA did not share Sen's deeply hostile attitude, or at least they were prepared to 'use' R2P in this instance in pursuit of India's narrow interests in Sri Lanka despite the fact that doing so may have contradicted India's wider stance against R2P. Later, after the LTTE's total destruction and the devastation of the Tamil homeland by heavy artillery, India provided assistance to rebuild Sri Lanka's human rights institutions as well as the shattered physical infrastructure in a manner contemplated by Pillar II (although India never explicitly mentioned Pillar II when explaining its aid policies).[107] On the other hand, too much should not be read into this: India was only invoking

100 New Delhi, 9 December 2013.

101 New Delhi, 13 November 2013.

102 I-1, New Delhi, 30 October 2014; I-4, 5 November 2014; I-5, 4 November 2014; I-6, 4 November 2014.

103 I-10, New Delhi, 9 December 2013.

104 Jaganathan and Kurtz, 'Singing the Tune', 471.

105 Ministry of External Affairs, 'Indo-Sri Lankan Joint Press Release', 26 October 2008.

106 Ministry of External Affairs, 'Statement by EAM on the Situation in Sri Lanka', 22 April 2009.

107 Avtar Singh Basin, *India's Foreign Policy – 2009 Documents* (New Delhi: Geetika Publishers, 2010), xliii.

Pillar I; it did not *threaten* to carry out a Pillar III-like intervention in Sri Lanka let alone dive back into the conflict 'combat-boots and all', so to speak. These sorts of reasons led Patrick Quinton-Brown, when surveying resistance to R2P in 2013, to list India as a 'cautious supporter' rather than an outright 'rejectionist'.[108]

As noted above, Jaganathan and Kurtz have argued that key policy-making individuals profoundly affect India's policy towards R2P, with Sen as their prime exhibit. But they also noted India's position on R2P shifted – not radically, but discernibly – when his successor Hardeep Puri Singh took over as New Delhi's UN Ambassador in May 2009. They claim Singh 'made it clear that India was taking a new tack on R2P', and that he was afforded more leeway to do so because after the 2009 general election the Congress-led coalition was not reliant on the Left Front parties to govern.[109] Despite a warning in his first statement directly addressing R2P against 'attempts to disingenuously use responsibility to protect', Singh also said 'it has been [India's] consistent view that the responsibility to protect its population' – so, Pillar I – 'is one of the foremost responsibilities of every state'.[110] A year later during an interactive Dialogue in the Assembly Singh stated India's position more explicitly:

> The responsibility to protect should in no way be seen as providing a pretext for humanitarian intervention or unilateral action. To do so would not only give R2P a bad name but also defeat its very purpose … . Let us remember that a solution to the avoidance of mass atrocities ultimately lies in strengthening the capacity and ability of states through various means so that they can effectively fulfil their human rights obligations rather than devising a Secretariat-driven mechanism [i.e. human rights oversight mechanisms were being discussed].[111]

The implications of this statement deserve close analysis. First, both India's official position, and especially the tone with which it addressed the issue of R2P, had changed since Sen's retirement in 2009; put simply, the vociferous denunciation and implacable resistance seemed to have been abandoned. Second, a generous reading might suggest India may, in particular circumstances, be open to a Pillar III intervention. Specifically, Singh said R2P should not be used as a 'pretext', which might mean that if India was convinced other states' invocations of R2P were genuine it may at least not oppose a Pillar III-style intervention (so long as the action was not 'unilateral', which presumably also means it was authorised

108 'Mapping Dissent: The R2P and its State Critics', *Global Responsibility to Protect* 5:3 (2013), 264.

109 Jaganathan and Kurtz, 'Singing the Tune', 472. Congress led the United Progressive Alliance with various small parties. Lacking a majority it sought support for various bills from outside the coalition, from either the Left Front, the BSP or the Samajwadi Party, meaning it did not 'rely on' any one of them exclusively.

110 A/63/PV.99, 24 July 2009.

111 A/65/877 – S/2011/393.9, 9 August 2010.

by the Security Council; this is consistent with India's long-standing position). Yet the general or wider meaning of Singh's statement is pretty clear, namely, that while India supports Pillar I and Pillar II it is at minimum very 'uncomfortable with' Pillar III. Singh never said outright that India would support Pillar III and the tone of his statement suggests that India would only do so in the most narrow, contingent and conditional of circumstances; his specific intent in this statement was, after all, to reject proposals for robust oversight and early warning mechanisms.

So much for India's official position on R2P in 2010, on the eve of its ascension to the Security Council in January 2011. Put in terms of this study's conceptual framework, India's position on R2P had shifted since 2001; for most of the decade the confrontational Nirupam Sen, channelling the anti-imperialist identity discourse and enjoying the tacit support of Left Front parties – and answering to political masters unwilling to rein him in – had vehemently opposed R2P, although perhaps India's 'true' position – if one believes Shyam Saran – was actually less antagonistic. The fact the Prime Minister overruled Sen at the 2005 World Summit is telling, and suggests the great power identity discourse, especially the enlightened-realist strain, was also shaping India's response. That is to say, despite India's 'point man' (Sen) opposing R2P 'on the ground' in New York, the key decision-makers in Cabinet were also determined to project the image of India as a responsible world power, worthy of being included in a reformed Council. Put simply, these policy-makers were *using* R2P to secure an elusive but highly-prized side-benefit. The Congress-led governments before 2009 had also been trying to implement the historic US-India civilian nuclear co-operation deal signed in 2005 in the face of stiff Left Front opposition (which largely explains the latter's exclusion from government after 2009), so Singh's softer line on R2P may have also been aimed at improving ties with America to move forward on this matter.[112] In other words, arguably the new government was using R2P to also pursue direct economic development interests in a manner hard-realists would approve of. Still, India's position on R2P in 2010 – cautious support for Pillars I and II and pointed discomfort with Pillar III – indicated sovereignty-friendly identity discourses still shaped Indian policy significantly more than R2P-friendly identity discourses.

Yet to conclude the liberal-democratic identity discourse played no part in shaping India's response to R2P up to 2010 – to argue that Indian policy-makers were not constituted by it at all – seems precipitous. Throughout the 2000s India had continued to contribute to various peacekeeping missions, including several in Africa (in the Sudan, and in Ethiopia and Eritrea) where India had few direct interests, suggesting at least some humanitarian motivations were behind these decisions (along with developing-world solidarity logic; and, to be sure, India's armed forces gained UN-subsidised out-of-region operational experience[113]). But

112 Jaganathan and Kurtz, 'Singing the Tune', 473.

113 Frank van Rooyen, 'Blue Helmets for Africa: India's Peacekeeping in Africa', *South African Institute for Race Relations – Occasional Working Paper* 60, May 2010, 21.

perhaps the most telling evidence for the influence of the shaping effect of the liberal democratic identity discourse is India's consistent support for the Protection of Civilians (PoC) norm throughout the 2000s.

The PoC norm was mentioned in Chapter 2 as a 'supporting' norm for R2P; the first specific application of the PoC norm took place in 1999 when the Security Council passed Resolution 1270 to directly protect civilians in Sierra Leone (see above).[114] There is an extensive literature exploring the relationship between PoC and R2P, but at the risk of over-simplification, the PoC norm contemplates a range of policy responses, from pleas to protect civilians, to prosecutions of war criminals, to the physical protection of civilians – or sometimes 'civilian areas' – directly threatened with harm. But, crucially, protecting forces are supposed to effectively remain neutral in the mould of traditional peacekeepers.[115] By contrast the sorts of measures contemplated under R2P (that is, its Pillar III component) may be much more robust, including blanket No-Fly Zones, active efforts to disarm abusers and – controversially, as the following chapters show – perhaps even regime change to remove the threat to civilians entirely.[116] Concerns have been raised about the potential overlap between PoC and R2P causing confusion and, in particular, that resistance to R2P may adversely affect the PoC norm.[117]

To risk over-simplification again, the PoC norm is arguably more sovereignty-friendly than the R2P norm, or at least there is good reason to conclude that *India* thinks it is. As far back as 2000 India's former-UN Ambassador endorsed the more robust peace enforcement role of UNAMSIL in Sierra Leone – very warily, to be sure – and stressed that peacekeepers must remain absolutely neutral.[118] In 2003 India called – again, only after further debates had been held and a wider consensus had been reached – for greater efforts[119] to implement what it called former-Secretary-General Kofi Annan's 'robust peacekeeping' agenda, which included policies which were obviously inspired or informed by the PoC norm.[120] By 2009 it seemed India had warmed to – or, put another way, Indian policy-makers might have become substantially constituted by – the PoC norm despite lingering concerns on specific issues. For example, a visiting Indian MP lectured

114 S/RES/1270, 22 October 1999.

115 S/2013/689, 22 November 2013.

116 Jennifer M. Welsh, 'Civilian Protection in Libya: Putting Coercion and Controversy Back into R2P', *Ethics & International Affairs* 25:3 (2011), 256–257; Lisa Hultman, 'UN Peace Operations and Protection of Civilians: Cheap Talk or Norm Implementation?', *Journal of Peace Research* 50:1 (2012), 61–64.

117 Jennifer M. Welsh, 'Implementing the "Responsibility to Protect": Where Expectations Meet Reality', *Ethics & International Affairs* 24:4 (2010), 415–430.

118 'Statement by Mr. Kamalesh Sharma, PR on November 9, 2000'. Available at: <https://www.pminewyork.org/adminpart/uploadpdf/2507568.pdf>.

119 'Statement by H.E. Ambassador V.K. Nambiar, Permanent Representative of India to the United Nations', 17 October 2003. Available at: <https://www.pminewyork.org/adminpart/uploadpdf/1208759.pdf>.

120 A/58/323, 2 September 2003.

the Security Council on the need to protect civilians at risk of harm and only criticised the lack of clarity regarding the permissible means of doing so and the funding shortfalls such missions typically suffered from.[121] By 2010 Ambassador Singh was praising the Security Council for its 'wisdom' in directly protecting civilians but lamented that 'the outcomes were not entirely satisfactory. Civilians continue to suffer today'. He confirmed that India remained fully committed to PoC missions, although he also stressed:

> There is only so much that peacekeepers can do. It is important to remember – at all times – that the primary responsibility of maintaining peace under a Chapter VI operation is that of the host government. The role of the United Nations is to support these authorities.[122]

The implications of this evolution in India's thinking are arguably two-fold. First, India seemed in 2010 to be genuinely committed to protecting civilians in ways compatible with the PoC norm. Second, India seemed to support PoC in preference to R2P; at minimum it was far less critical of PoC and its continual commitment of troops to peacekeeping operations with PoC mandates indicates its statements were not just empty rhetoric. One reason must be that the PoC norm is considered more compatible with Indian preferences for a relatively strong, traditional interpretation of the sovereignty norm. This may suggest India supports PoC in part strategically, namely, because it recognises there is significant support (especially from powerful Western states) for efforts to end atrocities when such occur, but India would prefer the PoC norm rather than the potentially more-interventionist R2P norm became entrenched as the primary norm shaping international responses to humanitarian crises.

Conclusion: India and R2P at the End of 2010

These findings (the last of which, regarding whether India might support the PoC norm strategically, is more of a speculation[123]) in turn suggest the sort of humanitarian logic at the heart of the liberal-democratic identity discourse did shape India's policy responses to humanitarian crises between 2001 and 2010; or, at least India was amenable to supporting a position which leaned towards the soft variety of liberal-democratic logic by which rhetorical support for

121 'Statement by Mr Dhurva Narayana Rangaswamy, MP, on Protection of Civilians in Armed Conflict at the United Nations Security Council', 11 November 2009. Available at: <https://www.pminewyork.org/adminpart/uploadpdf/18901ind1642.pdf>.

122 'Statement by Ambassador Manjeev Singh Puri on the thematic debate "Protection of Civilians" at the United Nations Security Council', 7 July 2010. Available at: <https://www.pminewyork.org/adminpart/uploadpdf/26169ind1707.pdf>.

123 Unfortunately, interviewees were not specifically queried about this.

human rights and democracy is offered, without entirely ruling out the robust variety of liberal-democratic logic (nevertheless, New Delhi seemingly remained quite 'uncomfortable' with such logic). One might therefore conclude that in 2010 the PoC norm, which is basically compatible with the soft variety of the liberal-democratic identity discourse, 'constituted India enough' to motivate it to want to 'do something' to alleviate humanitarian crisis, and aspects of the R2P norm (obviously Pillars I and II) were basically congruent with these preferences. Nevertheless, sovereignty-friendly identity discourses still exerted stronger shaping effects on New Delhi's responses to humanitarian crises and, as a consequence, the more-interventionist Pillar III of R2P did *not* substantially constitute India policy-makers.

One might therefore say that the great power identity discourse was the most influential identity discourse shaping India's responses to humanitarian crises in 2010, on the eve of India's entry onto the Security Council, especially the enlightened-realist strain. This is so because if the hard-realist strain was more influential India would not have been interested in taking part in peacekeeping missions shaped by the PoC norm, especially those in Africa. The enlightened-realist strain, by contrast, is more compatible with a 'marginally adjusted' conception of the sovereignty norm, namely, one in which sovereignty is only relaxed slightly to ensure, to the extent possible, that civilians are protected from harm without compromising the basic sovereignty of states. Its adherents see India's interests in wider terms; in other words, UN missions which first and foremost promote global stability by enhancing the stability of troubled states are judged to be good for India, and if protecting civilians can be achieved without compromising this core purpose, then they are worthwhile supporting. Regarding the anti-imperialist discourse, the developing-world solidarity logic obviously also supports this stance (and, again, helps explain why India so-readily contributes to UN missions in Africa). Of course, the anti-Western logic within it remained influential too – as we saw above, Sen found plenty of support at home for his vociferous attacks on R2P as recently as 2009, and his tireless agitations did not fatally jeopardise his career – although if this variety of the anti-imperial identity discourse had been truly dominant then, arguably, Manmohan Singh would not have signed off on an Outcome Document which endorsed R2P.

This is therefore the 'baseline' from which the analyses of the crises in Côte d'Ivoire, Libya and Syria draw in the following chapters. The next chapter begins in early January 2011 with an India entering the Security Council determined to burnish its reputation as a responsible power and make some meaningful progress towards its ultimate goal, permanent membership. The policy-makers in New Delhi must, if they thought about it at all, have vaguely hoped that debates over the R2P norm would not be especially high on the Council's agenda. But as things turned out India was blindsided by a series of acute humanitarian crises; the first of these crisis took place in Côte d'Ivoire, and India's response to it is examined in Chapter 4.

Chapter 4
India and the Crisis in Côte d'Ivoire

This chapter is the first to closely examine India's response to a humanitarian crisis while it sat on the Security Council in 2011 and 2012. It bears mentioning at the outset that Indian commentators paid relatively little attention to the Côte d'Ivoire crisis, meaning there is substantially less source material to draw upon compared to the Indian commentary on the Libyan and Syrian crises; accordingly, this chapter is relatively short. Nevertheless, India did vote for several Security Council resolutions which effectively authorised a humanitarian intervention – indeed, a regime change – in Côte d'Ivoire, so this crisis cannot be ignored.

Background to the Crisis in Côte d'Ivoire

Côte d'Ivoire had experienced unrest for over a decade before 2011. In the late 1990s the then-President Henri Konan Bédié had promoted 'Ivoirité' (i.e. 'Ivory-ness') to effectively deny citizenship and voting rights to about one quarter of the population. These persons, living mainly in the north, were allegedly 'foreigners' from Mali and Burkina Faso, although some such families had been present in Côte d'Ivoire for generations, and the 'Ivoirité' policy also effectively delegitimised Bédié's main political rival, the northern politician Alassane Ouattara.

Bédié was overthrown in a military coup in 1999 and replaced by General Robert Guéï, who presided over but lost a Presidential Election to Laurent Gbagbo in 2000, although the decision by the Supreme Court to prevent Ouattara from running on the grounds that he was not Ivorian caused unrest in the north. Eventually soldiers hailing from the north launched a coup on 19 September 2002, but while the rebels successfully took the northern provinces government forces rallied and held the south. Former President Guéï was killed in confused circumstances: Gbagbo's government claimed he had led the coup and that he had been killed in the fighting; the northern rebels denied he had been involved and claimed he had been murdered on Gbagbo's orders to provide a pretext for the repressive response.

Years of confused, sporadic fighting followed, with both sides recruiting local child soldiers and foreign mercenaries from the wars in neighbouring Sierra Leone and Liberia, and both sides allegedly committed serious atrocities.[1] The French led the first peacekeeping force into Côte d'Ivoire in 2003 after being invited

1 Alex J. Bellamy and Paul D. Williams, 'The New Politics of Protection? Côte d'Ivoire, Libya and the Responsibility to Protect', *International Affairs* 87:4 (2011), 829–831.

by the Economic Community of West African States (ECOWAS). The Security Council eventually passed Resolution 1528 on 4 April 2004 to form UNOCI, and about 8,000 peacekeepers were tasked with 'protect[ing] civilians under imminent threat of physical violence, within its capabilities, and areas of deployment'. This was certainly no mandate for regime change because it was hedged around with caveats; UNOCI couldn't go 'out of area to protect', and it could 'decline to protect if outgunned', etc. Nevertheless, the resolution referred to Chapter VII and called the situation in Côte d'Ivoire a 'threat to international peace and security'. The French did not formally join UNOCI but they were authorised by the Council to 'use all necessary means' to 'help protect civilians' and they demonstrated far greater willingness to use force than UN-badged forces; for example, after nine French troops were killed in an air-raid in November 2004 France destroyed the entire Ivorian air force in a single blow. Three peace agreements broke down rapidly, but a fourth signed in 2007 restored calm for several years.

The elections which had been due in 2004 were repeatedly postponed until 2010 when Ouattara ran against Gbagbo (who had remained in power since 2000). The first round on 31 October was relatively calm, but as the 27 November run-off election approached violence flared. Gbagbo was announced as the winner contrary to assessments by foreign election monitors that Ouattara had won, and after Gbagbo's swearing in ceremony on 4 December he told his supporters 'I will never give up our sovereignty'. The security forces began to fire on demonstrators and arrest Ouattara's supporters, and Ouattara himself sought UNOCI's protection. The Security Council reacted on 20 December 2010 with resolution 1962, which demanded Gbagbo 'respect the will of the people and the outcome of the election' and declared 'Alassane Dramane Ouattara is President-elect of Côte d'Ivoire' after noting both ECOWAS's and the African Union (AU) had recognised Ouattara too. The Council also expressed 'grave concern at the risk of escalation of violence, recalling that the Ivorian leaders 'bear primary responsibility for ensuring peace and protecting the civilian population' and it accordingly demanded 'all stakeholders and parties to the conflict act with maximum restraint … and ensure the protection of civilians'. Finally, it reinforced UNOCI with 500 troops but did not expand its mandate.

Intervention in Côte d'Ivoire

India, of course, was not on the Council when these resolutions were passed. But it had taken up its seat when Resolution 1967 was passed on 19 January 2011, to quell the escalating violence. This reiterated UNOCI's mandate to use 'all necessary means' to protect civilians and, crucially, it reinforced UNOCI with 2,000 additional troops, including several Ukrainian attack-helicopters. India did not sponsor the resolution or address the Council – no member state did – but it voted for the resolution (which passed unanimously). India voted for another resolution formally extending UNOCI's mandate on 16 February. But the violence continued and in March 2011

Ouattara's northern supporters launched a full-scale offensive, quickly capturing the capital Yamoussoukro in the centre of the county. Gbagbo's forces tightened their grip on Abidjan and other southern cities, killing hundreds of civilians.

The crucial Security Council meeting took place on 30 March 2011. Resolution 1975 began by reaffirming the Council's 'strong commitment to the sovereignty, independence, territorial integrity and unity of Côte d'Ivoire, and ... the principles of good-neighbourliness, non-interference and regional cooperation'. It went on to commend ECOWAS and the AU for their 'commitment to resolve the crisis', and noted that a full meeting of the AU on 10 March had recognised Ouattara as the rightful President. It then reaffirmed that it was 'the primary responsibility of each State to protect civilians'.[2] The Council therefore used language reminiscent of R2P – Pillar I in particular – and it also listed eight previous resolutions (all unrelated to Côte d'Ivoire) stretching back to 2000 which contained general statements about the requirement for states to protect their citizens. It then determined that the situation 'continues to constitute a threat to international peace and security'.

The operative paragraphs followed. The Council 'condemned' Gbagbo, 'urge[d] him to immediately step aside', and demanded 'all Ivorian State institutions, including the Defence and Security Forces of Côte d'Ivoire (FDSCI), yield to [Ouattara's] authority'. UNOCI's mandate was extended and it was authorised to:

> use all necessary means to carry out its mandate to protect civilians under imminent threat of physical violence, within its capabilities and its areas of deployment, including to prevent the use of heavy weapons against the civilian population.

This last statement about heavy weapons turned out to be crucial. On 17 March a rocket attack on an Abidjan suburb known to generally support Ouattara had caused over 100 casualties, and similar attacks in early April led to both UNOCI's Ukrainian helicopters and the French helicopters striking several locations where Gbagbo's forces were using heavy weapons on 4 April.[3] Ouattara's forces were fighting in the outskirts of Abidjan by then and Gbagbo's forces melted away over the next few days after being subjected to several more attacks by French and UNOCI forces. Gbagbo himself was arrested on 11 April, leaving Ouattara effectively in control of the country within about a week. Gbagbo was subsequently indicted by the International Criminal Court (ICC) and transferred to The Hague to await trial.

Indian Policy-Shapers' Views on the Côte d'Ivoire Crisis

As noted above, India had arrived at the Security Council with many of the elements of an intervention already in place: UNOCI and French forces had been

---

2 S/RES/1975, 30 March 2011.

3 Bellamy and Williams, 'The New Politics', 834.

in place for years and had been mandated to use force to protect civilians and, crucially, Ouattara had already been declared the rightful President; the fact both ECOWAS and the AU had ruled in Ouattara's favour formally was particularly important. But India did vote to send the Ukrainian attack helicopters to reinforce UNOCI in February, and it also voted for the key resolution on 30 March 2011 which widened UNOCI's mandate and, in effect, produced a regime change.

As explained at the end of Chapter 2, the analysis below first considers public sources which discuss the crisis. These are perused to determine whether the interpretation of the crisis and the advice tendered by policy-shapers about how to react to it reflect the core logics of various identity discourses. Then India's formal explanations for its policy responses are perused to determine if correlations between the broader public debate and the policy responses can be found, and then some hypothesis testing is also undertaken; together, these methods suggest certain identity discourses shaped the policy-response more than others. Then post-crisis sources are consulted later to consider how Indians reflected on it and to examine the lessons they drew from the conduct and outcome of the intervention.

Yet it must be said immediately the striking aspect of Indians' engagement with this crisis was their *lack* of engagement. The popular media largely ignored it: of the six English-language newspapers surveyed[4] relatively few articles appeared – 25 in total between 1 October 2010 and 1 May 2011 – of which 18 are essentially not amenable to the type of analysis this study undertakes. Specifically, seven of these were very short (under 50 words) and of the 11 longer articles (i.e. up to about 400 words), five were primarily focused on the fate of the Indian Ambassador (who escaped harm). The other six articles were all examples of 'reportage' – simple reporting of events – perhaps with a quote or two from key players in or UN officials, but they contained no interpretation of the crisis and offered no advice about what should be done. There were, however, seven op-ed articles; four written before the intervention and three after it. These are more relevant because they typically contain interpretations of history, demands for India to play a particular role, statements about other actors' trustworthiness, etc. In short, they provide evidence that the sorts of logics which inform the various identity discourses were affecting Indians policy-shapers' interpretation of the Côte d'Ivoire crisis.

The first op-ed, published on 10 December 2010, basically blamed Gbagbo for the crisis – he was accused of 'political chicanery and authoritarianism' – and its anonymous author worried about the effect on 'commodity markets' given Côte d'Ivoire's status as the premier global cocoa producer, and the potential for unrest to 'spill over into neighbouring countries'.[5] There was no mention of human rights abuses, let alone such justifying an intervention; nor did the author speculate about who should carry out an intervention. Indeed, the only concerns raised are the sort

4 *The Hindu*, *Times of India*, *Hindustan Times*, *Indian Express*, *New Indian Express* and *Asian Age*.

5 'Political Chicanery in Ivory Coast', *The Hindu*.

an enlightened-realist might have; in other words, by implication this author was suggesting intervention may be necessary to maintain stability, but this can only be tentatively inferred because no specific comments of this sort were offered.

Three op-ed articles were penned by John Cherian at *Frontline*, the only Indian journalist to write about Côte d'Ivoire more than once (two before the intervention, one after). In the first, in late January 2011, Cherian mainly provided background and reported the election results and the violence that followed, but he did note the presence of French troops and that France was applying diplomatic pressure to secure Gbagbo's resignation before observing 'the intervention of a former colonial power … in normal circumstances would not have gone down well … . But in the case of Ivory Coast, the international community so far has presented a united front'.[6] He also noted because Ouattara was the 'internationally recognised President … he can legitimately' request that the French intervene on his behalf. Cherian also noted the presence of UNOCI, but also reported that 'it does not have a mandate to intervene militarily'.

Another op-ed was published on 17 March. This noted the AU and ECOWAS had appropriately tried diplomacy, then sanctions, to persuade Gbagbo to step down, 'to no apparent effect'. The article conceded Ouattara's forces had 'created a condition of near-lawlessness' in parts of the country, but the anonymous author focused more on atrocities carried out by Gbagbo's forces, finishing with the conclusion that:

> What Mr Gbagbo is exposing, among other things, is that unless multilateral bodies create strong mandates for justifiable humanitarian intervention, the theory that national sovereignty has been vitiated in these purportedly globalised times is a vast overstatement.[7]

These last comments are especially interesting: they suggest the author accepted the sovereignty norm *should* be amended somewhat to allow occasional exceptions; in other words, while R2P is not specifically mentioned the article reflects logic consistent with the 'robust' variety of liberal-democratic logic which is most compatible with the R2P norm. The author did not declare a preference for *who* might intervene meaning there was no clear indication of anti-imperialist logic shaping their opinion (i.e. the AU or ECOWAS were not preferred to the French), nor did the author consider the effect of the crisis on regional or global stability, or on India's interests.

Then in late March Cherian reported again on the escalating violence, blamed both sides (although he apportioned more blame to Gbagbo), and delivered an off-hand remark about French reluctance to intervene directly because 'they would be accused of a "neo-colonial" intervention, given their dubious track record in the

6 'On the Brink', *Frontline* 28:2, 15–28 January 2011.

7 Opinion, 'Contrasting Elections', *The Hindu*, 17 March 2011.

region'.[8] Cherian then noted the AU had originally issued more robust statements but had later switched to calling for a 'negotiated settlement', which he felt was a 'major step backwards'. At this early stage, then, Cherian did not openly call for military action but the tone of this and the first article – and what he said after the intervention (see below) – strongly suggests he felt such would have been appropriate; if, that is, intervention was carried out by the AU and/or ECOWAS, and not by the French. Put in terms of this study's conceptual model Cherian's opinion reflected a mixture of the liberal-democratic and anti-colonial identity discourses; the great power discourse was conspicuously absent in that Cherian did not mention at all what India should do or what interests – direct or indirect – India might have had.

Overall there is evidence for all three identity discourses shaping the commentary from Indian policy-shapers about how to respond to the Côte d'Ivoire crisis. Cherian's views seem shaped mainly by the anti-imperial and liberal-democratic identity discourses, one anonymous author seemed more influenced by enlightened-realism (the variety which assumes interventions might enhance stability), while another's opinion was obviously shaped most by robust liberal-democratic logic. We should be very wary, however, about drawing firm conclusions about the relative strength of the various identity discourses for the obvious reason that the sample of such commentary is so small. We should also not rule out the shaping influence of hard-realism despite no commentator discussing India's direct interests. Indeed, the general silence in the Indian media arguably reflects what might be called the 'hidden power' of hard-realist logic; put another way, because Indians assumed India had few direct interests in West Africa they generally ignored what was going on there. This tendency was no doubt magnified by the fact NATO's intervention in Libya was taking place simultaneously and substantially distracting Indians, as the analysis in Chapter 5 amply demonstrates. We can now move on to consider the explanations India gave for its policy-response to the Côte d'Ivoire crisis.

New Delhi's Policy-Response to the Côte d'Ivoire Crisis

The relative silence about Côte d'Ivoire amongst Indian policy-shapers continues in those sources which might have provided evidence for why India voted for Resolution 1975; the MEA issued no press releases or media briefings, the matter was not discussed in parliament, and no Cabinet ministers spoke about it publically before the intervention.

The only direct evidence of New Delhi's policy response comes from the explanation India's UN Ambassador Hardeep Puri Singh offered to the Security Council when Resolution 1975 passed on 30 March. He confirmed India was 'seriously concerned' about the human rights situation and urged 'both parties [to]

8 'Looming Civil War', *Frontline* 28:7, 26 March–8 April 2011.

exercise maximum restraint and respect the outcome of the election'. The most important paragraph came next: Singh confirmed India had supported the AU's and ECOWAS's attempts to resolve the crisis 'peacefully and through dialogue' and with 'that objective in mind, we voted in favour of the resolution'. He also noted peacekeepers 'cannot be made agents of regime change' and 'UNOCI should not become a party to the political stalemate ... [and] also should not get involved in a civil war'. Singh then said 'we also want to put on record our growing concern at the tendency to hurry the process of adopting of resolutions',[9] a clear reference to Indian unease over Resolution 1973 vis-à-vis Libya, which had passed 13 days earlier (see Chapter 5). He also said that alleged war crimes should be investigated by national bodies, that India was not a member of the ICC, and was concerned Resolution 1975's referral of crimes to the ICC had not occurred in strict compliance with the relevant procedures. In other words, he stressed that India's 'yes' vote should not be taken as support for the ICC.

Regarding correlations between policy-shapers' commentary and India's policy-response – a 'yes' vote on a resolution which ultimately resulted in regime change – the most obvious correlation is with the developing-world solidarity aspect of the anti-imperial identity discourse. We should note, however, that Singh's words suggest India was not voting for regime change as such and was instead voting for, put colloquially, 'what the AU and ECOWAS said'. The statement is very clear on this point: Singh noted the AU and ECOWAS had resolved to end the crisis *peacefully* and India was supporting their efforts to do so, meaning New Delhi could technically absolve itself should the AU and ECOWAS depart from this course of action (which they – and the French and UNOCI – ultimately did less than a week later). Nevertheless, and while Cherian had argued the AU and ECOWAS should sort the crisis out and not the French, Singh said nothing about such matters and nor did he criticise France's role, meaning there was no correlation between the anti-Western aspect of anti-imperialist logic and New Delhi's policy-response.

There was, however, some evidence for a correlation with soft liberal-democratic logic given India rhetorically deplored the atrocities and called for the election results to be respected. But Singh did not use words reminiscent of R2P; he did not specify that Gbagbo's regime owed a Pillar I responsibility to its citizens (although he did cast a vote for a resolution which did use this terminology), nor did he suggest India recognised a Pillar III responsibility for the international community to intervene. What went unsaid was also important: in particular Singh did not *specifically* note Ouattara was the rightful president who deserved to be installed by the application of *force*. Instead Singh carefully noted India did not believe peacekeepers should be used to effect a regime change. There was, in short, no correlation with robust liberal-democratic logic. Finally, Singh did not refer to India acting in the interests of global or regional stability, let alone any direct interests India had in the matter.

9 S/PV 6508, 30 March 2011.

Hypothesis testing can shed further light on these matters. For example, if India had been motivated by fiercely anti-Western logic then one would expect this to have at least balanced out the shaping effect of the developing-world solidarity logic leading to an Indian abstention. Its ‘yes’ vote therefore reinforces the view that the latter variety of anti-imperialist logic exerted a powerful shaping influence, or at least more than anti-Western logic. And if robust liberal-democratic logic had exerted a profound shaping effect one would expect India to have referred to the international community’s responsibility to intervene using language reminiscent of Pillar III, and to possibly commit diplomatic, financial, or even military resources to the intervention. New Delhi did none of these things past expressing rhetorical support for human rights and democracy in general terms, suggesting that only soft liberal-democratic logic played any real shaping effect.

Regarding the shaping effect of enlightened-realist logic – especially the variety which assumes intervention enhances stability by ending crises which otherwise might drag on – India did vote ‘yes’ which at least suggests this logic played some part in India’s decision; or, put another way, the opposing enlightened-realist interpretation which assumes intervention *causes* instability seems to have *not* exerted much shaping influence. Yet it if India had been strongly motivated by the former logic then, again, one might have expected it to more enthusiastically and actively support the intervention. Instead, India expressed a general concern about these types of decisions becoming ‘hurried’, so at most we can conclude India’s policy-response was not shaped strongly by the notion that interventions always promote stability.

The situation is most interesting regarding the potential shaping effect of hard-realist logic. One might hypothesise that if Indian policy-makers did not consider India had any direct interests in Côte d’Ivoire or West Africa, they would have largely ignored the crisis and, in particular, they would have not spent any of India’s precious diplomatic or material resources. This is of course exactly what happened; New Delhi chose to follow the lead of the AU and ECOWAS, to not complain about French involvement, it didn’t offer any troops for UNOCI, and it also carefully hedged its position around with qualifications which indicated a strong preference for traditional interpretations of sovereignty while still, in effect, voting for a resolution which effectively authorised regime change, or at least the removal of the political leader currently ‘in charge’ (i.e. Laurent Gbagbo) in favour of a leader who had never been President before and who, despite winning an election, had not yet been sworn in (i.e. Alassane Ouattara). Indeed, India was arguably ‘forced’ to ‘engage’ with this crisis because it was sitting on the Security Council; if it hadn’t been present in the Council chamber New Delhi might have remained completely silent. All these considerations seemingly confirm what was said earlier about the hidden power of the hard-realist identity discourse.

These findings are supported by the interview data. First, all but one interviewee pleaded ignorance and declined to answer questions about Côte d’Ivoire. For example, when I-6 was asked broadly whether India was concerned by humanitarian crises, the response was ‘generally speaking the further away a crisis is, the less India cares', and when the author of this book asked 'do you mean Côte d'Ivoire?' I-6 unenthusiastically replied 'I suppose so'.[10] The fact 17 of 18 foreign policy experts considered themselves unqualified to discuss this crisis reinforces the notion that hard-realist logic exerts a powerful hidden or unarticulated shaping effect on Indian policy-responses; in other words, many policy-shapers didn't actually shape policy because they didn't consider India had any pressing interests and so they didn't bother offering any advice.

But some of the interviewees' more general comments about Indian attitudes to human rights are worth mentioning. Importantly, most interviewees reported that Indians, or at least the English-speaking Indian elites, are basically predisposed towards supporting liberal-democratic values – all 14 of those who were asked confirmed this – but 9 of the 14 also warned these are relatively easily *overridden* by other concerns. For example, I-4 talked of an 'impulse' to support democracy and human rights, but noted this is often overridden in specific circumstances and cited 'India's lessons in Burma, when we badgered them for too long about democracy and the Chinese, who don't care about that stuff, stole Burma away'.[11] I-6 (who self-described as a hard-realist) put it slightly differently:

> Indian elites are basically disposed favourably towards human rights. But often this is just "window-dressing" because they know they have to be careful about supporting tyrants. When there are direct national interests at stake, or if a traditional ally – like a non-aligned state – is the target, these considerations go straight out the same window.[12]

Second, the only interviewee who answered questions (I-16) had previously held a senior position in India's Côte d'Ivoire embassy. When specifically asked 'How did India view the R2P-motivated intervention in Côte d'Ivoire?', I-16 replied:

> R2P didn't really have anything to do with India's response, to be honest. The Libya crisis was breaking at the time and everyone was focused on that. But India did vote for [Resolution 1975], and I think it had two reasons for doing so. First, Ouattara had been elected already, so the UN action wasn't technically an intervention, or at least it was a consensual one [I-16 winked and chuckled at this juncture]. Second, the AU and ECOWAS were supporting intervention, and India usually backs what they want to do in their region. This reason was the really crucial one and it is the line we [i.e. he meant his former employer, the MEA] have taken for decades. India also wanted to be seen as supportive of peacekeeping: traditional peacekeeping mind you![13]

10 New Delhi, 4 December 2013.
11 New Delhi, 5 November 2013.
12 New Delhi, 4 November 2013.
13 New Delhi, 9 November 2013.

When asked what role humanitarian sentiments played I-16 noted 'India does of course prefer to respect human rights, but we don't like lecturing' although, interestingly, I-16 also said 'India always wants to be seen to be different to China; India wants to be seen to care'. When asked if French involvement provoked anti-imperial anxieties in India, I-16 explained 'there is a very complex relationship between France and French West Africa – India doesn't really have an opinion on the matter, or at least we keep it to ourselves'. Finally, I-16 confirmed India is typically not very concerned with events in West Africa, then observed wryly there had been as much media attention to the effect of the crisis on the price of chocolate as its humanitarian implications. I-16 immediately conceded, unprompted, that this was an exaggeration; but the author's research did in fact reveal the several such stories appeared in the Indian press.[14]

I-16 therefore confirmed the overall impression that India's policy-response to the crisis in Côte d'Ivoire was partly shaped by soft liberal-democratic logic in the sense that, at minimum, New Delhi didn't want to be seen to be too-actively opposed to a humanitarian intervention, and on balance some Indian policy-makers were probably genuinely concerned by the atrocities. India also seems to have been partly motivated by the sorts of concerns about instability in the region that enlightened-realists worry about. But the shaping effect of developing-world-solidarity logic and hard-realist logic ultimately exerted the strongest shaping influence on New Delhi's policy-response.

Indian Reflections on the Côte d'Ivoire Crisis

As noted in Chapter 2 this study is interested not just in determining whether the identity discourses may have shaped India's policy response to particular humanitarian crises but also in the lessons India drew from the conduct and/or outcome of these crises.

Notably, the general silence before the Côte d'Ivoire intervention continued afterwards; in other words, Indians didn't really draw many lessons, or at least not very important ones. This is especially so regarding formal responses by policy-makers. There was a fleeting mention of the crisis by the Minster of External Affairs on April 19 which simply acknowledged that India was pleased the violence had ended and wished President Ouattara well.[15] But the MEA issued no statements otherwise, and when Prime Minister Manmohan Singh addressed African states at an AU event in May 2011 – so, just weeks after ordering Ambassador Singh to vote for a resolution which effectively produced a regime

14 'Bitter Dreams', *Indian Express*, 31 January 2011; 'Choc a Block', *The Hindu*, 1 February 2011.

15 Speech, 'EAM's Remarks at the Release of India's National Security Annual Review 2010', S.M. Krishna, Ministry of External Affairs, New Delhi, 19 April 2011.

change – he declined to mention Côte d'Ivoire.[16] India's parliament also remained totally silent.

Only two op-ed pieces and one (very short) academic treatment of the crisis appeared after the intervention. John Cherian's article adopted a more indignant tone than those he had penned before the intervention. After noting France had been fighting alongside the United States in Libya and Afghanistan whilst intervening in Côte d'Ivoire, he accused the French President Nicholas Sarkozy of double standards by being 'noticeably quiet as far as the brutal repression of civilians in pro-Western authoritarian states in the Arab world is concerned' (i.e. he was referring to the situation in Bahrain, when the Gulf Cooperation Council intervened to quash unrest amongst that state's Shia population). He then hinted Sarkozy may have wanted to overturn the recent grants by Gbagbo of oil concessions to Russian and Angolan companies, as well as cynically boost his flagging poll numbers back in France. The article finished with Cherian chastising the AU and ECOWAS for 'pass[ing] the burden on to the UN and the French'. He also mused that the circumstances of Ouattara's ascension meant 'it will be difficult to shake off the allegation … that he assumed the presidency on the shoulders of the French' before predicting further trouble given that a foreign power had resolved the crisis.[17]

Cherian was clearly channelling anti-Western anti-imperialist logic. The French were heavily criticised in his article, and he expressed impatience with the African organisations which profess to want to manage their own affairs but then readily call in the former colonial power whenever things got serious. The fact Ouattara had been elected fairly and Gbagbo had illegally stayed on – the immediate cause of the violence – was ignored; in other words, Cherian failed to concede, let alone consider, whether intervention had been the only way to protect civilians and enforce the Ivorian people's democratic will. And no mention is made of India's interests in the region; indeed, Cherian failed to mention that India had voted for Resolution 1975. He also failed to consider whether Côte d'Ivoire might have had its best chance for stability in over a decade; to be fair, he was writing only weeks after Gbagbo's fall, but he nevertheless assumed the future would be gloomy simply because it had been the French who had resolved the crisis.

The other reflective op-ed article, penned by prominent strategic analyst Brahma Chellaney, was mainly focused on the simultaneous crisis in Libya. He did note the Côte d'Ivoire intervention had been justified, but he was concerned that because Côte d'Ivoire 'lacks strategic importance or oil' the intervention had come too late to save many civilians. Chellaney finished by observing 'if tyrants are to be stopped … any international intervention … must meet the test of impartiality'. This suggests robust liberal-democratic logic shaped his thinking to some degree,

16 Speech, 'Address by PM at the Plenary Session of the 2nd Africa-India Forum Summit', Manmohan Singh, Addis Ababa, 24 May 2011.

17 'African Adventure', *Frontline* 28:9, 23 April–6 May 2011.

along with enlightened-realist logic of the sort which assumes intervention might necessary to preserve stability – he declared his strong support for a 'rules-based international order' – although his support for such was also qualified, namely, he believed norms like R2P (which he did not mention specifically) should be applied *consistently* if they are to *actually* promote global stability.[18]

Interestingly, neither Cherian nor Chellaney commented on *India's* role in the Côte d'Ivoire crisis. The academic commentary is also very sparse; of the hundreds of publications produced by the five premier Indian foreign policy institutes[19] in 2011, only a single two-page article about Côte d'Ivoire appeared, penned by Anjana Varma.[20] She provided background information about the crisis and blamed both former Ivorian politicians for stoking ethnic tensions through their promotion of Ivoirité, and Gbagbo for selfishly refusing to relinquish office (and she also very obliquely assigned some blame to France, noting that Côte d'Ivoire's constitution 'is modelled on France's presidency model' which concentrates power too much). But Varma failed to comment at all on the propriety of the intervention itself and instead confined her remarks to advice about how to create 'more democratic accountability' in its wake. If anything, then, perhaps Varma's opinions about the crisis were shaped by the liberal-democratic identity discourse, but this can only be said tentatively because she said nothing about the propriety of the intervention or R2P more generally. Perhaps one might conclude enlightened-realist logic also played a part if one concedes more democratically-accountable governments are likely to be more stable; but she did not specifically say this, or discuss regional, let alone global stability. She also declined to comment on the AU and ECOWAS, the propriety of French or UNOCI involvement in the fighting, or India's role in the crisis.

Overall, then, there is little evidence of Indians drawing lessons from the Côte d'Ivoire crisis. It is particularly notable that two assessments of India's overall performance on the Security Council – one delivered after the first year, and the other at the conclusion of India's two-year term – completely ignored the Côte d'Ivoire crisis and India's part in it. Neither was very long (four and seven pages respectively[21]), but they were certainly long enough for Côte d'Ivoire to at least be mentioned; it is particularly telling the first article opened with the words '2011 began with the Arab Awakening and two countries, Libya and Syria, grabbed

18 'Saving Civilians: Murky Geopolitics', *The Hindu*, 6 April 2011.

19 Institute for Defence Studies and Analyses, Observer Research Foundation, Centre for Policy Research, Indian Council of World Affairs, and Institute for Peace and Conflict Studies.

20 Anjana Varma, 'Ivory Coast: A Crisis of Division', *Observer Research Foundation – Analysis*, 18 April 2011.

21 Saurabh Mishra Keerthi and Sampath Kumar, 'India's Two Years at the Horse-Shoe Table', *Institute for Defence Studies and Analyses – Issue Brief*, 8 March 2013; Rohan Mukherjee and David Malone, 'India and the UN Security Council: An Ambiguous Tale', *Economic & Political Weekly* 68:29, 20 July 2013.

most of the Security Council's attention'. These crises obviously grabbed Indians' attention too and, together with the general disinterest Indians show towards West Africa, led the authors to completely ignore Côte d'Ivoire which had, technically speaking, been the first crisis India dealt with in 2011. This, of course, further reinforces the conclusion that hard-realist logic was a powerful shaping factor in India's policy response; in other words, Indians were focused on events where they perceived India had direct and crucial interests – Libya – as the next chapter shows.

Chapter 5
India and the Crisis in Libya

As noted in the previous chapter, Indians were deeply engaged by the Libya crisis in early 2011. Indeed, as this chapter shows, the conduct and outcome of this application of the R2P norm[1] to resolving an acute – or perhaps just looming – humanitarian crisis not only engaged but also *enraged* many Indians. As a result serious damage has been done to R2P's 'image' in India, with consequences for R2P's wider fortunes going forward. But this last matter is addressed directly in the final chapter; this chapter instead closely analyses India's policy response (namely, abstaining when Resolution 1973 passed on 17 March 2011) and Indians' reflections on NATO's subsequent intervention.

Background to the Libyan Crisis before NATO's Intervention

The Libyan crisis was inextricably linked to the wider Middle Eastern unrest known as the 'Arab Spring'. The self-immolation of Mohamed Bouazizi, a Tunisian fruit-vendor driven to despair by corrupt and brutal local officials in December 2010, is usually considered the proximate cause of the protests and demonstrations which swept the Middle East and first caused the fall of Tunisia's dictatorial Ben Ali regime on 14 January 2011. Protests in Egypt began in earnest on 25 January, leading to the downfall of dictator Hosni Mubarak on 11 February 2011. The unrest spread to Libya too, but it has profoundly affected the entire Middle East; it sparked off the ongoing Syrian civil war (which later spilled into Iraq), precipitated the fall of Yemen's Saleh regime (and another ongoing civil war), provoked major demonstrations in Bahrain, Iran, Algeria and Lebanon, and induced Morocco, Kuwait, Jordan, Mauretania and Oman to offer mollifying reform packages to their restive populations.

---

1 Some believe the Libyan intervention was not an application of R2P because more traditional great power interests explain it: Aidan Hehir, 'The Permanence of Inconsistency: Libya, the Security Council, and the Responsibility to Protect', *International Security* 38:1 (2013), 137–159; Marie-Eve Loiselle, 'The Normative Status of the Responsibility to Protect', *Global Responsibility to Protect* 5:3 (2013), 317–341. But most scholars accept R2P was applied in Libya, whether they believe it was proper to do so (Alex J. Bellamy and Paul D. Williams, 'The New Politics of Protection? Côte d'Ivoire, Libya and the Responsibility to Protect', *International Affairs* 87:4 (2011), 825–850), or whether they believe it wasn't (Alan J. Kuperman, 'A Model Humanitarian Intervention? Reassessing NATO's Libya Campaign', *International Security* 38:1 (2013), 105–136).

Various deeper reasons have been offered to explain why the Arab Spring occurred, including: widespread frustration with corrupt, repressive and ineffective autocracies on the part of increasingly well-educated but disenfranchised middle classes; a so-called 'youth bulge' which produced a mass of un- or under-employed youth who, through the medium of social media, were both more aware of their own societies' failings and also able to mobilise very effectively; and more immediate causes like a sharp spike in food and utility prices in 2010.[2] In Libya, sporadic small protests against Muammar Gaddafi's regime took place in January 2011. Then in early February the writer and political commentator Jamal al-Hajji was arrested after calling for demonstrators to emulate those in Tunisia and Egypt. The first large protests took place on 15 February outside the police station in Benghazi where al-Hajji was being held. The next day it was overrun, many police joined the demonstrators, al-Hajji was freed, and regime loyalists fled, beginning the Libyan crisis.

Uprisings also took place in the larger western cities – Misurata in particular – but most were initially contained by loyalist forces. On 27 February the eastern rebels in Benghazi formed the Transitional National Council (TNC) which on 5 March proclaimed itself the 'only legitimate body representing the people of Libya'. France recognised it on 10 March and a steady stream of recognitions by other Western and some Arab states followed. But loyalists began to inflict battlefield defeats on the rebels; Misurata was put under siege and the initial rebel advances westward from their eastern stronghold in Benghazi were halted by a week of heavy fighting around Brega. Then loyalist forces rapidly drove eastwards, scattering the rebels and capturing Ajdabiya, the last city before Benghazi on 16 March. The fact Libya's air force could operate with near-total impunity conferred a major advantage on the loyalists.

Alan Kuperman has argued 'while the government did respond forcefully to the rebels, it never … resorted to "indiscriminate" force'.[3] Reports by Amnesty International and the International Crisis Group also concluded that despite there being no question the regime abused human rights – including shelling of civilian areas, torture and execution of activists and of soldiers who refused to fight, etc. – many reports had been exaggerated.[4] Nevertheless, the International Criminal Court (ICC) issued indictments against Gaddafi, his sons, and other senior regime figures. And Gaddafi himself issued blood-curdling threats of retribution, promising in late February to 'purify' rebel areas of 'cockroaches' and declaring

2 Lin Noueihed and Alex Warren, *The Battle for the Arab Spring: Revolution, Counter-Revolution and the Making of a New Era* (New Haven: Yale University Press, 2012), Part I; Paul Danahar, *The New Middle East: The World After the Arab Spring* (London: Bloomsbury, 2013).

3 'A Model', 110.

4 Patrick Cockburn, 'Amnesty Questions Claim that Gaddafi Ordered Rape as Weapon of War', *Independent*, 24 June 2011; Amnesty International, *The Battle for Libya: Killings, Disappearances and Torture* (London: Amnesty International, 13 September 2011).

'any Libyan who takes arms against Libya will be executed'.[5] As his forces approached Benghazi on 16 March he issued a chilling warning to the city: 'We are coming tonight. You will come out from inside. Prepare yourselves … . We will find you in your closets … . We will show no mercy and no pity'.[6] With hindsight it is clear that Gaddafi blundered badly because his rhetoric suggested a bloodbath of epic proportions was imminent and created a real sense of urgency amongst those international actors who eventually intervened to topple him. He arguably also made it harder for actors who might have otherwise opposed intervention from doing so.[7]

Resolutions 1970 and 1973

In late February various senior UN figures demanded the Gaddafi regime fulfil its Pillar I responsibilities, and Secretary-General Ban-Ki Moon warned failure to do so may mean Pillar III of R2P would become operable. On 22 February the League of Arab States (LAS) suspended Libya, and the African Union (AU) condemned the 'indiscriminate and excessive use of force' too. Bellamy and Williams have drawn a parallel between the 'gatekeeping' role of regional organisations in this crisis and the one which was unfolding simultaneously in Côte d'Ivoire.[8]

The Security Council first reacted on 26 February 2011 by passing Resolution 1970.[9] This recalled Libya's 'responsibility to protect its population' and demanded 'an immediate end to the violence', but it also reaffirmed the Council's 'strong commitment to the sovereignty, independence, territorial integrity and national unity' of Libya. It tasked the ICC with investigating abuses, imposed an arms embargo, travel ban, asset freeze and set up a sanctions committee to consider further action.

Resolution 1970 was adopted unanimously, meaning India voted for it (India's reasons are considered in more detail below). The U.S. Ambassador spoke of the Libyan government 'failing to meet [its] most basic responsibilities to [its] people' and others like South Africa, Nigeria and Colombia called for Libya to adhere to 'international humanitarian law' without directly referring to R2P. Indeed, only France directly invoked R2P by noting the resolution's text 'recalls the responsibility of each state to protect its own population' (which it did), but

5 Eleanor Hall, 'Defiant Gaddafi Issues Chilling Threat', *ABC: The World Today*, 23 February 2011.

6 Tom Heneghan, 'Gaddafi Tells Rebel City Benghazi "We Will Show no Mercy"', *Huffington Post*, 17 March 2011.

7 Alex J. Bellamy, 'Libya and the Responsibility to Protect: The Exception and the Norm', *Ethics & International Affairs* 25:3 (2011), 265–266; Hehir, 'The Permanence', 138.

8 Bellamy and Williams, 'The New Politics', 839.

9 S/RES/1970 (2011).

France also claimed the text referred to the responsibility of 'the international community to intervene when states fail in their duty' (which it didn't, at least not explicitly). Tellingly, after claiming it was 'deeply concerned' by the violence, China explained it had voted 'yes' after 'taking into account the special situation … and the views of the Arab and African countries'. Russia's Ambassador delivered a similar statement. Libya's representative had, in effect, 'gone rogue', and when he spoke he called Gaddafi 'the butcher of Tripoli' before endorsing intervention. Secretary-General Moon spoke last and noted the Council was 'determined to uphold its responsibilities for the maintenance of international peace and security' and thereby subtly suggested what was then essentially an internal disturbance (i.e. a mass refugee exodus had not yet occurred) could activate the Council's Article 42 powers.[10] But he also conceded the resolution 'cannot by itself end the violence', and so obliquely indicated a more robust future resolution may be needed.

Ban was proven correct: Gaddafi flatly rejected Resolution 1970 and refused to allow humanitarian aid deliveries to Benghazi. Britain and France pressed for more forceful action, and while Germany opposed a No-Fly Zone (and US support was lukewarm), NATO Command moved some assets southwards. Then several regional organisations decisively entered the fray. First, the Gulf Cooperation Council (GCC) called on 7 March for the Security Council to 'take all necessary measures to protect civilians, including enforcing a No-Fly Zone over Libya'. The next day the Organisation of Islamic Conference (OIC) echoed the call. The AU, however, was much less enthusiastic about intervening in Libya and on 10 March it proposed a detailed peace plan and tasked a high-powered panel which included five heads of state to seek a political solution. But events overtook this AU initiative, the key one being the LAS resolution on 12 March which called on the Council to:

> bear its responsibilities towards the deteriorating situation in Libya, and to take the necessary measures to impose immediately a No-Fly Zone … [and] to establish safe areas in places exposed to shelling … that allows the protection of the Libyan people. … [And] cooperate and communicate with the Transitional National Council [given] the Libyan authorities … [have] lost their legitimacy.[11]

The first few words quoted suggest the LAS recognised the Security Council, on behalf of the international community, had the authority – indeed the *responsibility* – to intervene in Libya to prevent atrocities. Yet many LAS states had other motivations too given Gaddafi had upset many neighbouring states repeatedly over the years: he had allegedly tried to have Saudi Arabia's Crown Prince Abdullah assassinated in 2003; and he had grandiosely declared himself the 'King of Kings' (of Africa) and the 'Iman of the Muslims', meaning 'Libya was in a position of

10 S/PV/6491, 26 February 2011.

11 Council of the League of Arab States, Resolution no. 7360, 12 March 2011.

extreme diplomatic isolation within the Arab world'.[12] Bellamy and Williams suspected some LAS members wanted to divert attention away from their own troubles and ultimately concluded that these states pursued ends other than strictly humanitarian ones.[13] Still, as discussed in Chapter 1, arguably 'mixed motives' do not automatically render a humanitarian intervention an example of abuse.

Whatever one thinks about these matters it is undeniable that the LAS's 12 March resolution was the crucial step leading to Resolution 1973 which authorised the intervention in Libya. Ten states voted for it and India, Germany, Brazil, Russia and China abstained. India's reasons are explored in a later section but the resolution's text and the reasons various states gave for their positions deserve consideration now.

While the preambular paragraphs of Resolution 1973 reaffirmed Libya's Pillar I responsibility they also made clear 'parties to armed conflict bear the primary responsibility ... to ensure the protection of civilians'; in other words, Pillar III of R2P was not directly invoked.[14] Scholars have argued about the relevance of this. Prominent R2P advocates like Gareth Evans[15] and Edward Luck[16] believe this failure to refer to the international community's responsibility mattered less than the *intent* behind Resolution 1973, and Ban-Ki Moon argued that the resolution affirmed 'clearly and unequivocally the international community's determination to fulfil its responsibility to protect civilians'.[17] But Marie-Eve Loiselle has argued the text did not demonstrate that 'a sense of legal obligation was guiding the actions of member states ... [indeed] some elements ... contradict this view'; in particular, the failure to mention Pillar III responsibilities 'is made even more salient by the reiteration ... [of] individual states' primary [Pillar I] responsibility'.[18]

Resolution 1973 also noted the AU's, LAS's and OIC's – and the Libyan Ambassador's – public statements before reaffirming Libya's sovereignty, and the final preambular paragraph declared that events within Libya constituted a threat to international peace and stability. The operative paragraphs followed. The single most important, the fourth, authorised member states to 'take all necessary measures ... to protect civilians and civilian populated areas under threat of attack ... while excluding a foreign occupation force of any form'. A No Fly-Zone was also established, and the arms embargo, asset freeze and travel bans were all tightened.

---

12 Shashank Joshi, 'The Complexity of Arab Support', in Adrian Johnson and Saqeb Mueen (eds), *Short War, Long Shadow: The Political and Military Legacies of the 2011 Libya Campaign* (London: RUSI, 2012), 66.

13 Bellamy and Williams, 'The New Politics', 842.

14 S/Res/1973/2011, 17 March 2011.

15 Speech, 'Ending Mass Atrocity Crimes', Leo Baeck Centre, Melbourne Australia, 31 July 2011.

16 'The Responsibility to Protect: The First Decade', *Global Responsibility to Protect* 3:4 (2011), 387–399. See also Hehir, 'The Permanence'.

17 SG/SM/13454-SC/10201-AFR/2144, 18 March 2011.

18 'The Normative', 331–332.

When explaining why it had voted 'yes' France referred to the 'burden of responsibility on our shoulders' and carefully explained what the resolution did – protect civilians, freeze assets, etc. – and so did not suggest it authorised regime change. Britain, however, noted the purpose was to 'protect civilians and to allow the people of Libya to determine their own future, free of the tyranny of the [Gaddafi] regime' and so at minimum the statement left the door to regime change ajar. Two other states provided somewhat cryptic remarks; Lebanon declared Gaddafi's regime had 'lost all legitimacy', although it also called for Libya's sovereignty to be respected; and Portugal first said 'for the international community, the [Gaddafi] regime … has come to an end by the will of the Libyan people', but then it declared Libya 'has to be reformed through a peaceful process'.

The US and the other five states which voted for the resolution were more circumspect; they typically reiterated exactly what the resolution authorised; referred to the LAS's 12 March resolution; and noted Libya had rejected Resolution 1970, meaning the Council must act to preserve its credibility. But none explicitly used R2P-like language and, in particular, none explicitly argued that because Libya had breached its Pillar I duties the international community's Pillar III responsibilities had been activated. South Africa's submission, for example, reveals much about how it understood Resolution 1973:

> We believe the Security Council has responded appropriately to the call of the countries in the region to strengthen the implementation of Resolution 1970, and has acted responsibly to protect and save the lives of defenceless civilians … . [Given] the necessary caveats to preserve [Libya's] sovereignty … it is our hope that this resolution will be implemented with full respect for both its letter and spirit.

South Africa did not therefore specifically refer to the responsibility to protect, but instead stressed that the *Security Council* should act responsibly, with the inference being that interveners should act with restraint (as an aside, South Africa later became very upset about the conduct and outcome of NATO's intervention: see Chapter 6).

The abstainers gave various reasons. Germany first declared Gaddafi had 'lost all legitimacy' and confirmed 'aspirations for democracy and human … rights merit our full support', but Berlin also worried that paragraph 4 might lead to 'a protracted military engagement that would affect the entire region'. Brazil said its abstention should not be interpreted as condoning Gaddafi's oppression, and while it supported the LAS's position, 'the text [of Resolution 1973] … goes far beyond' what the LAS had called for – which is not strictly accurate because the two resolutions were quite similar – and then Brazil declared it preferred the AU's diplomatic approach. Russia also condemned Gaddafi and acknowledged the LAS's call for action, but worried 'the text could potentially open the door to large-scale military intervention'. China also said it 'attached great importance to the relevant position by the [LAS]', but then also expressed concerns that questions about how the intervention would be conducted had not been not 'clarified or answered'.[19] The LAS's 12 March resolution was thus the crucial factor enabling the passage of Resolution 1973,[20] and we will see below how important it was in shaping India's decision to abstain.

The Indian Commentary About the Libyan Crisis

This section explores some of the contributions made by Indian policy-shapers who interpreted the crisis and offered advice about how India should respond. These are drawn from sources in February and March 2011, some before 17 March and some in the weeks after as India's policy-response continued. To be clear on this last point, arguably India's policy-response was not just confined to its vote on 17 March; we will see in the following section that Indian policy-makers continued to respond – mainly by criticising NATO's actions – in the weeks after Resolution 1973 was passed. So, the contributions to the public debates made by commentators before April 2011 are presented to demonstrate that logics inherent in various identity discourses shaped debate about 'what to *do*' vis-à-vis Libya. But by early April 2011 the true nature and implications of NATO's intervention began to dawn on Indians – it was clear regime change was in the offing rather than just direct protection of civilians – so, contributions from 1 April 2011 onward are more relevant to the question of 'what to *learn*' from the Libyan crisis. Accordingly, they are considered in a later section.

The contributions to public debates considered now are mainly drawn from the press, from a key parliamentary debate on 22 March 2011, and from a few foreign policy institutes' in-house publications. Longer academic contributions only appeared after 1 April 2011 so these are also considered later. Finally, because there were 680 articles about the Libya crisis in the six major newspapers between 15 February and 31 March 2011,[21] and because a formal content analysis was not carried out (see Chapter 2 for reasons), the analysis in this chapter cannot examine every contribution in detail as was possible vis-à-vis Côte d'Ivoire in Chapter 4. Instead the focuses is on op-ed pieces (and some *Frontline* magazine articles) to demonstrate logics reflecting the various identity discourses were 'out there' in the public sphere potentially shaping India's policy-response to the Libyan crisis.

---

19 S/PV.6498, 17 March 2011.

20 Bellamy and Williams, 'The New Politics', 842. See also Hehir, 'The Permanence', 138; Spencer Zifcak, 'The Responsibility to Protect after Libya and Syria', *Melbourne Journal of International Law* 13:1 (2012), 10; Justin Morris, 'Libya and Syria: The Spectre of the Swinging Pendulum', *International Affairs* 89:5 (2013), 1272; C. Raja Mohan, 'India, Libya and the Principle of Non-Intervention', *ISAS Insights*, No. 122, 13 April 2011, 6.

21 The *Factiva* database was surveyed and only one search term – 'libya' – was entered.

The first policy-shaper to mention the demonstrations in Libya wrote his article on 20 February 2011. Meghnad Desai, an Indian expatriate who holds the title Baron Desai in the British House of Lords, believed:

> what is now happening … is a real revolt against the dictators and the Fundamentalists. This is a belated demand by Muslims for the freedoms that many societies have enjoyed after they came to terms with western liberalism. The long overdue engagement with western modernity may yet happen in Arabia.[22]

Desai said nothing about R2P, did not call for intervention or offer advice to New Delhi, but his contribution clearly reflected soft liberal-democratic logic. At this early stage, however, most press articles explored the implications of the crisis for India's direct interests, especially the plight of 18,000 Indian citizens in Libya but also the spike in oil prices and falls on India's stock market, the SENSEX. Then on 28 February Atul Aneja wrote that Gaddafi

> is staring at defeat … because of his methods, which have revolved around authoritarianism, a personality cult and the use of brute force … . Soaring idealism has a better chance of realisation when it is premised, not on force, but on principles of transparency, grassroots organisation and a political culture which readily allows dissent and animated debate.[23]

So while Aneja's contribution reflects soft liberal-democratic logic, he did not mention R2P, armed intervention or discuss what India should do. India's parliament also debated the Arab Spring (briefly) on 23 February. The External Affairs Minister spoke only of Indian citizens' welfare, and in reply Mohan Jena (of Biju Janata Dal (BJD), aligned with the opposition Bharatiya Janata Party (BJP)) advised 'as a front-ranking democratic nation, it is our foremost duty to stand by the [Libyan] people'.[24]

What little commentary there was at this early stage either reflected hard-realist logic by focusing on India's direct interests – the papers were quite critical of New Delhi for bungling the evacuation effort[25] – or the liberal-democratic identity discourse, although only the soft variety; in other words, contributors expressed support for democracy and human rights but not necessarily armed intervention to promote such. But on 25 February Pratik Kanjilal mused that Western talk of 'smooth transition' in Libya was code 'for … "regime change" … [which] confers control over the destiny of the "Arab world"' in the name of 'the approved magical

22 'Muslim Renaissance', *New Indian Express*, 20 February 2011.

23 'Libya: in the Throes of Change', *The Hindu*, 28 February 2011.

24 Lok Sabha Debate, 15th Series, Vol. XVI, 7th Session, No. 20, 23 February 2011.

25 Manu Pubby, 'Out of Libya: India Crawls, the Rest are Safe at Home', *Indian Express*, 2 March 2011.

word: democracy'.[26] This was the first reference to the anti-Western variety of anti-imperial logic, although its tone was more ironic than vitriolic.

By early March it was becoming clearer that Resolution 1970 had achieved little and more forceful interventionist measures were being discussed in international forums. Indians accordingly began to contemplate such too, and on 3 March Bhaskar Balakrishnan, a retired diplomat, wrote that:

> the international community [must] step in with effective and coordinated action. The UN Security Council is the most appropriate body to take action, under the rubric of the right to protect … . to stop the violence and get Gaddafi out of power … . Robust UNSC action would receive broad-based international support, including from the G20 and key Arab and African countries … . India is a member of the UNSC at this critical juncture. It has an important role to play as the world's largest democracy and major developing country, in fashioning the UN and international response to the crisis.

Balakrishnan then called for 'an international intervention force' to be sent to ensure 'law and order [is] restored by the security forces, under impartial supervision'.[27] This contribution therefore reflects robust liberal-democratic logic closely compatible with the R2P norm (despite the fact he mistakenly talked of a 'right' not a 'responsibility' to protect). Specifically, Balakrishnan seems to have had measures which sort of straddled Pillars II and III in mind (so, not outright regime change).

On 6 March the Communist Party India (Marxist) (CPI(M)) entered the fray with a contribution clearly inspired by fiercely anti-Western anti-imperial logic; India must not support an intervention, the CPI(M) said, because doing so would

> be a tragedy and an abetment to imperialist designs. It will be another shift from the [traditional Indian] non-alignment foreign policy. The CPI demands that the Government of India keep away from the U.S. sponsored military actions … The U.S. wants to control Libya's oil … Let us support the people's struggle for democracy and freedom. Libyans are capable of winning their battle.[28]

Raja Mohan published an article on 7 March and came to a very different conclusion. He noted New Delhi was backing away from Resolution 1970 'because of domestic squeamishness about Western intervention in Libya', which he attributed to the Congress Party's 'humbug and hypocrisy about non-intervention as a high principle of India's foreign policy'. He then delivered advice clearly informed by the enlightened-realist logic:

---

26 'Wait While We Think of New Names', *Hindustan Times*, 25 February 2011.

27 Bhaskar Balakrishnan, 'UN Must Intervene to End the Crisis', *Indian Express*, 3 March 2011.

28 'Don't Get Involved in U.S. Imperialist Designs: CPI', *The Hindu*, 6 March 2011.

> The fact is that intervention in the internal affairs of nations is part of international life. As India rises … its interests become global and it is called on to contribute to regional and international peace and security, [so] the real question before India is not whether to intervene, but when, where and how … . It is about choosing between competing interests and balancing India's political values and strategic interests. Pious platitudes on non-intervention are neither credible nor helpful for an emerging India.[29]

Mohan was therefore channelling two varieties of enlightened-realist logic, namely, the view that a 'responsible' intervention might restore stability and also that New Delhi's support for such would likely have advanced India's long-term interests. Mohan did not, however, directly call for India to support a *military* intervention; but Meenakshi Ganguly from Human Rights Watch South Asia did after noting India 'supports governments no matter how they treat their people [which] … is simply not acceptable … India should once more stake out a position as a world leader defending the rights and aspirations of downtrodden people'.[30]

Then on 11 March an anonymous commentator advised it was in India's immediate and longer-term interests to oppose intervention because such would 'constitute acts of war against a sovereign state and must be condemned outright' as threatening global stability.[31] But on 16 March, the day before Resolution 1973 came before the Security Council, another policy-shaper wrote:

> the only hope the remnants of the jasmine revolution [i.e. Arab Spring] have today is international intervention … . Germany is hiding behind a position of non-intervention. India has taken the latter line, continuing a long tradition of preferring passivity when it comes to value-driven foreign policy.[32]

Some short contributions from foreign policy institutes also appeared around this time. K.P. Fabian wondered on 10 March whether 'Russia and China can resist the pressure' from the LAS, GCC and OIC, implying he thought an intervention was likely (but he declined to comment on the propriety of such). And India's reaction so far, he felt, was:

> measured and rational. While India believes that democracy is good in itself … she does understand that democracy to be sustainable should have firm roots in the soil. It cannot be transplanted … . It will be appropriate [for India] to render assistance when asked for.[33]

---

29 'How to intervene', *Indian Express*, 7 March 2011.
30 'India, Arab Democracy, and Human Rights', *OpenDemocracy*, 9 March 2011.
31 'Oppose Military Intervention', *The Hindu*, 10 March 2011.
32 'Withering of the Jasmine', *Hindustan Times*, 16 March 2011.
33 'An Arab Revolution?', *IDSA Issue Brief*, 10 March 2011.

A mix of hard-realist and soft liberal-democratic logics seemed to inform Fabian's thinking; he noted India prefers democracy, but didn't think India can, will, or should intervene to impose it, and he suggested it was in India's interests to not get involved until asked to offer non-lethal assistance once – or if – a nascent democracy was established. But another scholarly contribution, Saeed Naqvi, was much more critical of the West; he believed 'greed for oil' motivated the intervention, and urged India to oppose.[34] Clearly he was channelling the anti-Western variety of anti-imperial logic.

On the eve of the 17 March vote, then, opinions reflecting the logic of all the identity discourses had been delivered. The impression one gleans suggests hard-realist logic dominated – the press was very fixated on evacuating Indian nationals, but stories about rising oil prices and stock-market turmoil were common too – and liberal-democratic logic was also prominent; many contributors expressed support for the Libyan people's aspirations for freedom and wanted New Delhi to 'do something'. But we must be very cautious about concluding 'something' meant 'armed intervention'; only Ganguly and Balakrishnan advised India to support an armed intervention (and the latter was certainly not advising India support a regime change). All this suggests that while many Indians – or, again, maybe just the op-ed-writing elites interested in foreign policy – would like to see democracy and liberalism gain ground internationally (see the interviewees' opinions on this matter in Chapter 4), they are not necessarily strong supporters of the R2P norm, or at least not its Pillar III component.

After Resolution 1973 was passed on 17 March commentators continued to interpret events and offer advice in light of New Delhi's continuing policy-response (i.e. officials began to criticise NATO's operations: see below). On 21 March, after the first airstrikes, one contributor noted the intervention had been driven by mixed motives – 'emotional' (i.e. protecting human rights) and 'political', especially French President Nicholas Sarkozy's desire to boost his domestic standing – and this author was critical of India's role:

> India has continued its tradition of pleasing no one and sounding confused. It made sense to abstain … . However, [India's] subsequent denunciation of the airstrikes made India look naive. Enforcement of a no-fly zone would always … mean collateral civilian casualties. New Delhi's only saving grace is that not many capitals … paid much notice.[35]

This contribution to the public debate was informed mainly by hard-realist logic – India was right to stand on the sidelines – but it also suggested India should have stayed there, rhetorically speaking. Others noted India had been right to abstain to avoid 'being isolated among both Western powers and the Arab countries' but

34 'Can US Lead While Europe Scrambles for Oil?', *Observer Research Foundation: Analysis*, 14 March 2011.

35 'Into a Zone of Uncertainty', *Hindustan Times*, 21 March 2011.

didn't criticise New Delhi's subsequent opposition to NATO's air strikes.[36] And Pratik Kanjilal also argued it was not in India's interests to support the intervention, which he likened to 'pill-popping' (i.e. hasty, imprudent, and unlikely to be effective).[37] Then, a few days later Manoj Joshi delivered a withering broadside:

> After standing on the sidelines at the UNSC and then shedding crocodile tears over the developments in Libya, India is displaying its tendency to run with the hare and hunt with the hounds ... Like it or not, we cannot avoid intervening in the affairs of others. Should the world stand by when rulers decide to punish their own populace or, as in Rwanda, Cambodia and erstwhile Yugoslavia, wipe out entire groups of people? ... Obviously we need rules to undertake such ventures.[38]

Raja Mohan re-entered the fray and referred to the intervention being motivated in part by the 'moral "responsibility to protect" the people of Libya' and by the need to arrest the region's spiral into instability. Yet he too was critical of India's response. He discerned a clear disconnect between India's decision to abstain – 'which appears to be driven by a cold calculus of national interest' (which he also felt was reasonable given India's limited resources) – and like Joshi he criticised India's subsequent denunciations of NATO's airstrikes, arguing 'by sounding sceptical, India has looked wishy-washy and unattached to its own political values of democracy and the right to peaceful political change'. He felt the Congress Party-dominated government needed to, in effect, 'grow up' and stop pandering to the anti-American radical-left parties.[39]

These last two contributions were therefore both informed by similar enlightened-realist logic; both urged India to work to enhance global stability and burnish its reputation as a 'responsible great power', although Joshi felt India should support the intervention after also referring to robust liberal-democratic logic while Mohan's contribution included a dose of hard-realist appreciation of India's limited resources, leading him to endorse India's decision to avoid direct involvement in *this* crisis. Other contributions reflected the enlightened-realist logic by which New Delhi should support intervention to secure side-benefits more overtly; for example, Rajeswari Rajagopalan argued India should offer logistical support to enforce the No-Fly Zone to 'raise [India's] political capital in the US, France and UK'.[40]

---

36 Keerthi Sampath Kumar, 'Responsibility to Protect : The Case of Libya', *IDSA Comment*, 2 May 2011. See also Ramesh Phadke, 'India: An Uneasy Onlooker!', *IDSA Comment*, 21 March 2011.

37 'Intervention is more than just Popping a Pill', *Hindustan Times*, 25 March 2011.

38 'Dodgy Stand on Libya Crisis', *India Today*, 24 March 2011.

39 'It's not West vs the rest', *Indian Express*, 22 March 2011.

40 'Libya NFZ: An Opportunity for India', *Observer Research Foundation – Analysis*, 19 March 2011.

The far-left parties Mohan had lambasted were, unsurprisingly, deeply aggrieved by NATO's intervention. Sitaram Yechury, of the Community Party of India (Marxist) (CPI(M)), wrote on 21 March that Resolution 1973 'betrays imperialism's eagerness to retain its hegemonic control over the oil-rich region'. Marxist dogma permeated his article: for example, he somewhat implausibly blamed the uprising not on Gaddafi's repression but on globalisation, which allegedly 'increased the burden on the people through massive lay-offs and price rises'.[41] And one of the CPI(M)'s rivals on the left, the Socialist Unity Centre of India (Communist), scrambled to condemn NATO and the US in a similar manner.[42]

Yet contributions to the public debate reflecting 'garden variety' anti-Western anti-imperialist logic – less inspired by far-left ideology and more by general scepticism of Western motives – were more common. For example, *Frontline*'s Vijay Prasad argued the Arab Spring had ignited 'imperial anxieties' in America,[43] while his colleague John Cherian condemned the 'crude colonial-style intervention'.[44] Siddarth Vardarajan also condemned the intervention because, in his view,

> the motive is not humanitarian but political and strategic. … The 'responsibility to protect' doctrine which morally underpins the attack on Libya is still not a part of customary international law but even its advocates must agree that the selective and politically expedient invocation of R2P robs the doctrine of its normative force … . If there is one country in the Middle East which has threatened international peace and security for decades … it is Israel.[45]

This last piece also betrays hints of enlightened-realist logic, but the variety which assumes R2P undermines, not enhances, global stability. We saw above that Joshi and Mohan assumed the R2P norm – if properly applied – would likely enhance stability; as an aside, however, we will see enlightened-realist opinion shifting later in 2011 and into 2012 as post-intervention Libya descended into chaos.

But more generally, the sudden emergence of contributions reflecting the fiercely-anti-Western variety of anti-imperialist logic after Resolution 1973 passed – and after NATO began pursuing regime change – is striking. Other studies have noted this trend too; for example, Ian Hall concluded:

> the bulk of the Indian "establishment", left-leaning media and many academics … backed the stance taken by their government [i.e. abstaining but then criticising NATO's conduct] and weighed in with critical appraisals of R2P

41 'More Fuel to the Fire', *Hindustan Times*, 21 March 2011.
42 'US Criticised', *The Hindu*, 22 March 2011.
43 'Imperial Anxieties', *Frontline* 28:6, 12–25 March 2011.
44 'Colonel in his Labyrinth', *Frontline* 28:6, 12–25 March 2011.
45 'Odyssey Dawn, a Homeric Tragedy', *The Hindu*, 24 March 2011.

> [and] … they were bolstered by younger academics and journalists attached to postcolonial or critical theoretical ideas.[46]

And when a fiery parliamentary debate took place on 22 March it too was marked by anti-imperial sentiments (of both varieties). Unsurprisingly, the CPI(M)'s Basudeb Acharya condemned the 'brutal and unprovoked attack' on Libya and his colleague, Gurudas Dasgupta, said NATO 'had an eye on the oil'. But anti-imperialist logic was not restricted to far-left MPs: indeed, Bhartruhari Mahtab of the BJD – a right-wing party allied to the BJP opposition – noted 'Libya is a non-aligned country', urged solidarity with its government, and called for parliament to formally condemn the Western powers. The BJP itself then backed Mahtab's position, with Yaswant Sinha stating 'we are completely with the democratic forces struggling against an authoritarian regime [and w]e are against any military intervention to enforce regime change'. Tellingly, the Samajwadi Party – a democratic-socialist party which typically opposes the BJP – agreed, with its leader Mulayam Singh Yadav demanding the parliament 'condemn the attack on Libya'.

Mirza Mehboob Beg, from the Jammu and Kashmir National Congress (J&KNC), which was part of the Congress-led ruling coalition, took a more nuanced position, arguing (before he was shouted down):

> We have to find a middle ground. It is only one view that is being expressed in this house … . You cannot allow [Gaddafi] to slaughter his people and, at the same time, you cannot let America interfere and do the same there. So, a middle path has to be found to save the people of Libya and other people who are fighting for their democracy … (*interruptions end speech*)[47]

But Beg was very much in the minority. Immediately after he retired from the speaker's lectern another MP from the J&KNC declared 'America's coercive tactics have been increasing over years. It treats the UN Security Council as its pet cat'. A range of other small parties – the Shiromani Akali Dal (representing Sikhs), the Bahujan Samaj Party (representing mainly lower-castes in Uttar Pradesh), the Rashtriya Janata Dal (representing middle-castes and Muslims in Bihar state), the Muslim League, etc. – all called for a motion to condemn NATO.

Anti-imperialist logic was very much in the ascendant in the Lok Sabha on 22 March 2011. But we should not assume it entirely motivated the opinions expressed in the House that day because criticism of government policy by opposition MPs may reflect a determination to embarrass it politically more than a principled stance. In particular, the motion to condemn NATO was never

---

46 'Tilting at Windmills: The Indian Debate over the Responsibility to Protect after UNSC Resolution 1973', *Global Responsibility to Protect* 5:1 (2013), 98.

47 Lok Sabha Debate, 15th Series, Vol. XVI, 7th Session, No. 20, Tuesday 22 March 2011.

formally presented or voted on, suggesting MPs were more interested in producing rhetorical flourishes than formal resolutions. Nevertheless, the fact the debate was so dominated by anti-imperialist sentiment remains significant; it suggests, at minimum, that such 'plays well' with the general Indian population, or at least with supporters of parties which represented over half[48] the seats in the Lok Sabha. The next day India's upper house, the Rajya Sabha, saw a similar (if somewhat less raucous) debate take place.[49]

Several scholars also wrote about the Libyan crisis in foreign policy institutes' in-house publications. P.R. Kumaraswamy, writing for the Institute for Defence Studies and Analyses (IDSA), advised New Delhi to ignore the parliamentary backbenchers' anti-imperialist populism and avoid falling 'into the trap' of anti-Americanism. His advice essentially reflected hard-realist logic: India was right to have abstained, in his opinion, but he thought New Delhi should have stayed silent thereafter to carefully protect its wider diplomatic interests.[50] Prasanta Pradhan, also writing for the IDSA, focussed on India's direct interests too – like securing oil supplies and protecting exports to the Middle East – and counselled India to restrict itself to urging Arab regimes to pursue reforms.[51] These two opinions obviously reflected hard-realist logic.

These reactions by policy-shapers after the passage of Resolution 1973 tell an interesting story. The outpouring of anti-imperialist sentiment is particularly striking, especially in the parliament (subject to the caveats noted above), but it is also notable how hard-realist logic 'hardened'; in other words, most contributors thought India should evacuate its nationals and then not commit resources – diplomatic and especially material – to the intervention. To be sure, Rajagopalan urged India to offer some minor logistical support the intervention to curry-favour with the West, and Joshi referred to India's liberal-democratic traditions as a reason for supporting intervention too. But the general tenor of reactions to Resolution 1973 showed that when the crisis came to a head and decisions had to be made about supporting or opposing Western military intervention, Indian policy-shapers either opposed such or urged India to retreat to the sidelines. This suggests hard-realist logic was the single most dominant – or at least *prominent* – shaping influence once 'minds were focused', so to speak, while anti-imperialist logic was arguably the second most prominent shaping influence.

Data from the interviews supports this conclusion. As noted in Chapter 4 many interviewees told the author that Indians (or maybe just their elites) support liberal-democracy but are also uncomfortable with the idea of imposing it and, more importantly, most also agreed India does – and is right to – pursue

48 I.e. the Samajwadi Party's support for the opposition's stance tipped the scales; and four small parties in the United Progressive Alliance ruling coalition supported it too.

49 'RS Members Slam Libya Attack, Krishna Silent', *Indian Express*, 24 March 2011.

50 'Uprisings in the Arab World: Options for GOI', *IDSA Issue Brief*, 30 March 2011.

51 'Protests in the Arab World: Implications for the Region and India', *IDSA Issue Brief*, 31 March 2011.

other more traditional economic or security interests over interests grounded in liberal-democratic values when the two clash. For example, I-3 stated that 'when things get tough India generally reacts by thinking "don't get involved without thinking about the future", and then it rightly takes steps to protect its traditional interests',[52] while I-6 reported 'the default Indian setting is "abstain" and "avoid" when war threatens – before then India will publically support democracy and human rights',[53] and I-10 believed that 'India mainly focused on its interests – especially getting citizens out [of Libya] – because the media focused on this. India then properly stayed on the sidelines'.[54] Other interviewees gave responses which suggested anti-imperial logic remained strong in India; for example, I-7 reported 'India is very sensitive to maintaining solidarity with the developing world, which is why it abstained on [Resolution] 1973 and then criticised NATO's air strikes'. And of the 14 interviewees who were questioned directly, none thought India should have vigorously supported the intervention, especially with active participation.

The next section considers the Indian government's response to the Libyan crisis in more detail and, in particular, it examines whether the impression one gains from the analysis in this section – that hard-realist logic first and then anti-imperialist logic were the most dominant logics – is reflected in India's specific policy responses.

India's Policy Responses to the Libyan Crisis

As noted earlier, India voted for Resolution 1970 and abstained when Resolution 1973 passed. This section closely examines the explanations India gave with attention to statements delivered by Indian policy-makers and explores the linkages between these responses and the public debates considered in the previous section.

After India joined the Security Council its External Affairs Minister, S.M. Krishna, gave a short address on 11 February 2011. He spoke of India's proud peacekeeping tradition before calling for Council reform.[55] But his speech is otherwise unremarkable and did not mention R2P or events in the Middle East. Then, on 23 February the MEA released a statement advising India 'deplored' the use of force by Gaddafi's loyalist forces.[56] When Ambassador Hardeep Puri Singh explained India's vote for Resolution 1970 on 26 February he again spoke of India 'deploring' the violence and called for Libya to protect foreign nationals and facilitate their evacuation. But he spent the remainder – indeed, the majority

52 New Delhi, 1 November 2013.

53 New Delhi, 4 November 2013.

54 New Delhi, 10 November 2013.

55 Speech, 'Statement of EAM at the Security Council', New York (UN Security Council), 11 February 2011.

56 Sandeep Dikshit, 'India Condemns Libya Violence', *The Hindu*, 23 February 2011.

– of his statement explaining that India was not a member of the ICC and did not usually support its activities but had 'gone along with the consensus'.[57] And that was all; he did not refer to R2P, or to regional or global stability, or to any regional organisations' opinions about the crisis, or to India's interests.

MEA statements and press reports of Krishna's public statements later in February focused primarily on India's evacuation efforts. But on 27 February Krishna was asked why India had voted for Resolution 1970 and he declared 'India will certainly try to position itself to be of advantage to forces of democracy so dear to India's heart'. But he then very firmly stated 'India does not believe in interfering in the affairs of another country'.[58] The following day he reiterated India's position:

> Let us be very cautious in reacting to whatever is happening in Libya. The basic proposition has been spelt out with clarity. We do not interfere. But we are closely monitoring the situation. Our immediate concern is to see that those Indians who are eager to come out of Libya are [able to].[59]

These statements suggest that before more military intervention was being contemplated New Delhi's position reflected the tenor of the wider public debate, namely, India wanted to support democracy and human rights but was primarily focused on its direct interests, suggesting soft liberal-democratic and especially hard-realist logic were shaping Indian policy. But in early March, as Western states were discussing more forceful intervention, the Foreign Secretary Nirupama Rao was asked on 3 March about India's position and *The Hindu* reported that she had explained to journalists that:

> India's stand [on a second resolution] was echoed by many developing countries as well as the BRIC (Brazil, Russia, India and China) nations. However, India had not decided whether to abstain or vote against … . New Delhi would prefer to consult with its friends and then take a stand.[60]

A few days later India had consulted with Brazil and South Africa at the IBSA summit and a joint statement 'expressed their aversion to the move by some western countries to impose a military solution'.[61] But Rao's most revealing

57 S/PV.6491, 26 February 2011.

58 Sandeep Dikshit, 'India Can Help Build Democracy in Arab World', *The Hindu*, 27 February 2011.

59 Sandeep Dikshit, 'India Will Not Offer Unsolicited Advice to Arab Nations: Krishna', *The Hindu*, 28 February 2011.

60 Sandeep Dikshit, 'India Will Oppose Move to Use Force to End Civil War in Libya', *The Hindu*, 4 March 2011.

61 Sandeep Dikshit, 'IBSA Averse to No-Fly Zone Over Libya', *The Hindu*, 9 March 2011.

comments came on 10 March 2011. When asked whether India would support a No-Fly Zone she responded:

> We have to take into account what Egypt feels … What does the Arab League have to say about it, what does the African Union have to say about it. … And then we have the BRICS … . [We] are consulting with each other … . We will take a decision rather based on this, it won't be in isolation … . When you have a no-fly zone … it will involve bombings. … And that would again lead to a rapid escalation of violence.

And when Rao was asked what she thought about Gaddafi likening the situation in Libya with that in Kashmir, which he had done a few days earlier, she angrily declared India's 'very strong objections and reservations to Kashmir being referred to in that sort of context'.[62]

Only two days later the LAS delivered its 12 March call for action and the Indian government largely fell silent; only a single statement by Krishna confirming evacuations efforts were continuing[63] was issued in the week before 17 March. Interestingly, Gaddafi offered special oil-extraction rights to Indian companies on 13 March; but New Delhi issued no formal statements and it was left to the oil companies to report they had been told to decline because 'sending its oilmen to Libya would pitch India against the majority world view and cost it international goodwill'.[64] This incident is discussed again shortly.

The following day Resolution 1973 was voted on, and Hardeep Puri Singh explained India's abstention was motivated primarily by caution; he worried there was

> relatively little credible information about the situation on the ground … [and little] clarity about the details of enforcement measures, including who will participate and with what assets, and how these measures will exactly be carried out. It is of course very important that there be full respect for the sovereignty, unity and territorial integrity of Libya.

He finished by declaring:

> India continues to be gravely concerned about the deteriorating humanitarian situation in Libya and calls on the Libyan authorities to cease fire, protect the civilian population and address the legitimate demands of the Libyan people.[65]

---

62 'India consulting other nations on no-fly zone over Libya', *Times of India*, 10 March 2011.

63 'Will Bring Back Mideast Indians: SM Krishna', *Times of India*, 15 March 2011.

64 Sanjay Dutta, 'India Unlikely to Respond to Gaddafi Request for Oilmen to Fill Expat Void', *The Hindu*, 17 March 2011.

65 S/Res/1973/2011, 17 March 2011.

What was left out of this statement is arguably as important as what was included; Singh said nothing about India wanting to avoid antagonising Western states – which is perhaps not surprising – but he also failed to mention the LAS's position, which is strange given so many other states referred to it when explaining their votes on 17 March (see above). Only days before the LAS's 12 March resolution India's Foreign Secretary Rao had clearly stated India would 'consult with its friends' and 'take into account' their positions. And on 8 March India, South Africa and Brazil had jointly expressed 'aversion to … a military solution'. But on 17 March India only referred to the AU's relatively restrained position and didn't even try to finesse its position on the LAS resolution as Brazil had done. *The Hindu* reported on 26 March – so, nine days after Resolution 1973 had passed – that 'government sources' had explained India's abstention in the following terms:

> India has always opposed the use of force … But pragmatic considerations prevailed. The first was the uncertainty among … India, China and Russia over [Gaddafi's tactics] against his opponents … . their opposition to the no-fly-zone and air strikes [might] strengthen [Gaddafi's] resolve and [precipitate] mass killings … . The second was [India's] desire not to upset existing ties with the West and the Arabs. The other consideration was for civilians … . since the first Gulf War … . civilians were killed and maimed in large numbers.[66]

New Delhi was by then publically condemning NATO, first though an MEA spokesperson,[67] and then Krishna declared 'I am sure the air strikes will lead to more harm to innocent civilians'.[68] It was these statements, of course, which annoyed Joshi, Mohan and other policy-shapers (see above).

As noted in Chapter 2, to determine exactly why India abstained on Resolution 1973 it would be ideal to have access to transcripts of Cabinet records, advice memos from the Foreign Secretary, and diplomatic cables between India and LAS and BRICS states (etc.) to determine which factors really were the crucial ones for India. But these are not available so we must first search for correlations between the logics inherent in the various contributions to the public debates and New Delhi's explanations of its policy response.

We can, of course, see some evidence of liberal-democratic logic shaping the policy response – India condemned the violence and repeatedly called on the Libyan government to protect its people – but it never suggested it accepted that Libya's failure to fulfil its Pillar I obligations had activated a Pillar III responsibility for the international community. So, at best there is a correlation with the soft variety of liberal-democratic logic – rhetorical professions of support for democracy and

66 Ananth Krishnan and Sandeep Dikshit, 'India and China had Similar Considerations on Libya', *The Hindu*, 26 March 2011.

67 Manan Kumar, 'India Regrets Air Strikes on Libya', *New Indian Express*, 20 March 2011.

68 'Why India Regrets Attack', *Hindustan Times*, 22 March 2011.

human rights only – and the abstention. Instead, Singh's statement – and comments by Rao and Krishna prior to 17 March – emphasised India would make its decision *cautiously*, including by avoiding direct participation in the intervention; many contributors urged India to exercise caution, meaning there is a clear correlation between this aspect of hard-realist logic and India's abstention. Singh also referred in his statement to India's desire to secure 'the welfare … of foreigners' which obviously included the 18,000 Indians in Libya. There is therefore a clear correlation between the relentless clamour in the press for Indians to be evacuated safely (i.e. direct interests) and India's expressed reasons for abstaining.

A correlation between the shaping effect of enlightened-realist logic on India's policy response is, however, only faintly discernible. As noted above one variety of enlightened-realist logic holds intervention can enhance global stability which is in India's wider interests, and some contributions (Joshi's and Ganguly's especially) reflected this logic. But others (i.e. Vardarajan and the anonymous contributor to *The Hindu* on 11 March) disagreed, especially if R2P is applied selectively. New Delhi seems to have preferred the latter position, but this conclusion can only be made very tentatively given India did not directly say 'R2P is being abused and/or applied selectively, which undermines global stability' (although India hinted at such concerns 13 days later when it voted for Resolution 1975 vis-à-vis Côte d'Ivoire[69]: see Chapter 4).

Most strikingly, there is only a very faint correlation between the shaping effect of anti-imperialist contributions to the public debate – which as we saw above had been very prominent in the public debates – and India's explanation of its abstention. Ambassador Singh's failure to refer to the LAS's or the BRICS's position is particularly interesting given what Foreign Secretary Rao had said a week earlier; Singh only mentioned the AU's more-cautious position when addressing the Council. And Singh engaged in none of the outright condemnation of Western states' motives – or of R2P – which had been so favoured by his predecessor Nirupam Sen. Having said this, the fact Indian officials began to critique NATO in the weeks after 17 March *does* correlate with the outburst of anti-Western anti-imperialist sentiment expressed by numerous commentators and MPs. Still, there is no correlation with this and India's *formal* position in the Council, which remains significant.

These findings of correlations between the interpretations and advice offered by policy-shapers and India's policy-response to the Libyan crisis give some indication why India abstained on Resolution 1973, but to build a clearer picture requires hypothesis testing and the use of counterfactual logic. First, if India's policy-response had been shaped primarily by the robust variety of democratic-liberal logic one would expect it to have voted for Resolution 1973. India's abstention therefore suggests robust liberal-democratic logic had only a limited shaping effect, although the fact India did not vote *against* Resolution 1973 probably demonstrates a concern to not support Gaddafi, a noted human

69 India said 'we also want to put on record our growing concern at the tendency to hurry the process of adopting of resolutions': S/RES/1975, 30 March 2011.

rights abuser who had been graphically promising to exact bloody retribution on civilians. It is probably too cynical to conclude India *only* wanted to avoid being *seen* to support Gaddafi; no doubt this consideration played a part, but arguably India was also genuinely concerned about human rights abuses (but not concerned enough to wholeheartedly support an armed intervention). So it seems reasonable to conclude soft liberal-democratic logic did exert some shaping influence.

If India's policy response had been primarily shaped by the aspect of anti-imperialist logic which urged it to oppose Western states at every turn, then India would have opposed Resolution 1973 (and sharply criticised the West). This, of course, did not happen, suggesting New Delhi's reaction was not substantially shaped by this aspect of the anti-imperial identity discourse. But the situation is quite a bit more complex regarding its other aspect, namely, that which predisposes India to show solidarity with developing states.

If India's response had been primarily shaped by the desire to maintain solidarity with the LAS it would have voted 'yes'. But if India had been more concerned with maintaining solidarity with the BRICS then, given how we saw in Chapter 1 the BRICS have generally opposed Western military interventions since Kosovo and have consistently stated their preference for relatively strong, traditional understandings of sovereignty and their unease with (if not outright opposition to) Pillar III of R2P, then perhaps we would have expected India to have voted 'no'. Further, if the BRICS had maintained a united front against Western intervention in Libya India would have enjoyed two advantages when opposing Resolution 1973: first, the crucial no-votes would have been cast by China and Russia exercising their vetos and enabling India to 'hide' somewhat (i.e. China and Russia would have attracted much more criticism); second, if all the BRICS had opposed, then India would have enjoyed 'safety in numbers'.

But when the LAS called for military intervention on 12 March all the BRICS, including India, were put in a difficult situation; for them to vote 'no' would be to upset relations not only with the West but with much of the Arab world too. Indeed, Brazil, Russia and China all acknowledged the importance of the LAS's position when explaining why they abstained. India didn't, which is somewhat perplexing, but Rao's comments nine days earlier confirmed India *intended* to take account of the LAS's desires, suggesting it probably did so on 17 March. Ultimately the hypothesis that the shaping effect of developing-world solidarity logic – in this case solidarity with LAS states – was a strong shaping influence seems correct despite Singh's failure to explicitly mention this in his statement to the Council. Also, on 16 March South Africa broke ranks with the other BRICS; it was reported that U.S. President Obama convinced South Africa's President Jacob Zuma to vote for Resolution 1973 during a telephone call the night before.[70] In other words the BRICS were not just put in a difficult position by the LAS, they were also suddenly split, meaning the only

70 Harry Verhoeven, C.S.R. Murthy and Ricardo Soares de Oliveira, '"Our Identity is Our Currency": South Africa, the Responsibility to Protect, and the Logic of African Intervention', *Conflict, Security and Development* 14:4 (2014), 525.

way for India to maintain solidarity with *all* the BRICS – including the 'defecting' South Africa – *and* the LAS was to abstain and not try to block Resolution 1973. A week before the vote, as noted above, the joint IBSA statement expressed 'aversion' to a military intervention, so perhaps India (and, presumably, the other BRICS – especially Brazil) was a little annoyed with Pretoria on 17 March[71]; but whatever the case might be on this point, it adds further weight to the conclusion that the developing-world solidarity logic was a strong shaping factor.

We can also hypothesise that if India's policy response had been shaped primarily by the variety of enlightened-realist logic which assumes intervention enhances stability, India would have voted for Resolution 1973. But if India's decision had been shaped substantially by the rival interpretation it would have voted 'no'; certainly India had repeatedly warned in the early 2000s that R2P-inspired interventions threatened global stability (see Chapter 3). But if India wanted to improve relations with the West – or at least not damage such – by maintaining the general stance of cautious support for R2P it had adopted by 2010 to present itself as a responsible great power, then abstaining was arguably the best way to achieve such. This analysis adds some additional weight to the finding that enlightened-realist logic played some, albeit a minor, shaping role in India's policy response; more specifically, it probably shaped India away from voting 'yes' fairly strongly (i.e. because India leaned towards the view intervention is destabilising) but not strongly enough to cause it to vote 'no' (i.e. because India didn't want to upset the West too readily).

Finally, if India's policy response had been shaped primarily by hard-realist logic one would expect it to have exercised prudence and not imperil its direct interests (i.e. mainly evacuating citizens but also maintaining good relations with the Gulf Arab LAS members who supply much of India's energy[72]), and also to more generally conserve its scarce resources – diplomatic and material – by avoiding direct involvement in the crisis. Abstaining allowed it to do all these things, suggesting the shaping effect of hard-realist logic was relatively strong. Anger over Gaddafi's gratuitous comments about Kashmir the week before probably also played a part in shaping India's response. But Gaddafi's offer to Indian oil companies on 13 March requires more discussion.

The obvious inference is that Gaddafi tried to buy India's vote. If India had primarily wanted to leverage as many direct benefits as possible out of a desperate Gaddafi then this offer might have constituted a factor inducing India to vote 'no'; India is, after all, increasingly energy-hungry.[73] One way to explain India's

71 Hardeep Puri Singh hinted at India's annoyance in a press interview in March 2012: Vijay Prashad, 'Syria, Libya and the Security Council', *Frontline* 29:5, 10–23 March 2012.

72 U.S. Energy Information Administration, 'India: Overview', *Analysis Briefs*, 26 June 2014.

73 Dhirendra Dwivedi, 'India's Energy Needs in the 21st Century', in Shekha Adhikari and Sanjeev Bhadauria (eds), *India's Security in the 21st Century* (New Delhi: Pentagon Press, 2014).

decision to abstain is to acknowledge this temptation was 'overridden' by the other shaping influences discussed above. But India probably also expected Gaddafi to fall soon and to therefore be in no position to make good on his offer anyway; notably, the oil companies reported that New Delhi had warned them of the 'practical difficulties' of operating in strife-torn Libya.[74] In other words, arguably Gaddafi's desperate bid did not actually shape India towards voting 'no' because the application of hard-realist logic suggested it was an *ephemeral* offer.

The final conclusion seems clear; hard-realist logic shaped India's decision to abstain strongly, anti-imperialist logic – but only the developing-world solidarity and not the 'implacably oppose the West' aspect – was also very important, while soft liberal-democratic logic played only a minor role (and robust liberal-democratic logic was uninfluential). Enlightened-realist logic also might have played some part in shaping the policy response, but not as a factor shaping India to support intervention. Instead, any shaping influence it exerted was on the basis that intervention would undermine not enhance stability, shaping Indian policy in ways which suggested it should oppose – or at least not support – intervention, balanced with some appreciation of the need to avoid antagonising the West too severely.

So much for the relative influence of the various identity discourses and the shaping effects they had on India's policy-response to the Libyan crisis. But this study considers not just the ordinary direction of causation but is also interested in exploring the reflectivist direction which might involve some identity discourses being vindicated while others are discredited. The next and final section does so by considering some Indian reflections which draw lessons from the conduct and outcome of the Libyan crisis.

Reflections on the Libya Intervention

Because Indians reflected on the conduct and outcome of the Libyan intervention from the beginning of April 2011 and continued to do so for several years this section cannot survey each and every contribution. So examples are selected which demonstrate both policy-makers and policy-shapers reflecting on the Libyan crisis and its aftermath (and interviewee responses are presented too). Reflections from April and May 2011 are considered first, followed by those from later in 2011 – especially after Gaddafi's downfall – and on into 2012 and 2013 as Indians reflected on the chaotic mess Libya became. The impact of these ruminations on the relative influence of the various identity discourses is considered at the end of the section. But first, the course of events in Libya after NATO intervened up to the end of 2014 must be examined briefly to provide some context.

NATO air strikes began within hours of Resolution 1973 passing. The near-total destruction by French Rafale fighter jets of a loyalist Libyan armoured column near

74 Sanjay Dutta, 'India Unlikely to Respond to Gaddafi Request for Oilmen to Fill Expat Void', *The Hindu*, 17 March 2011.

Benghazi on 20 March 2011 was arguably consistent with the mandate established by Resolution 1973 – it was directly threatening the city – but on 26 March NATO aircraft attacked retreating Libyan forces in open desert which were not directly threatening civilians.[75] Similar attacks over the next few weeks suggested NATO was exceeding its mandate, and more overt breaches of Resolution 1973 occurred in May when the French air-dropped arms to rebels. Qatar and the UAE soon began to supply arms too and the increasingly well-supplied rebels began to gain the upper hand by mid-2011; in August Tripoli fell and, finally, on 20 October Gaddafi himself was dragged from a drainage ditch and summarily executed by a frenzied mob. NATO's intervention was undoubtedly crucial to this result – as Ben Barry has put it:

> without NATO's attacks … Gadhafi's forces would have defeated the rebels … . Although the rebels achieved modest improvements in fighting power, the principal factor in their victory was the attrition of regime forces, logistics, command and control and infrastructure by NATO attacks.[76]

At first the transition to democracy seemed reasonably smooth; the TNC appointed an interim Cabinet in November 2011, elections were held in July 2012, and the General National Congress (GNC) assumed sovereign authority over Libya on 8 August 2012. But trouble was brewing. In mid-2012 rebel groups flush with arms from Libya joined Islamist militants to overrun most of Northern Mali; they soon fell out and began fighting each other and were ultimately only defeated by French and AU intervention in 2013. The U.S. Ambassador, Christopher Stevens, was also killed by Islamist militants in Benghazi on 12 September 2011. More generally, Libya's government failed to disarm the various anti-Gaddafi militias – and the radical Islamist groups which emerged after Gaddafi's downfall – and the country steadily spiralled into anarchy. By the end of 2014 most GNC members had fled to Benghazi, heavy fighting which virtually destroyed Tripoli's airport left a coalition of Islamists and a militia from Misurata controlling the capital, planes from Egypt and the UEA had bombed them, and remnants of Gaddafi's forces were operating in southern districts. The aftermath of the Libyan crisis has therefore been spectacularly chaotic.

An early reflection on the implications of NATO's intervention was delivered by Brahma Chellaney in early April 2011: this was discussed in Chapter 4 because he spoke to Côte d'Ivoire too, but his article focused on Libya. While he did not mention R2P specifically he expressed general support for humanitarian interventions: if, that is, they were not carried out *selectively*. He feared the West was on this occasion motivated more by 'cold geopolitical calculation' and noted the obvious discrepancy between the West's – and the LAS's – willingness to intervene

---

75 Kareem Fahim and David D. Kirkpatrick, 'Airstrikes Clear Way for Rebels' First Major Advance', *New York Times*, 27 March 2011.

76 'Libya's Lessons', *Survival* 53:5 (2011), 5–14.

in Libya but not in Bahrain in what were ostensibly similar circumstances. He also worried about the potential 'costs ... in the form of rising Islamic extremism and terrorism'.[77]

Ashish Joy considered the implications of NATO's intervention for R2P more directly. He conceded 'the principle is noble' and sometimes intervention is necessary lest tyrants act with impunity and continually undermine stability. But he also claimed R2P 'requires exemplary standards of implementation' because it 'def[ies] national security' (i.e. sovereignty) and he noted, as Chellaney had, that Western powers had:

> turned a blind-eye toward several dictators across the region whose actions were not too different from Gaddafi's .... [While] there is some merit in the argument that it is better to intervene at least selectively rather than not intervening anywhere at all ... selective application of the R2P principle eventually corrodes its importance and effectiveness.[78]

So, only weeks after the intervention had begun some Indians were concluding NATO's operation was a selective application of R2P which would likely damage the norm. The most interesting aspect of these two reflections is the way both are grounded in a mix of liberal-democratic and enlightened-realist logic – they both basically accept R2P-interventions are necessary to protect human rights and to promote stability – but only *if* R2P is applied consistently.

By late April three prominent Indian émigrés reflected on the implications of India's decision to abstain on Resolution 1973. Harsh V. Pant (at King's College, London) wrote 'India claims to be a rising power [but it] ... needs to convince the world it has a legitimate claim to a permanent [UNSC] seat'. He also noted:

> India's decision to "sit on the fence" ... may perhaps arouse the suspicion that the emerging power remains unwilling to contribute to the management of global order. Moreover, the cleavage between India's much touted democratic credentials at home and its lack of leadership on democracy abroad seems to be widening. The world is taking note, especially as democracy is something that Indian leadership often underlines when distinguishing itself from another emerging power – China.[79]

Sumit Ganguly – now a US citizen and a professor at Indiana University – was even more critical. He wrote:

> Bluntly stated, the rationale behind India's position is untenable .... [I]t suggests that India is incapable of taking a clear-cut moral stance against a dictator

77 'Saving Civilians: Murky Geopolitics', *The Hindu*, 6 April 2011.

78 'The Crisis in Libya', *ORF Issue Brief* 28, April 2011, 17.

79 'Libya Exposes New Faultlines in Foreign Policy', *ISN Insights*, 21 April 2011.

> crushing a challenge to his regime. Nor is this an especially pragmatic stance as it puts India at odds with one of its principle strategic allies, the United States.[80]

For his part, Sadanand Dhume distinguished between those Indians who think 'Julian Assange is a modern saint', China should be trusted, the West should not, and Japan and Singapore are 'to be pitied as Western lackeys' – basically the radical-left, anti-Western anti-imperial position – and those who see 'India's interests in more sober terms', namely:

> In this reckoning America underpins the stable and open international order that India needs to fulfil its economic potential … . [China is] a powerful one-party ethno-state with a history of trying to resolve disputes by force … [and] Japan, South Korea and Singapore … immeasurably bettered the lives of their citizens by maintaining close ties with [America]. … With power comes both responsibility and scrutiny.[81]

Dhume is also a naturalised American citizen and the title of his article – 'It's time to Realign India' (with the West, obviously) – says a lot about his basic worldview. All three of these reflections are therefore grounded firmly in enlightened-realist logic: India, they all believed, should support the West (and R2P) to prove itself worthy of permanent elevation to the Security Council, and they also assumed the intervention would go smoothly and therefore enhance stability.

Back home in India others were less critical of New Delhi's policy responses to the Libyan crisis and, crucially, they typically exhibited pessimism regarding the prospects of the intervention. One was Arvind Gupta, a former senior diplomat who was at the time working at the highly influential IDSA; he would later become its Director and, in August 2014, he became the Deputy National Security Advisor (one interviewee described him in 2013 as a very influential policy-shaper with close links to the MEA[82]). Gupta wrote in late April 2011 that 'UNSC decisions always reflect realpolitik' and 'India's abstention … was on pragmatic grounds and not in opposition to R2P per se'. He therefore concluded that abstaining had been prudent, and he was also pessimistic about the prospects of NATO's intervention producing stability. He warned:

> R2P implies that state sovereignty is not absolute and can be violated. In the absence of common understanding what these conditions are … there is the potential for gross misuse … . Frequent use of military interventions in the name of R2P might destabilise the international system and do more harm than good.[83]

80 'A Pointless Abstention', *The Diplomat*, 23 April 2011.

81 'It's Time to Re-Align India', *Wall Street Journal*, 21 April 2011.

82 I-6, New Delhi, 4 November 2013.

83 'Mind the R2P', *Indian Express*, 22 April 2011.

This reflection demonstrates a clear appreciation of the potential danger posed by the Libyan intervention – to India's interests, but also to general global stability – and the wider implications should an under-specified R2P norm which is open to abuse become too entrenched. Gupta was clearly not especially convinced by liberal-democratic nor anti-imperial logic, and his contribution instead reflects hard-realism and enlightened-realism (namely, the variety which suspects intervention undermines stability).

Sanjeev Shrivastav, also at the IDSA, agreed New Delhi's abstention had been reasonable given 'domestic socio-political realities' and the need to maintain good relations with the West. But he also agreed with several other scholars – Kanti Bajpai and G. Parthasarathy – that the intervention may fuel Islamic extremism and general instability with negative consequences for India. He then noted India had acted responsibly on other international issues – by, for example, aligning against Iran's nuclear programme – but he also suggested 'the domestic constituency must be prepared through intense ... public debate' before India can consistently take similar stands (i.e. aligning with the West on any international issue).[84]

Raja Mohan directly addressed India's stance on R2P and the Libyan crisis in April 2011. He attacked leftists again for wanting India to return to a 'sterile' non-alignment posture, and elements of the government for pandering to them. But he also concluded India's abstention on 17 March had been reasonable given its limited resources, its 'strategic culture, which is very risk averse', and the possibility the intervention may 'leave the region in a far worse condition than before' which would not be in India's or, indeed, anyone's interests (he somewhat presciently, as it turned out, mentioned Somalia as an example of what might happen in Libya). He ultimately concluded 'the foreign policy establishment's reactions were clinical and entirely non-ideological', and therefore correct, although he also warned 'Delhi will be called upon to contribute more' to maintaining global stability in future, and that 'this debate is long overdue'.[85]

Both Mohan's and Shrivastav's reflections were therefore similar: both were basically grounded in hard-realist logic in the context of the *Libyan crisis* in the sense that India had been right to avoid entanglement and thereby avoid both spending its scarce resources and the possibility of suffering blowback. But they also both urged New Delhi pursue, or at least debate and prepare the public for, future policies shaped by enlightened-realist logic; in other words, they wanted India to contribute responsibly to international issues and avoid knee-jerk anti-Westernism. But both worried the intervention in Libya may not go smoothly, meaning their positions were relatively nuanced; they suspected the West had gotten it wrong *on this occasion*, but not that it always had or would do so.

So much for reflections delivered soon after NATO's intervention began; the Indian commentariat largely fell silent until later in 2011 when it looked

84 'India's response to the Libyan Crisis', *IDSA Issue Brief*, 13 April 2011, 7.

85 'India, Libya', 7–9.

like Gaddafi might fall. The policy-makers in New Delhi were also relatively quiet; as noted above, the MEA and the External Affairs Minister had condemned NATO's operations in the weeks immediately after 17 March, but the government offered no formal statements in April. Then on 4 May Hardeep Puri Singh addressed the Security Council and declined to condemn NATO. But a few days later, on 10 May, Singh addressed the Council again during an Open Debate on the Protection of Civilians norm. He endorsed Pillar I of R2P – he said 'it has been India's consistent view that the foremost responsibility of every State is to protect its population' – but some later comments were clearly made with Libya in mind:

> Protection of civilians when applied as a basis for Security Council action needs to respect … [the] sovereignty and integrity of the Member States. Any decision to intervene that is associated with political motives distracts from the noble principles and needs to be avoided … . [T]he principle of protecting civilians must be applied in a uniform manner … . [T]he United Nations has a mandate to intervene only in situations where there is a threat to international peace and stability.

His next words were especially revealing and must be understood in the context of continued unhappiness in New Delhi about NATO's intervention:

> I cannot but ask *quis custodiet ipsos custodies*? Who watches the guardians? There is a considerable sense of unease about the manner in which the humanitarian imperative of protecting civilians has been interpreted.[86]

So, seven weeks after NATO started operations in Libya, India was clearly unhappy with the way Resolution 1973 was being implemented, and Singh was explicitly criticising 'wide' or 'generous' interpretations of R2P. In other words, India was telling the world it was worried R2P – or at least the way its Pillar III was being implemented in Libya, namely as a 'license for regime change' – threatened global stability.

Over the next few months India addressed the Council regularly when the growing Syrian crisis was discussed; these statements are examined in detail in Chapter 6, but India typically warned that a narrow interventionist resolution might be interpreted widely by Western states. In particular, on 3 August 2011 India's Presidential Statement about Syria condemned the al-Assad regime's attacks on civilians but deliberately used language which could not in any way be interpreted as endorsing robust intervention of the sort which might lead to regime change. Several policy-shapers attributed India's reticence to the lessons it had drawn from NATO's conduct in Libya, namely, that Western states couldn't be

86 S/PV.6531.

trusted to not exceed Council mandates and that interventions of this type tended to undermine stability.[87]

Regarding Libya, India only recognised the TNC as the legitimate government on 16 September 2011 as Gaddafi's regime was visibly teetering, making it one of the very last states to do (and after China), saying much about how uncomfortable New Delhi was with the whole Libyan situation by that point. *The Hindu* reported that unnamed 'officials in Delhi' had expressed 'misgivings about the manner in which the West twisted the UNSC mandate to protecting civilians into one of regime change', and one was quoted as saying:

> India does not buy the argument that now NATO, UNSC and the West have got together everything will be rosy in Libya. The real problem ... would stem from the heavy flow of arms into Libya, led by the French.[88]

Then on 24 September 2011 India's Prime Minister Manmohan Singh addressed the General Assembly in New York and said:

> the observance of the rule of law is as important in international affairs as it is within countries. Societies cannot be reordered from outside through military force .... The international community has a role to play assisting in the processes of transition and institution building, but the idea that prescriptions have to be imposed from outside is fraught with danger ... [T]he United Nations must respect the unity, territorial integrity, sovereignty and independence of individual states. Correspondingly, governments are duty bound to their citizens to create conditions that enable them to freely determine their pathways to development.[89]

So, while Manmohan Singh gave a nod to Pillar I of R2P, he clearly communicated India's unhappiness with the looming regime change in Libya. He did not specifically say India expected it to go badly, but he did suggest strongly that it set a dangerous precedent. New Delhi had clearly made up its mind; it was deeply unhappy with the conduct of the intervention and strongly suspected that the outcome would be destabilising. Only days before Gaddafi's death, for example, the MEA told reporters India believed NATO was seeking 'regime change, which was against the spirit of the United Nations charter'.[90]

It was therefore not surprising that New Delhi responded to news of Gaddafi's death on 20 October 2011 with thinly-veiled indignation over the West's part in it. Journalists reported 'India's distaste for imposed external solutions' and that 'diplomats said they expected France, the UK, Italy and the US to reap [the] initial

---

87 'Deteriorating in Syria', *The Hindu*, 5 August 2011; Ravi Shankar, 'Arab Spring, American Winter, and Santa Obama', *The Hindu*, 6 August 2011.

88 Sandeep Dikshit, 'India Recognises Libyan Rebels', *The Hindu*, 17 September 2011.

89 A/66/PV.22.

90 'India to Help Libya Rebuild Economy', *New Indian Express*, 20 October 2011.

harvest of oil contracts'.[91] India did vote for a series of resolutions in late October and early November which unwound the sanctions, rescinded the authorisation for foreign forces to protect civilians, and tried to exert some control over the weapons used in the conflict.[92] But when Hardeep Puri Singh spoke about the last matter on 2 November he called it 'a major problem posing a threat to the stability of Libya [and] the larger region'.[93]

After Gaddafi's fall a flurry of reflections from Indian policy-shapers appeared which considered the wider implications of what had just happened. Some, like Preeti Nalwa (an intern at the IDSA), celebrated Gaddafi's fall enthusiastically; she concluded that 'military intervention was indispensable' because 'a peaceful resolution … was impossible'.[94] But few others were so enthusiastic. For example Atul Aneja, who in February had supported Libyans' aspirations to topple Gaddafi and establish a liberal democracy, was at best cautiously optimistic; he also warned that 'tensions between the Islamists and the secularists run high' and 'Libya is awash with unaccounted weapons'.[95] And while R.S. Kalha concluded the outcome was on balance a good one for Libya's people, he also expressed a great deal of caution, noting 'an earlier example, Iraq … is not very encouraging'.[96]

Most of the immediate reactions to Gaddafi's death, however, reflected fiercely anti-Western anti-imperialist logic. Unsurprisingly, various left-parties reacted very angrily: the CPI(M) called NATO's actions 'sheer hypocrisy' given Western support for other 'despotic regimes'; the Communist Party of India noted Gaddafi 'was once a fighter against imperialist powers' whose failure to carry out 'political reforms at an appropriate time' should not have condemned him to such an ignominious death; and the Communist Party of India (Marxist-Leninist) called NATO's intervention 'yet another instance when the imperialist quest for oil and strategic dominance was projected as support for democratic regime-change'.[97] But far-left Indian parties weren't alone in expressing outrage at Gaddafi's death; one story in the English-language press reported on a wave of pro-Gaddafi and anti-Western sentiment in India's Urdu press which printed somewhat implausible assessments like 'Gaddafi … was pitted against NATO, not his rebels. The people of Libya were with him till his end'.[98] These constitute relatively rare[99] examples of a more tightly-focused, ethnic-based identity – in

91 Sandeep Dikshit, 'India hopes peace will soon return to Libya', *The Hindu*, 20 October 2011.

92 S/RES/2016 (2011); S/RES/2017 (2011); S/RES/2022 (2011).

93 S/PV.6647, 2 November 2011.

94 'Gaddafi's Death: Mission Accomplished!', *IDSA Comment*, 29 October 2011.

95 'Libya Begins Risky Transition', *The Hindu*, 2 November 2011.

96 'Post-Gaddafi Libya: What Happens Next?', *IDSA Comment*, 19 November 2011.

97 'Let Libyans Decide, Say Left Parties', *The Hindu*, 22 October 2011.

98 Seema Chishti, 'Colonel's End', *Indian Express*, 28 October 2011.

99 This study focused on English language sources, meaning pro-Gaddafi sentiment might have been more common than is assumed herein.

this case a Muslim, or at least an Urdu-speaking[100] identity – contributing to the public debates.

One article said NATO's intervention had been justified 'on the pretext of protecting civilians'[101]; another savaged the 'sorry saga of violent regime change' disingenuously portrayed by the West 'ostensibly as a "humanitarian intervention"' and asked 'does the West want democracy in Libya or just any friendly regime that will give it access to the country's oil?'.[102] *Frontline* also took a very critical stance; Aijaz Ahmad's article in the wake of Gaddafi's downfall was titled 'Libya Recolonised' and he described NATO's intervention as 'filthy … human rights imperialism' and declared 'Empire goes where oil is'[103]; while John Cherian characterised NATO's intervention as just the first stage in a 'neocolonial' project which aimed at dominating access to other African states' resources.[104] The stridently anti-Western variety of anti-imperialist logic was therefore very common immediately after Gaddafi's downfall.

Some reflections which drew lessons for India concluded New Delhi had been embarrassed by the outcome in Libya. The deteriorating situation in Syria also led many policy-shapers to begin mixing advice about what India should do there with reflections on Libya. For example, Indrani Bagchi warned 'India's positions on Libya, Syria and Palestine – and increasingly Iran – draw scorn from Washington's administration elite' which was worrying for India's long-term interests and meant India should seriously consider supporting an intervention in Syria to repair its relations with the West.[105] Druhva Jaishankar also felt India should put its unease with what had happened in Libya aside and support intervention in Syria because with:

> considerable diplomatic capital being invested in a bid for permanent UN Security Council membership, India should be better attuned to the expectations which that privilege entails. Abstaining on key decisions as a UNSC member is hardly a marker of leadership … . With an eye on the future, setting a precedent for intervention on dire humanitarian grounds may be prudent.[106]

And Chinmaya Gharekhan speculated if:

---

100 Urdu is spoken by many Indian Muslims – it is a variety of Hindi with many Persian loan-words – although not all Indian Muslims speak it (e.g. Bengali is spoken more widely amongst Muslims in the state of West Bengal).

101 'Colonel's End', *Indian Express*, 22 October 2011.

102 'The Killing of Qadhafi', *The Hindu*, 22 October 2011.

103 *Frontline* 28:23, 5–18 November 2011.

104 'Scramble for Africa', *Frontline* 28:23, 5–18 November 2011.

105 'Bush-Era Warmth Over? US Seen Drifting from India', *Times of India*, 10 November 2011.

106 'Rocky Road to Damascus', *Indian Express*, 16 November 2011.

> Syria is heading for a civil war, a case could be made for abstention, since we would not like to take sides … . [But] if the Arab League were to make a formal request for sanctions, it would be difficult for us not to support them … . The people of India rightly want … an 'independent' foreign policy, but 'independence' should not mean merely a policy different from that of western powers. 'Genuine' independence calls for an approach designed to protect and further our interests, irrespective of whom it pleases or displeases.[107]

These sorts of reflections were obviously informed by the variety of enlightened-realist logic which assumes India should support R2P to secure side-benefits (they also implicitly assume intervention enhances stability). Others came to substantially the same conclusion – that India should support intervention in Syria – but from liberal-democratic premises. For example, several months later Meenakshi Ganguly, who had argued India should have supported intervention back in March, conceded 'some argue' NATO had 'misused the Libyan resolution', although she still urged India not to 'hide in the shadow of Russia' and to 'back Syria's people'.[108] One anonymous author felt the lesson for India should be that:

> intervention is one of the thorniest international issues … . Cynics say it is a throwback to imperialism. The more nuanced argue it is consequence of a post-sovereign concept … in which rights of the individual matter more than raison d'etat. India … has been a stout defender of sovereignty [and] is likely to remain so … . However, as … its own cross-border interests expand, New Delhi may wish to take a new look … . [and consider whether] intervention would help improve regional stability, would seek to measure popular support for such action and would consider the admixture of interests of nearby countries. This would not be an easy matrix to work out, but it is the sort of thing that is expected of a country of global significance … . The day will come, one suspects, when India will have to contemplate intervention in its own interests and it would be sensible to have the rules laid out well before hand.[109]

This author, whose contribution was remarkably sophisticated given the fact that it was delivered in a relatively short newspaper op-ed article, was obviously influenced by a mixture of liberal-democratic and enlightened-realist logic (i.e. the variety which assumes intervention might enhance stability).

Others, however, preferred the variety of enlightened-realism which assumed intervention *was* destabilising. For example, Saeed Naqvi claimed 'the scene is now set for a first class conflict within Islam (including Libya) stretching from Pakistan right across the Arab world [which] … will spill over as terrorism

107 'Slow but Certain Descent into Chaos', *The Hindu*, 19 November 2011.

108 'Back Syria's People, not Assad Regime', *Asian Age*, 3 February 2012.

109 'Lay Down the Rules Now', *Hindustan Times*, 22 October 2011.

abroad'[110]; others, like Sameena Hameed in late 2011, warned the Arab uprisings – including that in Libya – would likely 'ultimately be hijacked by Islamist forces'[111]; while Brahma Chellaney worried in early 2012 that events were taking an ominous turn because sectarianism and extremism were rising in post-Gaddafi Libya and across the region more generally.[112] And occasional reflections on India's role were informed by hard-realist logic, like Rohan Mukherjee's piece which concluded the Congress-led government's cautious approach had avoided upsetting both Muslims abroad who supply India's energy and Muslims at home who vote for it. India, he thought, should continue to 'not over-extend itself globally while trying to manage daunting challenges at home', meaning it should stay on the sidelines vis-à-vis Syria too.[113]

As Libya became ever-more anarchical over 2012 and 2013 the tenor of debate shifted markedly. Sameena Hameed, with the benefit of two years' hindsight, felt vindicated: under the title 'International Community should Desist from Attempting to Tip the Balance', she wrote 'Libya is infested with numerous armed militant groups, many of whom are "Salafists", some of whom killed the US Ambassador', and they were now destabilising Mali too.[114] A number of academic articles which drew lessons from the Libyan intervention directly relevant to the R2P norm itself began to appear. Dipankar Banerjee worried about the damage done to R2P itself:

> Libya became a test case for R2P and Resolution 1973 laid down the provisions of intervention. Regrettably, most of these were violated … . Instead, the focus was on bringing about regime change. … While there is agreement on international responsibility for protecting civilians … there is insufficient clarity over the means.[115]

The thesis that 'R2P-inspired interventions cause chaos' therefore steadily gained ground amongst Indian scholars.[116] By 2013 academic articles were appearing with titles like 'The "Spring" has had Contagious Effect Much Beyond'[117] and 'Fallout

---

110 'West Sets up the War Within Islam', *Observer Research Foundations – Analysis*, 24 October 2011.

111 'India Needs to Move from "Mild" to "Middle"', *Indian Foreign Affairs Journal* 6:2 (2011), 143.

112 'Lull after the Storm', *Hindustan Times*, 19 February 2012.

113 'Redefining Responsibility', *Pragati: The Indian National Interest*, 3 September 2011.

114 *Indian Foreign Affairs Journal* 8:2 (2013), 167–177.

115 'Responsibility to Protect: China's Version', *Institute for Peace and Conflict Studies – Article*, 14 November 2013.

116 Sandipani Dash, 'Responsibility to Protect: The Case of Libya', *Indian Council of World Affairs – Issue Brief*, 4 December 2012, 5; A. Gopinathan, 'The Arab Spring: Supporting Transition to Democracy', *Indian Foreign Affairs Journal* 7:4 (2012), 428.

117 Gulsham Dietl, *Indian Foreign Affairs Journal* 8:2 (2013), 134–141.

of the "Arab Spring": Challenges for India'. This last article concluded that while Western meddling was not wholly to blame, it had contributed significantly to making Libya ungovernable, destabilised several neighbouring states, exacerbated the Shia-Sunni split, energised political Islam and cemented authoritarianism in the Gulf.[118]

These scholars, when they considered India's role in the Libyan conflict, typically concluded New Delhi had been right to stay on the sidelines and reported that policy-makers' unhappiness with the conduct and outcome of the Libyan crisis in late 2011 had only deepened and hardened since then. For example, Sandipani Dash noted at the end of 2012 that R2P 'can be selectively used by the interventionist dominant powers to orchestrate regime change [and] cause destabilisations in societies already riddled with conflict. The misuse of the R2P principle evokes valid concerns from India'. He also quoted Hardeep Puri Singh to the effect 'the Libyan case has already given R2P a bad name' back in New Delhi.[119] Banerjee has written that, following Libya, India's stance against Pillar III-type interventions strengthened considerably,[120] and Manmohan Bahdur has made the same point,[121] as have Ian Hall,[122] Kudrat Virk,[123] and Jaganathan and Kurtz.[124]

The interviewees, when asked at the end of 2013, overwhelmingly told a similar story. All of the 18 who were asked agreed the conduct and outcome of the Libyan campaign had created a negative impression of R2P in India. All 18 believed the Indian government would be more wary of supporting similar future interventions because New Delhi viewed the R2P norm – or at least Pillar III – as dangerously destabilising and wanted to prevent further similar precedents accumulating. Four others also offered, unprompted, their view that New Delhi now assumed Islamist extremism was likely to flourish if further interventions in the Middle East took place given what had occurred in Libya. It is worth noting too that the interviewees – reflecting a general trend noticeable in the press and arguably in formal government statements as well – typically failed to distinguish between the Three Pillars of R2P. In other words, while technically speaking one might conclude Indians were unhappy with Pillar III alone, the interviewees tended to talk of unhappiness with the whole of the R2P norm, except when they were prompted by the author of this book to make a distinction.

---

118 Ranjit Gupta, *Indian Foreign Affairs Journal* 8:2 (2013), 142–155.

119 'Responsibility to Protect: The Case of Libya', *Indian Council of World Affairs – Issue Brief*, 4 December 2012.

120 Dipankar Banerjee, 'India and R2P: Reconciling the Tension Between Intervention and State Sovereignty', in *The Responsibility to Protect – From Evasive to Reluctant Action?* (Johannesburg: United Litho, 2012), 102.

121 'Interventionism and Human Security', *Strategic Analysis* 38:1 (2014), 7.

122 'Tilting at Windmills', 107.

123 'India and the Responsibility to Protect: A Tale of Ambiguity', *Global Responsibility to Protect* 5:1 (2013), 83.

124 Madhan Mohan Jaganathan and Gerrit Kurtz, 'Singing the Tune of Sovereignty? India and the Responsibility to Protect', *Conflict, Security and Development* 14:4 (2014), 475.

Just a few specific interviewee responses are worth exploring. I-1 said 'India was basically supportive of Resolution 1973 – until it turned into a blatant regime change – then it reinforced suspicions that R2P was just the old humanitarian intervention thing all over again'.[125] I-2 said 'Libya definitely undermined support in India for R2P, it exposed Western interests, it showed R2P was just a fig-leaf for Western hegemonic economic concerns'.[126] I-3 noted 'India was upset: it now assumes military interventions will be regime changes, inevitably, and it doesn't want to be associated with that'.[127] I-4 said the aftermath of Libya had 'reinforced India's preference for caution, and now many at the MEA view R2P through an "Islamist terror lens", which really preoccupies them and doesn't bode well for R2P in South Block'.[128] The list could go on – all 18 responses were substantially similar – but one more is worth noting. I-17 stated:

> Indians love to talk up democracy, and they really do mean it – they are very committed to it – and despite all sorts of specific problems all over the country and every day they are also committed to human rights. But at *home*. So, when the West intervenes in a place like Libya they revert to type and sagely say to each other "look, we were right to be sceptical of R2P!". The parliamentary debate was a classic example. And the aftermath – all the violence, the *jihadis* and so on – has led to Indians becoming even more indignant that their warnings were ignored; after all they love, like anyone does I suppose, to wag their finger at the always so superior Americans and French and so on, and say "I told you so!"[129]

Conclusion: Lessons Learned from the Libyan Crisis

The overwhelming conclusion is very clear; when Indians reflected on the conduct and outcome of the Libyan crisis with the benefit of hindsight they typically concluded it had been the wrong thing to do, that India was right to have not supported it, and that R2P is on balance a destabilising norm. Interestingly, the Indian government basically took this position all along, or at least after 17 March 2011; after expressing concern in the lead up to the vote on Resolution 1973, immediately after this date India began condemning NATO's air strikes, it continued to express ever-growing disquiet through the middle months of 2011, and even when Gaddafi fell in late October it refrained from celebrating and some of its officials were heard muttering – by the press – that the Western states who intervened had been 'oil hungry' and deceitful (or maybe just naïve).

125 New Delhi, 30 October 2013.

126 New Delhi, 30 October 2013.

127 New Delhi, 1 November 2013.

128 New Delhi, 5 November 2013. I.e. the wing of the Cabinet Secretariat in New Delhi where the MEA is located.

129 New Delhi, 13 December 2013.

By contrast, despite the fact that some of the reflections offered by policy-shapers in late 2011 were angry with the fall of Gaddafi and blamed India's government's failure to oppose NATO more forcefully, and a few others defended India's stance throughout to greater and lesser degrees, quite a few reflections at this early stage (i.e. soon after Gaddafi's fall) concluded India should probably have supported the intervention, or they drew the lesson that India should in future at least consider supporting similar interventions (especially in Syria, which was being discussed a lot at the time). But reflections of this nature substantially disappeared later in 2012 and thereafter as post-Gaddafi Libya spiralled into chaos. The overwhelming impression one gets from these later reflections is that New Delhi was both right to abstain in March 2011, and then also right to basically oppose the intervention thereafter, even if only rhetorically and diplomatically.

This has obvious implications for the relative shaping influence of the various identity discourses vis-à-vis one another. For one, hard-realist logic was strongly vindicated; India had safely extracted its citizens and had avoided expending resources by not actively supporting the intervention, and this decision had not otherwise damaged its interests. For another, the variety of enlightened-realism which assumes R2P *undermines* not enhances stability clearly became ascendant over the variety which assumes the opposite; the anarchy and chaos which followed NATO's intervention seemed to conclusively indicate that interventions, or at least robust military interventions leading to regime change, were likely to cause severe instability. And the anti-imperialist identity discourse – both aspects, the 'don't trust the West' and the 'show solidarity with the developing world' – had undeniably been vindicated; the West had shown it couldn't be trusted to stay within the bounds of a Council resolution, and India's alignment with its partners in IBSA and the key regional organisation, the LAS, had been strengthened over the course of the crisis. Conversely, substantial damage had been done to the perceived credibility and validity of the liberal-democratic identity discourse, particularly to the robust variety which contemplates or allows for the application of military force to protect human rights and promote democracy. This obviously had negative consequences for the prospects of India becoming a strong supporter of Pillar III and, arguably, of the whole R2P norm given the general tendency of Indians to not distinguish between its components.

But these findings also have implications for the way India reacted to the crisis in Syria which was running concurrently with the Libyan crisis (and its aftermath) through 2011 and 2012, and in turn the situation in Syria had implications for policy-shapers' and policy-makers' views on R2P too. Accordingly, a fuller account of the relative influence of the various identity discourses as shapers of Indian policy responses in humanitarian crisis cannot be made until after India's engagement with the crisis in Syria has been considered, which takes place in the next chapter.

Chapter 6
India and the Crisis in Syria

This chapter considers India's engagement with the humanitarian crisis in Syria. Given what was just said in Chapter 5 about Indians' reflections on the Libyan intervention one might expect India to have consistently opposed any and all efforts to intervene in Syria. But that is not exactly what happened.

While India did oppose any suggestion of intervention in 2011, it flirted with interventionism during the first half of 2012; to be sure, these flirtations were with two draft Security Council resolutions which, if they had passed, would have authorised forms of intervention falling well short of military intervention leading to regime change. But India nevertheless voted for them, which remains significant. By the end of 2012, however, India had reverted to opposing any form of intervention past applying diplomatic pressure on Syria's al-Assad regime. After leaving the Council India continued to oppose intervention – even after the chemical weapons attack in August 2013 – but it finally supported (if only in a very limited manner) a foreign intervention to combat Islamic State (IS) in the second half of 2014. One might say India's position towards *intervention* became somewhat more nuanced during the course of the Syrian crisis, although its position on the R2P norm changed little; in other words, New Delhi would only support the aspects of R2P which were compatible with the sovereignty norm (i.e. Pillars I and II) while it remained staunchly opposed to Pillar III, and only the emergence of a clear, relatively *traditional* security threat – the one posed by IS – could induce it to acquiesce to foreign military intervention in a sovereign state (i.e. Iraq, and tacitly in Syria too, at least to some extent).

Three key Indian policy-responses to the Syrian crisis are subjected to close analysis below: the Security Council Presidential Statement on 3 August 2011 (issued by India) and the Council vote on 4 October 2011 are considered together; then the crucial Council votes on 4 February 2012 and 19 July 2012 are considered in turn. The analytical method deployed in Chapters 4 and 5 is utilised again, namely, commentary and advice about the crisis offered by policy-shapers is examined first, then New Delhi's policy-response is considered, then informed speculation about the likely relationship between policy-shapers' advice and India's policy-responses follows, while some reflections by commentators on each of these policy-responses round out each section. Because this process is undertaken three times the chapter is relatively long. And while India continued to engage with events in Syria after leaving the Council it did not vote formally or offer detailed explanations for its policy-responses, making it difficult to analyse them as closely as the earlier ones; accordingly, the 2013–2014 period is covered relatively succinctly. But before the analysis proper can begin some background is required.

Background to the Syrian Crisis (Before October 2011)

The Syrian crisis was obviously connected to the wider Arab Spring unrest. Small protests took place in January and February 2011 but in early March, in Daraa, 15 young boys who had been spray-painting anti-government graffiti were arrested, tortured and summarily executed by police. This provided a spark analogous to the arrest of Jamal al-Hajji in Libya; anger erupted in Daraa, provoking a violent response on 18 March by security forces which only intensified the confrontations. By 22 April protests had broken out in 20 cities. Government forces typically reacted with brutality and by the end of May 2011 over 1,000 people were dead.[1] The initial demands for reform inexorably transformed into a campaign to overthrow Bashar al-Assad's regime. By July army defectors had formed the Free Syrian Army (FSA) which began to offer more sustained resistance, and by September 2011 a full-blown insurgency had erupted all over the country.

It is important to note several broad differences between the Libyan and the Syrian crises. First, the temporal and internal geographical dynamics were different. While the Libyan crisis erupted fast – within weeks rebels had captured the eastern third of the country[2] – stability in Syria degenerated more slowly and uprisings were more scattered. Second, while Libya is divided to some degree along tribal lines it is still predominantly Arab ethnically-speaking and overwhelmingly Sunni in faith; the situation inside Syria is very different. Third, the al-Assad regime was far less diplomatically isolated than Gaddafi had been. Finally, the diplomatic dynamics in key international institutions were very different. Each of these last three points is discussed in turn.

The Syrian crisis began at least in part as – and it has definitely since become – a sectarian conflict.[3] At its simplest, it pits the Sunni majority (about 75 per cent of the pre-war[4] population) against the dominant Alawite minority (12 per cent of the population; they follow a variety of Shia Islam). The French colonial authorities deliberately promoted minorities – especially Alawites – into key institutions like the army and the al-Assad regime intensified this policy.[5] Sunni Arabs, in turn, resented their marginalisation: Robert Kaplan has described the ascent to power of Hafez al-Assad in 1970 as akin to 'an untouchable becoming Maharajah in India'.[6] In February 1982 Sunnis rose up in Hama, provoking a devastating government response which killed over 10,000 people.

---

1 'Syria protests: Rights group warns of "Deraa massacre"', *BBC News*, 5 May 2011.

2 There were also important uprisings in western districts but these were either largely contained (i.e. in Misurata) or put down (i.e. in Zawiya) early in the crisis.

3 Robert G. Rabil, 'Syria and the Power of Sectarian Strife', *National Interest*, 2 July 2012.

4 Syria's demographics have now changed radically: of a pre-crisis population of 19 million around 3 million were refugees in neighbouring states and perhaps 6 million were internally displaced when 2014 ended.

5 Ted G. Carpenter, 'Tangled Web: The Syrian Civil War and Its Implications', *Mediterranean Quarterly* 24:1 (2013), 2.

6 'Syria: Identity Crisis', *The Atlantic*, 1 February 1993.

But Syria's demographics are actually much more complex: about 12 per cent are Christians of various ethnicities (Assyrian, Aramean, Armenian), about 3 per cent are Druze, 9 per cent are Sunni Kurds, and perhaps as much as 4 per cent of the population are Sunni Turks or Sunni Circassians too; so, a good proportion of Syria's Sunnis are not ethnic Arabs. These minorities have generally remained loyal to al-Assad, although many individuals joined the rebels and some Kurdish districts expelled government forces from their homelands (but then didn't actively fight regime forces in other regions). The early Sunni Arab versus Alawite dynamic also later devolved into a complex kaleidoscope of conflict as the rebels fractured into FSA-aligned secular groups and Islamists, making it a confusing struggle with (at least) three sides.[7]

Geopolitically, the situation is very different to that which prevailed vis-à-vis the Libyan crisis; as Ted Carpenter has put it, 'domestic divisions in [Syria] are very real and are the prime driver for the fighting, but regional rivalries also play an important role'.[8] Iran is the primary backer of the al-Assad regime, which has meant that Sunni states have generally backed the rebels and thereby grasped the opportunity to check and (hopefully, from their perspective) roll back Iran's (alleged) hegemonic regional ambitions which rest in part on supporting al-Assad.[9] Western states have also backed the rebels, although typically only with 'non-lethal' military equipment and this is also typically directed towards the FSA and not the Islamist rebel groups (to extent this is possible; rebel groups have pooled or traded resources at times). On the other hand Russia has supported al-Assad strongly. Direct interests in part explain this, but Russia's relationship with the West fractured more generally around this time; the split manifested itself most starkly in Ukraine in 2014,[10] but the confrontational dynamic gained real momentum after the Libyan crisis. Russia essentially concluded the West uses R2P to in effect 'pick off' anti-Western states, including Russian allies like al-Assad, meaning Russia has basically drawn its proverbial line in the sand against R2P in Syria.[11] China, too, had serious misgivings about R2P after Libya and it

7 Fred Dews, 'A Glossary of Forces in the Syrian Civil War', *Brookings Institute*, 27 May 2014.

8 Carpenter, 'Tangled Web', 4. Also see: Caitlin A. Buckley, 'Learning from Libya, Acting in Syria', *Journal of Strategic Security* 5:2 (2012), 91.

9 Hillel Fradkin and Lewis Libby, 'Why Sunnis Fear Shiites', *Commentary Magazine*, 20 December 2013; Carpenter, 'Tangled Web', 4, Buckley, 'Learning', 89–91; Saeed Naqvi, 'The Storm in the Arab Spring', *Observer Research Foundation – Discourse* 5:15, February 2012.

10 John J. Mearsheimer, 'Why the Ukraine Crisis Is the West's Fault: The Liberal Delusions That Provoked Putin', *Foreign Affairs* 93 (September/October 2014), 77–89.

11 Samuel Charap, 'Russia, Syria and the Doctrine of Non-Intervention', *Survival* 55:1 (2013), 35–41; Alex J. Bellamy, 'From Tripoli to Damascus? Lesson Learning and the Implementation of the Responsibility to Protect', *International Politics* 51:1 (2014), 23–44; J. Craig Barker, 'The Responsibility to Protect: Lessons from Libya and Syria', in Robert P. Barnidge (ed.), *The Liberal Way of War: Legal Perspectives* (Farnham: Ashgate, 2013).

routinely cast its veto with Russia's whenever the Syria crisis came before the Security Council (although China has assiduously avoided direct involvement).

These regional and global dynamics largely paralysed key international institutions in 2011. Western powers first proposed a draft Security Council press-statement condemning Syria's government on 25 April 2011. But the controversy swirling around NATO's intervention in Libya meant consensus was elusive; China, Russia, India, Brazil and South Africa dissented.[12] A draft resolution sponsored by Western states then circulated in May: it charged Syria's government with atrocities and demanded it fulfil its Pillar I responsibilities; but the same states opposed it and it was never voted on.[13] In August and September two further draft resolutions circulated: Britain's called for an arms embargo and asset freeze; and Russia's called on al-Assad to implement the reforms he had promised but did not threaten sanctions. It was a watered-down version of the British proposal that was eventually voted on – and vetoed – on 4 October (see below).

Unhappiness in the LAS with NATO's Libyan intervention also caused it to be much more divided over Syria than it had been vis-à-vis Libya. For example, when it condemned Syria's government in August Lebanon dissented, saying it stood by 'brotherly Syria'.[14] The LAS's position hardened later in 2011 when it became clear al-Assad was failing to implement the reforms he had promised: Syria was formally suspended in November by 18 votes to two (Lebanon and Yemen; with Iraq abstaining); travel bans and asset freezes were imposed; and unarmed LAS monitors were deployed in December. But it took until September 2014 before anything remotely resembling the 12 March 2011 LAS resolution vis-à-vis Libya was issued (and even this did not formally call for foreign military intervention). And as an aside, NATO's Secretary-General Anders Fogh Rasmussen stated clearly in November 'NATO has no intention whatsoever to intervene in Syria. I can completely rule that out'.[15]

So much for the broad outlines of the Syrian crisis before the end of 2011. The next section considers India's two key policy-responses in August and October 2011 as well as the advice about and reflections on these offered by Indian commentators.

India's Engagement with the Syrian Crisis in 2011

Because the crisis in Syria built relatively slowly through 2011 there was no burst of commentary by Indian policy-shapers like that which erupted vis-à-vis

12 'What's in Blue', *Insights on Syria*, Security Council Report, 27 April 2011.

13 Jess Gifkins, 'The UN Security Council Divided: Syria in Crisis', *Global Responsibility to Protect* 4:3 (2012), 382.

14 'Lebanon Stands by "Brotherly Syria" in Rejecting Arab League's Call to End Crackdown', *Haaretz*, 31 August 2011.

15 Kelly McEvers, 'Arab League's Syria Suspension Could Spur UN Action', *NPR*, 12 November, 2011.

Libya earlier in 2011. Instead, interest built slowly and sporadically. The first Indian op-ed article to discuss Syria at length[16] criticised Syria's government for disingenuously promising reforms while 'unleashing … repressive measures' and sympathised with the protesters' demands for 'democracy and freedom'. But the author also dismissed the Western-sponsored draft resolution circulating since May as 'questionable although, unlike the resolution in Libya, this does not call for military intervention. Any attempt to meddle … in Syria can only undermine the legitimacy of the protesters' demands'.[17] So, this contribution reflected soft liberal-democratic logic – mere rhetorical commitment to democracy and human rights – and it argued against intervention not because doing so would be destabilising or play into Western imperialists' hands, but because it would undermine the protesters (a somewhat implausible argument given protesters' repeated pleas for intervention[18]).

A week later Meenakshi Ganguly (from Human Rights Watch) entered the debate, criticising New Delhi's response:

> India [has] accepted the Syrian government's claims at face value … . India should know better … . As an emerging global power that aspires to a permanent seat in the UNSC, New Delhi needs to … speak for people and their aspirations. It can no longer stick to the comfort of 'good relations' with … rulers [who] are despised by their own citizens and have engaged in widespread human rights violations … . It is not only morally right for India to recognise these hopes, it is a prudent investment in the future.[19]

Ganguly was mixing robust liberal-democratic logic (which assumes democracy and human rights should be actively promoted, including by military intervention); enlightened-realist logic (i.e. support for a responsible intervention raises India's profile); and hard-realist logic (i.e. India would benefit from anti-regime forces' gratitude). But Chinmaya Gharekhan, a former senior diplomat and prime ministerial advisor, offered a very different opinion. He first condemned NATO's 'regime change in Tripoli' and charged the West with a 'barely concealed desire for regime change [in Syria] which most non-Western countries find difficult to reconcile with'. He felt:

> it makes sense for India to maintain relative silence on the events in West Asia[20] … [because] we have substantial interests in the region … . We should express

16 Previous op-eds had 'mentioned' unrest in Syria alongside discussion of the Arab Spring more generally.

17 'Syria on the Boil', *The Hindu*, 13 June 2011.

18 Liz Sly, 'Calls in Syria for weapons, NATO intervention', *Washington Post*, 28 August 2011.

19 'India: Speak up For Syrians', *Deccan Chronicle*, 20 June 2011.

20 The typical Indian description of the region Westerners call the Middle East.

> hope that at least some of the aspirations of the people for reform would be satisfied … [and] activate BRICS and/or IBSA and issue common statements agreed through diplomatic channels.[21]

So, Chinmaya's contribution was above all grounded in hard-realist logic, with some evidence of soft liberal-democratic logic and the developing-world solidarity aspect of anti-imperialist logic.

On 3 August 2011 India's UN Ambassador Hardeep Puri Singh issued a Security Council Presidential Statement. These are typically issued when there is insufficient consensus for a formal resolution to pass; they are non-binding, but issuing them requires some degree of consensus (only Lebanon formally dissented). The statement condemned 'the widespread violations of human rights … by the Syrian authorities', but it also strongly reaffirmed Syria's sovereignty and refrained from using R2P-like language entirely. This last point is important: instead of directly referring to Syria's Pillar I responsibilities the way resolutions from earlier in 2011 had (i.e. vis-à-vis both Côte d'Ivoire and Libya), a vaguer call for Syria's authorities to 'comply with their obligations under applicable international law' was issued.[22] This latter phrase was favoured in many of the key UN forums thereafter.[23] A week later an IBSA delegation was dispatched to Syria and upon arrival it declared 'there should not be any military intervention'.[24]

Singh confirmed in a *Frontline* interview six months later that New Delhi had deliberately decided to use the President's Chair to offer a high-profile initiative to break the Council deadlock and he had personally driven negotiations over the statement's wording. He also confirmed 'we stopped short of incorporating Chapter 7' (of the UN Charter; i.e. Article 41 sanctions and Article 42 military measures) to deliver 'a message we have given collectively … through IBSA'. Given the source – India's UN Ambassador – we can be very confident that India's first formal, active policy response to the Syrian crisis in August 2011 was in part shaped by liberal-democratic logic because India was genuinely concerned by the humanitarian situation in Syria. But the developing-world solidarity aspect of anti-imperialist logic was clearly a more influential shaping factor. The influence of the variety of enlightened-realist logic which assumes intervention is destabilising was also apparent: Singh reported that 'the unsettled state of Libya' had shaped India's thinking when it was deciding how to respond to events in Syria.[25]

---

21 'Is the Arab Spring Wishful Thinking?', *The Hindu*, 22 June 2011.

22 S/PRST/2011/16, 3 August 2011.

23 Bellamy notes R2P-like terminology became more frequently used *after* Libya than before (except when Syria was being discussed): 'From Tripoli', 39.

24 'IBSA Delivers Demarche; Syria Admits to "Mistakes"', *New Indian Express*, 10 August 2011.

25 Vijay Prashad, 'Syria, Libya and the Security Council', *Frontline* 29:5, 10–23 March 2012.

In late August the UN Human Rights Council (HCR) resolved to send a fact-finding mission to Syria; India abstained and repeated its view that engaging Syria in 'collaborative and constructive dialogue … is a more pragmatic and productive way forward. This is what India [and] IBSA … has done'. Put simply, India was motivated to 'do something' in August 2011, but not anything which might in any way lead to a regime change, and it was determined to give more time for its diplomatic initiatives to work.[26]

Policy-shapers delivered a flurry of reflections on New Delhi's August 2011 initiatives (which can also be treated, in effect, as offerings of advice given the Security Council's 4 October meeting was approaching). One commentator strongly criticised NATO's intervention in Libya and noted 'Russia, India and Brazil have copped some flak' for blocking similar action in Syria, but judged New Delhi's response so far as 'the right one'.[27] Ravi Shankar also delivered a rambling diatribe – U.S. President Barrack Obama was alternatively called 'Santa', a 'coward' and a 'milksop' – but the crux of his argument was that 'if Syria falls, the Islamic radicals will occupy power', creating 'a tyranny more terrible than the one before it'.[28]

While Shankar was not the first to oppose intervening in Syria because doing so would cause instability, he was the first to specifically claim intervention would empower radical Islamists. Much later some began to wonder whether an early intervention in Syria might have done the opposite by ending the conflict before Islamists became too strong; but in August 2011 many accepted the Libyan intervention had empowered Islamists, so it should not be repeated in Syria. For example, Indrani Bagchi noted:

> at the back of everyone's minds is the realisation that Syria still remains a reasonably secular country … . the removal of Assad … Indian officials say, could open the doors to Sunni extremist groups … . [H]aving Assad in power may well be the "least bad" option.[29]

Yet a few days later Bagchi warned that al-Assad showed no signs of actually pursuing reforms, which 'cuts into the Indian argument'.[30] Meenakshi Ganguly re-entered the debate and noted India's caution was attributable to it being 'anxious about protecting its own sovereignty and anxious about any criticism of its actions in Jammu and Kashmir' and to 'concerns over NATO action in Libya'. But she nevertheless claimed:

---

26 'India's Explanation of Vote in the HRC on the Resolution on Syria', *MEA – Speeches and Statements*, 23 August 2011.

27 'Deteriorating in Syria', *The Hindu*, 5 August 2011.

28 'Arab Spring, American Winter, and Santa Obama', *The Hindu*, 6 August 2011.

29 'US Pushes India, China to put Sanctions on Syria', *Times of India*, 13 August 2011.

30 'Indian Initiative on Syria May Run into Trouble', *Times of India*, 23 August 2011.

> India will have to make choices … . To avoid being labelled an eternal fence-sitter and a democracy that shies away from human rights protection abroad, India should urgently join in international efforts to escalate pressure on the Syrian government. It should take the lead.[31]

Ganguly was not alone in calling for India to pressure Syria's regime, although she was substantially alone in being motivated by robust liberal-democratic logic. For example, one anonymous policy-shaper chided New Delhi for framing its responses with reference to the 'north-south debate' and called for 'clear-eyed analysis, keeping our interests in mind';[32] hard-realist logic informed this contribution because the author assumed al-Assad would fall soon and that India should align itself, now, with his likely replacements.

But the weight of opinion concluded India had been right to act cautiously. Two authors lauded New Delhi for acting as a bridge between the developed and developing worlds and dampening the international acrimony stirred by Libya.[33] Anuradha Chenoy felt New Delhi was right 'to find its own balance' because 'teaming up with the US will have negative consequences for India' given the instability in Libya, but 'India … should [also] create an environment where Syrians can have their own democracy'.[34] Another author lauded Prime Minister Manmohan Singh for his 24 September General Assembly speech which had been very critical of the West's pursuit of regime change in Libya (see Chapter 5), and believed India's cautious approach was the most promising means of stabilising Syria and the region.[35] And Rajendra Abhyankar, a former Ambassador to Syria, pointed to the chaos in Libya as Gaddafi's regime teetered and agreed more time should be given for India's peace initiatives to bear fruit in Syria.[36] All these contributions approved of India's efforts to work through IBSA although, somewhat curiously, none discussed the LAS's initiatives, presumably because they were at the time very similar to IBSA's.

There was also relatively little evidence of contributions to the debates about Syria grounded in stridently anti-Western logic in 2011. The parliament largely ignored the Syrian crisis – both during 2011 and on into 2012 too – presumably because no intervention in Syria took place. There was instead notably more discussion of human rights abuses in Sri Lanka.[37] The Indian papers also didn't

31 'The Road to Damascus', *Hindustan Times*, 23 August 2011.

32 'Getting Real', *Indian Express*, 27 August 2011.

33 'India Bridges Old and New at UN', *Hindustan Times*, 31 August 2011; 'Take the Bull by its Horns', *Hindustan Times*, 4 September 2011.

34 'The Arab Spring and India', *New Indian Express*, 31 August 2011.

35 'Manmohan Singh Slams West for Using Force for Regime Change', *Times of India*, 25 September 2011.

36 'India Should Stay Out of West Asian Politics', *Hindustan Times*, 16 September 2011.

37 For example: Lok Sabha Debate, 15th Series, Vol. XVII, 8th Session, No. 7, 4 August 2011.

report much anti-Western sentiment, although one paper did report the Communist Party of India (Marxist)'s (CPI(M)) views on the Syrian conflict (unsurprisingly, the CPI(M) opposed intervention 'in the name of promoting "democracy"' because the West really wanted to 'control the hydro-carbon resources' despite the fact Syria has little in the way of oil reserves),[38] and in a string of articles written by John Cherian in *Frontline* the West was first accused of wanting to remove one of Israel's most ardent opponents,[39] then called hypocritical for seeking to topple Syria's but not Bahrain's government,[40] and finally judged guilty of hatching a grand conspiracy to dominate the Middle East.[41]

Still, the CPI(M)'s and *Frontline*'s interpretation of the matter was relatively unusual in the context of the wider Indian debates about Syria at this time, because the tenor of the sentiment amongst commentators in August and September 2011 was generally consistent with 'sovereignty-friendly' varieties of the various identity discourses. Soft liberal-democratic logic was clearly discernible – policy-shapers typically felt India should promote democracy and protect human rights rhetorically – but most also opposed intervention. Many also agreed India should maintain tight solidarity within IBSA and give this body's initiatives (with India in the driving seat) more time to work. There was also little discussion of India's direct interests, which is not surprising because India had few in Syria (see below). Instead, enlightened-realist logic was much more apparent (i.e. calls for India to play a bridging role between the developed and developing worlds to raise its international profile, acting cautiously to avoid destabilising the region, etc.).

The first key Security Council vote took place on 4 October. The draft first recalled 'the Syrian Government's primary responsibility to protect its population' – the last time this phrase was used – and other paragraphs noted the Syrian regime's promises to reform (but called for more progress), and commended various diplomatic efforts (including India's) to find a peaceful solution. The draft then demanded the regime stop abusing human rights, demanded the rebels reject extremism, requested – so, did not demand – that states not supply arms to either side, and called for the Council to meet again soon to 'consider its options, including measures under Article 41' (i.e. sanctions).[42]

The draft resolution did not therefore authorise or even threaten armed intervention, but the reference to the *possibility* of future sanctions doomed it. Russia cast its veto and referred repeatedly to NATO exceeding its mandate in Libya, saying 'these types of models [of intervention] should be excluded from global practices once and for all'. China was more circumspect and simply said 'sanctions or the threat thereof does not help … in the present circumstances' after

38 CJ. Manoj, 'India is Poorer?', *Indian Express*, 31 August 2011.

39 'Tough Target', *Frontline* 28:11, 21 May–3 June 2011.

40 'Stoking the Flames', *Frontline* 28:16, 30 July–12 August 2011.

41 'Next, Syria', *Frontline* 28:23, 5–18 November 2011.

42 S/2011/612, 4 October 2011.

it had cast its veto.[43] India abstained, along with Brazil, Lebanon and South Africa. Hardeep Puri Singh noted that India:

> recognises the responsibility of all States to respect the fundamental rights of their people … . [But] states also have the obligation to protect their citizens from armed groups and militants … . [E]ngaging Syria in a collaborative and constructive dialogue and partnership is the only … way forward … . [T]hrough the India-Brazil-South Africa initiative, we have urged restraint … . [We] should give time and space for [Syria's government] to implement the far-reaching reform measures … . [T]he international community should … not complicate the situation by threats of sanctions, regime change, et cetera … . The [draft] resolution [also] … does not condemn the violence perpetrated by the Syrian opposition.[44]

This explanation correlates closely with the prevailing opinions in the public debate; most policy-shapers had opposed intervention and offered advice broadly consistent with sovereignty-friendly varieties of the various identity discourses. This suggests New Delhi's policy-response was being shaped strongly by the variety of enlightened-realist logic which assumed R2P was generally destabilising; for example, Singh claimed the rebels' decision to 'resort to violence' deliberately exceeded 'the right of people to protest' (i.e. he was therefore essentially making the 'moral hazard' argument against R2P, namely, the possibility of foreign intervention induces rebels to 'go for broke' instead of seeking compromise solutions). There is also a hint of a correlation with hard-realist logic in these comments in that India may have had Kashmir in mind. But the correlation between the developing-world solidarity aspect of anti-imperialist logic which featured prominently in the public debates is much clearer given India stressed more time must be given for IBSA's initiatives to work.

Regarding liberal-democratic logic, India did also refer to Pillar I (for the last time) but balanced this against India's belief that Syria's government had a right to fight militants. And while Singh expressed concern about the violence he also stated India deplored 'all violence, irrespective of who its perpetrators are'. There was therefore also some correlation between India's explanation of its abstention with the soft variety of liberal-democratic logic, but the robust or full variety of liberal-democratic logic – represented by Pillar III of R2P – went unmentioned and was, by strong implication, opposed.

The results of hypothesis testing reinforce these findings. If India's decision to abstain had been primarily shaped by the robust variety of liberal-democratic logic it would have voted for the draft resolution. And if it had been shaped strongly by implacable anti-Western logic India would have voted against it. Instead, if it abstained India could maintain solidarity with Brazil and South Africa – and,

43 S/PV.6627, 4 October 2011.

44 Ibid.

by extension, the LAS (recall its position was similar to IBSA's in October 2011; Syria had not yet been expelled from or sanctioned by the LAS). India could also avoid directly opposing the West; according to one paper New Delhi was facing 'heat' from the US, Britain and France over its 'inconsistent' stance on Syria;[45] but another paper reported New Delhi's pleasure when Washington confirmed it still supported India joining the Council permanently despite their positions diverging in the narrower context of what to do about Syria.[46]

Further, if India on 4 October 2011 was aware Russia and/or China would likely veto any draft resolutions featuring interventionist measures – even those falling well short of armed intervention – then New Delhi could consider matters other than the strict effect of its vote on the situation in Syria. In other words, New Delhi could use its vote to shore up diplomatic relationships knowing an abstention would not attract much criticism because the West would direct most of its ire at Russia and/or China. India could indeed expect vetoes; reports from June 2011 suggested Russia would do so,[47] and another report just before 4 October suggested China might join it.[48] Ten of the 11 interviewees who were asked believed India's positions in the three crucial Council votes about Syria in 2011 and 2012 were made at least in part 'strategically', with wider or longer-term diplomatic considerations in mind.

More generally, we can hypothesise that one way of raising India's profile as a responsible power to burnish its credentials as permanent Council member – this remained a key Indian diplomatic objective after all – would be to promote cautious responses hoping they yielded positive results (namely, ending the crisis without an intervention). This would be a relatively risk-free diplomatic strategy given how similar the IBSA/Indian position was to the LAS position in October 2011; in other words, if non-interventionist peace initiatives succeeded India could claim a share of the credit, but if they failed India could retreat into a low profile and avoid the criticism which would likely (and as it turned out, did[49]) attach to the LAS as the premier regional organisation. The Council vote in October took place less than two months after India had launched its August initiative, making it reasonable to ask for more time.

All these considerations – India's desire to not upset the West with outright opposition, to align with its developing-world partners' positions, to seek an end to

45 Shubhajit Roy, 'India Faces Heat Over its "Inconsistent" Stand on Syria', *Indian Express*, 27 August 2011.

46 Chidanand Rajghatta, 'Ditched During Syria Vote, US Still Backs India's UNSC Bid', *Times of India*, 26 August 2011.

47 'Will Block Resolution on Syria: Russia', *The Hindu*, 21 June 2011.

48 'Security Council Divided Over Syria Sanctions', *Hindustan Times*, 1 October 2011.

49 For example, the rebels regularly associated each Friday – traditionally the best-attended day at Mosques – with particular 'issues'; they called the 16th of December 2011 'Friday of the Arab League Is Killing Us'.

the crisis without what it assumed would be a destabilising intervention, to pursue low-risk diplomatic gains while 'hiding' behind the likely Russian and Chinese vetoes and the greater expectations laid on the LAS – are all consistent with the notion that developing-world solidarity logic and enlightened-realist logic (i.e. especially the variety which judged R2P-inspired interventions to be destabilising; and, in this context, diplomatically *risky*) were the strongest shaping factors in India's decision to abstain.

Reflections by Indian commentators after 4 October were generally supportive of India's abstention. For example, Sanjay Kapoor concluded India had been right to want to give the peace initiatives more time to work.[50] Saurabh Mishra also explored various reasons for India's cautious approach – worries about rebels becoming radicalised, avoiding involvement in the deepening Sunni-Shia regional conflict, etc. – and finished with an insight no one else had mentioned yet, namely:

> the difference in the temperament of the leadership in Libya and Syria is visible. Assad seems to be a calculative politician while Gaddafi ... called the protesters cockroaches ... and threatened house-to-house killing ... . [Instead], Assad has been tactful ... . Assad has deliberately toned down at the right moment.[51]

This insight is important because it suggests India – indeed Russia, China, or indeed any actor which opposed intervention in October 2011 – were afforded the sort of 'rhetorical cover' by al-Assad that Gaddafi had so thoughtlessly denied them with his blood-curdling threats (see Chapter 5). Mishra noted India was still upset over Libya, meaning it wanted to prevent more Libya-like precedents accumulating. So, according to him, al-Assad's more restrained behaviour had not put New Delhi in the difficult position it had faced in March 2011 (i.e. being uncomfortable with the implications of Resolution 1973 but also not wanting to align with a bloodthirsty dictator), meaning when the Council considered the Syrian crisis in October 2011 India could follow its instincts, namely, 'respect to the sovereignty and integrity of all nations'.[52]

So, over the course of 2011 Indian policy-shapers had drawn important lessons from the intervention in Libya which caused them to reject robust intervention in Syria; and Indian policy-makers' responses were substantially in conformity. But, as 2011 ended some commentators began to muse about whether a change of course might be necessary given al-Assad seemed uncommitted to reforms and, as a consequence, conditions within Syria were worsening. The next section examines the second key Security Council vote about Syria on 4 February 2012 and shows New Delhi was also reconsidering its position.

---

50 'Syria: At the Threshold', *Observer Research Foundation: Analysis*, 27 October 2011.

51 'Why Syria is not Libya', *IDSA – Comment*, 21 October 2011.

52 'Reading the Veto on Syria', *IDSA – Comment*, 21 October 2011.

India's Engagement with the Syrian Crisis in Early 2012

Late in 2011 Western powers began to seek another Security Council resolution, so Indian policy-shapers offered advice about how New Delhi should react. For example, Dhruva Jaishankar noted that 'based on experiences in its own neighbourhood, India is suspicious about the feasibility of spreading democratic values', but he also wondered whether India should 'reconsider its traditional stances'; his reasons reflected mainly great power logic (i.e. both strains) because he felt aligning with majority opinion in the Arab world – against Syria's al-Assad regime – was generally in India's interests, and 'abstaining on key decisions as a UNSC member is hardly a marker of leadership' which burnishes India's claim to a permanent Council seat.[53] Similarly, while Rajendra Abhyankar still felt India had been right to oppose intervention and to search for compromise solutions in October, by the end of 2011 he felt al-Assad was reneging on his reform promises, meaning 'regime change looks like a better option than a creeping civil war', so 'for India, the time may have come to recalibrate'.[54]

Abhyankar's changing opinions reflect the contest between the two opposing interpretations of enlightened-realist logic regarding whether R2P-inspired interventions enhance or undermine stability. He had initially concluded non-intervention best maintained stability, but he wondered later whether the crisis might destabilise the region for years *without* an intervention. Unsurprisingly, Meenakshi Ganguly urged India to 'take the lead to ensure civilian protection'.[55] Equally unsurprisingly, John Cherian remained firmly opposed to such, believing the West's 'game plan is to not allow the Syrian government to implement … reforms' and instead to sought to 'enforce regime change'.[56]

Other policy-shapers also urged New Delhi to continue its cautious approach, but for different reasons; for example Zakir Hussain acknowledged the

> recent … news reports and analyses [which] have indicated India should revisit its Syrian policy and put pressure on the Asad [sic] regime … . However, the ambiguity involved … demands that India continues to follow its "principled stand" … India has shown a stable and consistent policy approach which shouldn't be abandoned without reasonable cause.[57]

Anuradha Chenoy, however, advised India not to align too closely with America on Syria after exploring various scenarios – mainly regarding Indo-Pakistan relations

53 'Rocky Road to Damascus', *Indian Express*, 16 November 2011.

54 'Time is Running out for Assad', *Daily Pioneer*, 20 November 2011.

55 'Back Syria's People, not Assad Regime', *Asian Age*, 3 February 2012.

56 'Looming Civil War', *Frontline* 28:26, 17–30 December 2011.

57 'Decoding the Syrian Blasts', *Indian Council of World Affairs – View Point*, 12 January 2012.

– where American and Indian interests diverged.[58] A few days later Chinmaya Gharekhan reiterated his advice from June 2011, namely, 'it makes sense to take a cautious stance' because intervention in such a complex conflict would only worsen it.[59]

There was in early 2012, therefore, a range of advice from policy-shapers. Ganguly's advice remained firmly grounded in robust liberal-democratic logic. And Cherian remained wedded to a fiercely anti-Western worldview. Advice consistent with great power logic (both strains) predominated, although commentators tended to split on the implications of such. Regarding hard-realism, Jaishankar thought India's interests lay in aligning with the rebels but Chenoy came to the opposite conclusion; the difference arose from the different assumptions underpinning their analyses (i.e. Jaishankar assumed the rebels would win, Chenoy assumed Indo-Pakistani issues were more crucial). The same occurred regarding enlightened-realist logic; Abhyankar assumed some sort of intervention might be needed to arrest Syria's seemingly inexorable descent into anarchy, while Hussain and Gharekhan assumed intervention would simply make matters worse.

As this advice was being delivered the LAS's position was changing. Frustration with Syria's government had built towards the end of 2011, and it boiled over in January 2012: on the 15th Qatar's Emir mused openly about possible LAS militarily action; on the 22nd an LAS resolution laid out a comprehensive plan for political settlement which included al-Assad stepping down; and on the 29th the LAS observer mission was frozen after it reported continual harassment. New Delhi was watching closely; MEA sources confirmed India 'awaits the next step of the Arab League' before it decided on what position to take in the looming Security Council showdown.[60]

When the Council met on 4 February 2012 it considered a draft resolution which condemned 'all violence, irrespective of where it comes from' (but it also apportioned relatively more blame to Syria's government), repeatedly demanded the LAS mission be facilitated, and demanded humanitarian organisations be given access. It also refrained from mentioning Syria's Pillar I responsibilities; indeed, it declined to even refer to Syria's obligations under international humanitarian law. The draft resolution also contained less threatening warnings than its 4 October predecessor – Article 41 (sanctions) was not mentioned, let alone Article 42 (military intervention) – and it merely committed the Council 'in the event of non-compliance, to consider further measures.[61]

But even this relatively benign draft failed to pass. The Russians vetoed, saying it 'sent a biased signal' after accusing 'some sitting at this table' of 'calling for regime change and encouraging the opposition'; while the Chinese repeated their

58 'The Road Ahead for India', *New Indian Express*, 10 January 2012.

59 'A Year after the Jasmine and Tahrir', *The Hindu*, 14 January 2011.

60 Parul Chandra, 'India Keeps Watch on Syria, Wants Stability', *Asian Age*, 21 January 2012.

61 S/2012/77, 4 February 2012.

earlier position that 'under the current circumstances to put undue emphasis on pressuring the Syrian government ... will not help'. The outcome enraged several Western powers: France's UN Ambassador said 'history will judge harshly those countries that have prevented the Council' from acting, while the U.S. Ambassador said America was 'disgusted'.[62]

India, however, voted for this draft with all other Council members apart from Russia and China. Hardeep Puri Singh explained India's position in the following terms:

> Prolonged instability and unrest in Syria have implications for peace and stability in the wider region ... . We strongly condemn all violence, irrespective of the perpetrators. We also condemn all human rights violations. India holds the rights of expression and peaceful assembly [dear] ..., while [also valuing] the stability and security of society. India has conveyed that message ... with our partners Brazil and South Africa ... . Our support for today's draft resolution is in accordance with our support for the efforts of the League of Arab States. ... We note that the draft resolution expressly rules out any measures under Article 42 of the Charter.[63]

This explanation correlates with the logics of several identity discourses. India talked up human rights and democracy, but noted its support had been contingent upon the absence of references to Article 42; in other words, there was an overt 'non-correlation' with – in effect an explicit rejection of – the robust variety of liberal-democratic logic. The draft resolution had also not specifically referred to Article 41 sanctions being applied in future, as the October 2011 draft had, but nor were such ruled out. Yet later reports suggested India had made its support contingent upon removal of the phrase 'automatic trigger for sanctions' from the draft during the negotiations which had proceeded the vote.[64] India's statement itself only correlates with soft liberal-democratic logic, and this extraneous evidence offers further proof that New Delhi was determined not support interventionist measures past placing diplomatic pressure on al-Assad, even those well short of military intervention.

India also specifically mentioned alignment with the other IBSA states and the LAS as important motivations. More to the point, the LAS had become more supportive of interventionism since October 2011 – not military intervention, to be sure, but sanctions – to pile the pressure on al-Assad. India did not specifically say 'the LAS has changed its mind, so we have too', but the pattern was clear; India's explanations for earlier votes in the Security Council in February and March (regarding Libya and Côte d'Ivoire), and in October (regarding Syria) had referred to developing-world solidarity logic repeatedly, but despite strident anti-Western logic featuring prominently in the public debates New Delhi studiously avoided

62 S/PV.6711, 4 February 2012.

63 Ibid.

64 Parul Chandra, 'UK Seeks India's Support on Syria', *Asian Age*, 17 July 2012.

mention of such in its formal policy statements.[65] This does not mean no policy-makers held anti-Western worldviews – several interviewees confirmed several such individuals remained influential in the MEA[66] – but it does suggest strongly such sentiments were not considered suitable for airing in public, whatever influence the officials who espoused them may have wielded behind closed doors.

Correlations with hard-realist logic are completely absent from Singh's statement, although this does not mean that they played no role in India's decision (see below). The most interesting aspect of Singh's statement is the reference to 'prolonged' instability in Syria adversely affecting the region; it hints at New Delhi beginning to lose patience with al-Assad's failure to reform and becoming more open to applying more pressure to force him to do so. Against this, Singh also clearly indicated India did not consider the rebels wholly blameless. It is not entirely clear, therefore, which variety of enlightened-realist logic – the variety which assumed intervention enhances stability, or the variety which assumes the opposite – shaped India's position on 4 February 2012.

Hypothesis testing can help clarify India's motivations for its 'yes' vote on 4 February. Regarding the last conundrum discussed above, if India's position had remain unchanged since October it would have probably abstained again and called for more time to be given for 'constructive and collaborative dialogue'. To be sure, the February draft itself was even less interventionist than the October 2011 draft had been. And India clearly stated it remained opposed to even mentioning Article 42 (and extraneous evidence showed it opposed mentioning Article 41 too). Nevertheless, the reference to 'prolonged instability' suggests India had shifted somewhat closer towards assuming *non*-intervention might be destabilising. More importantly, if India was aware Russia and China would likely veto *any* Western-sponsored draft resolution this is likely to have affected policy-makers' deliberations. India was indeed aware, as it had been back in October 2011, that the resolution would likely fail; on 2 February Russia, and this time China too, expressed clear intentions to exercise their vetoes.[67] This suggests strongly that we should focus attention on what India hoped to gain diplomatically rather than what it thought its vote would actually mean for events in Syria itself.

We know India has sought to improve relations with the West since at least 1991 to further its domestic development efforts, improve its prospects of securing elevation to the Security Council, and generally pursue various foreign policy interests more effectively.[68] Obviously a 'no' vote would pit India against the

65 Except for several indignant statements about 'Western hypocrisy' in Libya by anonymous MEA officials in October 2011: see Chapter 5.

66 I-3, New Delhi, 1 November 2013; I-6, New Delhi, 4 November 2013; I-10, New Delhi, 9 December 2013.

67 Atul Aneja, 'Russia, China oppose West-backed resolution on Syria', *The Hindu*, 2 February 2012; Prashad, 'Syria, Libya'.

68 Evan A. Feigenbaum, 'India's Rise, America's Interest: The Fate of the U.S.-Indian Partnership', *Foreign Affairs* 89:2 (2010), 76–91. Also see the discussion in Chapter 3 more generally.

West openly; India's cautious position in August 2011 had elicited some Western criticism,[69] and India's abstention in in October 2011 had drawn more[70] even though Russia and China suffered most in this regard.[71] So, if India was fairly sure the draft resolution would fail anyway it made sense to seek some side benefits by aligning with the West.

We also know India values working closely with – or within – developing-world organisations. By February 2012 the LAS was obviously at odds with two BRICS states, Russia and China. India therefore faced a choice; if it cleaved close to a Russia which seemed determined to confront the West and a China with whom it had long-standing disagreements and tensions,[72] it might imperil its relations with the West and LAS states (and be overshadowed by the veto-wielding permanent members). But if New Delhi found another developing-world grouping within which it enjoyed more relative influence it might be able to pursue various diplomatic ends, like acting as a bridge between the opposing camps, proposing initiatives the West couldn't twist into regime change and which might, if they worked, deliver diplomatic gains, etc.

India, of course, had chosen this latter course and had been leading IBSA's efforts since August 2011. For its part, while South Africa felt 'betrayed' by the West in Libya and 'anti-imperialist factions in the ANC' issued denunciations of Western states which India's CPI(M) would have been proud of, Pretoria never repudiated R2P entirely and confined itself to critiquing mandate-creep and regime change.[73] Brazil had also been unhappy with NATO's intervention in Libya, but Brasilia reacted by issuing the Responsibility while Protecting concept paper (RwP) which, while it sought to constrain Pillar III-inspired military interventions, did not rule them out entirely.[74] The IBSA states were therefore all substantially on the same page regarding Syria, at least until later in 2012 (see below). The IBSA states all delivered substantially similar explanations for their voting on 4 October 2011,[75] including strongly endorsing the LAS's position; and while Brazil had left the Council by 4 February 2012 it was still supporting IBSA's initiatives and the LAS diplomatically.[76] For its part, South Africa expressed strong support

69 'Deteriorating in Syria'; Roy, 'India Faces Heat'; Michele Keleman, 'US Underwhelmed by Emerging Powers at UN', *NPR*, 17 September 2011.

70 Howard Schaeffer, 'India & US at UN: A Complicated Dance', *The Hindu*, 8 October 2011.

71 'Anger as UN Action Against Syria Vetoed', *Indian Express*, 6 October 2011.

72 Mohan Malik, 'India and China: As China Rises, India Stirs', in Harsh V. Pant (ed.), *Indian Foreign Policy in a Unipolar World* (New Delhi: Routledge, 2009).

73 Harry Verhoeven, CSR Murthy and Ricardo Soares de Oliveira, '"Our Identity is Our Currency": South Africa, the Responsibility to Protect, and the Logic of African Intervention', *Conflict, Security and Development* 14:4 (2014), 526.

74 Oliver Stuenkel and Marco Tourinho, 'Regulating Intervention: Brazil and the Responsibility to Protect', *Conflict, Security and Development* 14:4 (2014), 391.

75 S/PV/6627, 4 October 2012.

76 Stuenkel and Tourinho, 'Regulating Intervention', 396.

for the LAS position on 4 February.[77] By voting 'yes' on 4 February India was therefore able to both maintain solidarity with its IBSA partners and, even better, to prominently lead IBSA's efforts to end the Syrian crisis.

Of course India also maintained solidarity with an LAS which had become more inclined to intervene in Syria. To be sure, the LAS (other than Qatar) was still not calling for military intervention – if it had been, India may have broken ranks with it; indeed, we will see below that this happened later in 2012 – but the LAS had nonetheless become more prepared to increase the pressure on al-Assad before the 4 February 2012 Council vote in ways that did not (yet) make India too uncomfortable. The conclusion is obvious: India's shift in position between October 2011 and February 2012 was primarily precipitated by the LAS's shift (and the fact the other IBSA states continued to support the LAS too). This demonstrates yet again how strongly developing-world solidarity logic shaped India's policy-responses to the Syrian crisis.

What of India's bilateral relationship with Syria? If India had wanted to maintain good relations with Syria – a developing-world state with whom India has traditionally enjoyed very a cordial if not especially close relationship – then India would have voted 'no'. But if India had stood with a human rights-abusing al-Assad regime it would have gone against the latent liberal-democratic 'urges' which animate many Indians (or maybe just their elites: again, see previous chapters). And it would have also tainted India by association; 10 of the 14 interviewees agreed India typically feels uncomfortable standing with tyrants and despots (and as an aside, four interviewees spontaneously mentioned China in this regard, saying India only stands with China when its interests overwhelmingly demand it do so[78]). This suggests the shaping effect of liberal-democratic logic – but only the soft variety – cannot be discounted as a shaping influence altogether; it was, at minimum, at least sufficiently influential to off-set the shaping influence of developing-world solidarity logic in the narrow context of the Indo-Syrian bilateral relationship.

And what of hard-realist logic? Some policy-shapers' had advised India to pursue various direct interests, but no correlation was found between these contributions to the public debate and Singh's statement to the Security Council. Yet we know states do not always explain the full reasoning behind their policy-responses, so we should consider whether direct interests shaped New Delhi's decision-making.

First, if New Delhi had believed the rebels were close to victory and had judged it prudent to make friendly gestures towards them, India would have voted 'yes' and expressed sympathy with them (or, at minimum, refrained from criticising them). India did of course vote 'yes', but it also apportioned blame equally between them and Syria's government. New Delhi was also aware that while al-Assad was under

77 S/PV.6711, 4 February 2012.

78 I-13, New Delhi 18 November 2013; I-10, New Delhi, 10 November 2013; I-15, New Delhi 2013; I-16, New Delhi, 9 December 2013.

great pressure the rebels were not yet close to unseating him.[79] It therefore seems likely India did not construe its interests in this hypothesised fashion. Second, if India felt its direct interests in Syria would have been imperilled by an intervention it would have voted 'no'. But India had no pressing interests: no military bases; relatively unimportant bilateral trade links;[80] and few energy-extraction interests.[81] Accordingly, there were very few Indians living in Syria; certainly far fewer than in Libya before March 2011. New Delhi could therefore vote 'yes' on 4 February without worrying too much about its direct interests either.

Finally, if India had other important interests in the region this may have affected its deliberations. And it did have an interest in the security and stability of the Gulf states, who also happen to be prominent members of the LAS (indeed, with Egypt in turmoil at the time, Saudi Arabia was dominating the LAS[82]). In 2012 India relied on imports for 70 per cent of its oil, with about half of that coming from Gulf states (Saudi Arabia supplied 19 per cent of total imports, the highest single source).[83] The Saudis also promised to make good the shortfall that India might otherwise suffer as sanctions against Iran were tightening in early 2012. And Riyadh extradited several terror suspects India had wanted to question for years. More generally, fully six million Indians worked in Gulf Arab states and sent significant remittances home.[84] There were therefore very pressing interests shaping India's decision to vote 'yes', both direct interests in backing its primary energy suppliers and more general ones in enhancing these states' security (or at least trying to).

The implications of this analysis are obvious. India's position did shift on 4 February 2012 – not radically, it was still not prepared to entertain anything approaching a Libya-style military intervention – but New Delhi had become prepared to back others' efforts to increase diplomatic pressure on al-Assad. The relative influence of the shaping effects of the various identity discourses also seems clear. The aspect of anti-imperial logic which stressed maintaining solidarity with IBSA and especially the LAS was very influential. But by voting 'yes' India could also protect vital interests in accordance with hard-realist logic,

---

79 S. Nihal Singh, 'UN Veto Takes Syria Nearer Civil War', *Political and Defence Weekly*, 16 February 2012.

80 Bilateral trade was $US364m in 2008–2009, $US345m in 2009–2010, and $US523m in 2010–2011, before plunging to $US258m in 2011–2012; 'India-Syria: Bilateral Relations', *Embassy of India – Damascus*, July 2013.

81 Kabir Taneja, 'India and China: Lessons From a Lost Oil Field in Syria', *The Diplomat*, 23 November 2014.

82 Bruce Maddy-Weitzman, 'The Arab League Comes Alive', *Middle East Quarterly* 19:3 (2012), 78.

83 US Energy Information Administration, 'India: Overview', *Analysis Briefs*, 26 June 2014; 'Table: India's Country-wise Crude Oil Imports Since 2001/02', *Reuters*, 6 August 2012.

84 Ramesh Thakur, 'R2P After Libya and Syria: Engaging Emerging Powers', *Washington Quarterly* 36:2 (2013), 71.

which would seem to have exercised a shaping influence which was probably at least equally if not more important. India could also reap some diplomatic benefits from aligning with the West, meaning the aspect of enlightened-realism which stresses the long-term benefits of acting as a responsible power also shaped India's 'yes' vote on 4 February too. And, as noted above, India seemed to have shifted somewhat – not decisively, but discernibly nonetheless – towards accepting that *non*-intervention might be destabilising, suggesting this variety of enlightened-realist logic exerted some shaping influence too.

The fact India voted 'yes' and thereby aligned itself with the West suggests in turn the shaping influence of anti-Western logic was relatively weak. And while a genuine concern with democracy and human rights in Syria cannot be discounted as a shaping influence – the human rights situation was markedly worse in February 2012 than it had been in October 2011 – it seems to have been a relatively minor consideration. At minimum, India's trenchant opposition to military solutions indicates that at best soft liberal-democratic logic played some minor part in New Delhi's deliberations on 4 February.

A burst of reflections on India's 4 February vote followed in the Indian press. Most concluded India had done the right thing and their reasoning was typically informed by varieties of great power logic. For example, Srinath Raghavan believed India now assumed non-intervention might imperil its interests in the Gulf, which explained its 'more active stance'. He was not suggesting India would have or should have voted for a military intervention – 'New Delhi', he said, 'does not favour … intervention aimed at regime change', and he stressed 'sovereignty … cannot be jettisoned casually' – but he did concede 'issues like the "Responsibility to Protect" need more discussion and consensus building' despite the fact 'the Western powers who led the intervention in Libya did a grave disservice to the principles they espouse'.[85] His contribution therefore primarily reflected the variety of enlightened-realist logic which assumed non-intervention might be destabilising and even gave a (very cautious) nod to robust liberal-democratic logic. Raja Mohan also re-entered the debate with a contribution clearly motivated by a mix of enlightened- and hard-realist logic:

> India's posturing on non-intervention, in Libya and Syria, has made little sense … . The time has come for India to view the [Middle East] through the cold lens of power politics. Anything else would undermine India's ability to secure its rapidly growing interests [including a permanent Council seat]. … The vote on Syria was a good start.[86]

And Chinmaya Gharekhan came to similar conclusions; he felt India had correctly supported the draft resolution 'as a demonstration of our readiness to adapt our positions to changed circumstances', pointing to India's interests the

85 'A Wider View of India's Syria Vote', *Asian Age*, 10 February 2012.

86 'Seeing Syria Straight', *Indian Express*, 11 February 2012.

Gulf primarily.[87] Gharekhan was channelling hard-realist logic and beginning to take more seriously the variety of enlightened-realist logic which assumed 'doing something' – pressuring the al-Assad regime, but stopping short of military intervention – was necessary to maintain stability in the Gulf.

Arun Sukumar responded directly to Gharekhan and argued India's position hadn't really changed between October 2011 and February 2012 because the latest draft resolution was so mild, meaning it actually reflected 'India's preference towards solutions that nudge adamant regimes [towards compromise] without muscular invocations of the "Responsibility to Protect"'. He called for India to forge consensus among the BRICS states and secure another 'draft – one that ultimately endorses much of what the previous version had to offer – that both Russia and China are amenable to'. A mix of developing-world solidarity and enlightened-realist logic – with a dash of soft liberal-democratic logic – was apparent; he endorsed India's backing of the Western-sponsored 4 February draft and urged India to play the bridging role to raise its profile as a candidate for elevation to the Security Council and, hopefully, also do some good for Syria's people.[88] Gharekhan then replied and made clear the different logics at play in each contribution, observing: '[Sukumar] believes that in voting for the [draft] resolution India set aside its geopolitical interests; I believe it is precisely these interests which dictated India's vote'.[89]

For his part, Prashanath Parameswaran disagreed with Raghavan's, Mohan's and Gharekhan's assessments and sided with Sukumar; he believed India's position hadn't really changed much from the cautious approach New Delhi had been pursuing since August 2011, and he felt the proof was in the fact 'the [draft] resolution was so weak that even Russia considered supporting it'. He ultimately concluded that 'while there remains a chance that India's position on Syria will shift … this seems doubtful at present … . India is trying to walk a tightrope and avoid taking bold stances'.[90] He therefore believed India's position was informed by a more-or-less even mix of hard-realist logic – protecting its interests in the Gulf – and the variety of enlightened-realist logic which assumes intervention is destabilising; and he focused more on analysing not judging India's position.

Atul Aneja, however, focused squarely on judging; by voting 'yes' and protecting its relationships with oil-rich Gulf Arabs and the West, he felt India had lost sight of the broader trends, namely, that 'the locus of global economic power has already shifted East'. He painted the conflict in Syria as the most acute manifestation of:

> the clash of two divergent and competing ideological positions. The West is undermining the principle of national sovereignty [using] … the doctrine of the

87 'New Great Game on West Asian Chessboard', *The Hindu*, 28 February 2012.

88 'A Test of India's Big Power Aspirations', *The Hindu*, 24 February 2011.

89 'Chinmaya R. Gharekhan Responds', *The Hindu*, 24 February 2011.

90 'India's position on Syria: A Tight Balancing Act', *East Asia Forum*, 8 March 2012.

> Right to Protect (R2P) … China and Russia … have staunchly defended … the principle of sovereignty … . [For them] the insistence on regime change in Syria is part of a long narrative scripted mainly by the United States to … control the world.

Aneja's reasoning was therefore grounded in a mix of anti-imperial logic – both aspects of it; the belief India should side with the developing world and also implacably oppose the West – with a strong dose of enlightened-realist logic. But, crucially, this was a variety of enlightened-realist logic not seen before, or at least never presented so starkly; it did not speak to stability, or to raising India's international profile in the *existing* configuration of global power, but instead argued India should 'play the long game' and align itself with the emerging powers which would one day be dominant. Aneja was also dismissive of hard-realist logic and patently hostile to liberal-democratic logic.[91]

Several scholars also offered reflections in foreign policy institutes' in-house publications. Rajesh Rajagopalan, for example, considered what influence liberal-democratic logic played in New Delhi's foreign policy more generally, but after determining that it played only a minor role he went on to declare that hard-realist logic alone *should* define most of India's foreign policy stances; for example, he argued that New Delhi was right to ignore Myanmar's human rights abuses to 'balanc[e] Chinese interests' in that state. On the question of Syria, Rajopagalan judged that India had been right to vote for the draft resolution on 4 February, but he made it crystal clear that 'none of this suggests human rights should be the basis of India's foreign policy'. Instead, and with regard to Syria, he claimed that 'India had essential interests to protect among the Gulf Arabs and in Washington', which led him back into criticism of India's policies towards Sri Lanka because they would 'rebound to China's and Pakistan's advantage'.[92]

To contextualise this last point, India voted for a US-sponsored resolution in the HCR on 22 March 2012 which condemned Colombo for various human rights failings. Rajagopalan noted the overriding influence on New Delhi of what was called earlier the ethnic-Tamil identity discourse (i.e. pressure from the DMK had shaped the Congress-led government's decision). But his colleague at the Observer Research Foundation, Sathiya Moorthy was less critical: he noted India had actually protected Sri Lanka by watering down the draft somewhat before the vote, and he lauded New Delhi for its adroit mollification of both domestic and Western opinion. Enlightened-realist logic shone thorough clearly in his contribution – New Delhi had cleverly secured several side-benefits by its handling of the matter – and he gave only the barest nod to the human rights situation in Sri Lanka having any real relevance to New Delhi's thoughts about the matter.[93]

91 'On the Wrong Side of History', *The Hindu*, 23 March 2011.

92 'Human Rights and India's Foreign Policy', *Observer Research Foundation – Analysis*, 26 March 2012.

93 'Shake-up time for Sri Lanka', *Observer Research Foundation – Analysis*, 26 March 2012.

This brief digression into the Indian debate about Sri Lanka is revealing because the analyses tendered by scholars at foreign policy institutes about India's vote on 4 February vis-à-vis Syria were overwhelmingly informed by variations of great power logic. Take just two additional examples: Stanly Johny deployed classic hard-realist logic to argue the West's and the LAS's policies towards Syria were not motivated by humanitarianism and they were instead advancing their interests by 'aggressively pursuing the regime change agenda', so it made sense for India do the same (i.e. pursue its interests, not regime change; Johny advised India to stay on the sidelines and pursue diplomatic gains);[94] and P.R. Kumaraswamy advised New Delhi to prudently restrict itself to diplomatic moves to increase the pressure on al-Assad, and thereby also keep India aligned with its key trading partners in the Gulf and the West.[95]

The broad trend was clear; when reflecting on India's 4 February vote most commentators concluded India had been right to vote 'yes'. Their reasoning was primarily informed by varieties of great power logic, with some concession to anti-imperialist logic, especially the developing-world solidarity variety. Few believed liberal-democratic logic played much part in New Delhi's thinking – only Sukumar referred to it at all, and then only the soft variety – and criticism of India's decision to vote with the West was also rare (Aneja's strident anti-Western critique was an outlier despite how strongly he put it). But the Syrian crisis continued to deteriorate, the West would continue to agitate for intervention, and India's preference for non-interventionist responses would begin to waver again, as the following section demonstrates.

India's Engagement with the Syrian Crisis in Mid- and Late 2012

After the Council's failure to act on 4 February the General Assembly passed a resolution on 16 February 2012 which was more critical of the Syrian government (and India voted for it). This eschewed R2P-like language and instead called for Syria's authorities to 'fully comply with their obligations under international human rights law'. It also asked the UN Secretary-General to appoint a Special Envoy[96] and Ban Ki-Moon acted swiftly by dispatching his predecessor Kofi Annan, who was enthusiastically backed by the LAS. But these moves had little effect on the crisis. The fighting steadily intensified and one Indian concluded the al-Assad regime had been 'emboldened by the veto' on 4 February.[97] By the beginning of March the UN reported that 7,500 people had died, but the death toll soared during that month as the government launched several offensives against the rebels.

94 'The Syrian Conundrum', *IDSA – Comment*, 14 February 2012.

95 'Silence on Syria is No Option', *IDSA – Comment*, 21 February 2012.

96 A/RES/66/253, 16 February 2012.

97 Jagdish N. Singh, 'A Gloomy Syrian Scenario', *IDSA – Comment*, 24 February 2012.

Annan delivered a Six-Point Plan which al-Assad promised to implement on 26 March. But the fighting intensified as the date for the start of the ceasefire, 14 April, approached. On that day and a week later the Security Council unanimously passed two resolutions which demanded all belligerents fully support Annan's plan to achieve a 'Syrian-led political transition leading to a democratic, plural political system'[98] and set up a formal UN Mission (UNSMIS) to deploy up to 300 unarmed ceasefire monitors.[99] Hardeep Puri Singh expressed India's strong support for Annan and UNSMIS, and confirmed India expected 'impartial implementation' of the peace plan.[100]

Yet these diplomatic moves also failed to alter the trajectory of the conflict; instead, monthly death tolls rose inexorably.[101] One especially disturbing incident grabbed international headlines. On 25 May, 108 residents of the village of Houla were killed by a regime-aligned militia, the *Shabiha*; all the victims were later found to have been executed, including 34 women and 49 children, which showed just how brutal the conflict generally, and especially al-Assad's forces, had become. In response the so-called 'Action Group' – comprising the five permanent Council members and 35 other states – met in June and released a Final Communiqué to drive Annan's Six-Point Plan forward and initiate a transition towards full representative democracy. But the major powers' unity began to unravel almost immediately.[102] Annan stayed in Syria hoping to turn the ever-deteriorating situation around, but he eventually resigned on 2 August 2012.

Although a degree of fatigue or perhaps resignation seems to have set in, some Indian policy-shapers continued to discuss what India should do about Syria before the next Council meeting on 19 July 2012. For example, prompted by the Houla massacre Mayuri Mukherjee asserted that 'al-Assad is responsible for the violence, but his opponents are no saints', and wondered 'when is it the right time to invoke the Responsibility to Protect?'. She concluded 'there are no easy yes-or-no answers [given] … the failure of a similar mission in Libya [which] … now teeters on the brink of anarchy', but she ultimately concluded unilaterally supplying arms to rebels – which some LAS states had begun to do after 4 February 2012 – was not ideal and wondered whether military intervention was needed to prevent 'another Afghanistan in Syria'.[103]

Mukherjee was therefore enunciating a mix of robust liberal-democratic logic and the variety of enlightened-realism which assumed instability might

98 S/RES/2042, 14 April 2012.

99 S/RES/2043, 21 April 2012.

100 S/PV.6751, 14 April 2012; S/PV.6756, 21 April 2012.

101 Over 8,000 died in August, the highest monthly total up to the end of 2014; 'only' 4,000 died per month on average for the rest of 2012: 'Syria: The Story of the Conflict', *BBC News*, 8 December 2014.

102 'UN Envoy Calls for Transitional Government in Syria', *BBC News*, 30 June 2012.

103 'Arming Rebels Won't Solve Syria Crisis', *Daily Pioneer*, 31 May 2012.

only be arrested by military intervention (although she hardly delivered a ringing endorsement of such). Firmer support for robust liberal-democratic logic was apparent when Salil Shetty, the Indian-born head of Amnesty International, expressed hope New Delhi's stance may be changing:

> Generally speaking, if the West votes one way, we'll vote the other … . [We] need to feel strong enough to say, 'No we won't toe the line. It doesn't matter [how the West] … votes, it doesn't matter [how] Russia and China vote. We, India, Brazil, and South Africa are democratic countries. We have grown up with human rights as part of our framework and we are not going to accept this'. However, we are not there yet … we did vote for the Syria resolution [in February], but that has only happened in the last few months.[104]

Significantly, regular commentator Chinmaya Gharekhan was edging towards a similar position (without quite reaching it). Recall that in September 2011 he had believed any intervention would cause instability, and he still held this view early in 2012 despite concluding India had been right to vote 'yes' on 4 February. But by June 2012 he concluded *non*-intervention might be imperilling India's interests (especially its energy supplies). He also wrote that 'we have to condemn all the atrocities, but not try too-much to strike a balance' between the sides; without referring to the Houla massacre directly he seems to have concluded al-Assad was primarily to blame for the ever-worsening situation. Still, he stopped short of endorsing military intervention and only advised New Delhi to support sanctions to increase the pressure on al-Assad. Specifically, he advised New Delhi to 'activate the BRICS forum' to develop a common position, before India could lead efforts to reconcile with the West and thereby find a way of restraining al-Assad.[105] So a mix of logics informed Gharekhan's position; he had by now basically accepted the variety of enlightened-realist logic which assumes non-intervention was destabilising, and also urged India to raise its diplomatic profile as a bridge-builder, but only from a position of solidarity with its developing-world partners.

Over at *Frontline* John Cherian, for his part, claimed the Syrian government was trying to implement reforms but the rebels 'want the Annan mission to fail and lead to a foreign military intervention'; according to his fiercely anti-Western logic:

> The Arab League [and] … the West rushed Syria's case to the UN Security Council in a bid to re-enact the Libyan regime change scenario. It was the timely veto by Russia and China that prevented Syria and the region from descending into more violence and chaos.[106]

---

104 Sarju Kaul, 'Amnesty Calls for India to Take Global Lead on Rights', *Asian Age*, 25 May 2012.

105 'Power Play in Damascus', *The Telegraph (Calcutta)*, 18 June 2011.

106 'Holding Out', *Frontline*, 19 May–1 June 2012.

Anuradha Chenoy re-entered the debate and characterised the wider grand-strategic debate in India as one between 'strategic thinkers that are a part of the military intelligence community [who] … want India to align with the US [because it] … . can make India a great power' and 'other strategic thinkers and independent civil society [who] … advocate India has a strongly independent foreign policy'. He positioned himself with the latter group and prescribed a mixture – but a very imprecise one – of logics to drive Indian policy in Syria, namely, India should adopt a 'case-by-case position based on a combination of ethics, international law and its people's interests'.[107] And that was it; logics compatible with all the identity discourses were presented – by a relatively small number of commentators – and no one logic dominated the public debate before the Council met again. But three authors from this small sample began to at least consider whether India should support more interventionist action against Syria's government.

The Western-sponsored draft Security Council resolution presented on 19 July condemned the rebels – especially for 'bombings … which are indicative of … well-organised terrorist groups' – but it condemned Syria's government more comprehensively and went on to demand compliance with the various international peace plans; it also used the phrase 'transition of power' repeatedly (but did not specifically demand al-Assad step down). Again, it did not use phrases reminiscent of Pillar I of R2P – or even remind Syria's government of its obligations under international law – but paragraph 14 did say the Council would meet again to consider imposing Article 41 sanctions.[108] Predictably, while 11 states voted for it and South Africa and Pakistan abstained, the draft was vetoed by Russia and China. The Russians ridiculed the Western powers and this time the Chinese were uncharacteristically assertive, calling the draft resolution 'flawed' and 'unbalanced' and a threat to regional security and trust between the major powers. The Western powers, also predictably, reacted with considerable anger,[109] but the fact this draft was noticeably tougher than the failed 4 February draft suggested the Russians may have been right to accuse the West of grandstanding. The next day an unremarkable resolution extending UNSMIS's mandate was passed unanimously and no one spoke which, ironically, spoke volumes about the degree of acrimony in the chamber; tellingly, no more Council meetings dealt directly with the Syrian conflict for the remainder of 2012.[110]

India voted for the draft on 19 July. The most pertinent statements made by Hardeep Puri Singh were as follows:

> India remains gravely concerned at the events unfolding in Syria … . We have called for the cessation of violence … irrespective of who its perpetrators are … . [W]e have consistently supported the [Annan] mission [and] … UNSMIS.

107 'India's Geopolitical Options', New Indian Express, 11 June 2012.

108 S/2012/528, 19 July 2012.

109 S/PV.6810, 19 July 2012.

110 S/RES/2059, 20 July 2012.

> ... Unfortunately, all parties have ... continued to pursue a military approach ... . Prolonged instability and unrest in Syria have ramifications for the entire region and beyond ... . We have therefore supported action ... that addresses the Syrian crisis in a balanced and impartial manner ... . [I]t would have been preferable for the Council members to show flexibility ... instead of pursuing domestic interests.

Various correlations between this statement and the advice offered by policy-shapers are discernible. For one, India was still concerned about the prospects of 'prolonged instability' and, notably, this draft, unlike the February draft, explicitly mentioned the possibility of sanctions (and there is no extraneous evidence to suggest India tried to have it removed). Additionally, India's statement of support for Annan and the UN mission UNSMIS correlates with enlightened-realist logic about the benefits – both to India and more generally – of acting responsibly. New Delhi also expressed concerns about the ever-worsening human rights situation – the fighting had intensified significantly since February after all – but it also continued to blame all the warring parties.

All these statements suggest New Delhi's decision might have been shaped in part by the aspect of enlightened-realist logic which assumes non-intervention might cause instability, and that responsible action is in India's wider interests. Soft liberal-democratic logic arguably also played a shaping role, but while New Delhi was prepared to now support moves to (possibly, in future) impose sanctions, it still opposed interventions of the sort contemplated by robust liberal-democratic logic (i.e. military intervention). Given what was said above about India's vote back in February several omissions from its statement in July are not surprising; again, there was no correlation with the anti-Western aspect of anti-imperialist logic; and there was no mention of India's direct interests to correlate with advice based in hard-realist logic. But Singh failed to mention the LAS or IBSA; he only told the Council India supported Annan's mission and UNSMIS.

Hypothesis testing can again shed additional light on India's decision to vote 'yes' on 19 July. If IBSA had begun to split, it might explain why India did not refer to having formed a joint position with its IBSA partners. And this had in fact happened. Brazil was off the Council by July 2012, and after February 2012 it steadily disengaged with events in the Middle East and, more specifically, with debates about R2P. Various reasons for this have been offered, including domestic-political factors; but Stuenkel and Tourinho, while not discounting these entirely, argue:

> it is no secret the global response to RwP was a surprise to Brazilian diplomats ... . [It] triggered some of the more risk-averse elements of Itamaraty's[111] foreign policy thinking. For an institution which prides itself on its historical tradition

111 Brazil's foreign ministry is housed in the architecturally renowned Itamaraty Palace.

> of pacifism and consensus-building, to engage in unrestrained discussions about the use of military force … carried immense risks … . [S]ince leaving the UN Security Council Brazil has played a far more modest role regarding the [Syrian] conflict, keeping with the typical diplomatic repertoire of expressing "deep concern".[112]

So, one of India's IBSA partners had, in effect, faded away. And South Africa's position also changed after Mali was almost overrun by Islamists in June 2012.[113] Pretoria therefore abstained after saying:

> We fail to see … how the [draft resolution] … would end the violence or contribute to the implementation of [Annan's] six-point plan. Instead, the text, in an unbalanced manner, threatens sanctions … without realistically allowing any action to be taken against the opposition … . In similar situations where the international community, including the Security Council, has preferred one side over the other, such bias has resulted in the polarization of the conflict.[114]

The shadow of the Libyan intervention – thrown into even sharper relief by the conflagration in northern Mali – therefore undermined the unity the IBSA states had shown before the middle of 2012 and prevented India from maintaining solidarity with this organisation.

It is a little harder to understand why Singh did not mention the LAS in his statement to the Council on 19 July. It was noted earlier that after the 4 February draft resolution failed, various LAS states – in particular Saudi Arabia and Qatar – began arming the rebels. One scholar has claimed Riyadh, after February 2012, essentially 'appropriated the Arab League … in its battle to overthrow the Syrian regime'.[115] This is probably an overstatement, but by mid-2012 the LAS proper – as opposed to particular members of the LAS – had definitely taken a back seat to the various other international efforts. The LAS did not retreat entirely – it attended the Action Group's Geneva Summit and it had endorsed Kofi Annan's efforts – nevertheless, the general impression is that LAS states threw up their hands in frustration after 4 February and individual members began to pursue their own interests directly.

So, if various LAS states were beginning to directly interfere in Syria in ways which discomforted India, and New Delhi had little or no interests in those countries, we should have expected India to at least abstain or possibly even vote 'no'. But of course India's interests in maintaining close relations with Gulf states – the primary meddlers – had not disappeared. Indeed, if anything they

---

112 'Regulating Intervention', 395–396.

113 Verhoeven et al., '"Our Identity is Our Currency"', 526.

114 S/PV.6810, 19 July 2012.

115 Bassel F. Salloukh, 'The Arab Uprisings and the Geopolitics of the Middle East', *The International Spectator: Italian Journal of International Affairs* 48:2 (2013), 40.

had become even more important as sanctions against Iran were now tightening significantly.[116] A careful search failed to unearth any formal statements by New Delhi indicating disquiet at the moves by various LAS states to arm Syria's rebels but, logically speaking, doing so ran counter to India's preference that all states be 'free to determine their own pathways' and India's preference for international crisis-resolution efforts being strictly 'impartial'. But on 19 July 2012, however much the policies of individual LAS states caused unease in New Delhi, the LAS itself had still not called for military intervention in Syria, or the imposition of sanctions. And, of course, India's interests in a generally good relationship with Western powers hadn't changed much either between February and July 2012; the July draft resolution had been sponsored by the West but it wasn't *significantly* more interventionist than the one India had voted for in February (and Western capitals were leaking signals indicating lukewarm enthusiasm at best for a Libya-style military intervention[117]). In these circumstances it made sense for India to vote 'yes' on 19 July 2012.

Yet on 22 July 2012 the LAS, clearly upset (again) with the Council's failure to act three days earlier, called on al-Assad to step down immediately and for all states to impose sanctions if he didn't. LAS members then proposed a very similar resolution in the General Assembly on 26 July 2012 (i.e. calling for sanctions to be imposed). But this was clearly beginning to test the limits of what New Delhi considered an acceptable level or form of intervention; when resolution 66/253B was put to the vote Singh declared 'we cannot welcome the League of Arab State's resolution of 22 July … it is unfortunate that [those interventionist] elements were not removed … . We therefore abstained'.[118] Clearly military intervention – and seemingly, the actual *implementation* of sanctions too – was, after Libya, a line in the sand New Delhi was simply not willing to cross no matter its interests in good relations with the Gulf states. Indeed, an unnamed 'senior official' in New Delhi reportedly said the LAS-sponsored Assembly resolution was 'a step too far' from India's perspective.[119] But it was clearly a difficult decision: one paper reported 'the pros and cons of the resolution w[ere] debated in South Block till late on Friday evening, and a decision to abstain was taken "in all caution" – moments before the vote'.[120]

And this was largely it regarding India's direct participation in efforts to end the Syria crisis. Prime Minister Manmohan Singh, at the Non-Aligned

116 Armin Rosen, 'Why India Is Finally Complying With Sanctions on Iran', *The Atlantic*, 15 March 2013.

117 Doug Bandow, 'Will NATO Intervene in Syria?', *National Interest*, 9 October 2012.

118 A/66/253B, 3 August 2012.

119 Parul Chandra, 'India Says UN Syria Resolution a "Step Too Far"', *The Hindu*, 5 August 2012.

120 Subhajit Roy, 'Cautious India Weighed Pros and Cons before Abstaining from UN's Syria Vote', *Indian Express*, 5 August 2012.

Movement's (NAM) late August 2012 conference, repeated India's now-familiar mantra regarding Syria, namely, 'as the world's largest democracy, India supports popular aspirations for a democratic and pluralistic order. Nevertheless, such transformations can't be prompted by external intervention'.[121] Then on 25 September, during a General Assembly debate on 'The Rule of Law' Hardeep Puri Singh did not mention Syria specifically but pointedly said:

> We strongly believe in the peaceful handling of any conflict situation ... by avoiding any unauthorised intervention in a state's internal affairs ... peaceful settlement of disputes is the key factor in the maintenance of international peace and security and in the promotion of the rule of law.[122]

As an aside, India voted for Resolution 2085 in December 2012 which authorised foreign intervention in Mali, although Mali's government had formally requested the operation and the AU and ECOWAS both supported and were participating in it.[123] Singh did not address the Council after this resolution passed unanimously. But he didn't need to: India's position had already crystalised in early August and it remained the same for the rest of 2012; India would support a consensual intervention because that was consistent with the sovereignty norm, but it would not countenance interventions, even sanctions, which were not.

Put in terms of this study's conceptual model, the following can be said about India's engagement with the Syrian crisis in mid-2012. First, hard-realist logic was clearly a very important shaping factor. India's 'yes' vote in February had very obviously been motivated by a desire to remain aligned with its main energy suppliers, and even though these states – especially the Saudis – had begun acting in ways New Delhi was not comfortable with by openly arming the Syrian rebels, India was still backing the Gulf states on 19 July 2012. Only when they went even further towards direct – or as India might have put it, 'partial' – intervention by calling for sanctions on 22 July did New Delhi begin to edge away (i.e. it still only abstained in the Assembly vote on 3 August).

The aspect of anti-imperialist logic which shaped India's preferences towards always seeking alignment with the developing world obviously also exerted a powerful shaping effect on India's policy-responses; but only up to a point. India had remained closely aligned with IBSA until Brazil faded away and South Africa broke ranks by abstaining in the Council on 19 July, and India remained aligned with the LAS as long as possible, namely, until the latter began to move ever-closer towards the sort of more-robust interventionism that New Delhi simply couldn't stomach (i.e. the 3 August Assembly vote). In other words, while ever the hard-

121 Varghese K. George, 'NAM Summit: India Says No to Foreign Intervention in Syria', *The Hindu*, 31 August 2012.

122 'India Against Unauthorised Internal Intervention', *New Indian Express*, 25 September 2012.

123 S/RES/2085, 20 December 2012.

realist and solidarity with the developing-world logics were complimentary, they shaped India's policy-responses decisively, but when maintaining solidarity with such states threatened India's strong preferences for traditional interpretations of the sovereignty norm, New Delhi began to squirm and deliver equivocal policy-responses (i.e. by abstaining).

The shaping effect of enlightened-realist logic in mid-2012 is perhaps the most interesting, or at least the most complex. For much of 2011 – namely, after NATO began exceeding its mandate in Libya – New Delhi clearly favoured the variety which assumed intervention was destabilising. In early 2012, however, some policy-shapers had begun to speculate whether *non*-intervention risked prolonging instability; and India's statements to the Council suggested New Delhi India was edging towards accepting that 'doing something' might be necessary to maintain stability in the region. To be sure, it remained adamantly opposed to 'doing too much' – to doing anything which could provide even the faintest hint of a pretext for a regime change – but it flirted with at least the 'possibility' of imposing sanctions on 19 July 2012.

This last point requires more elaboration: India voted for the 'future possibility of sanctions' on July19, but abstained on the 3 August General Assembly resolution which actually called for sanctions 'now' (even though it was technically non-binding). India was therefore treading a very fine line; it was arguably only prepared to ramp up pressure on al-Assad with *threats* of sanctions and to not *actually impose* sanctions. Overall, this suggests the variety of enlightened-realist discourse which assumes *interventionist measures past diplomatic pressure* are destabilising remained ascendant. In other words, New Delhi's policy-responses were shaped by a variety of enlightened-realist logic which ultimately remained compatible with India's long-standing preference for traditional interpretations of sovereignty.

The shaping influence of other aspects of the enlightened-realist identity discourse are clearer. First, India consistently avoided actively opposing the West – at least in 2012; we will see below that in 2013 its position changed – to ensure it didn't jeopardise the support of key Western states for its broader developmental and diplomatic goals. And the strategy paid off, with the U.S. State Department, for one, specifically singling India out for praise after 19 July.[124] Second, New Delhi assiduously and consistently looked to support multilateral efforts to end the Syrian crisis, including those by IBSA, the LAS, and when those fell away toward the middle of 2012, it switched to supporting the efforts by the UN, its envoys, and ad-hoc groups like the Action Group (so long as, that is, these bodies did not seek to end the crisis with a multilaterally-sanctioned military intervention or, as was suggested just above, even by the *multilateral imposition* rather than the mere 'multilateral threat' of sanctions).

In other words, India was deeply committed to work through multilateral bodies to seek stability-enhancing solutions to the Syrian crisis. This is of course

124 'US "Gratified" by India's Support on Syria', *Indian Express*, 25 July 2012.

also consistent with liberal-democratic logic, broadly speaking. So, India's policy responses were arguably also shaped to some degree by liberal-democratic logic; past its commitment to multilateralism, it would be overly cynical to entirely dismiss India's repeated professions of unease and concern about the human rights situation in Syria as completely insincere, empty rhetoric. But it nevertheless also seems clear this was, at best, only the soft variety of liberal-democratic logic involving rhetorical professions of support for democracy and human rights, supported by regular diplomatic missions and passionate entreaties, and maybe, just maybe, the *threat* of sanctions; but no more. The robust variety of liberal-democratic logic which most closely aligns with Pillar III of R2P was clearly *not* a shaping factor; indeed, quite the opposite, it had been so thoroughly discredited by the conduct, but especially the *outcome* in Libya (i.e. the true extent of post-Gaddafi chaos was only just becoming apparent in mid-2012) that India more-or-less broke ranks with the LAS in August 2012 over the passage of a non-binding Assembly resolution which stopped well-short of calling for military intervention.

Finally, it seems equally clear that the stridently anti-Western aspect of anti-imperialist logic was not shaping New Delhi's deliberations about Syria, or at least not strongly, in mid-2012. Of course, when India voted for Western-sponsored draft resolutions in February and July 2012 these were relatively benign and we know from what Singh told *Frontline* that India's position in October 2011 had been made with Libya in mind[125]; in other words, without saying so directly, he hinted strongly that India wanted to ensure the West would not be gifted another 'loose' Council resolution which could later be twisted into a regime change campaign. But Singh's statements to the Council across 2011 and into 2012 avoided any hint of outright criticism of the West, which must have caused much gnashing of teeth amongst fiercely anti-Western commentators back home.

Indeed, one such policy-shaper – or given what was just said, an 'aspiring' policy-shaper – gave vent to these frustrations when reflecting on India's 'yes' vote on 19 July 2012. Seema Mustafa delivered a diatribe against the US and Israel who, she claimed, 'justify terrorism so long as it is against an Arab regime' and took aim at R2P without naming it (i.e. 'the huge [Western] propaganda machinery [is used to] … convince the world that force is commendable to … get rid of "despots" and "dictators"'). She hailed Russia's and China's vetos as 'support for the Syrian … people's right to determine their own destiny', and chastised New Delhi for not joining them.[126] Sitaram Yechury of the CPI(M) also thoroughly denounced America's policy towards Syria which was designed to 'control the region and, hence, its resources', and he demanded India oppose the West implacably.[127]

125 Prashad, 'Syria, Libya'.

126 'West, Israel Using "Arab Spring" for Regime Change', *The Statesman*, 20 July 2012.

127 'The Agenda is Clear', *Hindustan Times*, 10 September 2012.

Prem Shankar Jha offered similar advice – he demanded India block all future Western initiatives in the Council – but while his reasoning contained hints of anti-Western logic his argument was primarily grounded in hard-realism, namely, there were 'striking parallels between what Damascus is facing today and what Delhi faced in Kashmir in the 1990s'. So, Jha worried military intervention would set a dangerous precedent for India.[128] And former ambassador and foreign secretary Kanwal Sibal called New Delhi's position 'craven', arguing that India's traditional 'abhorrence for externally enforced regime change' had been discarded in the pursuit of closer ties with the US and Gulf Arab states on 19 July. He warned India to not support 'the destruction of secular authoritarian regimes and their replacement by authoritarian Islamists ones' and he felt a 'compromise between principle and pragmatism dictated abstention by India'.[129]

But the general tenor of reflections on India's vote on 19 July offered a mixture of support for India's efforts to ramp up diplomatic pressure on al-Assad without allowing for military intervention, and a sense of weary resignation that these efforts had all failed, meaning India couldn't be expected to do much more. Alia Allana, for example, referred to ongoing Western talk of intervention and concluded 'this would be a misguided strategy, the Libya case should be proof enough' before musing whether the 'stalemate in the Security Council … creates a space for another push at diplomacy' (and if it did, Allana thought India should support it diplomatically).[130] Chinmaya Gharekhan's reflection was similar. He felt it 'made good sense for India to have voted in favour' on 19 July; specifically, after considering the human rights situation he concluded the Syrian government was mainly responsible, and because voting 'yes' furthered India's interests in the Gulf. But he again stopped short of advocating military intervention and suggested India had done about all it could other than offer the odd diplomatic gesture in future.[131]

And other policy-shapers were beginning to urge India to stealthily but steadily retreat from involvement in Syria and to simply look to its own interests; in other words, hard-realist logic was coming to the fore. In particular, a series of articles began to warn the Syrian conflict had seriously exacerbated the Shia-Sunni split, meaning India should studiously avoid getting sucked into the maelstrom. The titles of several articles speak volumes – 'Avoid this West Asian Drama',[132] 'India Walking Tightrope in Intra-Islam Cold War in West Asia',[133] 'Cold War in Middle East'[134] and 'Cold War Caliphate'[135] are illustrative.

128 'India Must Think Before it Acts on Syria', *The Hindu*, 7 August 2012.
129 'Delhi's Craven Policy on Syria', *Daily Mail Australia*, 24 July 2012.
130 'Arab Spring? The Season is Over', *The Hindu*, 24 July 2012.
131 'The Fog of War', *The Hindu*, 2 August 2012.
132 Barhat Karnad, *New Indian Express*, 10 August 2012.
133 Indrani Bagchi, *Times of India*, 25 August 2012.
134 C. Raja Mohan, *Indian Express*, 13 August 2012.
135 Pramit Pal Chaudhuri, *Hindustan Times*, 2 September 2012.

When the U.S. Ambassador Chris Stevens was killed by Islamists in Benghazi on 11 September 2012 a flurry of articles reflected on the implications for India; Atul Aneja, for example warned 'it is "regime change" which has led to a region-wide resurgence of the Al-Qaeda'.[136] Suhasini Haidar warned the West was in danger of repeating its mistake in Libya by arming the Syrian rebels, meaning it was now 'possible to understand India's nebulous stand on Syria at the UN where it has balanced two "yes" votes with … two "no" votes and two abstentions'; in other words, India's caution had been vindicated. For his part, R.S. Kalha argued that 'the Western powers are playing with fire' in Syria, and urged India to remain disengaged to avoid the 'blowback' more active involvement might precipitate.[137]

Chinmaya Gharekhan offered another especially important reflection in September 2011. By this point he had effectively come full circle. Gone were musings about the possibility of India backing a more robust intervention which had marked his writings in early and mid-2012 (short of military intervention of course; he had never quite reached that point). Now he urged India to stay clear of the worsening Sunni-Shia proxy war being fought in Syria by 'play[ing] non-alignment, or dual-alignment' between Riyadh and Tehran, which he thought New Delhi 'has been doing reasonably well'. Gharekhan had now switched positions twice, but the core of his argument had remained consistent; channelling hard-realist logic, he claimed 'consistency is not a virtue in international relations. The important thing is to look after one's national interests'.[138] In other words, India had been right to be cautious at first and support the various diplomatic efforts short of military intervention in late 2011; then it had correctly moved in lock-step with the LAS in the first half of 2012; and New Delhi was now right to back away given the abject failure of diplomatic solutions and rising tide of violence which flowed from such.

Zakir Hussein substantially agreed with Gharekhan,[139] as did Fazzur Siddiqui when he surveyed the implications, 18 months on, of the wider Arab Spring.[140] Indeed Indian scholars, whether writing in the policy institutes' in-house publications[141] or in the academic journals proper were drawing very similar conclusions on a range of points, including: that the chaos in Libya during 2012 generally vindicated India's cautious stance in Syria; that the Syrian conflict had now gotten out of hand due to geopolitical meddling India had little control over; and that India should

136 'In Benghazi, the Folly of Regime Change', *The Hindu*, 14 September 2012.

137 'The Wages of Naivety', *IDSA – Comment*, 18 September 2012.

138 'Raging Conflict', *Frontline* 29:18, 8–21 September 2012.

139 'Post-Assad Strategic Possibilities', *Indian Council of World Affairs – Issue Brief*, 6 August 2012.

140 'Arab Spring and the Changing Contours of Arab Politics', *Indian Council of World Affairs – Issue Brief*, 21 September 2012.

141 Vikram Sood, 'Oh What a Tangled Web We Weave', *Observer Research Foundation – Analysis*, 24 August 2012; Rajeev Agarwal, 'Arab Spring: Aspirations Met or Dreams Unfulfilled?', *Institute for Defence Studies and Analyses – Issue Brief*, 26 October 2012.

generally take a low profile as extremism flourished to avoid blowback. Hard-realist logic obviously underpins these sorts of findings: it was especially evident in every article in a special edition of the *Indian Foreign Affairs Journal* from mid-2013.[142] Sameena Hameed, for example, offered a classic statement of hard-realist logic when she considered India's policy towards the Syrian crisis:

> India has refused to extend a blanket endorsement of the Responsibility to Protect doctrine (R2P) … [India] was concerned about its selective implementation … . It is also relevant to India's rejection of any sort of external intervention in its own internal conflict zones … . India's stand has been vindicated in that any form of external intervention has proven to be disastrous.[143]

Regarding other identity discourses, soft liberal-democratic logic was only evident in one scholarly article from late 2012, and this author specifically refuted the notion that India's foreign policy was or should be shaped by robust liberal-democratic logic compatible with R2P (or at least Pillar III of such); instead, India should continue to promote 'constructive engagement, mediation, quiet diplomacy and dialogue as tools of international intervention'.[144] And the only mention of anti-imperialist logic (both varieties) came in the context of specific exhortations that New Delhi *not* be influenced by such; for example, after explaining India should generally avoid involvement in the Syrian crisis other than to protect its core interests, Ranjit Gupta claimed 'India's policy-makers should not be [swayed] by ideologically motivated domestic criticism about supposedly abandoning the so-called arbitrarily defined "independent" foreign policy'.[145]

Finally, several scholars assessed India's performance on the Security Council in early 2013 and, unsurprisingly, discussion of Libya and Syria dominated their papers. Regarding India's stance on R2P, Mishra and Kumar felt 'to a large extent, India took a consistent stand' by not rejecting it wholesale but 'seeking clarity with regard to certain aspects [of it, like] … "who guards the guardians"?'.[146] Regarding Syria, they explained how India had initially rejected interventionism and favoured dialogue, but that it changed its tune in July 2012 by voting for a draft resolution which raised the possibility of sanctions; they were not strongly critical, but they did suggest New Delhi had been right to revert later in August 2012 and

142 'India and Turmoil in the Arab World: Two Years Since the Advent of the "Arab Spring"', 8:2 (2012).

143 'International Community Should Desist from Attempting to Tip the Balance', *Indian Foreign Affairs Journal* 8:2 (2013), 176.

144 A. Gopinathan, 'The Arab Spring: Supporting Transition to Democracy', *Indian Foreign Affairs Journal* 7:4 (2012), 430.

145 Ranjit Gupta, 'Fallout of the "Arab Spring": Challenges for India', *Indian Foreign Affairs Journal* 8:2 (2013), 148.

146 Saurabh Mishra and Keerthi Sampath Kumar, 'India's Two Years at the Horse-Shoe Table', *Institute for Defence Studies and Analyses – Issue Brief*, 8 March 2013.

thereafter to opposing intervention past applying diplomatic pressure.[147] For their part, Mukherjee and Malone noted how after initially wanting to pursue Security Council reform India had been blindsided by the succession of humanitarian crises. These put India in a difficult position because:

> India's statements and stances on [R2P] … presented a coherent picture of conscientious objection, though one that resulted in it falling somewhere between … western pro-intervention and eastern anti-intervention. Consequently, India … at times found itself isolated, as in the case of its initial abstention on Syria in late 2011 that was followed by a change of course … largely provoked by representations from Saudi [Arabia] … . India was neither able to sway the council on specific issues nor able to emerge from debates with widely well-received positions.

Overall, however, they generally rated India's engagement with the Syrian crisis positively because, measured against New Delhi's own standards, 'by counselling restraint [India] … upheld its role as a guardian of the UN Charter and its goals'.[148] In other words, India's interpretation of what 'acting responsibly' meant was strongly shaped by its preference for traditional interpretations of the sovereignty norm. Thus while India could accept that a state was responsible for protecting its people (Pillar I), and that foreign states could be responsible for helping it do so (Pillar II), actual intervention in that sovereign state, even by means of sanctions, and especially by the use of force (Pillar III), was *not* 'a responsible act'.

This largely concludes the close analysis of India's engagement with the Syrian crisis. The next section of this chapter examines the lessons India learned from the Syria crisis when it stepped down from the Council at the end of 2012, before the final section briefly considers India's engagement with Syria in 2013 and 2014.

Lessons Learned from the Syrian Crisis

Put in terms of the conceptual model deployed herein, first and most obviously hard-realist logic had been strongly vindicated by the end of 2012. India had acted cautiously throughout its engagement with the Syrian crisis, not expended too many scarce and precious resources, successfully protected its most vital interests in the Gulf, and it had received tangible pay-offs while doing so, especially from Saudi Arabia. It had few direct interests to protect in Syria, so there was little to lose there. The Syrian crisis had not been resolved, but from the point of view of hard-realist logic, it had been 'managed' or 'contained' sufficiently (i.e. India's core interests were safe).

147 Ibid., 4.

148 Rohan Mukherjee and David Malone, 'India and the UN Security Council: An Ambiguous Tale', *Economic and Political Weekly* 48:29 (2013), 116.

Second, the variety of enlightened-realist logic which assumes that if India acts responsibly it can raise its international profile was basically vindicated; India had supported the various (non-interventionist) peace plans, and while none had borne fruit New Delhi could reasonably claim it had visibly and sincerely tried hard. And while India received occasional criticism from Western capitals for not supporting more interventionist measures it had also been the recipient of praise at times; at minimum in Western eyes New Delhi certainly looked good by comparison to some other powers (most obviously Russia, but China too). On balance, India managed what had been, in effect, a stance against the West's preference – more robust intervention than India could easily accept – without damaging its relationships with Western powers. India's diplomatic Holy Grail, permanent elevation to the Council, remained elusive, although the frantic agenda of and acrimonious atmosphere in the Council during 2011 and 2012 probably made hopes of significantly advancing that agenda unrealistic anyway.

Third, the tussle between the varieties of enlightened-realist logic which differ over whether intervention enhances or undermines stability was resolved, and decisively so. India had begun its engagement with the Syrian crisis in mid-2011 firmly convinced intervention undermines stability, however in the first half of 2012 it began to sway towards the opposite position. Yet the word 'sway' was used deliberately; India never quite got there, and after the LAS's 22 July resolution New Delhi took fright and retreated to an equivocal position by abstaining when the LAS presented an Assembly resolution on 3 August which demanded sanctions be imposed. Then as Libya continued to fall apart and Islamists advanced in Mali, Indian policy-shapers and policy-makers alike began to conclude ever-more firmly that they had been right all along; interventions, especially military interventions, *were* destabilising after all, and India should not support them. Notably, this lesson was not learned because robust intervention was tried and it failed in Syria, but because it had failed so miserably in *Libya*.

Fourth, the picture is mixed regarding the lessons learnt regarding the anti-imperialist identity discourse. Solidarity with Brazil and South Africa was maintained for the best part of a year before it broke down in mid-2012 (but not acrimoniously), and India's alignment with the LAS paid off directly (see above), although by mid-2012 the behaviour of some LAS members was making New Delhi increasingly uncomfortable. The early consensus within the BRICS over Libya broke down over Syria as Russia and China took hard-line stances at the outset. The India-led IBSA initiative had come to naught, as did every LAS initiative (India had backed all of these too before August 2012). Put simply, aligning with the developing world had not resolved the Syrian crisis.

Nevertheless, New Delhi had patiently 'invested' in its developing-world relationships and, generally speaking, its ties to these traditional partners had improved while it also avoided being sucked into the various diplomatic rifts (i.e. Russia versus the LAS/West, Sunni states versus Shia Iran, etc.) which became ever-more acrimonious. The 'align with the developing world' aspect of the anti-imperialist identity discourse was therefore vindicated, although perhaps not especially strongly. But the 'implacably oppose the West' aspect was undermined somewhat. The Western powers ultimately acted relatively more responsibly vis-à-vis Syria than they had in Libya – they had repeatedly and loudly called for intervention, but when authorisation to intervene was not forthcoming they had not gone ahead anyway and defied the Council – which undercut the core logic of this variety of anti-imperialism (i.e. that the West can't be trusted, that it ruthlessly pursues its interests, etc.). And despite the repeated, strong denunciations of the West by a number of anti-Western policy-shapers New Delhi voted with the West twice in 2012 and studiously avoided anti-Western rhetoric; the only conclusion possible is that the relative influence of this variety of anti-imperialist logic declined somewhat.

Fifth, and regarding the liberal-democratic identity discourse, on the face of it the soft variety of such was not vindicated; put simply, repeated rhetorical exhortations to respect human rights and begin the transition to democracy achieved little. But if all these statements had been entirely empty rhetoric India would have just mouthed the appropriate platitudes and then done nothing. New Delhi instead invested time and diplomatic capital – not enormous amounts, but a full year's worth of steady effort nonetheless – seeking a (non-interventionist) end to the Syrian crisis which would (hopefully) produce a democratic transition. Arguably this logic was undermined only marginally because Indians – or again, maybe just their elites – are very obviously, given their repeated references to soft liberal-democratic logic, constituted at least in part by this identity discourse. At minimum they remained committed to 'making an effort' to securing a peaceful, democratic Syria between August 2011 and August 2012.

Of course, after the Council became hopelessly deadlocked (after 19 July 2012) and the LAS subsequently shifted into a more confrontational position (in August 2012) India basically gave up; New Delhi was obviously not prepared to cross the line from rhetorical/diplomatic support for democracy and human rights to active, especially military, efforts to do so. This demonstrates clearly most Indian policy-shapers (apart from the odd one; Meenakshi Ganguly is the stand-out but almost lone example) are obviously not 'constituted enough' by robust liberal-democratic logic to be prepared to consistently support more robust interventionism to protect human rights and promote democracy (including by imposing sanctions). This much is absolutely clear; the robust variety of the liberal-democratic identity discourse which is most compatible with R2P's Pillar III was strongly undermined by the conduct and outcome of the Libyan intervention, and the fractured nature of and the unsavoury tactics employed by the Syrian rebels simply reinforced the impression amongst Indians that the use of force to protect human rights and promote democracy is fraught with danger.

These lessons have profound implications for India's approach to the broader contest between traditional interpretations of sovereignty and the newer R2P norm which seeks to modify the sovereignty norm to allow relatively more intervention in sovereign states, possibly including military intervention. Put simply, what have been called at times above sovereignty-friendly varieties of the various identity discourses – soft-liberal-democratic logic, hard-realist logic, the variety of enlightened-realism which assumes intervention caused instability, the anti-Western aspect of anti-imperialism, etc. – were noticeably more common in the public debates, especially when Indians reflected on the Libyan and Syrian crises towards the end of 2012. By contrast, R2P-friendly advice – grounded in robust liberal-democratic logic or the variety of enlightened-realist logic which assumes intervention might be necessary to arrest instability, for example – was tendered on occasion, but much less often.

New Delhi's policy-responses remained generally consistent with the weight of the sovereignty-friendly advice because policy-makers never seemed comfortable with the more interventionist measures being proposed to end the Syrian crisis. The clearest illustration is provided by consideration of developing-world solidarity logic; when other developing-world actors opposed intervention, India readily – even eagerly – aligned with them. But when these states (or their representative organisations) took R2P-friendly positions – when they favoured intervention, especially military intervention but also even less interventionist measures like the actual imposition of sanctions (i.e. the LAS in August 2012) – India distanced itself. The same sort of behaviour manifested regarding the aspect of enlightened-realist logic which purports to shape Indian policy-responses aimed at raising its profile in global affairs and pursuing diplomatic side-benefits; when 'acting responsibly' meant supporting relatively non-interventionist initiatives India would do so enthusiastically; but when other states concluded 'responsible behaviour' meant more interventionism, India would typically withhold its support for such, or only offer support when New Delhi was confident a Russian and/or Chinese veto would mean those initiatives would likely fail.

So, the clearest lesson India learned from the Syria crisis, by the end of 2012, was that its pre-2010 position on R2P need not change much. Recall that on the eve of India's ascension to the Security Council in 2011 the implacable opposition India had generally offered to R2P since 2001 had softened to some degree but had not changed radically; India had warmed somewhat to Pillars I and II but remained firmly opposed to Pillar III in 2010. Then India had abstained on Resolution 1973, flirting with qualified 'support' – really, 'non-opposition to' – what it thought would be an intervention which was basically consistent with a 'restrained' Pillar III operation (i.e. one which would only protect civilians directly threatened with harm). But this had quickly morphed into a regime change with ultimately catastrophic consequences for Libyan and regional stability, meaning New Delhi's position against Pillar-III-type interventions hardened considerably.

Events in 2011 and 2012 in Syria had basically reinforced this position; the primary lesson learned was that India's support for R2P must remain circumscribed with caveats, marked by caution, and informed by a firm desire to continue debating and negotiating the scope and meaning of the norm. Pillar I and Pillar II may be acceptable, but only because they are essentially compatible with traditional notions of sovereignty. Pillar III is not, and India's long-held suspicions about and scepticism toward this component of the R2P norm hardened even further during the Syrian crisis. India was not even prepared to impose sanctions let alone military measures designed to directly protect civilians, and it became adamantly opposed to anything which even hinted at the possibility of regime change. We will see in the next section that events in Syria after India stepped down from the Council changed India's position only marginally, if at all.

India's Engagement with the Syrian Crisis in 2013 and 2014

In August 2012, U.S. President Barrack Obama had warned that the use of chemical weapons by Syria's government was a 'red line' which, if crossed, would invite intervention.[149] But when the first well-verified reports[150] of such an attack appeared in late March both sides blamed each other,[151] and while the US and Britain formally investigated the matter, no intervention followed.

India's government had little to say in early 2013 after Hardeep Puri Singh stopped attending Security Council meetings on India's behalf; neither the Ministry of External Affairs (MEA) during March and April 2013, nor the Prime Minister at the BRICS forum on 27 March,[152] discussed Syria. When the General Assembly passed a resolution on 15 May 2013 which strongly condemned Syria's government,[153] New Delhi abstained after repeating its now-familiar mantra that 'unilateral action of any kind will not resolve the crisis. It will only exacerbate the problem'.[154] And the Indian commentators were relatively muted too; only a single op-ed considered the ramifications of the possible use of chemical weapons in early 2013, and its author wondered whether the West was repeating its strategy in Iraq a decade earlier (i.e. 'false allegations of ... weapons of mass destruction ... became the excuse for an illegal and ill-conceived invasion').[155]

But then a chemical attack on the Damascus suburb of Ghouta on 21 August 2013 killed around 1,000 people, and a UN investigative team reported in mid-September that sarin gas had been used, although it did not consider *who* was responsible.[156] Calls mounted – again – for a military intervention, and this time

149 James Ball, 'Obama Issues Syria a "Red Line" Warning on Chemical Weapons', *Washington Post*, 20 August 2012.

150 Earlier alleged attacks in December 2012 could not be verified due to the intensity of fighting in Aleppo; Asher Zeiger and Stuart Winer, 'Syrian Rebels Claim Recent Alleged Chemical Attack Not the First', *Times of Israel*, 25 December 2012.

151 William Branigin, Anne Gearan and Suzan Haidamous, 'Syria, Rebels Accuse Each Other of Firing a Chemical Weapon Near Aleppo', *Washington Post*, 19 March 2013.

152 Speech, Manmohan Singh, 'Prime Minister's Statement at the Plenary Session of the 5th BRICS Summit', Durban, 27 March 2012.

153 A/RES/67/262, 15 May 2012.

154 A/67/PV.80, 15 May 2013.

155 'A Turning Point in Syria', *The Hindu*, 27 April 2013.

156 Åke Sellström, Scott Cairns and Maurizio Barbeschi, 'Report on the Alleged Use of Chemical Weapons in the Ghouta Area of Damascus on 21 August 2013', *United Nations*, 13 September 2013.

the LAS backed military action (although not without some equivocation and dissention within its ranks[157]).

This woke Indians from their relative slumber vis-à-vis Syria; many articles focused on the likely negative consequences for India should the West intervene (mainly higher oil prices),[158] and others aired doubts about who was responsible for the attack.[159] On this last point, of the 16 interviewees asked nine suspected that the rebels had carried out the attack to precipitate a Western intervention – so, over half of the interviewees who were asked essentially raised the 'moral hazard' argument against R2P – while five declined to speculate and two assumed the Syrian government was responsible. This spread of opinions surprised the author (who is a Westerner[160]), but upon reflection it amply demonstrates that deep scepticism over the veracity of the justifications tendered by US policy-makers for its 2003 Iraq invasion continues to linger in India. Indeed anti-American conspiracy theorising arguably verges on pathological paranoia in some Indian circles: for example, while no interviewee said they *personally* believed the US was behind the August 2013 chemical attack, I-13 reported 'excitable and left-wing students – indeed, the odd colleague at this university[161] too – have speculated that maybe the US put [the rebels] up to it' in search of a pretext to invade.[162]

In the papers, only Frida Ghitis backed intervention in Syria after the chemical attack – her article was entitled 'The Consequences of Doing Nothing in Syria'[163] – but the overwhelming weight of opinion opposed intervention.[164] For example B.S.

---

157 'Arab League Chief: Confront ISIS', *The Hindu*, 8 September 2014.

158 Indrani Bagchi, 'US-led Military Action Against Syria Spells Bad News for India', *Times of India*, 28 August 2013; Pramit Chaudhari, 'It's all Connected: Why War in Syria May Hurt You', *Hindustan Times*, 28 August 2013; Maha Siddiqui, 'Syria Extracts Reassurance, India Eyes Crisis Apprehensively', *India Today*, 8 September 2013.

159 Ravi Joshi, 'Is Syria the Next Libya?', *Observer Research Foundation – Analysis*, 29 August 2013; Abhijit Iyer Mitra, 'The Evidence on Syria is Thin', *Observer Research Foundation – Analysis*, 3 September 2013; Arun Mohan Sukumar, 'Defending the Indefensible in Syria', *The Hindu*, 29 August 2013; 'Delay is Good', *Indian Express*, 2 September 2013.

160 The author grew up in Perth, Australia, has lived in Canada and Britain, and now lives in Sydney, Australia.

161 One of the leading universities in India, with a very strong Politics and IR department.

162 New Delhi, 18 November 2013.

163 *New Indian Express*, 8 September 2013.

164 'Attacking Syria is a Bad Idea', *The Hindu*, 26 August 2013; Rajeev Agrawal, 'Potential Military Strikes in Syria Threaten Regional Flare-Up', *Observer Research Foundation – Analysis*, 31 August 2013; 'International Order be Damned', *The Hindu*, 30 August 2013; Hardeep Puri Singh, 'No-win in Syria', *Indian Express*, 30 August 2013; 'Syria Hypocrisy', *Indian Express*, 4 September 2013; Kanwal Sibal, 'Two-Faced in West Asia', *The Hindu*, 4 September 2013; 'America, the New Colonial Power', *Asian Age*, 8 September 2013.

Chimni, a leading Indian scholar of international law and the only commentator to specifically refer to R2P in this context, noted the chemical attack 'would seem a textbook case for invoking the R2P doctrine'. But he ultimately concluded:

> military action is difficult to reconcile with the … legal principles of non-use of force and non-intervention … . [And] there are differences with respect to the understanding … of R2P … . [And] states have become wiser after the intervention in Libya … [And] there is a valid concern that military action will lead to an escalation of violence in Syria and the region … [And] there is a genuine fear that arms supplied to the rebels may end up with extremist rebel groups … [Instead we need] prudent internationalism [which] … refrains from undermining the normative consensus … on when military action is permissible [and] … acknowledges that democracy … cannot be exported … . [K]ey developing countries like Brazil, India, China and South Africa [must] … garner support for the diplomatic … Geneva-II process [i.e. another upcoming Action Group conference].[165]

Little has been said until now in this chapter about the Indian parliament because during 2011 and 2012 Syria was hardly discussed apart from occasional questions to ministers.[166] But when the prospect of Western intervention loomed the parliament reacted; it did not 'erupt' like it had back in March 2011 over NATO's bombing of Libya, but on 27 August 2013 MPs in the Rajya Sabha drew parallels with Iraq a decade earlier and urged India to oppose intervention (with the left parties, unsurprisingly, shrilly denouncing 'imperialist and reactionary powers'[167]). But the opposition BJP, led by former-Foreign Minister Jaswant Singh, also came out strongly against intervention in the Lok Sabha:

> The Western world are not the policemen, or the keepers of global peace. This is unacceptable [given they have] … already caused so much damage to our neighbourhood … India has to speak with much sounder and stronger voice against this kind of global policing or hegemony that we are witnessing.[168]

For its part the government (still a Congress-led coalition) obliged by resisting moves to intervene, although its position was nuanced because 'official sources' reported that 'there is a clash of two different principles which India supports

---

165 B.S. Chimni, 'R2P and Syria: Imperialism with a Human Face', *Open Democracy*, 11 September 2011.

166 Lok Sabha Debate, 15th Series, Vol. XXIII, 10th Session, No. 3, 14 March 2012; Lok Sabha Debate, 15th Series, Vol. XXVII, 11th Session, No. 6, 17 August 2012.

167 'Syria Crisis: MPs Ask Govt. to Take a Strong Stand', *New Indian Express*, 27 August 2013.

168 Lok Sabha Debate, 15th Session, Vo. XXXV, 14th Session, No. 19, 4 September 2013.

– the policy of non-intervention and backing for the CWC [Chemical Weapons Convention]'.[169] Then India's foreign minister, Salman Kurshid, admitted on 1 September 2013 to uncertainty over responsibility for the attacks, called for the Action Group to meet again and said 'we don't think we can be much help right now'.[170] Days later an MEA spokesperson reported policy-makers in South Block were grappling with the conundrum of opposing intervention and supporting efforts to eliminate chemical weapons; he declared 'we will prefer to await the full results of the UN inspection'.[171] A week later India strongly supported Russian moves to secure a compromise Security Council resolution.[172] A further week after that New Delhi enthusiastically endorsed the US-Russia deal that resulted in a resolution passing unanimously which avoided military intervention and instead began a multilateral process of destroying Syria's chemical weapons;[173] the MEA happily reported that this outcome was 'in alignment with India's consistent stance of supporting the complete destruction and elimination of chemical weapons worldwide'.[174]

It is easy to see why India was happy; a unanimous resolution had passed which authorised the Organisation for the Prohibition of Chemical Weapons, with the Syrian government's consent and the support of Western powers along with Russia and China, to eliminate an entire stockpile of chemical weapons without any foreign bombs being dropped. Of course, Syrians would continue to be killed in large numbers by conventional weapons, but that wasn't the point; the overwhelming weight of opinion in India had been unwilling to countenance a Pillar-III style intervention even if, as Chimni had noted, the chemical attack constituted 'textbook' circumstances for such. The logic of various sovereignty-friendly identity discourses had carried the day decisively.

This is not to say that logic consistent with R2P played no part at all because the disarmament effort would be conducted and paid for by an international coalition (India contributed US$1 million[175]). In other words, it was arguably the sort of measure contemplated by Pillar II of R2P: a state was 'helped' – under threat of Pillar III-style intervention, of course – by the international community to fulfil its Pillar I responsibilities, without an actual Pillar III intervention (or even the imposition of sanctions) taking place. Of the 16 interviewees asked: 'Is this

169 Parul Chandra, 'Action on Syria: India may do a Balancing Act', *Asian Age*, 29 August 2013.

170 'New Delhi Backs UN-led Process on Syria Crisis', *Indian Express*, 1 September 2013.

171 'No Military Solution to Conflict in Syria', *Hindustan Times*, 3 September 2013.

172 'Diplomacy has Saved the Day', *Hindustan Times*, 11 September 2013.

173 S/RES/2118, 27 September 2013.

174 'Delhi Welcomes US-Russia Pact on Syrian Chem Arms', *New Indian Express*, 16 September 2013.

175 Sachin Parashar, 'India Pledges $1 Million to Destroy Syria's Chemical Weapons', *Times of India*, 4 December 2013.

the sort of interpretation of R2P India is comfortable with?'; 14 agreed (the two dissenters disliked how the US and Russia had sidelined everyone else, including India). All 14 who agreed confirmed India liked this sort of interpretation of R2P because it was *narrow* and so was compatible with the sovereignty norm. For example, I-3 said that 'the deal is consistent with Pillar I – Syria would fulfil its responsibilities – under pressure, of course, but without bombs';[176] I-11 felt 'India was progressing on R2P, moving away from the old "strict sovereignty"; a "diluted R2P" is consistent with Pillar II, so India can back it';[177] and I-14 ticked-off the reasons why India was pleased: 'no invasion, a negotiated deal, Syria consented, the great powers agreed, WMD were eliminated, the UN was involved'.[178]

The August 2013 chemical attack in Syria therefore reinforced India's post-Libya position on R2P, namely, that only a narrow interpretation was acceptable (i.e. not including sanctions or military intervention, and definitely not regime change). But a year later New Delhi did not oppose an international military intervention into the 'Syrian' crisis (i.e. the conflict had by then spilled into Iraq) to combat the extremist group IS. Some context is required to explain why.

IS was once known in the West as 'al-Qaeda in Iraq'. It was largely defeated, as Biddle et al. put it, by a 'synergistic interaction between the [Bush] surge and the [Arab] Awakening' between 2005 and 2008.[179] But Iraq's Shia-dominated government led by Prime Minister Nouri al-Maliki alienated many Sunnis, al-Qaeda in Iraq survived,[180] and it was re-branded as the Islamic State of Iraq and the Levant/Syria (i.e. the ISIL and ISIS acronyms have been used interchangeably). In 2012, led by Abu Bakr al-Baghdadi, ISIL expanded its operations into Syria; specifically, militants were dispatched to form the al-Nusra Front, but the two groups later became estranged[181] which led to ISIL expanding directly into Syria from April 2013 by capturing Raqqa in the North-East. Open conflict with other rebel groups – including the FSA, the Islamic Front and, at times, also al-Nusra – started in late 2013 and intensified in early 2014. ISIL's ability to operate across the Syrian/Iraqi border conferred significant advantages on it, and in January 2014 it took the opportunity afforded by an outbreak of fighting between the Iraqi Army and Sunni tribes in Iraq's Anbar province to suddenly seize Fallujah.[182] But ISIL really burst onto the international scene, so to speak, in mid-2014 by launching a spectacularly

---

176 New Delhi, 1 November 2013.

177 New Delhi, 13 November 2013.

178 New Delhi, 19 November 2013.

179 Stephen Biddle, Jeffrey A. Friedman and Jacob N. Shapiro, 'Testing the Surge: Why Did Violence Decline in Iraq in 2007?', *International Security* 37:1 (2012), 10.

180 Hugh Tomlinson, 'Maliki Author of Nation's Chaos', *The Australian*, 16 June 2014.

181 Because al-Nusra refused to recognise al-Baghdadi's later attempt to supplant the 'original al-Qaeda', led by Ayman al-Zawahiri after Osama bin-Laden's death in 2011.

182 Liz Sly, 'Al-Qaeda Claims Key Iraqi City of Fallujah', *Sydney Morning Herald*, 5 January 2014.

successful campaign in Iraq's north. Three whole Iraqi Army divisions were routed and Mosul, a city of 1.8 million, was captured in early June; then ISIL declared the Sykes-Picot borders meaningless;[183] and finally, in late June 2014, al-Baghdadi declared the establishment of the Islamic State (IS) with himself as Caliph.[184]

The international response led by the US was slow but measured: Washington first carried out a few airstrikes in support of Kurdish Peshmerga forces which were under pressure from IS but the Americans refused to go further until Iraq's Prime Minister al-Maliki resigned (which occurred in mid-August). US operations against IS in other areas of Iraq and also in Syria increased steadily thereafter, and five LAS members conducted their first air strikes against IS targets on 23 September.[185] The US-led coalition eventually grew to about 20 states, although there was considerable difference in members' contributions (i.e. the US conducted strikes in both Iraq and Syria while its Western allies tended to only operate in Iraq and LAS members only operated in Syria).

IS rapidly gained a reputation for unrelenting barbarity in the areas it controlled; it openly sold captured Yazidi women as slaves; it summarily executed thousands of captured Iraqi army troops; and it beheaded a number of Western hostages.[186] The case for intervention being consistent with the R2P norm was made by both Gareth Evans[187] and Secretary-General Ban Ki-Moon,[188] but while it would be inaccurate to claim humanitarianism played *no* role in motivating the intervention in what had now become a linked Syrian/Iraqi crisis, it would seem reasonable to accept the interveners were primarily protecting direct interests in Iraq and acting to preserve the general stability of the oil-rich Middle East. In particular the *timing* of the intervention suggested this was the case – in other words, if humanitarianism had been the paramount motivation intervention in the conflict in Syria would have come much earlier – and it is also notable that American public opinion also turned sharply in favour of intervention after James Foley, a US citizen, was beheaded.[189] For the sake of clarity, while Iraq's government specifically requested foreign assistance the US-led coalition was not prepared to formally work with al-Assad,[190] who in turn never formally requested nor authorised strikes be carried

183 Michael Knights, 'Iraq War III has Now Begun', *Foreign Policy*, 11 June 2014.

184 'Sunni Rebels Declare new "Islamic Caliphate"', *Al-Jazeera*, 30 June 2014.

185 John Lyons and Dennis Shanahan, 'Arab Nations Join US Strikes on ISIS in Syria', *The Australian*, 24 September 2014.

186 Stephanie Nebehay, 'Islamic State Committing Staggering Crimes in Iraq: UN Report', *The Age*, 3 October 2014.

187 'A Legitimate, Humane Mission in Iraq to Halt IS Extremism', *The Australian*, 2 September 2014.

188 Jared Owens, 'UN Comments Leave the Greens, Left Isolated on Iraq', *The Australian*, 3 September 2014.

189 Leon Hadar, 'Has Rand Paul's Moment Already Passed?', *American Conservative*, 31 October 2014.

190 Sam Dagher, Maria Abi-Habib and Felicia Schwartz, 'Syria Says U.S. Told It of Coming Airstrikes Against Islamic State', *Wall Street Journal*, 23 September 2014.

out within Syria's borders; but given the air strikes were directed against one of his enemies (i.e. IS) al-Assad essentially consented *tacitly*.[191]

Indian commentators were slow to realise the significance of IS's advances in early 2014 with only a few articles reporting the seizure of Fallujah;[192] most remained focused on the crisis in Syria proper.[193] In May, one commentator bemoaned how the 'chamber of horrors of the Syrian civil war has spawned a terrorist group so extreme that it has been rejected even by al-Qaeda',[194] although it wasn't until mid-June 2014 that Indians really took note. Arvind Sivaramakrishnan, for one, blamed the emergence of IS on the US (for its Iraq invasion) and al-Maliki (for his sectarian policies) after Mosul fell, and while he noted the West was currently ruling out intervention, he thought it might be necessary in light of the dire threat to everyone – India included – that IS posed.[195]

This last sentiment was a quite sudden reversal from the general trend of strong opposition to intervention that had prevailed amongst Indians for several years now; as noted earlier several commentators had flirted with advising India to support some sort of intervention in Syria – at least sanctions – in mid-2012 before anti-intervention sentiment later hardened; but now some began to reassess this position again. For example, the calls by prominent Indian Shia clerics for New Delhi to support military intervention were reported in one paper,[196] while another paper concluded the failure to intervene in Syria meant it had 'become the biggest training ground for *jihadis*'.[197] Suhasini Haidar judged the situation now demanded New Delhi consider abandoning its

> confused path, voting with the U.S. and the EU … on a Security Council vote that Russia and China eventually vetoed, but then turning around against the West on others. With each successive flip-flop voting at the UN and the UNHRC, (two for, three against, three abstentions), India's voice has lost its timbre.[198]

Haidar did not specify exactly what to do, but one paper reported 'security establishment sources' had warned Narendra Modi's newly-elected BJP-led

---

191 Ian Black and Mona Mahmood, 'Coalition Air Strikes Against Isis Aid Bashar al-Assad, Syrian Rebels Claim', *The Guardian*, 10 October 2014.

192 'Al-Qaeda Militants in Iraq Claim Falluja as "Independent State"', *New Indian Express*, 5 January 2014; 'Iraqis Seek Political Solution to Avert Army Attack on Falluja', *Times of India*, 12 January 2014.

193 'India's Syria Juggling Act', *The Diplomat*, 14 January 2014; 'India's Syrian Venture', *The Hindu*, 28 January 2014.

194 'A Nightmare Group in Syria', *The Hindu*, 15 May 2014.

195 'Teetering on the Edge', *The Hindu*, 14 June 2014.

196 'City Muslims Follow Iraq Crisis with Bated Breath', *Times of India*, 16 June 2014.

197 Kounteya Sinha, 'Caravan of *Jihadists* Coming from Afghanistan to Liberate Kashmir: Al-Qaida', *Times of India*, 15 June 2014.

198 'India Must Find its Voice in West Asia', *The Hindu*, 19 June 2014.

government that IS had 'global ambitions and aims to create an Islamic World Dominion of which even India would be a part' and urged India to consider supporting military intervention.[199]

New Delhi was indeed seemingly prompted into a more activist response by the emergence of the IS threat; the first official MEA statement expressed concerns about 'the direct threat to the security and territorial integrity of Iraq'[200] and India's stance against intervention seemed to shift towards support for intervention (although it remained logically consistent; the Iraqi *government* was under threat and any foreign intervention would therefore be *consensual*). The shift was no doubt also a function of the newly-self-proclaimed Caliph al-Baghdadi's call for *jihadis* in India (amongst other places) to rise up and join IS's holy war.[201] But, crucially, almost 100 Indians were being held hostage in Mosul. One commentator, while acknowledging New Delhi's bind, began to wonder whether India was on the verge of a fundamental foreign policy realignment.[202] When the US began bombing – with the Iraqi government's permission – in early August 2014, New Delhi declined to comment. But comments by the newly-appointed Deputy National Security Advisor Arvind Gupta a few days later were telling; he noted that 'on a scale of brutality, [IS] scores 10 out of 10. Al-Qaeda scores 6 out of 10', although he also conceded caution was necessary to ensure 'the negotiations for the release of the Indians are not jeopardised'.[203]

The press began to report on IS's human rights abuses,[204] although only one commentator, Vijay Prashad urged New Delhi to adopt a 'moral foundation' for its foreign policy and support direct intervention.[205] It was, however, reported that Indian Shias were lobbying the government to intervene directly (and somewhere between 25,000 and 200,000 reportedly 'signed up' to fight IS: conflicting reports gave wildly different figures[206]). IS's execution of the American hostage James Foley elicited condemnation in India of the group's 'barbarism' later in August

---

199 Deeptiman Tiwari, 'ISIS has Designs on India: Experts', *Times of India*, 20 June 2014.

200 'India Slams Terror Attack in Iraq Cities', *Asian Age*, 17 June 2014.

201 Praveen Swami, 'India Among Jihad Targets of ISIS', *The Hindu*, 2 July 2014.

202 Amirah Bhattacharyya, 'Climate Change in New Delhi', *Hindustan Times*, 26 July 2014.

203 'ISIS More Brutal than al-Qaeda, Says Dy NSA', *Indian Express*, 12 August 2014.

204 'Women Stoned to Death in Syria for Adultery', *Times of India*, 10 August 2014; Vijay Prashad, 'Metastasis of the IS', *The Hindu*, 11 August 2014; Ginu Zacharia Oommen, 'In West Asia, a Faith Under Siege', *The Hindu*, 13 August 2014.

205 The Yazidis are a minority whose faith resembles ancient Zoroastrianism. IS considered them heretics and treated them appallingly; 'A Moral Foundation for Foreign Policy', *The Hindu*, 18 August 2014.

206 Ishaan Tharoor, 'Shiites in India Want to Join the Fight Against the IS in Iraq', *Washington Post*, 6 August 2014; Stephanie March, '200,000 Indians Volunteer to Join Effort Against Islamic State Militants in Iraq, Mosque Says', *ABC News*, 6 October 2014.

2014,[207] but other articles appeared which did not oppose intervention per se but instead blamed the US for creating the enemy it was now fighting (i.e. US support for the Afghanistan *mujahedeen* in the 1980s, its 2003 Iraq invasion, its support of allegedly radical Sunni states like Pakistan and Saudi Arabia, etc., were cited[208]).

Then in September, al-Qaeda – the 'original' *jihadi* group established by Osama bin-Laden – announced the establishment of an Indian al-Qaeda branch in what many interpreted as a somewhat desperate move to grab back some of the limelight stolen by the newly-prominent (and estranged) *jihadis* running IS.[209] This prodded New Delhi further towards an activist response. Ministers and security chiefs first announced a range of measures to 'stamp out *jihadism*' within India,[210] and just before Prime Minister Modi travelled to New York India's position became clearer. First, the MEA announced India would likely share intelligence with the US, and that it may extend logistical support to the US-led coalition's air campaign, but ruled out Indian forces participating directly.[211] Then, when Modi addressed the General Assembly on 27 September, he said India 'welcomes efforts to combat terrorism's resurgence in West Asia, which is affecting countries near and far'.[212] Finally, Modi and Obama held a joint press conference at which they 'reaffirmed their deep concern over the continued threat posed by terrorism, most recently highlighted by the dangers presented by the [IS]'.[213]

India had now, in effect, come down off the fence – not decisively, because it didn't join the anti-IS coalition apart from offering to share intelligence; its concerns about Indian hostages remained an important constraint[214] – but India was in effect tacitly supporting foreign military operations in Iraq and, by extension, in Syria too (i.e. the US-led coalition was bombing targets in Syria; but not Syrian *government* targets). Obviously the fact the Iraqi government actively sought foreign assistance was crucial; while New Delhi never said so explicitly, its position was consistent with Pillars I and II of R2P (i.e. Iraq had requested 'military assistance'). Nevertheless India had in effect climbed down from its

---

207 'No Limit to the Brutality of ISIS', *Hindustan Times*, 22 August; 'Dealing with Barbarism' *The Hindu*, 23 August 2014.

208 Upendra Nath Sharma, 'US War on Terror is Skewed', *New Indian Express*, 25 August 2014; 'US Should Shelve Bias in Its War on Terror', *New Indian Express*, 26 August 2014; Brahma Chellaney, 'IS, Frankenstein's Monster Unleashed', *The Hindu*, 27 August 2014; Vijay Prashad, 'The Pendulum of the IS', *The Hindu*, 6 September 2014.

209 'Don't Ignore the Call of the Vile', *Hindustan Times*, 5 September 2014.

210 'India Sounds Alert as al Qaeda Sets up a Sub-continent Wing', *Hindustan Times*, 5 September 2014; Bernard Haykel, 'A *Jihadi* Battle of Brands', *The Hindu*, 11 September 2014.

211 Suhasini Haidar, 'Delhi May Share Intelligence in Fight Against IS', *The Hindu*, 25 September 2014.

212 Speech, 'Statement by H.E. Narendra Modi, Prime Minister of India, General Debate of 69th Session of the United Nations General Assembly', New York, 27 September 2014.

213 'Joint Statement During the Visit of Prime Minister to USA', Ministry of External Affairs (India), 30 September 2014.

214 'Joining Global War Against ISIS: Two Scenarios that India Needs to Consider', *MSN News*, 20 October 2014.

stance against the use of foreign military intervention to resolve internal disputes which it had stuck to since the Libyan intervention (apart from the occasional wobble in early 2012).

The shaping effect of various great power logics on India's policy-response to the shocking emergence of IS in 2014 is obvious; India, like many other states, had suddenly concluded *non*-intervention was destabilising given the grave threat IS posed to Middle Eastern stability and, potentially, to India directly. India was also aligning itself with its oil-suppliers in the Gulf and with Western actors (especially with the US). Anti-imperialist logic, however, seems to not have shaped India's response appreciably because India did not consult with BRICS or IBSA states, or the LAS. Of course, India was demonstrating solidarity with the LAS states in the anti-IS coalition, and the LAS itself basically supported the military campaign. But, tellingly, India's policy shift had followed Modi's visit to *New York*, not to an IBSA, BRICS or LAS summit. This, and the fact India tacitly supported a US-led air campaign against targets in Syria without Syria's government formally consenting, also suggests the fiercely anti-Western variety of anti-imperialist logic played little or no role in shaping New Delhi's policy response. Liberal-democratic logic may have provided some limited shaping effect – Modi had said 'democracy is trying to find a voice in West Asia and North Africa; Tunisia's success makes us believe that it is possible' – although he was really only expressing 'soft' liberal-democratic logic (i.e. he did not specifically endorse foreign military intervention to promote democracy and protect human rights).

Conclusion: India and R2P at the End of 2014

None of the discussion in the section above suggests India had shifted much at the end of 2014 from its position on R2P at the end of 2012. The outcome of the chemical attack – a diplomatic deal to disarm Syria of its chemical weapons – had pleased New Delhi, but it had been consistent with Pillars I and II of R2P and had it had been specifically predicated on *avoiding* a Pillar III-style intervention. India also only supported the intervention against IS in the most minimal way, and humanitarian sentiment seems to have played only a minor role given the timing of India's change in policy. In other words, if India had been strongly motivated by liberal-democratic logic (of either variety) it would have supported intervention much earlier; instead its support was only forthcoming when a seemingly more dire and direct security traditional threat emerged dramatically and began to threaten India (if only rhetorically, but still very directly and graphically).

This concludes the empirical analysis of India's position on R2P after 2010. The following chapter is a short one which summarises the findings in terms of the philosophical framework established in Chapter 2, namely, the contest between traditional interpretations of the norm of sovereignty and the challenge to such posed by R2P. It then puts this finding into broader perspective by considering what India's position might mean for the effort to entrench the R2P norm more generally.

Conclusion

India and the Responsibility to Protect after the Crises in Côte d'Ivoire, Libya and Syria

This concluding chapter contextualises previous chapters' findings about India's position towards the responsibility to protect (R2P) in terms of the broad contest between traditional interpretations of the sovereignty norm and the challenge to this status quo posed by the R2P norm. The discussion then turns briefly to consider what India's stance on the R2P norm at the end of 2014 might mean for the wider effort to entrench R2P in international law and global governance structures, before it finishes with some equally brief findings about the prospects of India's position on R2P changing in future and what this might mean for R2P advocates' efforts.

India, and the R2P and Sovereignty Norms

The introductory chapter noted the debate about the meaning and status of R2P features prominently in contemporary debates about the nature of modern sovereignty, and Chapter 1 explored in more detail what this meant, namely, that efforts to promote the R2P norm do not typically focus on replacing the sovereignty norm wholesale. Instead, R2P's advocates usually seek to *modify* the contemporary understanding of sovereignty. Specifically, Pillar I of R2P is designed to explicitly establish what was arguably already implicit in the sovereignty norm, namely, that states are responsible for protecting their citizens from harm; but not just from external threats, because according to Pillar I states are also obliged to refrain from posing a threat to their own citizens. Pillar II is somewhat more novel given that it seeks to establish a more overt responsibility for Pillar I-compliant states to help other states fulfil their Pillar I responsibilities, although its novelty should not be overstated; many states have for many years provided foreign aid to boost governance and human rights protections, not just to directly alleviate the effects of famine or disease, etc. However the R2P norm also contains Pillar III which is arguably quite a bit more novel or, given that a number of humanitarian interventions took place in the 1990s, at least the Pillar III responsibility for the international community to intervene in states which are grievously failing to comply with Pillar I (including with military force) is more *controversial* and therefore *contested.* Notwithstanding this, R2P's advocates ultimately hope all states will 'internalise' the R2P norm – they hope it will become part of the properties of all states' identities – meaning all states would construe their interests in such a way that incidences of gross human rights abuses were greatly reduced or even eliminated entirely.

Chapter 3 established that India was historically uncomfortable with, and especially after the 1999 Kosovo war, was basically opposed to humanitarian intervention. This meant that for much of the decade after R2P was first proposed in 2001, India was highly sceptical of it too. To be sure, Jaganath and Kurtz are probably right to attribute some degree of this opposition to the influence wielded by one man, India's long-serving UN Ambassador Nirupam Sen,[1] but this study's findings strongly suggest the roots of India's opposition went much deeper than the preferences of single individual. This is because, put in terms of the conceptual model outlined in Chapter 2, Indians – both policy-shapers and policy-makers – were strongly *constituted* by the norm of sovereignty.

This means the properties of India's collective identity were (for most of the decade after 2001) such that policy-responses to humanitarian crises which were broadly consistent with the sovereignty norm were *enabled*, they were made 'more conceivable' or rendered 'proper' in Indians' eyes, while policy-responses which were more compatible with the R2P norm and especially Pillar III of such were *constrained*, they seemed 'less conceivable' or perhaps 'more improper' when Indians grappled with how to respond to humanitarian crises. This was apparent when the various identity discourses (and their 'strains') identified in Chapter 2 were applied in Chapter 3 to understanding India's policy-responses to a number of humanitarian crisis before 2010; what were called in earlier chapters sovereignty-friendly logics – soft-liberal-democratic logic, the anti-Western aspect of anti-imperialism, hard-realist logic, and the variety of enlightened-realism which assumes intervention caused instability – tended to shape India's policy-responses more strongly than R2P-friendly or relatively more interventionist logics (i.e. robust liberal-democratic logic or the variety of enlightened-realist logic which assumes intervention might sometimes be necessary to arrest instability).

Of course, Chapter 3 also established that India's formal position on R2P changed somewhat after India's new UN Ambassador Hardeep Puri Singh began to consistently articulate in UN forums what former-Foreign Minister Shyam Saran said was India's 'true' position on R2P, one which was arguably more nuanced than Nirupam Sen's trademark hard-line rejectionism. In other words, in 2009 and 2010 India indicated that it had become more *discriminating* when it came to R2P. In particular New Delhi indicated that it was more prepared to support Pillars I and II, suggesting the sorts of measures envisaged by these components of R2P as appropriate responses to humanitarian crises were beginning to be regarded in New Delhi as *conceivable* or *proper* given the prevailing properties of India's identity. And India had also warmed noticeably to the Protection of Civilians norm over the decade prior to 2011, suggesting even a few of the less-interventionist measures – prosecuting the perpetrators of genocide, directly protecting civilians at risk of

1 'Singing the Tune of Sovereignty? India and the Responsibility to Protect', *Conflict, Security and Development* 14:4 (2014), 469.

harm, etc. – which might be judged to be broadly compatible with Pillar III were also coming to be regarded as 'less improper'.

Nevertheless, we should not conclude India's identity had changed radically by 2010. Indeed, India's basic position – scepticism towards interventionism – remained substantially unaltered because Pillars I and II were essentially compatible with the sovereignty norm while Pillar III was not, in the main. Most of the sorts of interventionist measures, especially the more robust *military* options envisaged under Pillar III of R2P, typically remained *inconceivable* or *improper* given the prevailing properties of India's collective identity in 2010. Put another way, India's identity remained substantially more constituted by domestic-level sovereignty-compatible identity discourses – which themselves drew support from the global-level sovereignty norm – than it was constituted by R2P-compatible identity discourses (i.e. which draw similar support from the R2P and other human rights norms). And, in 2010, this marginally more nuanced position on R2P had not yet been *tested*, it remained essentially *hypothetical* because no serious humanitarian crises broke in 2009 and 2010, or at least India had not yet ascended to the Security Council, a forum where it would soon be *forced* to grapple extensively with exactly how to respond to humanitarian crises.

The detailed examination in Chapters 4, 5 and 6 of India's responses to the three humanitarian crises which broke during 2011 and 2012 then demonstrated that India's position on R2P changed only marginally overall as a result of its Security Council tenure. In particular, these chapters showed that, if anything, India backpedalled to some degree, that its opposition to R2P *hardened* somewhat; at the end of 2014, while India remained basically supportive of measures to resolve humanitarian crises which were compatible with Pillars I and II – rhetorical exhortations to respect human rights and democratic processes, high-profile diplomatic missions to facilitate political reconciliation between warring parties, unarmed monitoring missions, etc. – New Delhi had also become noticeably more opposed to the sorts of measures which are usually thought to fall under Pillar III of R2P, like the imposition of sanctions, the use of military force to impose No-Fly Zones, other even more coercive measures to directly protect civilians and, especially, military operations directed towards achieving regime change. How India got to this position requires more detailed consideration.

India began its stint on the Council with Côte d'Ivoire already in crisis and deteriorating rapidly. Crucially, a number of key steps towards resolving the crisis by essentially carrying out a regime change had already been taken before New Delhi took its seat; in particular UNOCI had been established and the situation in Côte d'Ivoire had been declared a threat to international peace and stability (years before), and Alassane Ouattara had been declared the rightful President (in late 2010). India did vote for UNOCI to be reinforced, including with attack helicopters, and it voted for Resolution 1975 on 30 March 2011 which in effect precipitated a regime change, but the analysis in Chapter 4 demonstrated that its decision had been primarily shaped by developing-world solidarity logic – India closely followed the AU's and ECOWAS's lead regarding how to respond to the crisis –

and not by the sort of robust liberal-democratic logic which is most compatible with Pillar III of R2P. Chapter 4 also established that hard-realist logic meant India was not especially concerned with or interested in what was happening in West Africa, especially given the powerful distraction of contemporaneous events in Libya; in other words hard-realist logic played a 'hidden' but still profound shaping role in the sense that New Delhi didn't consider that it had many interests in that region. Instead, the Libyan crisis – which occurred in a region in which India did have pressing interests – played the most crucial role shaping India's position on R2P. This position then became clearer as the Syrian crisis progressed despite India seeming to waver at times.

Regarding Libya, India abstained on Resolution 1973 on 17 March 2011 and its decision was most strongly shaped by a mixture of hard-realist logic and developing-world solidarity logic, especially the desire to not oppose the League of Arab States (LAS) and to also maintain a sort of unity with its BRICS partners. The discussion in Chapter 5 also established that New Delhi's decision was to some degree shaped by enlightened-realist logic, mainly the desire to not upset the West by directly opposing it, although it wasn't really clear which of two other interpretations of enlightened-realism – that which assumes R2P-inspired interventions are destabilising, or that which assumes the opposite – exerted more shaping influence. Perhaps soft-liberal-democratic logic played some role, at least by suggesting India shouldn't be seen to align with a dictator graphically threatening his own people, and it also seems overly cynical to claim that New Delhi did not care at all about the fate of Benghazi's population. But, crucially, the sort of robust-liberal-democratic logic which is most compatible with Pillar III of R2P seems to have played little or no part shaping India's decision to abstain, and arguably the anti-Western variety of anti-imperialist logic also exerted little shaping effect (i.e. if it had India would likely have voted 'no').

But then the conduct and outcome of NATO's Libyan intervention delivered powerful lessons which caused India's position against R2P to harden, especially with regard to Pillar III. Regarding conduct, the way NATO almost immediately after 17 March began to exceed its mandate and blatantly pursue regime change left Indians feeling duped and betrayed, which vindicated the anti-Western strain of anti-imperial logic. Regarding the outcome, a year or two's worth of hindsight convinced Indians that R2P-inspired interventions in humanitarian crises – or perhaps just measures compatible with Pillar III, to the extent they drew the distinction – risked anarchy, which powerfully vindicated the variety of enlightened-realist logic which assumed R2P-inspired intervention produces instability. Hard-realist logic was vindicated too by both the outcome and the conduct of NATO's intervention in Libya given India had basically protected its interests – India's citizens were successfully evacuated, it had not wasted resources and its wider interests were not damaged substantially more than any other actors' in anarchical post-Gaddafi Libya – and Western states were shown to behave like all states are assumed to do (i.e. motivated by the pursuit of traditional interests, not humanitarianism).

On the other hand, the relative influence of robust liberal-democratic logic as a shaper of Indian policy responses to humanitarian crises was undermined quite substantially, perhaps even 'near-fatally' as later events in Syria suggested (and recall that the interviewees were unanimous on this point). It is harder to tell exactly what the effect of the Libyan crisis was on its stablemate, soft liberal-democratic logic, because it was never given a chance to shape the conduct of outcome of the international response – the Libyan crisis developed too fast for international luminaries to be dispatched or multilateral conferences to be held, as happened vis-à-vis Syria – but it is probably fair to conclude that this variety of the liberal democratic identity discourse to some degree 'suffered by association' with its more interventionist sibling. The effect of the Libyan crisis on the developing-world solidarity aspect of the anti-imperial identity discourse is also difficult to determine definitively because the developing world split (i.e. the AU called for restraint, the LAS called for intervention). Perhaps we should conclude that the *cautious* developing-world position – so, the AU's – was vindicated, meaning the lesson India learned was to align with those developing-world actors which counsel restraint.

This hardening of India's stance against R2P was then illustrated during New Delhi's engagement with the Syrian crisis (to clarify, perhaps Indian attitudes only hardened against Pillar III, although the interviews this author conducted suggested strongly that some Indian policy-shapers at least do not always make a concerted effort to distinguish it from the other pillars). With the Libyan crisis fresh in their minds Indian policy-shapers and policy-makers alike were generally opposed to interventionism of any kind in Syria – even the 'mention' of the 'possibility' of sanctions, let alone military intervention of any sort – in the early stages. This was illustrated most clearly by India's abstention in the Security Council on 4 October 2011.

Then in the first half of 2012 India voted for draft Council resolutions on 4 February and 19 July which proposed 'mildly interventionist' measures to deal with the Syrian crisis. The analysis in Chapter 6 demonstrated the powerful shaping influence of developing-world solidarity logic (i.e. with the LAS) and hard-realist logic (because LAS members were offering direct benefits to India for its support) in these decisions. Arguably soft liberal-democratic logic played some role too given the humanitarian situation was steadily deteriorating into what has become the worst humanitarian disaster of the contemporary era, and Chapter 6 also showed New Delhi was starting to 'come around to' the variety of enlightened-realist logic which assumed *non*-intervention may be destabilising as the crisis persisted with no end in sight. Crucially, however, the analysis also showed India was very much aware these two resolutions would very likely fail no matter how India voted, leaving it free to pursue both direct and diplomatic side-benefits; it did this most obviously vis-à-vis the Gulf Arab members of the LAS, but it also aligned with the West in accordance with the aspect of enlightened-realist logic which urges New Delhi to burnish its image as a 'responsible' player in global affairs who also wants to develop economically with Western goodwill and assistance.

But ultimately events in Syria – or, more accurately, in the international forums where solutions to the crisis were being proposed, debated and voted on – provided a clear illustration of the *limits* of India's support for the R2P norm. New Delhi was prepared to vote for a draft resolution presented to the Council on 19 July which ramped up the diplomatic pressure on the al-Assad regime by *threatening* sanctions; but only two weeks later when the LAS proposed a non-binding General Assembly resolution which called for the actual *imposition* of sanctions the Indian policy-makers in South Block debated how to respond long into the night and ultimately took fright, retreating back to an equivocal position by abstaining. Even a shocking atrocity – a chemical weapons attack on civilians – a year later was not enough to change India's opposition to robust interventionist measures to end the humanitarian crisis in Syria; India wasn't on the Security Council then but for the first time it openly stood against the West and the LAS before rejoicing at the eventual solution which involved Syria consenting to the destruction of its arsenal of chemical weapons. A year after that India did tacitly support a foreign military intervention in what had become a joint Syrian/Iraqi crisis in response to the shocking emergence of Islamic State; but this decision seems to have been shaped only minimally by humanitarian sentiment and it was consensual in any event (or at least *Iraq* formally requested assistance; the Syrian government's consent was tacit).

The reader is referred back to the extended discussion in Chapter 6 for the details about the relative influence the various identity discourses enjoyed vis-à-vis one another by the end of 2014; the various effects of India's engagement with the Syrian crisis (while Libya was also simultaneously sliding ever-further into anarchy) were very complex. But more importantly in the context of this chapter the *limit* on the sorts of non-consensual interventionist measures New Delhi will support seemed to have been set, at least in the context of the Syrian crisis, by the *threat of sanctions*. Arguably sanctions are a non-consensual interventionist measure of the sort envisaged under Pillar III; to threaten sanctions is to apply direct pressure on another state which technically goes further than the sort of 'assistance' measures envisaged under Pillar II. But it is not a *very* coercive measure; indeed, it is amongst the least-most interventionist measures possible, especially if the actor making the threat is not prepared to follow through on it (as India failed to). By strong implication the other sorts of measures envisaged by Pillar III – actual imposition of sanctions, enforcement of a No-Fly Zone, the insertion of military forces to directly protect civilians, and most especially military operations leading to regime change – were beyond what India considered an acceptable response.

All this means Indian policy-makers, after their state had spent two years on the Security Council, were 'constituted enough' by R2P norm – or put another way, India's policy-responses to humanitarian crises were shaped by R2P-friendly identity discourses – to support the sorts of responses contemplated under Pillar I and Pillar II; but only the sorts of measures compatible with these, and not Pillar III-compatible measures, had been enabled or 'made possible'. In other words, New Delhi was prepared to support minimally-interventionist measures which remained substantially in compliance with the norm of sovereignty. The constitutive *constraining* effect of the sovereignty norm therefore remained very powerful; while India seemed motivated by humanitarianism to at least try to help resolve crises in ways which promoted democracy and protected human rights, it was clearly unprepared to do so in ways which might weaken the sovereignty norm substantially as 2014 came to a close.

Two important caveats to this general finding must be noted. First, India is obviously more amenable to more interventionist measures – including military intervention – when a state *requests* such, but this should come as little surprise given consensual intervention is compatible with the sovereignty norm, and so therefore Pillar II of R2P. Second, the debates about intervention in Syria took place in a particular geopolitical and temporal context, implying India may well be prepared to go further and support more interventionist measures in different circumstances. Indeed, a range of possible differences in context – geographical, diplomatic, economic factors, etc. – mean we cannot be sure the line India refused to cross in Syria will always define the limit on the sorts of interventionist measures India will support; certainly India was not vehemently opposed to what was effectively a regime change in Côte d'Ivoire in early 2011. But we can conclude with more confidence that the more-extreme Pillar III measures, especially military intervention leading to regime change, will likely remain unacceptable from New Delhi's perspective for quite some time.

Accordingly, and keeping in mind the need to remain sensitive to the contextual peculiarities of any future humanitarian crisis, it is possible to draw some conclusions about which of the identity discourses were more/less influential at the end of 2014. The preceding analysis demonstrated that at least six identity discourses were 'out there' in the public sphere, being promoted by policy-shapers and present as potential shapers of India's policy responses; several others (Hindutva and some 'ethnic' identity discourses) were considered, but only ethnic-Tamil logic was found to have any real effect on policy (and not on the responses to the three crises examined in detail). So, it seems very clear that the two most dominant discourses at the end of 2014 were hard-realism and developing-world solidarity. Hard-realist logic was clearly shaping all the responses India made to the three crises, sometimes overtly in the sense that India would act directly to protect its interests, at other times implicitly by causing Indian policy-makers to not prioritise a crisis (i.e. Côte d'Ivoire). There was also a marked tendency for India to try to align itself with the developing world. This was not always easy because at times the developing world split over how to respond to a crisis; perhaps one might conclude that India's inherent preference was to align with at least *some* developing-world actors, and hard-realist-like consideration of its direct interests influenced this choice.

On the other hand the anti-Western aspect of the anti-imperialist identity discourse clearly wasn't dominant because if it had been India would have likely voted 'no' whenever the Security Council considered a Western-sponsored draft resolution (i.e. every resolution considered in Chapters 4, 5 and 6). Still, this logic clearly exerted some influence; it appeared regularly in the public debates, prominent opposition politicians (and some MPs formally in the governing coalition) delivered anti-Western remarks in parliament, and even leaks from the Ministry of External Affairs (MEA) suggested that some degree of anti-Western sentiment was lurking in the halls of that key institution. But it is telling that key policy-makers – the Foreign Secretary, the UN Ambassador, cabinet ministers, etc. – consistently declined to deploy this sort of rhetoric in public. Its influence should therefore probably be considered a sort of 'background factor' which policy-makers have to be aware of and which sets limits on their freedom of action by preventing them siding too readily or openly with Western actors and initiatives.

The shaping influence of enlightened-realist logic seems very mixed and somewhat contradictory. First, the aspect of it which warns against upsetting powerful Western actors too much seems to exert some degree of influence, although we shouldn't go too far and judge it to be 'very' influential; we should probably see it as providing a counterweight to the influence of anti-Western logic. This might suggest that the influence of these two logics is roughly equal, but it is probably better to see them as exerting influence in different *places* or on different *actors*; in other words, the anti-Western logic finds expression in populist parties and in the popular press while the pro-Western logic holds a greater sway in professional policy-making circles, namely, among MEA officials but also politicians who are actually in government and who have to make decisions which may affect India's wider diplomatic relations. The exact weight of these logics relative to one another will therefore arguably vary according to context, including the nature of the crisis under consideration and the relative power and influence of the various Indian domestic actors at the time.

There was also clearly an ongoing tussle between a strain of enlightened-realist logic which assumed that intervening to protect human rights tended to enhance stability, and another which assumed intervention was typically destabilising. The outcome in Libya certainly provided powerful vindication of the latter position, but India also shifted at times towards the former – especially in early 2012 as the deadlock over Syria seemed to fuel ever-greater instability – and when IS posed a sort of 'full spectrum' challenge to regional stability India backed foreign intervention. But this latter intervention was basically a consensual one, and in any event India's direct involvement was minimal, so overall we must conclude the strain which assumes intervention should be avoided because it tends to be destabilising was more influential than its competitor as 2014 ended.

Regarding the relative influence of the liberal-democratic identity discourse, the analysis in previous chapters makes clear that the soft variety does exert some influence on Indian policy-making; India consistently condemned human rights abuses, it backed its words with repeated attempts to resolve the crisis in Syria in particular with diplomatic initiatives, and it seems to genuinely prefer that all states respect human rights and operate in accordance with democratic principles. But there were clear limits on these preferences, namely, as a result of what went on in Libya, India was not prepared to use military force to promote democracy and protect human rights, and it was also ultimately not prepared to impose sanctions on Syria to do so either. This has obvious implications for the robust variety of liberal-democratic logic: clearly it remains quite uninfluential in policy-making circles, and despite the fact that some policy-shapers delivered advice reflecting its core logic even these sorts of contributions were relatively few and far between.

To sum up India's position on R2P at the end of 2014, while policy-makers remained relatively supportive of or at least 'open to' responses to crises which are consistent with Pillar I and Pillar II of R2P, India was arguably less supportive of or open to Pillar III-type responses than it had before it entered the Security Council, especially those responses which involved non-consensual military intervention, and in particular, any response which might even vaguely suggest a regime change could occur. Given the observations above about the tendency for Indians to conflate R2P's components, this study concludes that India's position on R2P overall has shifted since 2010 and New Delhi is now more opposed to the norm than it was in 2010; in other words, India's greater opposition to Pillar III is sort of 'bleeding over into' and 'tainting' its position on the other two pillars.

The next and final section of the book considers what this might mean for the R2P norm's fortunes more broadly, which requires some initial discussion about the wider, global status of R2P at the end of 2014 and what scholars have been saying about the effects of the crises in Libya and Syria on the R2P norm. The chapter, and therefore the book, then ends by considering the prospect of India substantially changing its position on R2P in future, which really hinges on it changing its opposition to Pillar III .

Implications of India's Position for the Effort to Entrench R2P

Ramesh Thakur – who along with Gareth Evans was a principal author of the 2001 International Commission on Intervention and State Sovereignty report – has remained a staunch R2P supporter despite being disarmingly honest at times about the reasonableness of some of the critiques which have been levelled against it.[2] In a 2013 article in *The Washington Quarterly* in which he examined the status of R2P after Libya and Syria, Thakur acknowledged:

> The Libyan operation proved particularly controversial among the emerging powers, and the price of exceeding the mandate there has been paid by Syrians. Nevertheless, it would be premature to conclude that R2P can be branded "RIP".[3]

2 'Global Norms and International Humanitarian Law: An Asian Perspective', *International Review of the Red Cross* 83:841 (2001), 19–44; 'The Responsibility to Protect and the North-South Divide', in S.R. Silverberg (ed.), *International Law: Readings on Contemporary Problems and Future Issues* (Boulder: Westview Press, 2011).

3 Ramesh Thakur, 'R2P after Libya and Syria: Engaging Emerging Powers', *Washington Quarterly* 36:2 (2013), 61.

The finding that the conduct and outcome of NATO's operation in Libya was a substantial cause of the failure to apply R2P (or at least Pillar III) to end the Syrian crisis, and that this in turn has undermined the prospects for R2P's further entrenchment, has been disputed by Alex Bellamy. He concedes Russian intransigence over Syria was clearly motivated by events in Libya; he finds numerous Russian statements directly confirming the outcome in Libya profoundly affected Moscow's thinking vis-à-vis Syria. But he argues 'there is relatively little evidence to suggest that concerns arising out of Libya were determinants of the Security Council's decision-making on Syria', mainly because he doesn't find many other similar overt statements (other than a few from South Africa) which link Council members' voting on Syria with what took place in Libya.[4]

Unfortunately, it is difficult to escape the conclusion that Bellamy (who is another very prominent champion of R2P) is trying to put the best face on what is a difficult time for promoters of the R2P norm. Specifically, he has arguably fallen into the trap this study took great pains to avoid, namely, he has failed to adequately acknowledge that states do not always publically articulate every reason behind or motivation for their policy-responses to international crises. In particular, and given we are talking about *humanitarian* crises here, there are obvious reasons why states may want to finesse their positions and avoid bluntly stating that they oppose ending atrocities and alleviating mass suffering. Thomas Weiss (also a very prominent advocate of R2P) has basically supported Bellamy's interpretation of the Libyan and Syrian crises,[5] but the overwhelming weight of scholarly opinion is with Thakur, namely, that NATO's intervention in Libyan was the primary reason why no substantially *humanitarian* intervention[6] had taken place in Syria before the end of 2014, and together these outcomes have significantly damaged the R2P norm's prospects of becoming further entrenched in international law and global governance structures.[7]

4 'From Tripoli to Damascus? Lesson Learning and the Implementation of the Responsibility to Protect', *International Politics* 51:1 (2014), 26.

5 'Military Humanism: Syria Hasn't Killed it', *Washington Quarterly* 37:1 (2014), 7–20.

6 I.e. the 2014 intervention in Syria/Iraq was not primarily motivated by humanitarianism: see Chapter 6.

7 For just a few example, see: Gareth Evans, 'The Responsibility to Protect After Libya and Syria', speech, Annual Castan Centre for Human Rights Law Conference, Melbourne, 20 July 2012; Lloyd Axworthy and Allan Rock, 'A Reflection on Responsibility: What Does Syria Mean for R2P?', *Diplomatica*, 4 October 2012; Jennifer M. Welsh, 'Norm Contestation and the Responsibility to Protect', *Global Responsibility to Protect* 5:1 (2013), 382–384; Philipp Rotmann, Gerrit Kurtz and Sarah Brockmeier, 'Major Powers and the Contested Evolution of a Responsibility to Protect', *Conflict, Security and Development* 14:4 (2014), 355–377; J. Craig Baker, The Responsibility to Protect: Lessons from Libya and Syria', in Robert P. Barnidge (ed.), *The Liberal Way of War: Legal Perspectives* (Farnham: Ashgate, 2013); Mohammed Nurazzaman, 'The "Responsibility to Protect" Doctrine: Revived in Libya, Buried in Syria', *Insight Turkey* 15:2 (2013), 57–66; Robert Murray, 'Conclusion: The Responsibility to Protect after Libya', in Aidan Hehir and Robert Murray (eds), *Libya:*

The reader will recall that Chapter 1 concluded by noting that despite some ups and downs during the 2000s 'by 2010 the effort to entrench R2P as an international norm seemed to have some *momentum* behind it'. But by the end of 2014 the prospects of R2P becoming entrenched would seem, if not exactly 'bleak' then at least 'less promising' when compared to the position at the end of 2010. In other words, R2P's momentum seemed to have been arrested by the end of 2014 and, perhaps, the R2P norm may have even lost some ground and been rolled back to some degree. But this book is not the appropriate place to make conclusive findings about this complex and controversial matter; instead, it is the right place to consider what impact *India's position* on R2P may have on the wider prospects of the R2P norm becoming further entrenched.

The introductory chapter positioned this study at the intersection of two broad debates in the academic field of international relations, namely, the contest between the R2P norm and more traditional interpretations of the meaning of sovereignty, and the debate about the emergence of rising non-Western powers and their impact on the international system.[8] Other studies of R2P have positioned themselves at this intersection too,[9] and because China's rise has made it the most conspicuous new international player in recent decades much time and effort has been spent on assessing what China's position on R2P means for the prospects of the R2P norm becoming entrenched in international law and structures of global governance more broadly. China has not featured heavily in this study but when it has been mentioned it has typically been portrayed as an opponent of R2P, although a 2014 study by two Chinese scholars[10] broadly agrees with Patrick Quinton-Brown's 2013 determination that China is a 'cautious supporter' of R2P in a manner that is roughly analogous to India's position (i.e. cautious support for Pillars I and II but general opposition to Pillar III).[11]

The Introduction argued further that China and a few other key international actors (i.e. Russia, Western powers, the UN Secretary-General, etc.) were probably more important actors when we consider the prospect of R2P becoming entrenched. But the Introduction also claimed that 'India is already an important international actor, and one whose stake in and influence over debates about the management of global affairs, including debates about R2P, is likely to increase'. Notably, Thakur

---

The Responsibility to Protect and the Future of Humanitarian Intervention (Basingstoke: Palgrave Macmillan, 2013), 224.

8 Pu Xiayou, 'Socialisation as a Two-Way Process: Emerging Powers and the Diffusion of International Norms', *Chinese Journal of International Politics* 5:4 (2012), 341–367.

9 Thakur, 'R2P after Libya'; Rotmann et al., 'Major Powers'; Oliver Stuenkel, 'The BRICS and the Future of R2P', *Global Responsibility to Protect* 6:1 (2014), 3–28.

10 Teiwa Lui and Haibin Zhang, 'Debates in China About the Responsibility to Protect as a Developing International Norm: A General Assessment', *Conflict, Security and Development* 14:4 (2014), 403–427.

11 'Mapping Dissent: The R2P and its State Critics', *Global Responsibility to Protect* 5:3 (2013), 260–282.

agrees; he went on in his 2013 *Washington Quarterly* article to invest considerable hope for R2P's future in efforts to 'engag[e] the emerging powers on developing the criteria for, and conduct of, R2P interventions'.[12] He made clear, however, that we should not be too sanguine at present about the prospects of emerging powers driving R2P forward because:

> so far the signs show that these new players are more interested in the status and trappings of power than in assuming the burdens of leadership … . Brazil, South Africa and especially India with its more than six decades of constitutional democratic governance – do not demonstrate that that hard or soft human rights promotion is an integral element of their foreign policy.[13]

This study's findings align strongly with Thakur's thoughts on this matter, at least as far as India is concerned. And this conclusion is substantially in accordance with a number of shorter article-length studies of India's position on R2P; for example, Dipankar Banerjee has concluded that when it comes to R2P (after Libya) 'the overwhelming view [in India] has been that of restraint' and that New Delhi's basic position against regime change and military intervention more generally was 'fundamental and long-lasting';[14] Ian Hall found that India's engagement with the Libyan crisis strongly reinforced a tendency that Pratap Mehta had observed in 2009, namely, India is profoundly reluctant to 'endorse new principles in the international order that formally question sovereignty';[15] Urvashi Aneja found India remained firmly wedded to philosophically-pluralist conceptions of sovereignty which meant New Delhi would likely continue to favour 'contain[ing] the meaning of [R2P within] a pluralist view' by limiting international efforts to protect persons under threat to the tendering of 'technical and capacity-building assistance … to the affected state';[16] and Jaganath and Kurtz, after repeatedly noting 'India's respect for sovereignty underlies its basic position on R2P' and 'the notion of sovereignty is critical [and] can be considered a background variable setting the tone of India's position' on R2P, concluded 'India's support for R2P is based on the premise that the sovereign state will not be circumvented but rather rendered functional so as to discharge its duty in a responsible manner'.[17] These

---

12 Thakur, 'R2P after Libya', 63.

13 Ibid., 62.

14 'India and R2P: Reconciling the Tension Between Intervention and State Sovereignty', in *The Responsibility to Protect – From Evasive to Reluctant Action?* (Johannesburg: United Litho, 2012), 103.

15 'Tilting at Windmills: The Indian Debate over the Responsibility to Protect after UNSC Resolution 1973', *Global Responsibility to Protect* 5:1 (2013), 106.

16 'India, R2P and Humanitarian Assistance', *Global Responsibility to Protect* 6:2 (2014), 243.

17 'Singing the Tune of Sovereignty? India and the Responsibility to Protect', *Conflict, Security and Development* 14:4 (2014), 480.

scholars therefore all believe India is likely to continue to be at best a cautious supporter of the R2P norm and only back measures to alleviate humanitarian crises which are broadly compatible with the sovereignty norm (i.e. measures under Pillars I and II) while consistently rejecting those which don't (i.e. most Pillar III measures), and their findings align with this longer and more detailed study's findings on the matter.

This should be sobering for advocates of R2P. They are typically unwilling to jettison Pillar III given doing so would risk removing an important 'final option', namely, direct action to prevent atrocities when all other less-coercive steps to end a humanitarian crisis have failed. Perhaps even more importantly, ruling out Pillar III measures would also reduce the credibility of attempts the international community might make to pressure a state to bow to the less-coercive initiatives short of military intervention.[18] So, absent substantial changes in the foreign policy stances of major emerging democratic powers, including and especially changes in India's position, the slow but steady shift of relative power from developed to developing states that marks contemporary international politics does not bode well for the effort to further entrench the R2P norm, or at least to entrench an R2P norm containing a functioning and credible Pillar III 'last resort' or 'big stick' option.

But what of the prospects for change? Might India one day become a more wholehearted supporter of R2P's Pillar III? Some have certainly called for more debate in India about the possibility of New Delhi supporting future Pillar-III type interventions; Sanjeev Shrivastav's call to do so was considered in Chapter 5 and Srinath Raghavan also echoed this sentiment (discussed in Chapter 6). Most notably we saw Raja Mohan, one of the most influential thinkers in contemporary Indian strategic circles, repeatedly urging Indians and their policy-makers to seriously consider whether India should become a more active and responsible international player more generally. For example, Mohan wrote in a widely-cited scholarly piece that:

> the Indian strategic community needs to debate on when, where and how India might use or support the use of force … . As India's weight in the international system increases Delhi will be called upon to contribute more to the maintenance of international peace and security. This debate is long overdue and can only be kick-started by the political leadership at the highest levels … . An activist approach and a willingness to take the lead in resolving [humanitarian crises] might in fact lend credibility to India's claim for a seat at the international high table.[19]

18 Weiss, 'Military Humanism'; Jennifer M. Welsh, Patrick Quinton-Brown and Victor MacDiarmid, 'Brazil's "Responsibility While Protecting" Proposal: A Canadian Perspective', *CCRtoP*, 12 July 2012.

19 'India, Libya and the Principle of Non-Intervention', *ISAS Insights* 122, 13 April 2011, 9.

Kudrat Virk has also noted that if India:

> wants to shape and manage the international order as a great power, India has to move beyond reactiveness and further clarify its stance on R2P-based intervention … . India's leadership must deal with the challenge in order to realise their ambitions on the world stage. A wider, more sustained and public debate within India on humanitarian intervention and R2P … would be a crucial first step towards identifying the guiding elements of India's approach to the norm and building some sort of consensus at home.[20]

So, at least some commentators are calling for more debate about and wholehearted engagement with R2P, and this at least holds out the possibility that such might end with India becoming more supportive of Pillar-III-like responses to humanitarian crises. Yet it remains telling that Mohan and Virk did not premise their advice primarily on the basis that it would be *morally right* for India to be more prepared to intervene more but, instead, on the assumption that it would be politically and/or diplomatically *expedient* for India to do so. Ian Hall observed something similar when he surveyed the Indian debates about the Libyan crisis; he concluded 'instead of debating [R2P's] merit … Indian[s] chose instead to "tilt at windmills", whether their particular target was Western "neo-colonialism" or India's great power ambitions'.[21]

This arguably means that if India's position on R2P changed merely because New Delhi wanted to project a more 'responsible face' to the world in pursuit of diplomatic and economic side-benefits such a change would rest on relatively shallow grounds, namely, on the sorts of calculations about India's long-term self-interests that enlightened-realists are wont to make, which in turn suggests India's new position on R2P would be a relatively superficial or unstable one. If the global configuration of power were then to change substantially – for example, if Western R2P-supporting states became significantly less influential while authoritarian states like China or Russia rose in power and influence – would future Indians judge it expedient to retreat from their new position on R2P to curry favour with the more-powerful R2P-sceptics and R2P-opponents? We cannot know for sure, but it seems reasonable to suspect that only a deeper, more profound change in India's identity – which is the wellspring of its interests after all – would be required before India became more *enduringly* supportive of all aspects of the R2P norm.

There are of course some reasons to think a fundamental shift of this nature might be possible; in particular, the study showed there are some Indian policy-shapers who consistently offered advice which was primarily motivated by robust liberal-democratic logic (Meenakshi Ganguly was the standout example) during 2011 and 2012. And others presented robust liberal-democratic logic as one

20 'India and the Responsibility to Protect: A Tale of Ambiguity', *Global Responsibility to Protect* 5:1 (2013), 83.

21 'Tilting at Windmills', 106.

element of a mixture of logics which informed their opinion that India should support interventionist measures at certain times. This means that, at minimum, while this study found the robust liberal-democratic position is clearly not very influential *now* it is at least 'out there' in the public sphere competing for attention and offering itself as a possible framework to think about and shape India's responses to humanitarian crises.

In other words the mere existence of robust liberal-democratic logic as 'one option' in India's public culture means it is 'available' to policy-makers grappling with future humanitarian crises. To fully grasp the significance of this requires delving briefly into the prevailing view of what *culture* is and does. In the sociological literature it has become common to think of culture as a sort of 'toolbox' which contains multiple 'strategies of action' which are 'culturally available ways of organizing collective behaviour'.[22] Charles Tilly, for example, calls cultures 'repertoires' which contain 'most, if not all, the strategies we need to successfully navigate our way through the social world of everyday collective human interaction'.[23] In this study, of course, these culturally-available tools have been called identity discourses.

What this means is that when confronted by new contexts, like a new humanitarian crisis, in which the 'old tools' don't seem to hold out much prospect of working, or they have already been tried and failed, Indian policy-makers might reach into the cultural toolbox to find robust liberal-democratic logic provides an available and, crucially, a viable and credible strategy of action to guide their deliberations. We arguably saw something like this occurring in the first half of 2012 vis-à-vis Syria: as India's preferred responses failed to end the violence and regional stability deteriorated New Delhi began considering whether a change of direction was necessary, and in the course of doing so it voted for two Council resolutions which were interventionist in nature, if only mildly so. But we also saw that New Delhi later retreated, demonstrating that humans are creatures of habit who tend to favour the status quo,[24] or to continue the toolbox metaphor, humans tend to favour using the cultural tools with which they are most familiar (which in the context of this study are the hard-realist and the developing-world solidarity logics). Nevertheless, the very presence of robust liberal-democratic logic makes it one available means for Indians to respond to a future humanitarian crisis; it is certainly 'more available' in democratic India's cultural context than is the case in authoritarian China's.

22 Ann Swidler, 'Culture in Action: Symbols and Strategies', *American Sociological Review* 57:2 (1986), 273–86.

23 'How to Detect, Describe and Explain Repertoires of Contention', *Working Paper* 150, Centre of Study of Social Change, New School of Social Research, 1992, 17. See also: Paul DiMaggio, 'Culture and Cognition', *Annual Review of Sociology* 23 (1997), 263–287.

24 Jeffrey Legro, 'The Transformation of Policy Ideas', *American Journal of Political Science* 44:3 (2000), 426–429; James Mahoney, 'Path Dependence in Historical Sociology', *Theory and Society* 29:4 (2000), 513–515.

Alternatively – and arguably more positively from the perspective of an R2P-advocate – the study also found that the soft variety of the liberal-democratic identity discourse was very deep-seated; consideration of both the textual sources and the interviewees' responses demonstrates that Indians really are very committed to liberal-democratic values, at least when it comes to how *India* should be governed. Indeed, one interviewee – a former General Staff-level officer in India's armed services – explained that in his more than 40 years of service:

> never did I perceive even a whiff of sentiment amongst my comrades about putting undue pressure on the elected government in Delhi, let alone staging a coup. This is independent India's greatest triumph and it makes our Pakistani cousins look very shabby by comparison.[25]

The point is that India has the 'cultural/discursive raw material' from which the robust liberal-democratic identity discourse might slowly but steadily gain more adherents amongst Indian policy-shapers and the wider public and possibly, one day, exert more influence over policy-making.

This is not to say robust liberal-democratic logic would necessarily become dominant any time soon; but it wouldn't necessarily need to become truly dominant for India's position on R2P to change sufficiently for India to become a net-contributor to the wider effort to entrench the R2P norm. Instead, robust liberal-democratic logic would only need to become *more influential* than it is now: past humanitarian interventions have rarely been 'purely' motivated by humanitarianism, and the analytical chapters demonstrated how India's policy-responses to the various crises it engaged with during 2011 and 2012 were typically shaped by a mix of logics. In other words, if the robust liberal-democratic identity discourse were to grow in influence then in the peculiar contexts of some future humanitarian crises this logic might align with the shaping influence of other identity discourses and contribute to shaping New Delhi's policy-responses in ways which lead India to support measures of the sort envisaged by Pillar III of R2P.

Finally, what are the prospects of such a change taking place? Admittedly, there are many reasons to be sceptical about India's identity changing in the manner just outlined (i.e. 'quite substantially') even given the latent strength of the soft variety of liberal-democratic discourse. Still, it is certainly not impossible to imagine such occurring: one interviewee, I-10, noted the generation of Indians born after 1990 – the first to grow up with more than a single, state-owned television station – has been much more exposed to, and generally more accepting of, Western culture and norms than their parents ever were.[26] Sarang Shidore has explained this as a shift in broader Indian identity towards one in which the West – and especially the United States – is no longer widely seen as the 'adversarial Other'; instead, Shidore claims that the US has already, or at least is becoming, the 'aspirational Other' in key sections of Indian society, and he traces the beginnings of this process

25 I-10, New Delhi, 9 December 2013.

26 New Delhi, 10 November 2013.

to the rude shock delivered to India's sense of Self by the twin crises of 1991 (i.e. the collapse of the Soviet Union and the acute contemporaneous Indian economic crisis), claiming that the cultural shift continued to gather pace as the reforms of the 1990s facilitated the emergence of:

> a large and articulate Indian urban middle class with consumerist tendencies. Many of India's foreign policy elites, media commentators, and corporate professionals [are drawn] from this class – a class which increasingly identified itself with the aspirations of the American model of society.[27]

Another interviewee, I-3, also noted a new generation of elite-Indians, many educated in Western universities, was steadily replacing the older generation in the MEA who had typically been weaned on Nehruvian Third Worldism and educated in Soviet-era Moscow.[28]

I-10 also warned, however, that many of these rising Western-educated Indian diplomats were realists: realist discourses are strongly represented in the halls of Western academia after all.[29] This study has also shown that leftist ideology is far from dead in India's public culture, and while ever hundreds of millions of Indians struggle with grinding poverty one would expect this worldview to retain a relatively strong foothold. And Pratap Mehta has provided a slew of reasons to explain why India is, and is likely to remain, unwilling to adopt the promotion of democracy and human rights play as a key part of its foreign policy: Indian domestic politics is too contentious to enable anything but foreign policy caution; India's developmental needs are so pressing it is forced to subordinate other preferences; and it remains riven with internal frictions and threats to central authority.[30] In short, we should entirely abandon the lazy assumption that there is some sort of teleological *certainty* that India's identity will shift towards a liberal-democratic position of the sort which will *necessarily* fundamentally transform India's position on Pillar III of R2P.

Ultimately these sorts of musings about how the collective identity of an actor whose borders encompass over 1.25 billion individuals might change become too speculative to treat too seriously; but at least they indicate what scholars might look for in future when exploring the question of whether New Delhi's position on R2P might change fundamentally. It also hints at the sorts of tactics and strategies R2P's advocates might need to consider deploying to promote the harder-to-achieve but deeper, more enduring societal changes which may hold the key to emerging states like India internalising and thus supporting all the pillars of the R2P norm more wholeheartedly.

27 'Iran in a Reconsidered Indian Grand Strategy', in Kanti Bajpai, Saira Basit and V. Krishnappa, *India's Grand Strategy: History, Theory, Cases* (Routledge: New Delhi, 2014), 438–441.

28 New Delhi, 1 November 2013.

29 New Delhi, 9 December 2013.

30 'Reluctant India', *Journal of Democracy* 22:4 (2011), 102.

Bibliography

ABC News. Australian Broadcasting Corporation. Canberra.

Abdelal, Rawi, Yoshiko M. Herrera, Alistair Iain Johnston and Rose McDermott. 'Identity as a Variable'. *Perspectives on Politics* 4:4 (2006): 695–711.

Acharya, Amitav. 'How Ideas Spread'. *International Organization* 58:2 (2004): 239–75.

Acharya, Amitav. 'Norm Subsidiarity and Regional Orders: Sovereignty, Regionalism, and Rule-Making in the Third World'. *International Studies Quarterly* 55:1 (2011): 95–123.

Acharya, Amitav. 'The R2P and Norm Diffusion: Towards a Framework of Norm Circulation'. *Global Responsibility to Protect* 5:1 (2013): 466–479.

Adhikari, Shekha, and Sanjeev Bhadauria (eds). *India's Security in the 21st Century*. New Delhi: Pentagon Press, 2014.

Adler, Emanuel. 'Seizing the Middle Ground: Constructivism in World Politics'. *European Journal of International Relations* 3:3 (1997): 319–363.

Agarwal, Rajeev. 'Arab Spring: Aspirations Met or Dreams Unfulfilled?'. *Institute for Defence Studies and Analyses – Issue Brief*, 26 October 2012.

Age, The. Fairfax Media. Melbourne.

Agrawal, Rajeev. 'Potential Military Strikes in Syria Threaten Regional Flare-Up'. *Observer Research Foundation – Analysis*, 31 August 2013.

Amin, Samir. 'US Hegemony: Need to Reshape European Politics'. *Economic and Political Weekly* 34:21 (1999).

Anderson, John R. *Cognitive Psychology and its Implications*. New York: Freeman, 1990.

Aneja, Urvashi. 'India, R2P and Humanitarian Assistance'. *Global Responsibility to Protect* 6:2 (2014): 227–245.

Annan, Kofi. 'Two Concepts of Sovereignty'. *The Economist*, 18 September 1999.

Annan, Kofi. *In Larger Freedom*. New York: United Nations, 2005.

Arbour, Louise. 'The Responsibility to Protect as a Duty of Care in International Law and Practice'. *Review of International Studies* 34:3 (2008): 445–458.

Asian Age, The. Deccan Chronicle Holdings Ltd. Hyderabad.

Atlantic, The. Atlantic Media. Washington.

Australian, The. News Corp Australia. Sydney.

Ayoob, Mohammed. 'Humanitarian Intervention and International Society'. *Global Governance* 7:3 (2001): 225–230.

Ayoob, Mohammed. 'Humanitarian Intervention and State Sovereignty'. *International Journal of Human Rights* 6:1 (2002): 81–102.

Badescu, Christina G., and Thomas G. Weiss. 'Misrepresenting R2P and Advancing Norms: An Alternative Spiral?'. *International Studies Perspectives* 11 (2010): 354–374.

Bahdur, Manmohan. 'Interventionism and Human Security'. *Strategic Analysis* 38:1 (2014): 6–11.

Bajpai, Kanti. *Future Strategic Balances and Alliances*. Carlisle: Strategic Studies Institute, 2002.

Bajpai, Kanti, Saira Basit and V. Krishnappa (eds). *India's Grand Strategy: History, Theory, Cases*. Routledge: New Delhi, 2014.

Banerjee, Dipankar. 'Responsibility to Protect: China's Version'. *Institute for Peace and Conflict Studies – Article*, 14 November 2013.

Bardam, Pranab. *Awakening Giants, Feet of Clay: Assessing the Economic Rise of China and India*. Princeton: Princeton University Press, 2012.

Barkum, Michael. *Law Without Sanctions: Order in Primitive Societies and the World Community*. New Haven: Yale University Press, 1968.

Barnidge, Robert P. (ed.). *The Liberal Way of War: Legal Perspectives*. Farnham: Ashgate, 2013.

Barry, Ben. 'Libya's Lessons'. *Survival* 53:5 (2011): 5–14.

Basin, Avtar S. *India's Foreign Policy – 2009 Documents*. New Delhi: Geetika Publishers, 2010.

Bass, Gary. *Freedom's Battle: Origins of Humanitarian Interventionism*. New York: Alfred A. Knopf, 2008.

BBC News. British Broadcasting Corporation. London.

Beachler, Donald W. *The Genocide Debate: Politicians, Academics, and Victims*. New York: Palgrave Macmillan, 2011.

Bell, Holy A. 'Status of the "BRICs": An Analysis of Growth Factors'. *International Research Journal of Finance and Economics* 69:2 (2011): 19–25.

Bellamy, Alex J. 'Responsibility to Protect or Trojan Horse? The Crisis in Darfur and Humanitarian Intervention after Iraq'. *Ethics & International Affairs* 19:2 (2005): 31–54.

Bellamy, Alex J. *Responsibility to Protect: The Global Effort to End Mass Atrocities*. Cambridge: Polity Press, 2009.

Bellamy, Alex J. *Global Politics and the Responsibility to Protect: From Words to Deeds*. Oxon: Routledge, 2011.

Bellamy, Alex J., and Paul D. Williams. 'The New Politics of Protection? Côte d'Ivoire, Libya and the Responsibility to Protect'. *International Affairs* 87:4 (2011): 829–831.

Bellamy, Alex J. 'Libya and the Responsibility to Protect: The Exception and the Norm'. *Ethics & International Affairs* 25:3 (2011): 263–269.

Bhaskar, Roy. *A Realist Theory of Science*. New York: Humanities Press, 1975.

Biddle, Stephen, Jeffrey A. Friedman and Jacob N. Shapiro. 'Testing the Surge: Why Did Violence Decline in Iraq in 2007?'. *International Security* 37:1 (2012): 7–40.

Brown, Chris. *International Relations Theory: New Normative Approaches*. New York: Columbia University Press, 1992.

Brunnée, Jutta, and Stephen Toope. *Legitimacy and Legality in International Law*. Cambridge: Cambridge University Press, 2010.

Buckley, Caitlin A. 'Learning from Libya, Acting in Syria'. *Journal of Strategic Security* 5:2 (2012): 81–104.

Bull, Hedley. *Intervention in World Politics*. Oxford: Oxford University Press, 1984.

Bull, Hedley, and Adam Watson (eds). *The Expansion of International Society*. Oxford: Clarendon Press, 1984.

Bullion, Alan. 'India in Sierra Leone: A Case of Muscular Peacekeeping?'. *International Peacekeeping* 8:4 (2001): 77–91.

Butterfield, Herbert, and Martin Wight (eds). *Diplomatic Investigations*. London: Allen & Unwin, 1966.

Byrd, B. Sharon, and Joachim Hruschka. 'From the State of Nature to the Juridical State of States'. *Law and Philosophy* 27:6 (2008): 599–641.

Chacko, Priya. *Indian Foreign Policy: The Politics of Postcolonial Identity from 1947 to 2004*. Oxon: Routledge, 2012.

Campbell, David. *Writing Security: United States Foreign Policy and the Politics of Identity*. Minneapolis: University of Minnesota Press, 1992.

Campbell, John L. 'Ideas, Politics and Public Policy'. *Annual Review of Sociology* 28:1 (2002): 21–38.

Chandra, Bipan, Aditya Mukherjee, Mridula Mukherjee (eds). *India After Independence*. New Delhi: Penguin, 1999.

Carpenter, Ted G. 'Tangled Web: The Syrian Civil War and Its Implications'. *Mediterranean Quarterly* 24:1 (2013): 1–11.

Charap, Samuel. 'Russia, Syria and the Doctrine of Non-Intervention'. *Survival* 55:1 (2013): 35–41.

Chatterjee, Partha. *Nationalist Thought and the Colonial World: A Derivative Discourse*. Minneapolis: University of Minnesota Press, 1986.

Chatterjee-Miller, Manjari. *Wronged By Empire: Post-Imperial Ideology and Foreign Policy in India and China*. Stanford: Stanford University Press, 2013.

Checkel, Jeffrey. 'Norms, Institutions, and National Identity in Contemporary Europe'. *International Studies Quarterly* 43:1 (1999): 84–114.

Chesterman, Simon. *Just War or Just Peace: Humanitarian Intervention and International Law*. Oxford: Oxford University Press, 2001.

Chomsky, Noam. *The New Military Humanism: Lessons From Kosovo*. Monroe: Common Courage Press, 1999.

Cohen, Stephen P. *India: Emerging Power*. Washington: Brookings Institution, 2001.

Cooper, Andrew F., Richard A. Higgott and Kim Richard Nossal. *Relocating Middle Powers: Australia and Canada in a Changing World Order*. Carlton: Melbourne University Press, 1993.

Cortell, Andrew P., and James W. Davis. 'Understanding the Domestic Impact of International Norms: A Research Agenda'. *International Studies Review* 2:1 (2000): 65–87.

Cortell, Andrew P., and James W. Davis, 'When Norms Clash: International Norms, Domestic Practices, and Japan's Internalisation of the GATT/WTO'. *Review of International Studies* 31:1 (2005): 3–25.

Cox, Robert W., and Timothy J. Sinclair (eds). *Approaches to World Order*. Cambridge: Cambridge University Press, 1996.

Cunliffe, Philip (ed.). *Critical Perspectives on the Responsibility to Protect: Interrogating Theory and Practice*. Oxon: Routledge, 2011.

Dalgaard-Neilsen, Anja. 'The Test of Strategic Culture: Germany, Pacifism and Pre-emptive Strikes'. *Security Dialogue* 36:3 (2005): 339–359.

Danahar, Paul. *The New Middle East: The World After the Arab Spring*. London: Bloomsbury, 2013.

Das, Gurcharan. 'The India Model'. *Foreign Affairs* 85:4 (2006): 2–16.

Das, Samir K., and Achin Vanaik (eds). *ICSSR Research Surveys and Explorations: Political Science – Volume 1, The Indian State*. New Delhi: Oxford University Press, 2013.

Dash Sandipani. 'Responsibility to Protect: The Case of Libya'. *Indian Council of World Affairs – Issue Brief*, 4 December 2012.

Denemark, Robert A. (ed.). *The International Studies Encyclopedia*. Blackwell Publishing, 2010.

Deng, Francis, and Roberta Cohen. *Masses in Flight: The Global Crisis of Internal Displacement*. Washington: Brookings, 1998.

Denzau, Arthur, and Douglass North. 'Shared Mental Models: Ideologies and Institutions'. *Kyklos* 47:1 (1994): 3–31.

Dews, Fred. 'A Glossary of Forces in the Syrian Civil War'. *Brookings Now*, 27 May 2014.

Dietl, Gulsham. 'The "Spring" has had Contagious Effect Much Beyond'. *Indian Foreign Affairs Journal* 8:2 (2013): 134–141.

DiMaggio, Paul. 'Culture and Cognition'. *Annual Review of Sociology* 23 (1997): 263–287.

Dixit, J.N. *India's Foreign Policy, 1947–2003*. Delhi: Picus Books, 2003.

Dunne, Tim, and Jess Gifkin. 'Libya and the State of Intervention'. *Australian Journal of International Affairs* 65:5 (2011): 515–529.

Economist, The. Economist Group. London.

Enloe, Cynthia. *Bananas, Beaches and Bases: Making Feminist Sense of International Politics*. Berkley: University of California Press, 1990.

Epstein, Charlotte. *The Power of Words in International Relations: The Birth of an Anti-Whaling Discourse*. Cambridge, Mass.: MIT Press, 2008.

Fabian, K.P. 'An Arab Revolution?'. *IDSA Issue Brief*, 10 March 2011.

Fay, Brian. *Social Theory and Political Practice*. London: George Allen & Unwin, 1975.

Farrell, Theo. 'Transnational Norms and Military Development: Constructing Ireland's National Army'. *European Journal of International Relations* 7:1 (2001): 63–102.

Fearon, James D. 'What is Identity (as we now use the word?)'. Unpublished manuscript, Stanford University, 3 November 1999.

Feigenbaum, Evan A. 'India's Rise, America's Interest: The Fate of the U.S.-Indian Partnership'. *Foreign Affairs* 89:2 (2010): 76–91.

Finnemore, Martha, and Kathryn Sikkink. 'International Norm Dynamics and Political Change'. *International Organization* 52:4 (1998): 887–917.

Franck, Thomas M., and Nigel S. Rodley. 'After Bangladesh: The Law of Humanitarian Intervention by Military Force'. *American Journal of International Law* 67:2 (1973): 275–305.

Frank, Andre G. *The Development of Underdevelopment.* Boston: New England Free Press, 1966.

Frontline. Hindu Group. Chennai.

Gallagher, Adrian. 'A Clash of Responsibilities: Engaging with Realist Critiques of the R2P'. *Global Responsibility to Protect* 4:3 (2012): 334–357.

Ganguly, Sumit (ed.). *India's Foreign Policy: Retrospect and Prospect.* New Delhi: Oxford University Press, 2010.

Ganguly, Sumit. 'A Pointless Abstention', *The Diplomat*, 23 April 2011.

Geertz, Clifford. *The Interpretation of Cultures: Selected Essays*. New York: Basic Books, 1973.

Geertz, Clifford. *Negara: The Theatre State in Nineteenth-Century Bali.* Princeton: Princeton University Press, 1980.

Giddens, Anthony. *The Constitution of Society*. Cambridge: Blackwell, 1984.

Gifkins, Jess. 'The UN Security Council Divided: Syria in Crisis'. *Global Responsibility to Protect* 4:3 (2012): 377–393.

Glaser, Charles. 'Realists as Optimists: Cooperation as Self-Help'. *International Security* 19:3 (1994/5): 50–90.

Global Centre for the Responsibility to Protect. *Implementing the Responsibility to Protect: The 2009 General Assembly Debate: An Assessment*. August 2009.

Goldgeier, James, and Philip E. Tetlock. 'Psychology and International Relations Theory'. *Annual Review of Political Science* 4 (2001): 67–92.

Golwalkar, M.S. *Bunch of Thoughts*, 3rd ed. Bangalore: Sahitya Sindu Prakahana, 1996.

Gopinathan, A. 'The Arab Spring: Supporting Transition to Democracy'. *Indian Foreign Affairs Journal* 7:4 (2012): 423–432.

Guha, Ramachandra. *India After Ghandi: The History of the World's Largest Democracy*. New York: Harper Perennial, 2008.

Gupta, Ranjit. 'Fallout of the "Arab Spring": Challenges for India'. *Indian Foreign Affairs Journal* 8:2 (2013): 142–155.

Guicherd, Catherine. 'International Law and the War in Kosovo'. *Survival* 41:2 (1999): 19–34.

Hacking, Ian. *The Social Construction of What?*. Cambridge: Harvard University Press, 1999.

Hameed, Sameena. 'India Needs to Move from "Mild" to "Middle"'. *Indian Foreign Affairs Journal* 6:2 (2011): 143–151.

Hameed, Sameena. 'India and Turmoil in the Arab World: Two Years Since the Advent of the "Arab Spring"'. *Indian Foreign Affairs Journal* 8:2 (2012): 111–151.

Hameed, Sameena. 'International Community should Desist from Attempting to Tip the Balance Libya'. *Indian Foreign Affairs Journal* 8:2 (2013): 167–177.

Hagerty, Devin T. 'India's Regional Security Doctrine'. *Asian Survey* 31:4 (1991): 351–363.

Hall, Ian. 'The Other Exception? India as a rising Power'. *Australian Journal of International Affairs* 64:5 (2010): 601–611.

Hall, Ian. 'Tilting at Windmills? The Indian Debate over the Responsibility to Protect after UNSC Resolution 1973'. *Global Responsibility to Protect* 5:1 (2013): 84–108.

Hehir, Aidan. 'The Permanence of Inconsistency: Libya, the Security Council, and the Responsibility to Protect'. *International Security* 38:1 (2013): 137–159.

Hehir, Aidan, and Robert Murray (eds). *Libya: The Responsibility to Protect and the Future of Humanitarian Intervention.* Basingstoke: Palgrave Macmillan, 2013.

Henriksen, Andres, and Marc Schack. 'The Crisis in Syria and Humanitarian Intervention'. *Journal of the Use of Force and International Law* 1:1 (2014): 122–147.

High Level Panel. *A More Secure World: Our Shared Responsibility.* New York: United Nations, 2004.

Hindu, The. Kasturi and Sons. Chennai.

Hindustan Times. HT Media. New Delhi.

Hollis, Martin. *The Philosophy of Social Science*, 2nd ed. Cambridge: Cambridge University Press, 2002 [1994].

Holsti, Ole. 'Public Opinion and Foreign Policy'. *International Studies Quarterly* 36:4 (1992): 439–466.

Hopf, Ted. 'The Promise of Constructivism'. *International Security* 23:1 (1998): 171–200.

Hopf, Ted. *Social Construction of International Politics: Identities and Foreign Policies, Moscow, 1955 & 1999*. Ithaca: Cornell University Press, 2002.

Hopf, Ted. *Reconstructing the Cold War: The Early Years, 1945–1958*. Oxford: Oxford University Press, 2012.

Huffington Post, The. Huffington Post Media Group. New York.

Hultman, Lisa. 'UN Peace Operations and Protection of Civilians: Cheap Talk or Norm Implementation?'. *Journal of Peace Research* 50:1 (2012): 59–73.

Huntington, Samuel P. 'New Contingencies, Old Roles'. *Joint Forces Quarterly* 2 (Autumn 1992): 38–43.

Hussain, Zakir. 'Decoding the Syrian Blasts'. *Indian Council of World Affairs – View Point*, 12 January 2012.
Hussain, Zakir. 'Post-Assad Strategic Possibilities'. *Indian Council of World Affairs – Issue Brief*, 6 August 2012.
Ignatieff, Michael. *Empire Lite: Nation-Building in Bosnia, Kosovo and Afghanistan*. London: Vintage, 2003.
Independent, The. Independent Print Limited. London.
Independent International Commission on Kosovo. *The Kosovo Report: Conflict, International Response, Lessons Learned*. Oxford: Oxford University Press, 2000.
Indian Express, The. Indian Express Group. Mumbai.
India Today. Living Media. Noida.
International Commission on Intervention and State Sovereignty (ICISS). *The Responsibility to Protect: Supplementary Volume*. Ottawa: International Development Research Centre, 2001.
Jackson, Robert. *South Asian Crisis: India-Pakistan-Bangladesh*. London: Chatto & Windus, 1975.
Jackson, Robert. *Quasi-States: Sovereignty, International Relations and the Third World*. Cambridge: Cambridge University Press, 1990.
Jaganathan, Madhan M., and Gerrit Kurtz. 'Singing the Tune of Sovereignty? India and the Responsibility to Protect'. *Conflict, Security and Development* 14:4 (2014): 461–487.
Jha, Nalini K. 'The Cultural and Philosophical Roots of Indian Foreign Policy'. *International Studies* 26:1 (1989): 45–67.
Johnson, Adrian, and Saqueb Mueen. *Short War, Long Shadow: The Political and Military Legacies of the 2011 Libya Campaign*. London: Royal United Services Institute, 2012.
Johny, Stanly. 'The Syrian Conundrum'. *IDSA – Comment*, 14 February 2012.
Joshi, Ravi. 'Is Syria the Next Libya?'. *Observer Research Foundation – Analysis*, 29 August 2013.
Joy, Ashish. 'The Crisis in Libya'. *ORF Issue Brief* 28, April 2011.
Kaldor, Mary. *New and Old Wars: Organized Violence in a Global Era*. Stanford: Stanford University Press, 1999.
Kalha, R.S. 'Post-Gaddafi Libya: What Happens Next?'. *IDSA Comment*, 19 November 2011.
Kalha, R.S. 'The Wages of Naivety'. *IDSA – Comment*, 18 September 2012.
Kapoor, Sanjay. 'Syria: At the Threshold'. *Observer Research Foundation: Analysis*, 27 October 2011.
Kapur, Ashok. *India: From Regional to World Power*. Oxon: Routledge, 2006.
Katzenstein, Peter J. (ed.). *The Culture of National Security: Norms and Identity in World Politics*. New York: Columbia University Press, 1996.
Keay, John. *India: A History*, 2nd ed. London: HarperPress, 2010 [2000].
Keerthi, Saurabh M., and Sampath Kumar. 'India's Two Years at the Horse-Shoe Table'. *Institute for Defence Studies and Analyses – Issue Brief*, 8 March 2013.

Kilnani, Sunil, Rajiv Kumar, Pratap B. Mehta, Prakash Menon, Nandan Nilekani, Srinath Raghavan, Shyam Saran and Siddharth Varadarajan. *Nonalignment 2.0: A Foreign and Strategic Policy for India in the Twenty First Century*. Centre for Policy Research, *Working Paper*, January 2012.

Klotz, Audie. *Norms in International Relations: The Struggle Against Apartheid*. Ithaca: Cornell University Press, 1999.

Knights, Michael. 'Iraq War III has Now Begun'. *Foreign Policy*, 11 June 2014.

Koshy, Ninan. 'Sidelining the United Nations'. *Economic & Political Weekly* 35:15, 8–14 April 2001.

Kratochwil, Friedrich V. *Rules, Norms and Decisions: On the Conditions of Practical and Legal Reasoning in International Relations and Domestic Affairs*. Cambridge: University of Cambridge, 1989.

Krishna, Sankaran. 'India and Sri Lanka: A Fatal Convergence'. *Studies in Conflict & Terrorism* 15:4 (1992): 267–281.

Kumar, Radha. 'India as a Foreign Policy Actor – Normative Redux'. *CEPS Working Document* No. 285, February 2008.

Kumar, Keerthi S. 'Responsibility to Protect : The Case of Libya'. *IDSA Comment*, 2 May 2011.

Kumaraswamy, P.R. 'Uprisings in the Arab World: Options for GOI'. *IDSA Issue Brief*, 30 March 2011.

Kumaraswamy, P.R. 'Silence on Syria is No Option'. *IDSA – Comment*, 21 February 2012.

Kuperman, Alan J. 'A Model Humanitarian Intervention? Reassessing NATO's Libya Campaign'. *International Security* 38:1 (2013): 105–136.

Kurki, Milja. 'Causes of a Divided Discipline: A Critical Examination of the Concept of Cause in International Relations Theory'. *Global Politics Network* (2002): 3–41.

Kurki, Milja. 'Causes of a Divided Discipline: Rethinking the Concept of Cause in International Relations Theory'. *Review of International Studies* 32:2 (2006): 189–216.

Kux, Dennis. *India and the United States: Estranged Democracies, 1941–1991*. Washington: Diane Publishing, 1993.

Laffey, Mark, and Jutta Weldes. 'Beyond Belief: Ideas and Symbolic Technologies in the Study of International Relations'. *European Journal of International Relations* 3:2 (1997): 193–237.

Lauterpacht, Hersch. 'The Grotian Tradition in International Law'. *British Year Book of International Law* 23:1 (1946): 1–54.

Legro, Jeffrey W. 'The Transformation of Policy Ideas'. *American Journal of Political Science* 44:3 (2000): 419–432.

Lenin, Vladimir. *Imperialism, The Highest Stage of Capitalism*. Chippendale: Resistance Books, 1999 [1917].

Liebig, Michael. 'Kautilya's Relevance for India Today'. *India Quarterly* 69:2 (2013): 99–116.

Lillich, Richard. *Humanitarian Intervention and the United Nations*. Charlottesville: University Press of Virginia, 1973.
Lok Sabha (lower house). Parliament of India. New Delhi.
Loiselle, Marie-Eve. 'The Normative Status of the Responsibility to Protect after Libya'. *Global Responsibility to Protect* 5:3 (2013): 317–341.
Luck, Edward C. 'The R2P: The First Decade'. *Global Responsibility to Protect* 3:4 (2011): 387–399.
Lui, Teiwa, and Haibin Zhang. 'Debates in China About the Responsibility to Protect as a Developing International Norm: A General Assessment'. *Conflict, Security and Development* 14:4 (2014): 403–427.
Maddy-Weitzman, Bruce. 'The Arab League Comes Alive'. *Middle East Quarterly* 19:3 (2012): 71–78.
Mahoney, James. 'Path Dependence in Historical Sociology'. *Theory and Society* 29:4 (2000): 507–548.
Malik, J. Mohan. 'India Goes Nuclear: Rationale, Benefits, Costs and Implications'. *Contemporary Southeast Asia* 20:2 (1998): 191–215.
Malone, David. *Can the Elephant Dance?: Contemporary Indian Foreign Policy*. Oxford: Oxford University Press, 2011.
Mearsheimer, John J. *The Tragedy of Great Power Politics*. New York: Norton & Norton, 2001.
Mearsheimer, John J. 'Why the Ukraine Crisis Is the West's Fault: The Liberal Delusions That Provoked Putin'. *Foreign Affairs* 93 (September/October 2014): 77–89.
Mehta, Pratap B. 'Still Under Nehru's Shadow? The Absence of Foreign Policy Frameworks in India'. *India Review* 8:3 (2009): 209–233.
Mehta, Pratap B. 'Do New Democracies Support Democracy?: Reluctant India'. *Journal of Democracy* 22:4 (2011): 101–113.
Milliken, Jennifer. 'The Study of Discourse in International Relations: A Critique of Research and Methods'. *European Journal of International Relations* 5:2 (1999): 225–254.
Ministry of External Affairs (India), Republic of India. New Delhi.
Mishra, Saurabh. 'Why Syria is not Libya'. *IDSA – Comment*, 21 October 2011.
Mishra, Saurabh. 'Reading the Veto on Syria'. *IDSA – Comment*, 21 October 2011.
Mishra, Saurabh, and Keerthi S. Kumar. 'India's Two Years at the Horse-Shoe Table'. *Institute for Defence Studies and Analyses – Issue Brief*, 8 March 2013.
Mitra, Abhijit I. 'The Evidence on Syria is Thin'. *Observer Research Foundation – Analysis*, 3 September 2013.
Mohan, C. Raja. *Crossing the Rubicon: The Shaping of India's New Foreign Policy*. New Delhi: Viking, 2003.
Mohan, C. Raja. 'Balancing Interests and Values: India's Struggle with Democracy Promotion'. *Washington Quarterly* 30:3 (2007): 99–115.
Mohan, C. Raja. 'The Making of Indian Foreign Policy: The Role of Scholarship and Public Opinion'. *ISAS Working Paper* 73, 13 July 2009.

Mohan, C. Raja. 'Rising India: Partner in Shaping the Global Commons?'. *Washington Quarterly* 33:3 (2010): 133–148.

Mohan, C. Raja. 'India, Libya and the Principle of Non-Intervention'. *ISAS Insights* 122, 13 April 2011.

Moorthy, Sathiya N. 'Shake-up time for Sri Lanka'. *Observer Research Foundation: Analysis*, 26 March 2012.

Morgenthau, Hans J. *Politics Among Nations: The Struggle for Power and Peace*, 5th ed. New York: Alfred A. Knopf, 1948.

Morris, Justin. 'Libya and Syria: The Spectre of the Swinging Pendulum'. *International Affairs* 89:5 (2013): 1265–1283.

Mukherjee, Rohan and David Malone. 'India and the UN Security Council: An Ambiguous Tale'. *Economic and Political Weekly* 48:29 (2013): 110–117.

Nalwa, Preeti. 'Gaddafi's Death: Mission Accomplished!'. *IDSA Comment*, 29 October 2011.

Nambiar, Satish. 'The Emerging Principle of the Responsibility to Protect: An Asian Perspective'. *Strategic Analysis* 35:6 (2011): 955–965.

National Interest, The. Center for the National Interest. Washington.

Naqvi, Saeed. 'Can US Lead While Europe Scrambles for Oil?'. *Observer Research Foundation: Analysis*, 14 March 2011.

Naqvi, Saeed. 'West Sets up the War Within Islam'. *Observer Research Foundations: Analysis*, 24 October 2011.

Naqvi, Saeed. 'The Storm in the Arab Spring'. *Observer Research Foundation: Discourse* 5:15, February 2012.

Narlikar, Amrita. 'Is India a Responsible Great Power?'. *Third World Quarterly* 32:9 (2011): 1607–1621.

Nayar, Baldev Raj and T.V. Paul. *India in the World Order: Searching for Major-Power Status*. Cambridge: Cambridge University Press, 2003.

Nehru, Jawaharlal. *India's Foreign Policy: Selected Speeches, September 1946–April 1961*. New Delhi: Ministry of Information, 1961.

New Indian Express, The. Express Publications. Chennai.

New York Times, The. New York Times Company. New York.

Nizami, Taufiq. *The Communist Party and India's Foreign Policy*. New Delhi: Associated Publishing House, 1971.

Noueihed, Lin, and Alex Warren. *The Battle for the Arab Spring: Revolution, Counter-Revolution and the Making of a New Era*. New Haven: Yale University Press, 2012.

NPR. National Public Radio, Inc. Washington.

Nurazzaman, Mohammed. 'The "Responsibility to Protect" Doctrine: Revived in Libya, Buried in Syria'. *Insight Turkey* 15:2 (2013): 57–66.

Ollapally, Deepa and Rajesh Rajapagolan. 'The Pragmatic Challenge to Indian Foreign Policy'. *Washington Quarterly* 34:2 (2011): 145–162.

Ollapally, Deepa. 'India: the Ambivalent Power in Asia'. *International Studies* 48:3–4 (2011): 201–222.

O'Neill, Jim. 'Building Better Global Economic BRICs', *Global Economics Paper* 66 (Goldman Sachs), 30 November 2001.
openDemocracy. openDemocracy Foundation for the Advancement of Global Education. London.
Pangariya, Arvind. *India: The Emerging Giant*. New York: Oxford University Press, 2008.
Pant, Harsh V. *Contemporary Debates in Indian Foreign and Security Policy*. New York: Palgrave Macmillan, 2008.
Pant, Harsh V. 'A Rising India's Search for a Foreign Policy'. *Orbis* 53:2 (2009): 250–264.
Pant, Harsh V. (ed.). *Indian Foreign Policy in a Unipolar World*. New Delhi: Routledge, 2009.
Pant, Harsh V. *The China Syndrome: Grappling with an Uneasy Relationship*. New Delhi: HarperCollins, 2010.
Pant, Harsh V. 'Libya Exposes New Faultlines in Foreign Policy'. *ISN Insights*, 21 April 2011.
Parekh, Bhikhu. 'Rethinking Humanitarian Intervention'. *International Political Science Review* 18:1 (1997): 49–69.
Pattanayak, Satya. 'India as an Emerging Power'. *India Quarterly* 63:1 (2007): 79–110.
Pattison, James. *Humanitarian Intervention and the Responsibility to Protect: Who Should Intervene?*. Oxford: Oxford University Press, 2010.
Paul, T.V. (ed.). *South Asia's Weak States: Understanding the Regional Insecurity Predicament*. Stanford: Stanford University Press, 2010.
Pfaffenberger, Bryan. 'Sri Lanka in 1987: Indian Intervention and Resurgence of the JVP'. *Asian Survey* 28:2 (1988): 137–147.
Phadke, Ramesh. 'India: An Uneasy Onlooker!'. *IDSA Comment*, 21 March 2011.
Philpott, Daniel. *Revolutions in Sovereignty*. Princeton: Princeton University Press, 2001.
Pethiyagoda, Kadira. 'India's Approach to Humanitarian Intervention and the Responsibility to Protect'. *Oxford Institute for Ethics, Law and Armed Conflict Working Paper*, November 2013.
Prasanta, Pradhan. 'Protests in the Arab World: Implications for the Region and India'. *IDSA Issue Brief*, 31 March 2011.
Price, Richard. 'Reversing the Gun Sights: Transnational Civil Society Targets Land Mines'. *International Organization* 52:3 (1998): 613–644.
Prys, Miriam. *Redefining Regional Power in International Relations: Indian and South African Perspectives*. Oxon: Routledge, 2012.
Quinton-Brown, Patrick. 'Mapping Dissent: The R2P and its State Critics'. *Global Responsibility to Protect* 5:3 (2013): 260–282.
Raghavan, Srinath. *1971: A Global History of the Creation of Bangladesh*. Ranikert: Permanent Black, 2013.
Rajan, M.S. 'The New Interventionism'. *International Studies* 37:1 (2000): 31–40.

Rajan, M.S. 'Sovereignty of States and Intervention'. *International Studies* 40:3 (2003): 277–281.

Rajagopalan, Rajesh, and Varun Singh. 'India and the Great Powers: Strategic Imperatives, Normative Necessities'. *South Asian Survey* 15:5 (2008): 5–32.

Rajagopalan, Rajesh. 'Human Rights and India's Foreign Policy'. *Observer Research Foundation – Analysis*, 26 March 2012.

Rao, Rahul. 'The UN and NATO in the New World Order: Legal Issues'. *International Studies* 37:3 (2000): 157–181.

Recchia, Stefano, and Jennifer M. Welsh (eds). *Just and Unjust Military Intervention: European Thinkers from Vitoria to Mill*. Cambridge: Cambridge University Press, 2013.

Report of the Secretary-General Pursuant to General Assembly Resolution 53/35: The Fall of Srebrenica (United Nations). 15 November 1999, A/54/549.

Roberts, Adam. 'Humanitarian War: Military Intervention and Human Rights'. *International Affairs* 69:3 (1993): 429–449.

Roberts, Adam. 'NATO's "Humanitarian War" Over Kosovo'. *Survival* 41:3 (1999): 102–123.

Roberts, Adam. 'Law and the Use of Force after Iraq'. *Survival* 45:2 (2003): 31–56.

Roff, Heather. *Global Justice, Kant, and the Responsibility to Protect: A Provisional Duty*. Oxon: Routledge, 2013.

van Rooyen, Frank. 'Blue Helmets for Africa: India's Peacekeeping in Africa'. *South African Institute for Race Relations – Occasional Working Paper* 60, May 2010.

Rotmann, Philipp, Gerrit Kurtz and Sarah Brockmeier. 'Major Powers and the Contested Evolution of a Responsibility to Protect'. *Conflict, Security and Development* 14:4 (2014): 355–377.

Kohli, Atul, and Prema Singh (eds). *Routledge Handbook of Indian Politics*. Oxon: Routledge, 2013.

Sagar, Rahul. 'State of Mind: What Sort of Power will India Become?'. *International Affairs* 85:4 (2009): 801–816.

Salloukh, Bassel F. 'The Arab Uprisings and the Geopolitics of the Middle East'. *The International Spectator: Italian Journal of International Affairs* 48:2 (2013): 32–46.

Savarkar, Vinayak. *Hindutva*. New Delhi: The Central Hindu Yuvak Sabha, 1938.

Schnabel, Albrecht, and Ramesh Thakur (eds). *Kosovo and the Challenge of Humanitarian Intervention*. Tokyo: United Nations University Press, 2000.

Scott, Shirley V. *International Law in World Politics*, 2nd ed. Boulder: Lynne Rienner, 2010.

Sellström, Åke, Scott Cairns and Maurizio Barbeschi. 'Report on the Alleged Use of Chemical Weapons in the Ghouta Area of Damascus on 21 August 2013'. *United Nations*, 13 September 2013.

Shapiro, Ian, and Alexander Wendt. 'The Difference that Realism Makes: Social Science and the Politics of Consent'. *Politics and Society* 20:2 (1997): 197–223.

Shrivastava, B.K., and Manmohan Agarwal. 'Politics of Intervention and the Bosnian-Herzegovina Conflict', *International Studies* 40:1 (2003): 69–84.

Shrivastav, Sanjeev. 'India's response to the Libyan Crisis'. *IDSA Issue Brief*, 13 April 2011.

Shore, Bradd. *Culture in Mind: Cognition, Culture and the Problem of Meaning*. New York: Harper, 1996.

Siddiqui, Fazzur. 'Arab Spring and the Changing Contours of Arab Politics'. *Indian Council of World Affairs: Issue Brief*, 21 September 2012.

Sidhu, W.P.S., and Ramesh Thakur (eds). *The Iraq Crisis and World Order: Structural, Institutional and Normative Challenges*. New York: United Nations Press, 2006.

Sikri, Rajiv. *Challenge and Strategy: Rethinking India's Foreign Policy*. New Delhi: Sage, 2009.

Silverberg, S.R. (ed.). *International Law: Readings on Contemporary Problems and Future Issues*. Boulder: Westview Press, 2011.

Singh, Jagdish N. 'A Gloomy Syrian Scenario'. *IDSA – Comment*, 24 February 2012.

Smith, Michael J. 'Humanitarian Intervention: An Overview of the Ethical Issues'. *Ethics and International Affairs* 12:1 (1998): 63–79.

Stein, Janis G. 'Political Learning by Doing: Gorbachev as Uncommitted Thinker and Motivated Learner'. *International Organization* 48:2 (1994): 155–184.

Sood, Vikram. 'Oh What a Tangled Web We Weave'. *Observer Research Foundation: Analysis*, 24 August 2012.

Stowell, Ellery. *Intervention in International Law*. Washington: L.J. Byrne, 1921.

Stuenkel, Oliver. 'The BRICS and the Future of R2P'. *Global Responsibility to Protect* 6:1 (2014): 3–28.

Stuenkel, Oliver, and Marco Tourinho, 'Regulating Intervention: Brazil and the Responsibility to Protect'. *Conflict, Security and Development* 14:4 (2014): 379–402.

Swain, Ashok, Ramses Amer and Joakim Öjendal (eds). *Globalization and Challenges to Building Peace*. London: Anthem Press, 2008.

Swidler, Ann. 'Culture in Action: Symbols and Strategies'. *American Sociological Review* 57:2 (1986): 273–286.

Taneja, Kabir. 'India and China: Lessons From a Lost Oil Field in Syria'. *The Diplomat*, 23 November 2014.

Tanham, George. *Indian Strategic Thought: An Interpretive Essay*. Santa Monica: RAND Corporation, 1992.

Thakur, Ramesh. 'India after Nonalignment'. *Foreign Affairs* 71 (1992): 165–182.

Thakur, Ramesh. 'Global Norms and International Humanitarian Law: An Asian Perspective'. *International Review of the Red Cross* 83:841 (2001): 19–44.

Thakur, Ramesh. *The United Nations, Peace and Security: From Collective Security to the Responsibility to Protect*. Cambridge: Cambridge University Press, 2006.

Thakur, Ramesh, and Thomas G Weiss. 'R2P: From Idea to Norm – and Action?'. *Global Responsibility to Protect* 1:1 (2009): 22–53.

Thakur, Ramesh. *The Responsibility to Protect: Norms, Laws and the Use of Force*. Oxon: Routledge, 2011.

Thakur, Ramesh. 'R2P after Libya and Syria: Engaging Emerging Powers'. *Washington Quarterly* 36:2 (2013): 61–76.

The Battle for Libya: Killings, Disappearances and Torture. London: Amnesty International, 13 September 2011.

The Responsibility to Protect – From Evasive to Reluctant Action? The Role of Global Middle Powers. Johannesburg: United Litho, 2012.

Tilly, Charles. 'How to Detect, Describe and Explain Repertoires of Contention'. *Working Paper* 150, Centre of Study of Social Change, New School of Social Research, 1992.

Times of India, The. The Times Group. New Delhi.

Timms, D.J.B., and Brendan Simms (eds). *Humanitarian Intervention: A History*. Cambridge: Cambridge University Press, 2011.

Tudor, Maya. *The Promise of Power: The Origins of Democracy in India and Autocracy in Pakistan*. Cambridge: Cambridge University Press, 2013.

Traub, James. *The Best Intentions: Kofi Annan and the UN in an Era of American Power*. London: Bloomsbury, 2006.

U.S. Energy Information Administration. 'India: Overview'. *Analysis Briefs*, 26 June 2014.

Varma, Anjana. 'Ivory Coast: A Crisis of Division'. *Observer Research Foundation: Analysis*, 18 April 2011.

Verhoeven, Harry, C.S.R. Murthy and Ricardo Soares de Oliveira. '"Our Identity is Our Currency": South Africa, the Responsibility to Protect, and the Logic of African Intervention'. *Conflict, Security and Development* 14:4 (2014): 509–534.

Vincent, R.J. *Human Rights and International Relations*. Cambridge: Cambridge University Press, 1986.

Virk, Kudrat. 'India and the Responsibility to Protect: A Tale of Ambiguity'. *Global Responsibility to Protect* 5:1 (2013): 56–83.

Walker, R.J.B. *Inside/Outside: International Relations as Political Theory*. Cambridge: Cambridge University Press, 1993.

Wallace, Victor H. (ed.). *Paths to Peace*. London: Cambridge University Press, 1956.

Wall Street Journal, The. Dow Jones & Company. New York.

K. Waltz, Kenneth. *The Theory of International Politics*. Reading: Addison-Wesley, 1979.

Walzer, Michael. *Just and Unjust Wars: A Moral Argument with Historical Illustrations*. New York: Basic Books, 1977.

Weiss, Thomas G. *Humanitarian Intervention*, 2nd ed. Cambridge: Polity Press, 2012.

Weiss, Thomas G. 'Military Humanism: Syria Hasn't Killed it'. *Washington Quarterly* 37:1 (2014): 7–20.

Welsh, Jennifer M. (ed.). *Humanitarian Intervention and International Relations*. Oxford: Oxford University Press, 2004.

Welsh, Jennifer M., and Maria Banda. 'International Law and the Responsibility to Protect'. *Global Responsibility to Protect* 2:3 (2010): 213–231.

Welsh, Jennifer M. 'Implementing the "Responsibility to Protect": Where Expectations Meet Reality'. *Ethics & International Affairs* 24:4 (2010): 415–430.

Welsh, Jennifer M. 'Civilian Protection in Libya: Putting Coercion and Controversy Back into R2P'. *Ethics & International Affairs* 25:3 (2011): 255–262.

Welsh, Jennifer M., Patrick Quinton-Brown and Victor MacDiarmid. 'Brazil's "Responsibility While Protecting" Proposal: A Canadian Perspective'. *CCRtoP*, 12 July 2012.

Welsh, Jennifer M. 'Norm Contestation and the Responsibility to Protect'. *Global Responsibility to Protect* 5:4 (2013): 365–396.

Weldes, Jutta. 'Constructing National Interests'. *European Journal of International Relations* 2:3 (1996): 275–318.

Weldes, Jutta, Mark Laffey, Hugh Gusterson and Raymond Duvall (eds). *Cultures of Insecurity: States, Communities, and the Production of Danger*. Minneapolis: University of Minnesota Press, 1999.

Wendt, Alexander. 'The Agent-Structure Problem in International Relations Theory'. *International Organization* 41:3 (1987): 335–370.

Wendt, Alexander. 'On Constitution and Causation in International Relations'. *Review of International Studies* 24:5 (1998): 101–117.

Wendt, Alexander. 'Anarchy is What States Make of It: The Social Construction of Power Politics'. *International Organization* 46:2 (1992): 391–425.

Wheeler, Nicholas J. *Saving Strangers: Humanitarian Intervention and International Society*. Oxford: Oxford University Press, 2000.

Winch, Peter. *The Idea of a Social Science*. London: Routledge & Kegan Paul, 1958.

Wittgenstein, Ludwig. *Philosophical Investigations*. Oxford: Blackwell, 1953.

Wolf, Jr., Charles, Siddhartha Dalal, Julie DaVanzo, Eric V. Larson, Alisher Akhmedjonov, Harun Dogo, Meilinda Huang and Silvia Montoya. *China and India, 2025: A Comparative Assessment*. Santa Monica: RAND Corporation, 2011.

Xiayou, Pu. 'Socialisation as a Two-Way Process: Emerging Powers and the Diffusion of International Norms'. *Chinese Journal of International Politics* 5:4 (2012): 341–367.

Yearbook of International Humanitarian Law 2000, Volume 3. The Hague: T.M.C. Asser, 2002.

Yearbook of the International Law Commission 1966, Vol. II. New York: United Nations, 1967.

Yee, Albert. 'The Causal Effect of Ideas on Policies'. *International Organization* 50:1 (1996): 69–108.

Zaman, Rashed U. 'Kautilya: The Indian Strategic Thinker and Indian Strategic Culture'. *Comparative Strategy* 25:3 (2006): 231–247.

Zifcak, Spencer. 'The Responsibility to Protect after Libya and Syria'. *Melbourne Journal of International Law* 13:1 (2012): 60–93.

Index

For Product Safety Concerns and Information please contact our EU representative GPSR@taylorandfrancis.com Taylor & Francis Verlag GmbH, Kaufingerstraße 24, 80331 München, Germany